THE
COMPLETE
SCRIMGEOUR

THE COMPLETE SCRIMGEOUR

FROM DARTMOUTH TO JUTLAND: 1913–16

COMPILED BY RICHARD HALLAM AND MARK BEYNON

CONWAY

BLOOMSBURY

LONDON · OXFORD · NEW YORK · NEW DELHI · SYDNEY

Published by Conway
An imprint of Bloomsbury Publishing Plc

www.bloomsbury.com

50 Bedford Square
London
WC1B 3DP
UK

1385 Broadway
New York
NY 10018
USA

BLOOMSBURY and the Diana logo are trademarks of Bloomsbury Publishing Plc
CONWAY and the 'C' logo are trademarks of Bloomsbury Publishing Plc

First published 2016

British Library Cataloguing-in-Publication Data
A catalogue record for this book is available from the British Library.

ISBN: HB: 978-1-8448-6310-5
ePDF: 978-1-8448-6311-2
ePub: 978-1-8448-6312-9

10 9 8 7 6 5 4 3 2 1

Typeset in Minion Pro by Deanta Global Publishing Services, Chennai, India
Printed and bound in Great Britain by CPI Group (UK) Ltd, Croydon CR0 4YY

To find out more about our authors and books visit www.bloomsbury.com.
Here you will find extracts, author interviews, details of forthcoming events and
the option to sign up for our newsletters.

CONTENTS

LIST OF CHARTS AND ILLUSTRATIONS

PREFACE

I have known of, and lived with, Alexander Scrimgeour's diaries since I was a child. As a young boy I grew up in Thorncombe House, near Godalming, Surrey, with my mother, grandmother and step-grandfather, Toby Scrimgeour. Toby, whom I regarded as my surrogate father and patriarch, would often regale me with fascinating accounts from his wealth of family history, including the tale of Alexander Scrimgeour, his brave uncle who had lost his life at sea during the First World War.

When he told me that he had been handed down Alexander's war diaries and letters by his father (Alexander's younger brother, Jim) and that they were safely concealed in his grand chest of drawers, I couldn't wait to cast my eager young eyes over them. I have many fond memories of Thorncombe, which to an inquisitive child was a real den of antiquity, rich in a secretive past, but Alexander's diaries and his portrait hanging on the wall are what I remember most vividly.

Toby would often reiterate his desire to see the diaries published, and left the responsibility to my mother. When he passed away, my mother and I felt it would be a fitting tribute to both Toby and Alexander to publish the diaries he cherished, so we set about fulfilling his wish.

It was during the editing process that my mother was diagnosed with cancer, and after a brave battle, she sadly succumbed to her illness. Having been handed the baton, so to speak, I feel proud and privileged to have been part of bringing this humbling collection to a wider audience. I sincerely hope it inspires you as much as it did me.

Richard Hallam

For the 1026 men who lost their
lives on board HMS *Invincible*,
and for Caroline Hallam.

ACKNOWLEDGEMENTS

It has been our good fortune to work alongside several people who have shared our enthusiasm for Alexander Scrimgeour's writing, and without whom this compelling collection would never have seen the light of day. First, Sonia Land, whose belief in the diaries was paramount; secondly, the editor of the first edition, Alison Moss, whose tireless hard work and guidance were integral; and our original publisher, John Lee, whose vision and passion for the project has been nothing less than overwhelming. For this new edition, we are grateful for the support from Lisa Thomas at Bloomsbury.

We are indebted to Andrew Lambert for his wonderful words; Nick Swan at Aldro School for supplying us with Alexander's school photographs; Alan Jones for his local knowledge, and to Rick Beynon for slaving over a scanning machine for the best part of a day. On a more personal note, we would both like to thank our partners, Jodie and Vicky, for their patience and understanding.

Toby Hallam, who was born during the editing of these diaries, inherits the moniker of the Scrimgeour gentlemen, ensuring their legacy lives on.

Richard Hallam and Mark Beynon

INTRODUCTION

Born on 5 March 1897, Alexander Scrimgeour grew up in the picturesque Kentish village of Wickhambreaux, five miles outside Canterbury. At the time of his birth, the name Scrimgeour was synonymous with London stockbroking – the family would later go on to achieve greater success under his younger brother, Jim. Alexander led a privileged upbringing as the eldest of four children, reaping the benefits of his father's (Alexander Caron Scrimgeour's) wealth and status, both educationally and socially. As well as Jim, Alexander had a much younger brother called Billy and a sister, Peggy.

To best understand his aspirations (or perhaps his father's aspirations for him) as a boy born at the turn of the century, it is important to consider Edwardian society, which, although brief, was undeniably fascinating in its attitudes. Most historians agree that the Edwardian era covers the period from the turn of the twentieth century to the outbreak of the First World War. The ambitions of a young upper-middle-class gentleman would have been dictated by a stringent list of professions. Many young Edwardians would follow in their father's footsteps, but Alexander joined the Royal Navy, a profession chosen for him by his father when he was still a child, and this would have been deemed suitable by his family and their peers at a time when Britain was at the height of her imperial power.

Edwardian Britain afforded the affluent every chance in life. While the rich seemed to get richer and richer, the poor descended further into poverty. The dissent arising from this fanned a turbulent political climate. Britain was slowly coming to terms with the idea of the suffrage movement and the role of working women in its society – this would, of course, become commonplace throughout the First World War in the munitions factories.

The theatre, which was enjoying a renaissance of its own, was suddenly inundated with strong and dominant female characters and an upturn in plays that shocked contemporary audiences with their frank portrayals of everyday life and sexuality. Similar female characters would make their mark on literature, too. At a time when an enormous number of novels and short stories were being written and consumed, many would reflect the issues of the day. The emergence of socialism, the age of the self-educated man, and a middle-class society that refused to support the flamboyant and gaudy trends of Edward VII and the upper classes, would also be represented by a new era of fiction, which evolved from its Victorian predecessor.

Seemingly inspired by the many great writers of his era, Alexander decided to keep a day-to-day diary, which displayed his own adroit ability with prose. The diaries that have survived start in 1910, and cover his formative years from cadet training right through to his active service in war, and his cherished time spent at home with family and friends. Indeed, it is important to emphasise that this collection is not just a war diary. Alexander was efficient in writing his accounts and recording events as they happened, displaying a self-discipline that has left us with a sharp insight into the era, untouched by the vagaries of memory and post-war analysis.

The Scrimgeour family owned two properties: the first was The Quaives in Wickhambreaux; and the second was a flat at Cumberland Terrace near Regent's Park. Still considered to be one of the more desirable properties in London, the John Nash-designed Cumberland Terrace has seen many illustrious dignitaries reside there over the years, such as the composer Bernard Herrmann. Indeed, in the front of his 1913 diary, Alexander lists the properties to which his diary should be sent if lost. As well as his home addresses, Alexander also lists Hatton Court, Threadneedle Street, London, and Dudhope Castle in Dundee. It is fair to assume that Hatton Court was his father's place of work as it is situated right in the heart of the London banking district, and Dudhope Castle was, and still is, the seat of Clan Scrimgeour in Scotland. Before moving to The Quaives, the Scrimgeours lived at Batemans in East Sussex, eventually selling the property to Rudyard Kipling in 1902 when Alexander was five.

Alexander also enjoyed the benefits of a first-class education, initially at Aldro School in Eastbourne, East Sussex. Having been groomed for a career in the armed forces, in 1910, at the age of thirteen, he joined the Royal Navy as a cadet, and forged the friendships that would last until his death. Together with his contemporaries, Thomas Cobb, Leopold Johnstone, Alexander Richardson, Richard Henderson, Desmond Tottenham, William Hutchinson (WSH was Alexander's 'best friend') and 'Fober' Robinson, Alexander went through four years of rigorous tuition, two at Osborne Naval College, Isle of Wight, and two at Dartmouth Royal Naval College, before being approved to train on board HMS *Cornwall* in the first half of 1914. (The *Cornwall*, a 9,800-ton Monmouth-class armoured cruiser, would later go on to sink the German light cruiser *Leipzig* in the Battle of the Falklands and support the Dardanelles campaign.)

The group of cadets flourished and excelled in the demanding training conditions on board the *Cornwall*, and they were fortunate to find themselves frequently harboured in glamorous locations with ample free time on their hands. Unsurprisingly, they would make the most of their leave, often resulting in tales of high jinks. In the first half of 1914 alone, the *Cornwall* was permanently away from Britain, including a three-month stay in the Mediterranean during which she visited Monte Carlo, Malta, Gibraltar, Nice, Cannes, Florence and Algiers. Sport provided another source of distraction for the cadets looking to wile away their recreation. It occupied much of Alexander's spare time, and he regularly partook in rugby and cricket matches, both at college and while on leave abroad. Indeed, spectator sport enjoyed a boom throughout the Edwardian era, and many young men wished to emulate the sportsmen they would have seen at Lord's and Twickenham.

In July 1914, Alexander and the *Cornwall* returned to England, and on Saturday, 18 July, Winston Churchill, the then First Lord of the Admiralty, came on board to visit the crew during the Royal Fleet Review, perhaps to herald what was to come. Just two weeks later, and after less than a week of leave, Alexander was summoned to the naval barracks at Portsmouth where he and his fellow cadets were assigned to HMS

Crescent (a first-class cruiser of the Edgar class) as midshipmen. The First World War had begun, quite remarkably just as Alexander had finished his training.

The build-up to war had been gradual and inevitable. Germany looked to emulate Britain's empire and relations between the two nations became increasingly strained in the early 1900s following the 'scramble for Africa' and the alarming escalation of the arms race following the introduction of HMS *Dreadnought* in 1906.

Under Rear-Admiral Dudley de Chair, who was in command of the Tenth Cruiser Squadron and who was assigned the *Crescent* as his flagship, Alexander and company were given the unenviable task of maintaining a blockade with a view to intercept all German commerce. Following severe damage to the *Crescent* during a storm, de Chair and the cadets were transferred to the armed merchant cruiser *Alsatian* in December 1914. Continuing their strict blockade, it was during 1915 that the *Alsatian* had been at sea a phenomenal 262 days. She had steamed 71,500 miles and had burned 40,287 tons of coal, all the while negotiating the perils of mines (which they came close to hitting on more than one occasion) and the ever-present threat of U-boats. In recognition of the work of the Tenth Cruiser Squadron, Rear-Admiral de Chair would receive the KCB.

On the infrequent occasions that Alexander was entitled leave, his diary entries offer a tantalising glimpse into how a footloose young Edwardian gentleman spent his time. Frequenting many of the hotspots of London, Liverpool and Edinburgh, Alexander recorded the details of his social life, which, despite the war, was not short of frivolity. Indeed, before the outbreak of hostilities, London had a reputation for being the most glamorous city in the world, and although the reality of war had an effect on its glitz (in particular, the infrequent Zeppelin air raids), it merely dimmed the city's many lights but never extinguished them.

The most fashionable district was Piccadilly and Regent Street, in particular the Trocadero, Criterion, Monico and Café Royal restaurants. They were all grand affairs, afforded by only the middle and upper classes.

Nearby, the Strand was equally chic: the Savoy, Simpson's, the Drury Lane and Covent Garden theatre district, and the new hotels in and around Aldwych and Holborn (including the Strand Palace and the Waldorf) provided the main sources of entertainment. It is unsurprising that Alexander would visit them all during his leave in London.

Similarly, in Liverpool Alexander enjoyed visiting the Olympia Theatre and Adelphi Hotel. After he was transferred to HMS *Invincible* in July 1915 and joined the Battle Cruiser Fleet based at Rosyth in the Firth of Forth, as an officer he was able to make the most of all the delights of Scotland's capital city, frequenting the Waverley on Princes Street, the Café Royal on West Register Street and the Haymarket Ice Rink in particular.

In August 1914, the House of Commons passed the Defence of the Realm Act (DORA) without debate. Fearing that the war effort was becoming hampered by drunkenness, the legislation allowed the government to control civilian behaviour, including the consumption of alcohol. David Lloyd George, the Chancellor of the Exchequer, famously claimed that Britain was 'fighting the Germans, Austrians and drink, and as far as I can see the greatest of these foes is drink'. Pub drinkers were the hardest hit by the new legislation, which limited opening times. But perhaps the most shocking change of all was the introduction of watered-down beer.

However, restaurants and hotels experienced an influx of young party-goers keen to avoid watered-down beer in favour of wine, spirits and cocktails, which, although heavily taxed, were still affordable. Following the Licensing (Consolidation) Act of 1910, those who were sixteen and over were able to purchase alcoholic beverages, and Alexander as a seventeen-year-old in 1914 certainly made the most of his fortuitous position.

It was around this time that Alexander fell in love with 'Joko' Robertson (having previously fallen for her friend, Doris Champion), a family friend and an aspiring actress, who lived a short distance from The Quaives in a house called Westenhanger in neighbouring Ickham.

However, their brief relationship was tragically cut short when he was assigned to HMS *Invincible*. It was to be the first and last battle cruiser Alexander would serve in. Upon hearing of Alexander's death at the Battle of Jutland in May 1916, his heartbroken father, flexing his financial muscle, used his society status to investigate his son's last moments. Much like the aforementioned Rudyard Kipling did when his son Jack died at the Battle of Loos, Alexander Caron Scrimgeour interviewed the two highest-ranking officers of the six survivors from HMS *Invincible*. Not every family of the 1,026 dead would have been able to persuade Commander Dannreuther and Lieutenant Sandford to make a house call. But Alexander's father did.

When we examine and contextualise the diaries of Alexander Scrimgeour we are immediately struck by just how articulate and intelligent he was. Juxtaposing the rigours of life at sea during the war and the glamour of Edwardian society in London and Kent, Scrimgeour seamlessly goes from love-struck teenage squire to proud midshipman. His love for his family is very much evident throughout, particularly in his letters to his mother, Helen, which although displaying a golden sarcastic wit, are always touching and heartfelt. Alexander signs his letters off as 'Toby', which was a long-standing moniker for the Scrimgeour gentlemen named Alexander – of which there have been many. His ability to poke fun at his own expense is charming, especially when he has an off day at the countryside shoot.

Perhaps the most significant feature of the diaries is Alexander's willingness to record highly confidential information, including government cover-ups and the movement of a German spy. This would have resulted in his court martial and expulsion from the Navy should his diaries have been discovered. On numerous occasions, one has the feeling that he was writing his diary, not just for his own personal record and gratification, but for something far grander.

The shift in tone from 1914 to 1915 is also worth noting. December 1914 saw Alexander spend his first Christmas away from his family, and the poignancy of the occasion is marked in his diary entries. The following year he barely acknowledges the holiday season at all. Indeed, his style of writing changes, too, as do his opinions of the war. Initially Alexander comes across as an eager patriot, and this is reflected in his prose. By 1915, however, a matter-of-fact bluntness replaces his initial enthusiasm. Bearing in mind the vast majority of those serving in the First World War believed it would all be over by Christmas 1914, it seems evident that a year at sea during wartime had sapped Alexander's spirits.

As part of their training, midshipmen were required to keep a detailed journal of their daily duties at sea (without personal opinion or conjecture). Supplied by the Admiralty, their purpose was to hone and improve the midshipman's knowledge and understanding of all things nautical. It was by chance that we discovered Alexander's Midshipman's Journal covering his time on board *Crescent* and *Alsatian* during the editing of these diaries. We have seen fit to incorporate some of his hand-drawn charts and illustrations as well as supplement his journal entries when, for whatever reason, he hadn't recorded an entry in his personal diary.

During 1915, Alexander left his diary at home for weeks at a time. We can only speculate as to why he did this, although it is fair to assume that he was concerned that his diary would fall into the wrong hands as the war dragged on. This is supported by the fact that his more controversial diary entries were written as amendments on scrap pieces of paper, and included loose.

In editing the diaries, we have kept Alexander's spellings, particularly of place names, which may differ from modern usage, but have corrected his punctuation when necessary. Alexander made extra notes at the end of his 1914 diary regarding the characters of the officers of the *Crescent* and *Alsatian*. We have left them in place.

As stated, Alexander's surviving diaries begin in 1910 and continue until 1915 (we are left to assume that his 1916 diary would have gone down with him at Jutland). For this new edition, which commemorates the centenary of the Battle of Jutland, we have transcribed earlier, unpublished material. This edition starts in August 1913, when Alexander became a more confident diarist, and takes in his training at Dartmouth Royal Naval College, his enthralling time abroad on HMS *Cornwall*, as well as the build-up to war through his eyes.

Both sides of Alexander's life are vividly brought to life in his writing. At once we get an idea of what the drab conditions were like in the ships of the British fleet in the First World War, and yet the thrill of Edwardian society is so often brilliantly described. One wonders what might have become of Alexander had he survived Jutland and the war. It must be remembered that both Jellicoe and Beatty entered the Navy as midshipmen, and Alexander's friend at Osborne, John Tovey, was Admiral of the Fleet during the Second World War and sank the *Bismarck*.

From what these diaries tell us about Alexander's character, apart from putting a very human face on a faceless war, perhaps a similar position would have been bestowed upon him, too. As it is, we have a treasured record of a talented young life suddenly cut short – a tragedy of war.

Mark Beynon

'RULE BRITANNIA'

THE ROYAL NAVY IN 1914

Alexander Scrimgeour served in the world's most successful fighting service, heir to Nelson, Trafalgar and an almost unbroken run of success that stretched back even further still. The Royal Navy was responsible for the security, prosperity and power of the British state, the overseas empire and the trade that connected it. For a century it had provided the visible proof of British power that backed up the financial services, in which the elder Srimgeour made his money; and deterred war. Unrivalled in size, reputation and reach, the Edwardian Navy formed the armoured centre of British power, and the core of its culture, from sailor suits to Navy Days and Trafalgar Square.

Britain was a maritime nation with a global empire and no one doubted the sea was the natural element of her people. The effortless superiority that Scrimgeour and his contemporaries assumed reflected an unchallenged reality – this was *the* Navy. Such organisations do not promote doubt or introspection. Furthermore, the culture of Edwardian Britain was dominated by values that amplified key elements of officer-like behaviour: 'self-restraint, perseverance, strenuous effort, courage in the face of adversity' and 'an abiding sense of duty'.*

OFFICER EDUCATION

At the turn of the twentieth century British naval education underwent a radical transformation. Cadets joined the service at 12 or 13 at the new Osborne College on the Isle of Wight, built amid the stable blocks of Queen Victoria's favourite home, where they would spend the first two years. Then they moved to Dartmouth, where the old *Britannia* stationary

---

* Collini, S. *Public Moralists: Political Thought and Intellectual Life in Britain 1850–1930.* Oxford: Clarendon Press; 1991. p.100.

training ship for officer cadets, a wooden wall left over from the 1850s, had been replaced by a massive new shoreside college. In addition, the curriculum was brought up to date to include engineering and modern languages – subjects in which Scrimgeour demonstrated considerable ability – English, history and seamanship.

Under Alfred Ewing, Director of Naval Education and wartime code-breaker, the curriculum was strikingly modern, lacking the ancient languages and other mental exercises that continued to dominate in the public schools. Ewing recruited a high-quality staff. The object was to produce commissioned officers ready for active duty in a highly technical profession by the age of 20. The architect of these reforms, Admiral Fisher, wanted all cadets to be educated together, to a common curriculum, whether they were destined for engineering, the marines or paymaster duty. This modern educational system was administered by naval officers who imbued the pupils with a rigid code of honour, one that led to a major *cause célèbre* in the Archer-Shee case of 1908, the basis for the drama *The Winslow Boy*. This was the structure in place in 1910 and 13-year-old Alexander Scrimgeour joined Osborne under the shadow of the Archer-Shee case.*

After four years at College, cadets of Scrimgeour's generation went to sea in a training ship before being rated as midshipmen and joining the regular service. They would be 16 or 17. They were well equipped for the task. In August 1914 newly minted midshipman Scrimgeour was about to be posted to his first ship. By contrast, the term below his were rushed into service at the outbreak of war, and many were lost in the armoured cruisers *Aboukir, Cressy* and *Hogue* in September.

The benefits of Fisher's new education system are obvious to any reader of Scrimgeour's diary. He was soon employed as an interpreter when seizing German trawlers, and made a useful effort at working on Norwegian radio messages. Furthermore, he was comfortable working with the latest fire control instruments, gunsights and engines. As a

---

* Partridge, MS. *The Royal Naval College Osborne: A History 1903–1921*. Stroud: Sutton Publishing; 1999. Davies, EL, Grove, EJ. *The Royal Naval College Dartmouth*. Portsmouth: Gieves & Hawkes; 1980.

well-connected young man from a prosperous upper-middle-class background it would be expected that Scrimgeour was destined for a career in the regular service, but by 1915 his obvious mechanical aptitude led him to consider shifting to engineering.

The diaries and letters that survive are those of a well-educated, technically sophisticated young man. The speed with which he adjusted to the demands of war, and the key role he and others like him played in providing up-to-date expertise for older reserve officers indicates the success of the system. His work on the *Crescent*, rebuilding gunsights, adding fire control gear, handling range finding and gunnery direction demonstrate the success of the Osborne/Dartmouth system in generating the necessary young officers ready for service.

However, midshipmen at sea were still, in effect, under training. They did not qualify for a commission, as sub-lieutenants, until they had been examined in a wide range of specialist aspects of the profession: seamanship, gunnery, navigation, torpedoes and electricity. Throughout the diaries Scrimgeour expresses his anxiety to get first-class marks in his five examinations, which would accelerate his promotion to lieutenant, and the limits of his instruction and instructors while serving with the Tenth Cruiser Squadron and on *Invincible*. Without quality instruction from the naval instructor and experienced officers on the ships, he could not produce the necessary journals and exercises, or master the subjects to the requisite standard. It may be surmised that Rear-Admiral de Chair was motivated to send him to the Grand Fleet to ensure a fine young officer was ready for the examinations. By May 1916 Scrimgeour was an acting sub-lieutenant in recognition of his experience and his ability pending the examination. He had spent much of his time on *Invincible* working through the different departments of the ship, gunnery, engineering, etc., making the necessary drawings and journals.

GRAND STRATEGY

In August 1914 Britain went to war with well-prepared plans for global war. The government defence co-ordinating body, the Committee of

Imperial Defence, had developed a plan to harness the power of the empire and protect the commercial shipping that linked the various dominions and colonies with the home islands, while crushing German overseas trade and colonies through a tough economic blockade. This maritime war would complement the military efforts of Britain's Entente partners, France and Russia, who were expected to defeat the German and Austro-Hungarian armies in Europe. The small British Expeditionary Force would contribute to the defence of France and Belgium, but the government had no intention of raising or using mass armies on the continental model. They preferred to rely on the Royal Navy, while maintaining British trade and industry.

The linchpin of British strategy was the Grand Fleet at Scapa Flow, which controlled access to the North Sea. By placing a superior fleet across Germany's international trade routes Britain ensured the destruction of her commerce and her empire, while protecting her own trade. This situation would only change if the Grand Fleet was defeated. The rest of the naval effort operated behind the strategic cover provided by Vice-Admiral Sir John Jellicoe's dreadnought battleships. There was no need for the British to seek out the German High Seas Fleet, because they expected the economic blockade to win the war and that when the Germans recognised this they would be obliged to take the initiative – to attack the British in the waters between Scotland and Norway.

THE BLOCKADE: HMS *CRESCENT* AND
THE TENTH CRUISER SQUADRON

On the eve of war the Royal Navy quickly and efficiently mobilised its officers and men. Scrimgeour was ordered to HMS *Crescent*, a 7,700-ton protected cruiser of the Edgar class.* By 1914 these ships were twenty years old and woefully outdated; their obsolescent guns, fire control and

---

* HMS *Crescent* was built in Portsmouth Dockyard in 1890–94: 360 ft long, 60 ft beam; speed of 20 knots when built, no more than 18 by 1914; one 9.2-inch gun, twelve 6-inch guns and twelve 6-pounder guns.

engines denied them a place in the main fleet. However, they remained effective seaworthy vessels and gave good service through the war.

The *Crescent*, the flagship of the Tenth Cruiser Squadron, and her seven sister ships were ordered to the seas off the north of Scotland for blockade service under Rear-Admiral Sir Dudley de Chair. Unfortunately, they soon encountered threats they were ill-equipped for. U-boat torpedoes sank HMS *Hawke* while mountainous seas sent many back to base for extended repairs. Scrimgeour's striking description of one particular storm adds power and resonance to the usual laconic official report: Boats were smashed, forty men injured and many compartments simply washed out.

The Tenth Cruiser Squadron occupied the front line of the economic war effort, the main British contribution to the defeat of Germany before mid-1916. The operation of the blockade depended on the interpretation of International Law dealing with the rights of belligerent states and neutrals. German merchant ships were fair game, and a few were taken trying to get home, but the real problem lay in the shipment of goods to Germany in neutral ships, and via neutral third parties. Britain asserted the right to stop neutral merchant ships on the high seas, and inspect their cargo for contraband; that is goods defined as likely to aid the enemy war effort – anything from guns and fuel to army reservists and food.

On 4 August 1914 the British listed obvious war materials destined for Germany as absolute contraband, while food and other items as conditional contraband, liable to seizure if destined for enemy armed forces. On 20 August, the application of this regime was widened to include cargoes destined for contiguous neutrals, Denmark, the Netherlands and Sweden. Six days later rumours that the army had taken control of all German food stocks saw food added to the list of absolute contraband, a serious change in the nature of the blockade, now clearly aimed at the entire population.

The list was widened yet further as the year went on and the USA showed itself favourable to the Anglo-French alliance. The North Sea was defined as a war zone, and all neutral merchant ships were obliged to stop for inspection in the Strait of Dover, with the exception of the Scandinavians. On 11 March 1915 an Order in Council established a complete blockade of Germany, and began to limit the imports of the Scandinavian powers, to stop them exporting any surplus to Germany. This was based on two coercive instruments, British naval power and control of the world's steam coal supply. While most ships were prepared to accept British demands, the Tenth Cruiser Squadron still had to patrol a vast area of rough and dangerous sea to intercept potential blockade breakers, facing the perils of U-boat attack, mines and a surface sortie by heavy German forces.

As might be expected the Scandinavian states and the Netherlands saw neutrality as an opportunity for profit, quickly generating large agricultural industries to supply Germany with processed animal fats, from butter to bacon. Swedish iron and copper, industrial products and horses all helped to sustain the German war effort while her manpower was detained in uniform. The British government, unlike the Navy which simply assumed all would bend before the will of Britannia, was anxious to keep on good terms with these powers. This would ensure their merchant ships carried goods for the Allies, and prevent them from joining Germany.

The German response – unrestricted submarine warfare – proved to be a diplomatic disaster. With a little help from British propaganda – the same machine that fed Scrimgeour and his friends with 'Hun' atrocity stories – the U-boats persuaded neutrals that Germany was more dangerous than Britain. As a result, the blockade was never perfect, and took time to reach a level at which it began to seriously weaken the German war effort. But it was an effective instrument, well handled at all levels.*

---

* Grainger, J, editor. *The Maritime Blockade of Germany in the Great War: The Northern Patrol 1914–1918.* Aldershot: Navy Records Society; 2003. This provides an extensive documentary collection on the work of the Tenth Cruiser Squadron. The official history is: Bell, AC. *A History of the Blockade of Germany and the Central Powers.* London: HMSO; 1937.

Scrimgeour's first-hand account of the business of blockade and patrol reveals the combination of boredom and excitement (bad weather, poor food, discomfort and coaling ship (refuelling)) as they boarded ships and countered German efforts to break blockade with munitions, food, and reservists from the USA and elsewhere. Throughout the war naval officers constantly complained that the Foreign Office was weakening to blockade, kow-towing to the Americans and allowing neutral powers to act as conduits for German imports. This was a particular concern for the Tenth Cruiser Squadron, whose harsh and demanding regime must have been softened by the expectation of a rich haul of prize money.

In the event the naval prize fund was homogenised and paid out *pro rata* to every man in the service. The complaints of naval officers were serious, but missed the bigger picture. The British government was highly successful in persuading, or coercing neutrals into self-regulation; while the compliance of the US administration and covert intelligence operations predicted most suspect sailings, and positioned ships to intercept. As cipher officer on the *Alsatian* Scrimgeour was ideally placed to see how these intelligence-led operations worked, and clearly understood how intelligence was used. Admiral de Chair understood the wider ramifications of the blockade, and remained involved in the economic war when he went ashore.

HMS *ALSATIAN*

Before the war the Admiralty had recognised the need to supplement the Navy's cruiser fleet with Armed Merchant Cruisers. Initially they looked at big Atlantic liners, such as the *Lusitania*, but by 1914 the choice had fallen on smaller, more economic ships that combined long endurance with good seaworthiness. Within months the first of these ships joined the Tenth Cruiser Squadron, replacing the elderly *Crescent* and her sisters over the winter of 1914–15. Scrimgeour moved to HMS *Alsatian*, a nearly new 18,000-ton Allan Line steamer built for the Liverpool–Canada trade. Armed with eight 6-inch guns, she became the flagship.

In 1915 she spent 262 days at sea, covering 71,500 miles and burning 40,287 tons of coal.*

This was the grim reality of the economic blockade, hard sea service, for extended periods, stopping and searching merchant ships: Scrimgeour notes that between 8 March and 19 April 1915 367 ships were intercepted, and 129 sent in for inspection with a prize crew on board. Every detail of the work was hard, not least the business of lowering a boat, rowing across to the suspect vessel and getting on board. Scrimgeour only went once or twice, but he got very wet. More significantly, he was involved with *Alsatian*'s modern guns and fire control equipment. These ships were ideally suited to the task, and well equipped.

While Scrimgeour was apt to be dismissive of his admiral (an opinion that others have repeated), de Chair knew that his young officers were the future of the Navy. He did not keep the best midshipmen in his squadron, where their education would suffer, and once the Armed Merchant Cruisers were up to standard he was content to get by with reserve officers and volunteers. If old 'Duds' had a soft spot for Scrimgeour, it was because the young officer had shown great promise in all aspects of his work. Clearly he had good links and impressed the men who mattered.

The dramatic, crushing British victory off the Falklands Islands in December 1914 ended the oceanic phase of the war at sea. This allowed the British to concentrate their naval effort in the main theatres, especially the North Sea where all modern capital ships were assembled. It also simplified the work of the Tenth Cruiser Squadron, which no longer needed to look over its shoulder in case German warships came in from the west.

HMS *INVINCIBLE*

In July 1915 Scrimgeour exchanged the hard graft of the blockade for the most glamorous posting in the Navy, the battle cruiser HMS *Invincible*,

---

* Osborne, R, Spong, H, Gover, T. *Armed Merchant Cruisers 1873–1945*. Windsor: World Ship Society; 2007. This is the essential guide to these ships and their operations. The *Alsatian* was 600 ft by 72.4 ft, with a speed of 18 knots and with eight 6-inch guns. See p.93.

flagship of Rear-Admiral Sir Horace Hood's Third Battle Cruiser Squadron. The Battle Cruiser Fleet was based at Rosyth in the Firth of Forth. Completed in 1908, the 18,000-ton, 26-knot *Invincible* was the first of her type, a dreadnought armed with eight 12-inch guns, and powerful turbine engines.* Conceived by Admiral Sir John Fisher to combine the speed and firepower needed to deal with threats to ocean shipping, the battle cruisers quickly became iconic. With three mighty funnels belching smoke to set off the high freeboard hulls and a powerful bow wave, they looked every inch the ideal warship, and after action at the Heligoland Bight in August 1914 and the battle of the Falkland Islands in December, *Invincible* had a high profile.

Under the dynamic leadership of Vice-Admiral Sir David Beatty the Battle Cruiser Fleet saw themselves as the elite of the service, and played hard living up to the image: The new boy soon discovered this was an expensive posting. Nevertheless, coaling ship remained a monumental task for the entire ship's company.

However, the battle cruiser type bought their speed, 6 or 7 knots faster than contemporary battleships, at the expense of reduced armour protection. After Jutland it was argued that this caused the loss of three of the type, and their glittering reputation suffered a sudden reverse.[†]

Hood, the third son of the Fourth Lord Hood, was a direct descendant of Nelson's mentor, Admiral Samuel, Lord Hood. While Scrimgeour manages to confuse a little of the family tree in one of his letters home, he was well aware of the powerful dynastic connections between his admiral and the greatest names in naval history. He also noted that Hood, like Beatty, had married an American woman, and picked up some of the speech and mannerisms of his in-laws. Hood was also a familiar figure; he had been captain of the Osborne College during Scrimgeour's time.

---

* Built in Newcastle, the 567 ft long, 78 ft 6 in broad *Invincible* weighed 17,330 tons. Her engines produced 41,000 horse power.

† Tarrent, VE. *Battle Cruiser Invincible: The History of the First Battle Cruiser, 1909–1916*. London: Arms & Armour; 1986. This provides a full-length biography of the ship.

In one vital respect the Battle Cruiser Fleet mirrored the Tenth Cruiser Squadron: Both operated on intelligence leads provided by the Admiralty's code-breaking unit, Room 40. Poor German radio discipline gave the British precious insights into their plans, opportunities to intercept their infrequent sorties, and the luxury of waiting in harbour rather than patrol. In late November/early December 1915 a fleet exercise tested one scenario, a German battle cruiser sortie into the Atlantic. Scrimgeour and several of his contemporaries sat their examinations for sub-lieutenant early in 1916, and he passed. This brought him into the Navy as an officer holding the King's commission, and increased his responsibilities.

In March and April 1916 the fleet went to sea, first to support a seaplane raid, and then to intercept a German sortie, and only missed contact by fifty or sixty miles. Returning from the second cruise *Invincible* collided with an armed yacht, and suffered considerable damage. The enforced docking gave Scrimgeour his last shore leave.

THE BATTLE OF JUTLAND

After the ship returned to sea the Third Battle Cruiser Squadron was detached to Scapa Flow for long overdue gunnery exercises: They could not conduct full-calibre shoots at Rosyth without breaking all the windows in Kirkcaldy. In their absence the Battle Cruiser Fleet was supplemented by the Fifth Battle Squadron. The exercises at Scapa were 'highly satisfactory'. Before they could return to Rosyth the fleet sortied, and the Third formed up with Jellicoe's Grand Fleet, while the Fifth Battle Squadron took its place in the Battle Cruiser Fleet. This time they would meet the Germans, the long-awaited day had come. Contemporary accounts, both those sent to Scrimgeour's parents and others, make it clear the fleet set out with high hopes of battle and victory, having the chance to do their bit.

Acting ahead of Jellicoe's Grand Fleet, Hood's force missed the opening exchanges of the Run to the South, during which Beatty lost two of his battle cruisers. On a day when most British flag officers proved too cautious, and a few, such as Beatty (HMS *Lion*) and Robert

Arbuthnot (HMS *Defence*), overly aggressive, Hood stands out. Listening to incomplete and confusing hints from the radio he used his initiative to bring his squadron into battle, and achieved decisive effect, smashing the German scouting forces that were looking for Jellicoe's main fleet, and crippling the flagship enemy battle cruiser *Lützow* in a high-speed medium-range engagement, between 9000 and 10,000 yards. The last words that Scrimgeour, as the officer of X turret, would have heard were Hood's ringing endorsement of the ship's gunnery: 'Your firing is very good, keep at it as quickly as you can, every shot is telling.'

Then the smoke of battle parted and a second German battle cruiser, the *Derfflinger*, also opened fire. At 6.34pm a German salvo, two 12-inch shells, hit *Invincible* amidships, smashing through the 7-inch-thick frontal armour of Q turret, exploding in the loading chamber. The explosion set off the loose cordite charges, blowing the roof off the turret, and instantaneously passed down through the ammunition hoists to the main amidships magazine, which exploded with catastrophic force. A vast crimson flame, followed by a hellish pall of cordite and coal smoke, covered a gaping void which, only seconds before, had been occupied by the centre of the ship. When the smoke cleared *Invincible's* bow and stern were left pointing up to heaven like twin tombstones. Only six officers and men survived, most of them from the fire control top high on the foremast: 1026 had died in an instant, among them Hood, Scrimgeour and every man in X turret. It was, as David Beatty observed, 'a glorious death', but it was also entirely unnecessary.

Invincible was the third British battle cruiser to blow up that day. *Indefatigable* and *Queen Mary* had preceded her into eternity, in exactly the same way, with the same terrible human cost. At the loss of *Queen Mary* Beatty laconically observed: 'There seems to be something wrong with our bloody ships today.' After the battle an expert investigation concluded that the explosions were caused by human error, not design weakness. Following the action on the Dogger Bank in January 1915 Beatty had concluded that the answer to his tactical problems was to increase the rate of fire: His ships removed the air-tight safety interlocks in the ammunition hoists and allowed cordite charges to be stowed in exposed areas to achieve this. There is a hint of this ammunition production in the diary. As a result, any hit on a heavy gun turret risked the fire reaching the magazines. Only one ship in Beatty's force had replaced the interlocks, and reintroduced proper ammunition-handling practice – his flagship HMS *Lion*. As a result, the *Lion* survived the destruction of her Q turret during the heavy fighting in the Run to the South.

Rather than admit the real cause of the triple catastrophe lay in human error, his own human error, Beatty had the report suppressed, blamed the disaster on inadequate armour and had unnecessary and largely useless additional armour put on the ships. The reputation of the battle cruiser type never recovered. Had the designed safety systems been in place on 31 May 1916 it is highly unlikely that the *Invincible* would have exploded. Q turret would have been wrecked, and the gun crews killed, but the ship would have survived.* What tales Alexander Scrimgeour would have had to tell, like another Jutland turret officer, the future King George VI.

CONCLUSION

These diaries offer another priceless insight into the mental world of the Edwardian Navy. While we usually see the First World War as the play of vast numbers of faceless men in a mechanised war across the globe, the men who went to sea in Fisher's dreadnoughts were all too human. Scrimgeour is so obviously an 18-year-old boy with all the cultural baggage of Edwardian England, from his effortless assumption of innate superiority, his contempt for the beastly Huns and distrust of foreigners more generally, to the mores of dating and courtship among his social class. Class differences are accepted, and are reason enough to exclude men from the officer class. He and his generation went to war willingly, laid down their lives to do their duty, and accepted the human cost. While much of this might seem a very long way from the modern

---

* Roberts, J. *Battlecruisers*. London: Chatham Publishing; 1997. pp.118–20. The final word on the subject of British battle cruiser design.

world, Scrimgeour's emotions, his delight in the company of pretty girls and readiness to party hard are enduring aspects of the human condition.

That his parents were consoled by the thought that he met his end happy and glorious, tells us much about the age. A young life full of promise, snuffed out in an instant by a single catastrophic explosion, Alexander Scrimgeour would join a long list of Edwardian boys whose names will live in the memory for as long as the memorials of the Great War remain in place, bearing witness to the sacrifice of a generation. Unlike his army contemporaries, who lie in a neatly tended foreign field under a simple gravestone, his remains are entombed in the wreck of the *Invincible*, along with the last volume of his diary. There they rest, as part of a massive war grave in a shallow, dark North Sea, strewn with fishing nets and surrounded by empty cordite cases.

LIST OF ABBREVIATIONS

AP	Assistant Paymaster
ASC	Army Service Corps
BCS	Battle Cruiser Squadron
CERA	Chief Engine Room Artificer
CG	Coastguard
C-in-C	Commander-in-Chief
CPO	Chief Petty Officer
DR	Dead Reckoning
DSC	Distinguished Service Cross
DSO	Distinguished Service Order
ER	Engine Room
'Flags'	Flag-Lieutenant
Fx.	Forecastle (fo'c'sle)
GQs	General Quarters
GR	Gunroom
'Guns'	Gunnery-Lieutenant (GL)
HMS	Her Majesty's Ship
MAA	Master-at-Arms
No. 1	First Lieutenant
NO	Naval Officer
OOW	Officer of the Watch

PO	Petty Officer
QD	Quarterdeck
RA	Rear-Admiral
RFR	Royal Fleet Reserve
RMLI	Royal Marine Light Infantry
RNR	Royal Naval Reserve
RNVR	Royal Naval Volunteer Reserve
Snotties	Midshipmen
SM	Sergeant-Major
SNO	Senior Naval Officer
TBD	Torpedo Boat Destroyer
'Torps'	Torpedo-Lieutenant
VC	Victoria Cross
WO	Warrant Officer
WR	Wardroom
WT	Wireless Telegraphy

THE
SCRIMGEOUR
DIARIES

From Dartmouth to Jutland
1913–16

1913

AUGUST

Thursday 7

Came home on leave. Went in to the cricket at Canterbury. Ladies' day.
Notts got 308. Play dull. Saw Doris but did not have much time to talk
to her, as Percy and Mrs Champion remained there all the time.

Friday 8

Saw Wetherall from Dartmouth and JJK Shaw in the old Blakes, whom
funnily enough Doris says she knows. Had a chat with her in the
pavilion before lunch. Woolley, Humphreys and Hardinge played well.*
Saw a lot of Sophie.

Saturday 9

Went in to the cricket just in time to see Notts collapse before the rain
came on and stopped play for the day. Thunderstorm. Bad fair at Byron's
barn at Ickham Court.

Sunday 10

Played golf with Doris and beat her. She went home to tea early.

Monday 11

All the family went off to Hemsby. I was left alone at Quaives. Golf week
began. Played with Dolly against Boris and Lizzie Bony in the mixed
foursomes and we won 6 and 5. Saw Harry Baird.

---

* Frank Woolley, Edward Humphreys and Wally Hardinge, part of the Kent side
who won the County Championship in 1913. Woolley and Hardinge would go on
to play for England.

Tuesday 12

Played against Bogey with Jack and did badly. Went and played tennis with the Kelseys in the evening, but found I was very weak. Met the Cohens and Young. Bob came to supper.

Wednesday 13

Played with Dolly against Jack and Fanny and won on the nineteenth green after a terrific match. Jack Gordon came down. In the afternoon we beat Aubrey Cohen and Nora on the eighteenth. Picnicked with the Robertsons, the Champions and Alfred Schiff. Still very much in love with Doris and I am very fond of her, but do not know what she thinks of me and am afraid her parents are suspicious of me.

Thursday 14

The governor had a row with his men. Dolly and I played Col. and Mrs Rodwell in the final and were just beaten after a tremendous game. Their putting was brilliant. The Champions went to Sarre, so I saw nothing of Doris.

Friday 15

Heard from home. Played with Jack against Bogey. Bob won the men's comp. Doris won the girl's comp. Played tennis at Westenhanger. Dined at Seaton with the Drakes, and thoroughly enjoyed myself.

Saturday 16

We quarrelled about Alfred Schiff. Six of us, Bertie, Jackie, Alfred, Joko, Doris and myself went on the river at Grove Ferry; we did not enjoy ourselves. I bathed. We all had tea at Quaives. Head over heels in love with Doris, but I found to my chagrin that I have lost all my letters from her. Cannot think where they are. Dined with the Cohens at Frogwell and played baccarat until 3.

Sunday 17

Went to church at Ickham. Lunched and played tennis at Seaton. Capt. Barmby, an old Osborne friend, came over with Capt. Rawlings and invited me to go to Eastchurch.

Monday 18

I took nine people in the taxi to the cricket, including Nita, Joko, Alfred Schiff, Trevor, Elsie, Doris and Margot Folliot. Kent v Leicestershire. Who should we see but dear old Jack Burgess.* He batted jolly well and made 28. I gave the whole party tea at the café and then went off with Doris and bought her some handkerchiefs. More than ever in love with her. Am a bit more hopeful as to her feelings to me.

Tuesday 19

Went to the cricket again. Sat with Doris and the Champions all day. Lunched with the Wachers. Liked Jack Wacher. Allen, Selby Lowndes' enemy, was rude to us.

Wednesday 20

Last day of the cricket. Jack Burgess batted well. He came out to Quaives to spend the night and I did him as well as I could, which I am afraid was not very well. In the afternoon we all went to a tennis party at the Champions. I played better. Jack was too good for most of them. He was rather struck by Margery Champion, who returned home today, and also liked Doris. He said she was going to be 'the prettiest of the lot'.

---

* John 'Jack' Burgess was a first-class cricketer for Leicestershire. As a batsman and wicketkeeper, he made twelve appearances for his county between 1902 and 1913.

Thursday 21

I took Joko, the Champions and Jack Wacher to Dover cricket week in a taxi. Mr Abercrombie was playing for Hants and I had a long chat with him.* Had a bit of a huff with the girls coming back.

Friday 22

Went to the cricket again. Travelled down with the Nesbitts. Got back in time for a dance at the village hall, which was a great success. Still cool with Joko. Did not dance with Doris till the end of the evening, and felt fearfully jealous of her dancing with Schiff, etc., but had a lovely sit out with her at the end. We made up all our quarrels and she let me kiss her, the little darling. Our tête-à-tête was all too short. Ernest Baker came to Quaives.

Saturday 23

More in love with Doris than ever. Quite see the disadvantage of early marriage, especially with her, but begin to feel I shall have to marry her someday. Went to play tennis with the Robertsons. Lunched at the Kelseys. Dined with the Champions in the evening. Played hide and seek and it was great fun in the dark. Margery was very rude to me, so I went home.

Sunday 24

Did not get up till late. Doris came round to play golf but it rained and we had a lovely afternoon all by ourselves at Quaives. Wrote letters in the evening.

Monday 25

Went to the cricket at Dover again. I drove Doris and Margot to the station; Elsie bicycled. Met Jack Wacher at Dover. Good day's cricket.

---

* Cecil Abercrombie was a Scottish rugby union player and a first-class cricketer. He was capped six times for Scotland between 1910 and 1913, and played cricket for Hampshire in 1913. He also died at the Battle of Jutland in 1916 when he was serving on HMS *Defence*.

We put the pony up at Ernest Baker's. No lamps – we had to borrow returning. Came back with John Robertson and Mr Wacher. Belly band broke and we had to mend it. Went round to Westenhanger, the club and the Kelseys after supper, and did not get to bed until 2.30. Wrote to Tentworth and Capt. Barmby.

Tuesday 26
Drove Toots in to Canterbury and did some shopping. Went round to play tennis at the Champions in the afternoon. Arranged pony to Dover the next day. Mac came back from abroad.

Wednesday 27
Took Doris, Margery and a friend in taxi to the cricket at Dover. Sophie, Willie and Bertie came too. Good game. Kent won. Doris did not come round to see me in the evening although I waited for her for ages.

Thursday 28
Walked into Canterbury. Very hot day. Gave out that I had been to Eastchurch. Went round to Willie's cottage. Lost my cap. Saw but little of Doris, but thought of her all day. I wonder if she cares for me as much as I do for her.

Friday 29
Still saw but little of Doris. Played golf with Joko against Sophie and Mr Whitefield and took 2 up. We then played Alfred and Gladys and won 4 up and 2. I had to go or else we should probably have won the whole competition. I went to London and then down to Tentworth.

Saturday 30
Lost my bag in London, so had to borrow John's clothes. Went up to Stubbs' to see Auntie Maud. Peter and Sammie very sweet. Bella growing quite pretty and rather taken with me. I was disappointed to find that neither the Gedges nor the Salamans were there. Met Lady

Betty Clifton. Played polo in the evening. I played well. Jolly good game and I enjoyed it very much.

Sunday 31
Rained hard all day. Awful nuisance. Had supper at Stubbs'.

SEPTEMBER

Monday 1
Left Tentworth and came home to Quaives. Bella drove me to the station. Heard from Mr Hodgson, Culme's friend, inviting me to go and shoot. Saw Bob and Byron. Refused Hodgson's invitation.

Tuesday 2
Played golf with Joko against Alfred and Doris and won on the last green. Excellent performances. On the afternoon we all went for a picnic on the river; Margery, Elsie, Doris, Joko, Eileen Hills, Paddy Barrow, Jack Wacher, Trevor and myself. I have now determined to confront Doris with the Mac and Dolly smile, and tell her I am not such a fool as I look. I am very fond of her.

Wednesday 3
Doris came round to see me early, but I was slack and did not get up. Went round to Westenhanger. I went over with the Champions to the Sarre Champions – a tennis party. Quite good fun. I won two sets. Had tea and supper there. Paddy Barrow is quite a decent chap, but rather an ass. Doris looked sweet, and I saw all too little of her. We drove back together with Paddy Barrow. I adore Doris.

Thursday 4
Doris played golf with Paddy – I was furious. Everyone went to play tennis at the Champions. I was not asked either by accident or design,

and this increased my fury. I should not have gone if they had asked me. I drove Bob to Canterbury; saw a pretty girl at the Rose. General meeting of ICGC. Dined at Westenhanger; Elmleigh party came round, and had quite good fun. Did not leave till 2, and then rode up and down past the treasury thinking of Doris. I would do anything for her. Does she care for me? Tomorrow I shall settle everything finally.

Friday 5

Went to play cricket against Mr Ramsay's XI. I captained our side. Match drawn owing to rain in our favour. I did not bat. Dance in the evening at Ickham. Met DH Browne. I danced ten times with Doris and sat out four times, but had not pluck to settle. Still enjoyed myself very much with her. She looked simply sweet and I adore her. Left at about 1.30, but did not go to bed till 4 as I played gramophone records, etc., at home.

Saturday 6

Got up late. Club golf v Elmleigh and Westenhanger. Singles and foursomes. We won 17–6. I beat Whitefield 10 and 8, and Miss Byng and I beat Whitefield and Ethel Escombe 8 and 7. The Champions asked me to go to the cinema, but they did not go, and I had supper there. Margery rude to me again. I adore Doris but cannot make out whether she is only playing with me, or whether she really loves me a little. I love her, every inch of her. She is sweet, I adore her, I do. I think I shall find out her feelings by pumping Joko. The suspense makes me ill.

Sunday 7

Feeling rather miserable about Doris. Played tennis at Seaton. Had a good chance to tackle Joko about Doris but funked it. Very windy day.

Monday 8

Slacked about in the morning. Family came home. Daddy and Mother seemed rather funny. Dined at Westenhanger. Gladys and Bertie, Alfred and Doris came round. They dressed up. I was sulky and got worse when Doris flirted with Bertie. Got worse and went home in a tearing rage. Wrote to Doris asking whether she preferred Bertie or me and in case of a negative answer said I would have no more to do with her.

Tuesday 9

Got up early and posted my letter to Doris, got no answer and felt miserable. I adore her and cannot imagine why she prefers Bertie (if she does). I thought of her all day and every minute. Refused an invitation to go to Canterbury with Nita, Bertie, Gladys, Joko and the Schiffs. I am certain Joko is in love with me and so fosters my quarrel with Doris. Our children are flourishing but Daddy seems rather funny. Mother well.

Wednesday 10

Doris came round at breakfast; I was rather cool but fearfully pleased to see her. I think she must have decided on me but am not sure. Daddy, Governor and I went shooting. Lunched out; had an excellent day and got eleven-and-a-half brace partridges and six hares. I shot three-and-a-half brace and one hare, Daddy shot five brace and five hare, and Gov shot three brace. Old man very tired. Robertsons all went to Margate with Capt. Gould. Bertie, Gladys and Joko came round to see me after supper.

Thursday 11

Walked about with Peg and Jim in the morning. Played tennis at Westenhanger with Doris against Joko and Bertie and won. Played well. Tennis party at the Kelseys in the afternoon. I played badly. Asked Doris if she had got my letter; she said she had, but was too young to decide (she said she told Elsie). Why doesn't she love me? I adore her, I worship her. I crave for her love. Daddy gave me a bottle of champagne and we dined at Westenhanger. Doris was not there, alas.

Friday 12

Daddy, Gov and I shot again and got ten brace and four hares. I shot two-and-a-half brace and one hare, Daddy shot four-and-a-half brace, and

Gov shot three brace and three hares. Daddy got sciatica. Went round to the cottage to play tennis. Doris was not there. Bertie is as much in love with her as I am. I wonder who she likes best. Bertie and Alfred ragged Trevor. Sophie, Governor and Mother came to dinner. Daddy still not well. Talked with Mother about a motor.

Saturday 13

Huge party of us drove over to Shuart for the day. Sixteen people. Toby, Peggy, Jimmy, Bobbie Drake, Joko, Jackie, Jerram, Mr Whitefield, Alfred, Ernest, Gladys, Bertie, Edith, Doris, Trevor (and Luff). Good day; children thoroughly enjoyed themselves, bathing, etc. I swam a long way. Four of us went in to Birchington to the cinema. Saw Doris' school. Doris is a beastly little flirt; she flirted with Bertie and Alfred as well as me! I am absolutely fascinated with her, and am dying to get her alone. Daddy motored over to Aldington with Selby Lowndes. John Parish and Fanny to dinner. JP played piano.

Sunday 14

Doris came round to tea and supper. We played cards and Ludo. I took her home and I adore her. I think of her all day long.

Monday 15

Played cricket at St Lawrence v Mr Ramsay's XI, and were beaten. I batted well. Jimmy played, Doris scored. Large crowd watching. Doris, Joko, Alfred, Bertie and I dined at the Rose and went to the cinema after. Had a fine time with Doris; gave her the hat pins. I believe she likes me better than Bertie after all. Bertie is a dear old chap, but I adore Doris. She is divine. She is a fascinating, but elusive, darling.

Tuesday 16

Played golf with Doris against Joko and Alfred and won easily. Gave them six strokes. Arranged to meet Doris in churchyard, but she stood me up. Nita had another row with the Cohens. Had a chat with Bob and

Mac. Paid Anchor's bill. Doris came round to supper and looked simply sweet. I love her. We played cards after. I drove her home, but Trevor came to fetch her and so spoilt our tête-à-tête.

Wednesday 17

Loafed about in the morning. Lunched with Mac at Bob's. Mac, Bob, Byron and I played the Doctor in the afternoon and he beat us. Went to tea at the Champions. Said Sunday goodbyes. Although it was my last day, Doris flirted with Alfred and Bertie! Still I think she really likes me best. They all came round after supper and I got rather cross and swore at her. I hope she did not mind. She has promised to write to me, the dear.

Thursday 18

Just missed George and Daddy. Said goodbye to everyone, but did not get Doris alone. Felt severe heart burnings at leaving her. I realise how much she means to me, and I think of her continually. Left Grove Ferry with Nita. Went to shop at 37 Warwick Road. In the evening Sophie, Nita and I went to a variety show at the Victoria Palace. Quite good turns. Ragtime rotten!

Friday 19

Went to see Aunt Do. Bought a bracelet for Doris' birthday present. Called on Bengie Young, 8 Queens Gate Place, but he was out. Went to the Natural History Museum. Went down by the 3.30 to Dartmouth. Hutcher left behind in the train. Had quite good fun and broke several windows! Left my Bellagio stud box behind at Sophie's. Took a deckchair back.

Saturday 20

Started work again. I am taking the Exmouth term with Lieut. Sturges. The other skippers are Stromeyer, AS Russell and Roxburgh. Made up logs and slack party.* Danced in the evening, and unpacked. Same

---

* A group of cadets performing a punishment detail.

masters as last term. Saw old Browne. Wrote home, several letters, and wrote to Doris.

Sunday 21

Drake Open List. Captain jawed with skippers. Tottenham, Branson, Hutchinson and I chatted with Sturges and Blagrove.

Monday 22

Heard from Mother, Daddy and Peggy with photos of the Shuart expedition. Went to the gym, did rifle drill and started row time in earnest. First tutor set prep. Regatta practice on the river. I left my old gig and went out with Johnstone, Cockburn and Pyke-Nott, with Nicholson (cox). Fair crew; I pulled badly. Too slack to go in a skiff.

Tuesday 23

Practised in gig again and also sculling – rowed badly. Received my stud box from Sophie, and also heard from Jimmy. Inaugurated slack party in Exmouth term. Feeling rather slack; think I must pull myself together and buck up. Also think I stop up too late at nights! Hoping to hear from Doris. I wonder if she has forgotten all about me or not. She goes back to school today.

Wednesday 24

Went to seamanship room and got into a scrape. Still feel rather off work. Am reading *David Copperfield* hard. On the river again; sculled fairly well and did much better in gig. Heard from Jimmy.

Thursday 25

Punted about for training on upper ground. Carried out a coal and efficiency test in the Power House at Sandquay in the afternoon.* It was

---

* Sandquay was home to Dartmouth Naval College's boat maintenance operation.

quite interesting. Slack party steadily getting licked into shape. Went to bed early. CPO Saunders complained about mess in the wash houses.

Friday 26

Heard from Aunt Do. She sent me petition forms against Home Rule and £2.* Went on the river again. Went out with Culme-Seymour in a skiff as he wished to train. Johnstone and Willis joined up. Had some fun in the seamanship room. Am dying to hear from Doris.

Saturday 27

Johnstone took my place in our gig. Had a strenuous scrum practice. I ran quite well I think. I shall ask Cantrell if I may play three-quarters. Wrote to Aunt Do. Raynes and I did well in lab. Finished *David Copperfield*. Had a great rag in dancing. Stopped up till half past 12 in Legge's cabin. Legge got quite angry. Still dying to hear from Doris.

Sunday 28

My cold got worse. Went for a picnic up the river with Cantrell, Sturrock, Hutchinson, Tottenham, Bury and Payne. My day on. Turned in early.

Monday 29

Cold still bad. Did 'life-saving' practice in the swimming bath. We had to stop in water for over half an hour and it was very cold. Went on the river again in the afternoon and practised class gigs. Regatta heats went up on board in QD. Very sick at not having heard from Doris.

Tuesday 30

Pulled in my sculls heat, and although I had practically no opposition, made an ass of myself. Slacked in navigation prep; I am beginning to realise that it is about time I began to work hard.

---

* Petition against the third Irish Home Rule Bill.

OCTOBER

Wednesday 1

A terrific storm. Pair oar heats. I ran to Hemborough in 45 minutes. Enjoyed the run. Had a good feed at the canteen. Bury, Hutchinson, Tottenham and Trollope played bridge. Made several people sing in the gym room; great fun!

Thursday 2

Regatta skiff heats. Drakes did badly. Garside, Cobb and Raynes beaten. Went to sea in the *Roebuck* (TBD) in the afternoon. Quite calm; very hot in the engine room, but I thoroughly enjoyed it. Eng.-Lieutenant Carlisle of the *Roebuck* very decent. My day on again. Clothes came from home.

Friday 3

Gig heats. We did very well and got ten places out of thirty, and only one crew did not get a place. Our best crew, however, did none too well. HEARD FROM DORIS AT LAST! A very nice letter, which I simply loved getting. My work showed instantaneous improvement. Turned in early.

Saturday 4

Regatta heats continued; we did very fairly. Had a slack morning in the lab. It rained hard. Wrote six letters. Ordered cream for Doris at canteen, and wrote to her.

Sunday 5

Wrote six letters. Gave Mother a drubbing about Mrs Steele. Had a bath in 'A' block. Finished *A Pack of Many Tales*.

Monday 6

Very cold day. Rifle drill in gym. Regatta heats continued. We did badly again, but had bad luck. Had a row with AS Russell and Roxburgh;

put them in to Cobb, and they got squashed. Told Smith to run to Hemborough for log shirking.

Tuesday 7

Bought stamps. Very windy, with intermittent showers. Our gigs did well on the river, but Branson and Tweedy were beaten in the pair oar. Wrote and blackguarded Gieve, Matthews and Seagrove.* Heard from Aunt Do.

Wednesday 8

Class gigs. PA did hopelessly. I rowed for PA; SB won, SA second. Did scrum practice in the afternoon. Had a row with Sturges about beating; he was cross but very decent. It made me in the dickens of a funk. Engineering prep. I sent Doris a gold bracelet for her birthday.

Thursday 9

Glorious day. I am afraid our row has permanently spoilt conditions with Sturges, which is a great pity as I like him very much, and I think he liked me before. Went out in the TB to take sights; Mr Pope took us. I did not show great skill, but I think I learnt something, and anyhow I thoroughly enjoyed myself. Had a good feed.

Friday 10

Doris' birthday (14th). Very windy day. Went out with pilotage class again. Although it was not my day, it was too rough to go to sea. We ravaged Lieut. Maxwell's cabin for provisions and ate all his food. The PO on duty prophesied trouble on his return. Had a very boring morning at Sandquay. Kicked about with Goddard in the afternoon.

---

* Gieve, Matthews and Seagrove was an Army and Navy outfitter based in Portsmouth.

Saturday 11

First round of cutter races. Drakes beat Exmouths, Hawkes beat
St Vincents, and Blakes beat Grenvilles.* We had scrum practice at
Norton. Cantrell very sick as we complained of the state of the grounds.
Shot at the range; better than last week, but none too well. Stromeyer
returned from hospital. Had a jaw from the man about the ravaging of
Maxwell's cabin. Roome's brother in the Old Grenville's came over.

Sunday 12

Did not go to church in the morning. Played golf. Hutchinson,
Johnstone, Henderson and Cockburn went out with Culme; I was rather
hurt at not going. Had a chat with Roome, of the Old Grenville's, now a
midshipman in the *Bellerophon*.

Monday 13

Cutter race rowed. We tied with the Hawkes, Blakes were second. I went
to the hospital for my eyesight and dental tests. Passed eyesight test with
flying colours but my teeth were rather patchy. Had a chat with Brown in
Tutor Set Prep. It is about time I received the photos of Doris from Peggy.

Tuesday 14

Did a very strenuous afternoon's exercise. Punted about and ran around
hard for over an hour on the 2nd XV ground, then punched the ball
in the gym and finished up in the swimming bath. Gave out about the
block race to the term. Reported slack party to Sturges, but am afraid he
will not keep his resolutions to punish them.

Wednesday 15

Regatta day. Our gigs came in first and second, but Dickson beat
Branson in the sculls, and Gardner and Goddard got second in the pair

---

* The six Houses at Dartmouth Naval College – Blake, Drake, Exmouth, Grenville,
Hawke and St Vincent.

oar. On the whole we did very fairly. Great fun in the block race. I ran to the pinnace and in spite of breaking both stroke oars we did very well and knocked 'B' block into a cocked hat. 'C' block did quite well, but 'A' block won. Stomley fell overboard and Dickson jumped to save him and succeeded. Cookson got mobbed. Heard from Bob.

Thursday 16

Final cutter – Hawkes knocked us into a cocked hat. We were all dog sick. They pulled jolly well. Worked hard down at Sandquay. Had a row with Blood and Nicholson. Had a great rag in the evening after rounds. Entered for a golf competition.

Friday 17

First games of rugger. AC Chapman broke his wrist. The outfitter came and fitted on my clothes. I captained one side, but only played moderately. Cannot decide whether to play rugger or soccer. I am beginning to think it is about time Doris wrote to me again after all the presents I have sent her.

Saturday 18

Played in a pick-up, but was nothing marvellous. We were overweighted in the scrum. First XV played D&M and lost 23–11, but played very well as they were very strong. Hutchinson played very well. The draw for the golf competition came out, ninety-four entries. I drew Bumaly. Wrote to Mother, Peggy and Bob. Doris is jolly slack about her letters.

Sunday 19

Played golf with Henderson, Trollope and Blood. Trollope beat me 2 up, beat Blood 3 and 1 and beat Henderson 5 and 3. I beat Blood 1 up and Henderson 3 and 1. Blood beat Henderson 1 up.

Monday 20

Played for Drake II v Grenville A and we won 42–0. I played abominably. Nasty wet ground. Heard from Doris. A very brief letter.

Mr Broadbent and Mr Keywin came down. Am feeling the side effects of last night's dissipation.

Tuesday 21

Mr Broadbent and Mr Piggott came down to Sandquay and visited us in the electrical shop. In the afternoon I walked round and chatted with Mr Broadbent about Osborne, our work, etc., etc. Had a talk with Culme. Bean and Keywin came into electricity with Megson. I think Bean has thoroughly enjoyed his visit, and I certainly have greatly enjoyed seeing him.

Wednesday 22

Heard from Peggy. Mr Keywin and Mr Broadbent left. Played in a pickup; good game. O&M beat the cadets. Went and had tea with Culme-Seymour and had a chat. Ponsomby asked out to tea on Sunday.

Thursday 23

Cold day. A row brewing about all the holes being bored in the Round House partitions. No one in Exmouth term has owned up. Mr Crabb, at my request, reports matter to Sturges. Went out in TB to lake. Quite rough, nearly everyone sick. I was not, of course, but did not enjoy it very much.

Friday 24

1st and 2nd XV scrum practices. Another party went out in TB. Exmouth term severely punished for the holes. Talked for nearly an hour with Megson, Raynes and Robinson.

Saturday 25

1st XV v HMS *Highflyer*. Jolly good match before a very large crowd of cadets and visitors. Won by college unexpectedly by 26–3. Hutchinson, Henderson and Chevallier played very well. I played for the 2nd XV. We won 9–6. Very rough game. I played fairly well but had a fight, which I am afraid did not please the authorities. *Highflyer* people came up to the dance. 3rd XV lost to Dartmouth reserves 5–17, and soccer XI lost 1–3. Was sent the photos of Doris, looking awfully sweet.

Sunday 26

Capt. Trench came over from the *Highflyer*. (He was imprisoned in Germany as a spy.*) Played golf and beat Bumaly. Went to tea with Ponsomby; a most interesting time as we had much in common.

Monday 27

Wet day; our game v Hawke scratched, so I kicked about and went early to Sandquay. Had a row with old Haswell. Had a great rag with Blagrove in the evening. The hack on my ankle, which I received on Saturday, became oppressive. Did life-saving in the swimming bath. Weather very wet and cold. Stopped up very late roasting chestnuts.

Tuesday 28

Wet again. Our game v Blake scratched. General runs. I ran to Hemborough in forty. Received green ink from Mother. My leg still bad. Am getting quite excited as to whether I shall be playing for the 2nd or not on Saturday.

Wednesday 29

Still very wet. I unexpectedly captained 2nd XV v Vanstone's team, and we won 22–3. I did not shine much. Find it hard to shout and play as well. Other matches scratched owing to scarlet fever.

Thursday 30

Rain continued incessantly, fourth day running. Term run to Pound House – I did not go, but punted about on scrum practice ground.

---

* Captain Trench, the physical training instructor of HMS *Highflyer*, was sentenced to four years in prison in Berlin on charges of espionage in 1910. He served half his sentence.

Plymouth teams went up for Saturday; I am skippering the 2nd XV. Heard from and wrote to Uncle Jack.

Friday 31

Rain still continuous. 1st and 2nd XV scrum practice. 2nd XV match scratched again. Hawkes licked the Blakes in league match.

NOVEMBER

Saturday 1

1st Whole Holiday. I went with the 1st XV to Plymouth. Lunched at Royal Hotel. Had my photos taken. We won the match 8–6; very close game. Bury played well. The team had tea in the *Highflyer*. The spectators at Keyham Engineering College,* Bury and I went to the Green Room mess of the *Colossus* with Thomas and Hall. They were awfully decent. We missed our dinner with the team at the Royal, and had a separate meal and plenty of whisky at Newton Abbot. We tried to cheer up Cantrell, who seemed lonely, and made an awful faux pas for our pain. Got done in for 7/- by the guard. Bumaly, WJ Russell, Bayne, Harrison, Martineau tight.

Sunday 2

Played golf with Hutchinson and Henderson. I won 7 and 6, and played well. Did pilotage. Thrashed Martineau hard for being tight.

Monday 3

Heard from Uncle Jack. Received photos from Novelty Studio, 184 Union Street, Plymouth. 1st and 2nd XV scrum practice. Drake II beat Blake II 99–0. The score would have been 145–0 but for missed place kicks. PA hammock slinging party.

---

* The Royal Naval Engineering College was founded in Keyham, Devon, in 1880. The site eventually closed in 1958.

Tuesday 4

Drake II beaten by Hawke A 9–0. Our great chagrin. First defeat for over a year. Wrote to Balls for a motor for Sunday, and to the photo people, Novelty Studio, 184 Union Street, Plymouth.

Wednesday 5

1st XV game v a scratch team of officers and cadets, for which I was playing. Had quite a good game, which they won 27–14, but it was really quite equal. I did not move too well, but sprained my thumb rather nastily. Hutchinson, Passmore and Millar all played well. Exciting 1st XI soccer match v Paignton Rovers AFC. Draw 3–3. Great enthusiasm aroused for once in a way. Bury, Tottenham and I had a row with the linesman. Had a row with Bairstow.

Thursday 6

Drake river day. I had my arm in a sling on account of my sprained thumb. Outfitter came down. Pilotage class cancelled.

Friday 7

1st and 2nd XV scrum practice. Got invitation to dine with the captain tomorrow. Drake II beat Exmouth I 46–3. Drake III beat St Vincent 49–3. My thumb better. Had toothache.

Saturday 8

1st XV beat University College 13–3. Excellent performance, as we were not expected to win. 2nd XV beat Dartmouth reserves 14–0. I captained them. Soccer team badly beaten. Dined with the captain. Met Lord and Lady Ampthill. Completed a week of abstinence (first time in my memory).

Sunday 9

Went up to Natsworthy. Met Alfred Jackson, Mother and Daddy's old Porthgwarra friend.

Monday 10

College scrum practice. I made a fool of myself. Hammock slinging party. I was last, of course. In rotten form altogether. Heard from Bob.

Tuesday 11

All the term had scrum practice. My photos arrived from Plymouth. Heard from Doris. Put in pilotage notes. Garside and I had a row with a CERA. Chellew at Sandquay.

Wednesday 12

Played in a fearful mud scramble for 2nd XV v Vanstone's XV and drew 3–3. Mr Vanstone broke his collarbone. Soccer XI won a match for a change.

Thursday 13

Heard from and wrote to Joko. Had 2-hour lecture at Sandquay. Went on putting in buoys in my pilotage notes.

Friday 14

Punted about. Blakes (minus Scrimgeour and WJ Russell) beat Grenvilles in a friendly Term comp 33–0.

Saturday 15

1st XV match v St Lukes won easily. Silly rugger pick up 2nd v 3rd XV. We also won easily, 46–5. Soccer lost as usual. Boxing: Mr Patway beat Lieut. Kenworthy of the TB. Bad fight.

Sunday 16

Went to Salcombe with Culme, Mr Hodgson, Johnstone and Gardner. Had a jolly good time. Confirmation Sunday.

Monday 17

Played in a Term soccer pick up. Term XI drew 2–2 with a side from Seaton. I got a goal, but we did none too well. I was in a bad temper as usual on Mondays. Discussed possibility of Hendon flying with Johnstone, Cobb and Garside. Mr Brown went sick. Went to camp for tutor set.

Tuesday 18

Wet day. Wanted to play golf with Johnstone but we were stopped by PO and could not get permission. So we were obliged to toss up for our round of the competition, and of course he won. Was very angry and annoyed. Wrote home about the dentist.

Wednesday 19

Played the Hawkes and won 30–0. Henderson played very well, Fitzroy very badly. The forwards never got really together. The Hawkes did well, good game, but I did none too well. Soccer game v the 0 & 17, which we won 3–2; an excellent performance. The outfitter came down.

Thursday 20

Our river day, but it rained, so I punted and trained. Had a long and fruitless workshop lecture with Sturrock at Sandquay. Skipped English with Hope on account of poetry.

Friday 21

Wet day. Term run to Black Cottage. I did not go, but kicked about. Cut my finger badly down at Sandquay. Had a row with Tottenham. Painted in buoys. Collected money for Willis' trombone.

Saturday 22

2nd Whole Holiday. I played for College A team v Exeter A (a pretty classy game) at Exeter. Good game. We won 16–0. I got quite tight afterwards and was put to bed by Stromeyer and AJ Russell. I broke two teeth and my nose, got a kick on the thigh, and felt very dizzy and miserable, but had a very jovial evening at the Regiment College. Full strength drew with Exeter 1st 21–21 after a terrific game. Blagrove excelled.

Sunday 23

Played golf in competition against Johnstone and lost 4 down and 2. Afterwards, Cobb and I beat Hutchinson and Henderson 2 and 1. I felt an awful wreck after yesterday.

Monday 24

My teeth and nose still very sore. Played the Hawkes at soccer and won 3–1. We played abominably – last year we won 12–2! Heard from 'Beans'.

Tuesday 25

Played Blakes at soccer and won 6–3 after being down 2–3 at half time. An excellent performance. We all played very well, myself included. The Vincents beat Exmouths at rugger.

Wednesday 26

Played Blakes at rugger and won 34–3. This making two cups in one day. Wrote to Bob.

Thursday 27

All the skippers had a jaw with the captain about the food. Heard from Doris; she promised to play golf with me in mixed foursomes at Xmas. My toothache bad; am looking forward to seeing the dentist. Played for 1st XV v *Colossus* and *Conquest* and won 36–3. Many old Hawkes, Blakes etc. playing. We won relay race.

Friday 28

Drake term river. 1st and 2nd XV scrum practices. Keys' kid (Charles Edward Keys) came up and played about. Grenvilles beat Vincents 2–1; Vincents did very well. Had a lovely chat with Megson.

Saturday 29

Mr JW Mercer came over. 1st and 2nd XV Blundells matches.* We
won 2nd XV (which I captained) 38–0, and 1st XV 36–5. Splendid
performances, everyone did well and fearfully tucked. Cantrell and all
the officers jubilant. Hutchinson played the game of his life. We gave the
Blundells people a rotten tea. All the skippers had a jaw with the captain
about the food again. Entertainment in the evening not bad. Stopped up
very late, all the officers tight.

Sunday 30

Our Old Testament exam. I did not bother about it much. Several
colours given. I got my 2nd XV colours.

DECEMBER

Monday 1

Slacked about. Did Drawing Office exam at Sandquay. Term photos
went up. I bullied Crowe.

Tuesday 2

Felt much better. Scrum practice. Drake term life-saving exam. All
competitors got bronze medal. I rather wish I had gone in for it.

Wednesday 3

1st XV played the *Highflyer* again and won 43–4. Everyone did well.
Hutchinson still brilliant. Very nasty day. Had a Morse flashing
examination. Must start training for Sherborne now.

Thursday 4

Drake river. Very cold day. Got in a row with Orr and Sturrock for
wearing a blazer at Sandquay. A damned swizzle as everybody else does

---

* Blundells School in Tiverton, Devon.

it, and he seemed to think I did it on purpose to annoy him, although I had no idea it was not allowed. Received an anniversary ornament as a present from Hodgson, Culme's friend.

Friday 5

Scrum practice. 1st and 2nd XV photos. I only had a rather insignificant position in the photo, which rather disappointed me after captaining the side the whole season. In fact, Hutcher and I damned sick. Hammock slinging competition won by SB. My semaphore exam. Sherborne arrived.

Saturday 6

Sherborne beaten 18–6. Everyone jubilant. All the team played magnificently. Unluckily there was no 2nd XV match as they did not bring a side. Stromeyer's brother came over. Received a letter from Uncle Jack about Mr Jackson.

Sunday 7

Wrote home. Finished off as much revision as possible. Turned in early.

Monday 8

Pilotage exam in the morning. I think I did pretty well, but of course I don't know. Last Sandquay day, took fond farewells off all the instructors. Last tutor set.

Tuesday 9

We beat Fleet (full-strength match) 6–0. Very wet ground. I was third in pilotage. History and seamanship exams. I think I did fairly well in history, but rottenly in seamanship. Turned in early.

Wednesday 10

German oral. I did badly. Mechanics exam; I think I did well. 1st XI drew with Vanstone's XI. I packed some of my books.

Thursday 11

German and engineering 1 exam. I did moderately in both. Exams going fairly well.

Friday 12

Maths 2 exam. Did very poorly. Cobb heard from Mr Wilson.

Saturday 13

Navigation exam. I did fairly well. Nine of our skippers went to a dance at the captain's house so I had to take chief skippers' rounds, but could not keep a straight face. Received £2 from Daddy.

Sunday 14

Wrote labels, etc. Tottenham, Bumaly and I went to tea with old Brown at the hostel. Drake term life-saving medals presented.

Monday 15

Maths 1 and English exams. Had a great rag on the soccer ground in the afternoon. Fearful row about immorality. Everyone jawed. It appeared Mitchell and co. complained, and Roxburgh was moved out of this term and Warburton came instead. I vowed vengeance on the Exmouth term.

Tuesday 16

All the skippers jawed about Roxburgh's case. He was publicly disrated.* Engineering 2 very easy. King's Medal presented to Gardner. Bury, Cockburn and I were the three to be disrated for the cruiser. I was fearfully disappointed in contrast with my jubilance this time two terms ago. Both Bury and I were altered for Johnstone and Tottenham, owing to the skipper's favouritism. I said goodbye to old Lavers. Felt very miserable.

---

* Naval term, being reduced to a lower rank.

Wednesday 17

Last night we had a great rag. Branson, Hutchinson, Henderson, Bury and I all went up to Norton for the last term. Had a long farewell chat with Sturges in his cabin on my return. I like him very much. Got to bed at 3.30, up again at 6 still feeling very miserable. Hutchinson, Bury, Tottenham and I breakfasted at Exeter. Decided to have a spree tonight. Daddy met me at Paddington and I went to the dentist, Dr Field, at 117 Park Street. Stopped at the flat at 73 New Cavendish Street. Dined with Tottenham, Bury and Hutchinson at Lord Athlumney's.* We all went on to the Alhambra revue, and then to Hatchetts for supper. Had a terrific evening. Thoroughly enjoyed myself. Hutchinson came and slept at the flat. Met Arthur Russell at the flat.

Thursday 18

Went to the dentist again. Went home by the 12.20 from Holborn.

Friday 19

Played golf with the Dr against the Colonel and Bob. We won 5 and 3. I played quite well. Saw George and Byron. Jack and Toots came down with Daddy. Wrote to Bench. Went round to Westenhanger after supper.

Saturday 20

Got up late. I drove Byron, Peggy and Johnny with Bob to Canterbury; we had an accident and broke the shafts, so I went back and fetched the motor. Did a lot of my shopping in Canterbury. Had tea with Byron. Gave Dolly a lift home. Looked in at the Tango tea at the county; saw Toots, Nita, Olive and Henry.

Doris is due to come home today, but have seen nothing of her. Saw Margery on the links, but took no notice of her.

---

* James Somerville, 2nd Baron Athlumney, was an Irish peer and an officer of the British Army.

Sunday 21

Played golf with Daddy against George and Bob and lost 2 and 1.
I played well but Daddy's play was weak. Wrote letters. Have not seen
Doris yet.

Monday 22

Went up to town by the boat-train. Did some shopping; bought an
expensive wrist watch for Doris, but do not know whether I'll give it to
her or not. I wonder if whooping cough has had anything to do with
her not being round at Quaives. Went to the dentist and had four teeth
stopped. A Sub-Lieut. Blunt, a friend of Arthur Russell's, came to stop
at the flat. I thought he was our Mr Blunt from the stock exchange. We
dined together and drank freely, and then went on to 'Cachez Ça' at the
Middlesex.

Tuesday 23

Went to the dentist again and had six teeth stopped. Went home by
the 12.20 from Victoria. It was pouring with rain. Peggy in bed with a
cold. Daddy and George went hunting. They wore red. Packed up Xmas
parcels and cards. Heard from Bench; he piqued me considerably by
addressing me as cadet captain. Still saw nothing of Doris.

Wednesday 24

The hounds met at Quaives, and we had quite good fun on the whole.
Quite an average number of farmers turned up. A jolly fine array of
food and drink supplied at Quaives. All the Kelsey girls came in and
had drinks. Saw Doris and the Champions, but they would not come in.
I am just as fond of her as ever. She was dressed in white and I thought
looked topping. I adore her. She was quite sweet to me, although I saw
nothing of her. Had a terrific lot of drink and had a little flunk at home,
which I am uncertain at present as to how it will develop.

I love my mother, but Doris is divine.

Thursday 25

Xmas Day. Billy thoroughly enjoyed himself. George and Bob came to lunch, and George to dinner. Byron and I played Bob and George in the afternoon and lost. The Dr came to Quaives to tea. I went to the Rectory; saw the Gov, etc.

Friday 26

In the morning I went to Ickham and got Doris to play with me in the competition. I played an extraordinarily fine game and won the competition easily in 76. Henry Handy was second. Doris tore up; she looked very sweet in a white jersey (but told me she could not play with me in the mixed foursomes, owing to a dance, which rather piqued me). In the afternoon I took Reggie Cox, Jackie and Jimmy to Canterbury, and then went to a rehearsal of the Ickham revue at the Bairds. Daddy and George hunted.

Saturday 27

Hunted. Meet at New House, Mersham. Dull morning, but very good fun in the afternoon. McNeill, Kit Davidson and George Green in attendance. Green and McNeill came to grief. Went back past Smeeth station and had great fun jumping the Smeeth dyke. Four men in, only George, Daddy, I and two others got over. Went on and had a meal at Viv Nickalls' place with Selby.* Got home in time for entertainment at Ickham. It was a great success. Chatted with Byron till 1. Very tired. Only saw Doris in the distance at the show, not near enough to speak to.

Sunday 28

Mooched about. Lunched with George. Met Doris and Margery in the village and had a chat. Very cold day indeed. Went to tea at the Rectory.

---

* Vivian Nickalls was a British rower who won the Wingfield Sculls three times and the Diamond Challenge Sculls at the Henley Royal Regatta in 1891. He was on the winning side of three University Boat Races for Oxford.

Monday 29

Daddy and Mother went to London. Rode to the meet at Halfway House, but it was too frosty to hunt. Had tea at cottage with Aunts Arabella, Jessie and Adelaide. Supped with the Kelseys and played games and had my leg pulled. Met George Byron, a returned paymaster, just off to Assam, and we, along with George GW and Bob, had a very thick evening indeed. Feel miserable about Doris. She and Margery have gone to dance in Canterbury. I am very jealous. She is an extraordinary girl and I cannot understand whether she is fond of me or not. I wish I knew. I adore her, but am seeing simply nothing of her this holiday.

Tuesday 30

Shot with Governor, Jack, Dr, Blake Wacher, Tom Wacher, George Wacher and George Finn. Very cold and snowy day. Terribly cold shooting. Jimmy loaded for me. Got nine-and-a-half brace and two hares, fair under the circumstances. I got two brace and did well in the afternoon. Sent a brace round to the Champions; I wonder what they will think. Went to a dance at Seaton with the Kelseys; fearfully dull show – no one there. I long for Doris, and am moping for her.

Wednesday 31

Went up by the early train to London. Saw Cag, Uncle John and Robert at the office. Went to the dentist. Lunch with Bench at the flat. Went on to Queens Club. Navy v Harlequins. They won 5–11. Met Mr Gibbons, Mr Eldridge, Mr Blagrove, Mr Haines, Bairstow, Buchanan and WJ Russell. Called on Mac Hilton. Bench and I lunched at Gatti's and went on to 'Oh I Say!'. Very funny piece. Went back to the flat to see in the New Year. Had a great rag, then Arthur Russell and four friends took us six to the Covent Garden Ball on top of a taxi. Had tremendous rag at the dance and thoroughly enjoyed it.

1914

JANUARY

Thursday 1

Returned from dance at Covent Garden, at which point I met
AM Cohen, and got cursed by CAC Russell. Felt I had thoroughly
enjoyed it. Got to bed at 6.30, got up at 9. Left Bench and Arthur
Russell in bed. Called on Bertie and Gladys Robertson and
returned home.

Had a thorough mould; the reaction of last night's enjoyment and the
fact that I am seeing absolutely nothing of Doris. Went to supper with
Bob at George Goodson's.

Friday 2

Very snowy. Had a mould still. Helped Jack break in his pony with
Hucklesby, Jackie and Reggie Cox. Had tea with Jack at Westenhanger.
Went to see the Champions; found Doris had gone to Dover and
Margery to London. Had a lovely chat with Percy Champion, which
made me feel better. Daddy returned home in great form.

Saturday 3

Hunted. Meet at Alkham. Still very snowy; only a small field.
Had quite good fun around the hills above Dover. Daddy went
back to Alkham early, but I stopped on until the end with old
Downs, Selby and his son. Finished up near Lydden. We dined at
Westenhanger.

Had a note from Mrs Champion, thanking me for the game, on my
return from hunting. I am still dying to see Doris.

Sunday 4

Had another note from Mrs Champion asking me to a dance at Birchington on Friday. Daddy and I beat George and Byron 2 and 1, conceding 1 stroke. I played brilliantly.

Harold Wacher and Capt. Gould dined at Quaives. Supped with the Kelseys.

Monday 5

Hunted. Meet at Knowlton; had a jolly good breakfast. Very wet day. Drew Knowlton Court woods blank, Tye Wood blank. Lord Guilford would not let Selby Lowndes draw Waldershare Park, so we drew Easling and had a fair run. Went home fairly early. Miss Pym, Ramsay, John Robinson, the Miss Penns, GW Walker, Missy Baker, Lord and Lady Guilford, the Lowndes family, old Downs, Harries, etc., among the field. Had a large meal on our return and contracted a very bad temper.

Tuesday 6

Sloped about all the morning. Had lunch at Westenhanger. Helped Jack break the pony again with Hucklesby and Jackie; also with the chimney pot. Byron, Dolly, Nora, George, Doris and I went to the pantomime at Canterbury. Rotten show, but I loved being with Doris of course. Took Doris home afterwards and gave her the wrist watch, which she seemed very pleased with. She is a funny little thing, but I love her.

Wednesday 7

Hunted. Meet at Guinea Park, Sellindge. Vivien Nickalls' farewell meet. Very hard frost and dangerous going. Murdoch out. We had a very long chat with him. We went home early, but they had more fun after we left. Took old Harries home and had a large meal at Elham. Ernest Baker out. Heard that poor old Edwin Kelsey was very seriously ill indeed, two doctors and a nurse. Byron very worried. I went over to Seaton after dinner and met Capt. Wilson from Deal.

Thursday 8

Daddy went to town. Mother rather worried; all the children rather run down after their whooping cough. It has been an awful nuisance their having whooping cough this leave, as I have been unable to have Doris into Quaives and so have seen very little of her. Played golf with her in the morning, and she looked very sweet. I am afraid her teeth rather spoil her looks. I wish they would improve, but I love her nevertheless (I am afraid I am a young jackass). Lunched at Westenhanger. Old Kelsey still very bad indeed.

Friday 9

My last day's hunting this season. Met at Denton; dull morning, good hunt in the afternoon. Long hack home. Ernest Baker, Murdoch, George Goodson, George Green and many others out. Motored Doris over to Sarre. Mr and Mrs Champion took us all up to Birchington to a dance at the Tetts. Very few pretty girls, the two Misses Heath excepted. Had a lovely evening with Doris; out of twenty dances, I danced seven with her and sat out five. Danced one with each Miss Heath, one with Miss Hilda Brown, five with wallflowers for charity, and stopped the other two for drinks.

Saturday 10

Got up late. Doris, Mrs S Champion, Jack Wacher and I went in to Canterbury from Sarre, and met Ernest Baker and Mrs P Champion there. Gave Doris and the two Mrs Champions lunch. Had my hair cut. Drove home with Doris in pony cart. Hutchinson came down to stop night. Daddy and George had a good day hunting. We two went to a dance given by Mrs Drake. Forty people there. Quite good fun. It would have been much better had the Kelseys, Doreen King and Dorothy Green been there. Hutchinson enjoyed himself and fell in love with Miss Page. Doris very tired; I enjoyed myself with her. We supped at Willie's cottage. Capt. Gould and Kit Davidson came to Quaives for a whisky toddy. Bed 3am.

Sunday 11

Goodson and I played Hutchinson and GGW. We halved; good game.
Very cold day. Played cards afterwards. Old Kelsey better. Daddy gave
me my accounts, but they would not tally. The Robertson Westenhanger
house party left.

Monday 12

Hutchinson went off by the 9.39. Went round to Westenhanger. Had
intended to ride with Doris, but she was not very well and it was
very cold. Saw Pongo and Gracie Baines. Went to see Doris in the
afternoon and took her some photos. She looked sweet. Danced tango at
Westenhanger. Florence Lomax left. All the family left Quaives for a spree
in London. Went to a dull dance at Seaton. Capt. Wilson slept at Quaives.

Tuesday 13

Capt. Wilson left. Heard of poor old Edwin Kelsey's death. A universal
gloom spread around. Everyone very cut up. Wrote to Mrs Kelsey
and Byron in condolence. I went up to London. Met Mr Denniston,
Mr Heberden, Lieut. GTA Scott, Armstrong and Cobb. Lunched at
Trocadero. Went to 'Charley's Aunt' at the Prince of Wales theatre.
Saw W Shalford and Thomas. Went home by the 6.15. Had supper at
Westenhanger. Very sad about old Kelsey.

Wednesday 14

Family still in London. Hard frost stopped hunting. Heard from Mother.
Saw nothing of the Kelseys, as they were terribly cut up by Edwin's
death. Saw Nita, Toots, Jack and the Bairds. Played golf with George
and Bob. Selby Lowndes, Harries and Lee came over to see the puppies.
Had good fun and heaps of drink; they stopped to tea and saw over
stables before going. Saw Doris in Ickham, but took no notice of her,
chiefly because Margery, my *bête noire*, had returned (she ain't a bad
sort really). Dined with Mother and Governor at Rectory and played
coon-can.

Thursday 15

Went to see Susie Baird. Lunched at Westenhanger. Took Doris for a ride through Wingham, Preston and Grove. I think she enjoyed it, and may ride well some day with practice, as she is very plucky. Had tea with the Champions. The family came home. George dined at Quaives. Saw the Baines.

Friday 16

Took Trevor for a ride and then Doris for a long one. We went up over Adisham Downs and had several nice canters. She is a sweet little thing, and I really believe she is at last beginning to get fond of me; I shall be very sorry to lose her. Selby and Harries came to lunch, and we all went to dear old Edwin Kelsey's funeral after. It was terribly sad, as we all loved him without exception. Heaps of people there. John Parish came down especially for it. Norrie took the service as the old Governor was so weepy. We chewed up afterwards, and they all hunted me down the marshes to Deadmill with the puppies.

Saturday 17

Daddy and George went for an expedition with Harries. I went to London, met Norrie Robertson and Kit Davidson and the Miss Wachers. Called on Sophie. Went to England v Wales match at Twickenham with Bench. Very good game. We won 10–9, but did not deserve to. Poulton, LG Brown and Maynard played fine games, Pillman good.* Enormous crowd of 30,000. Met Crebbin, P Buchanan, Bairstow and Cookson. Did not get home till late. Col. and Gracie Baines came to dinner. Daddy and Mother peckish. The kitchen maid attempted to commit suicide, but failed. Had a row with Daddy, Mother and George. Heard from dear old Byron and Culme.

---

* Ronald Poulton-Palmer, captain, was considered one of the finest centres in rugby before he was killed by a sniper on the Western Front in 1915. Alfred Maynard, hooker, was killed on the first day of the Battle of Ancre, 1916, having survived being shot in Gallipoli.

Sunday 18

Dull day. Wrote letters. Mr Steele came to lunch. The Baines came to tea again. Dined at Westenhanger. Row with George continued, with people all night. Had a great rag singing, etc. Settled up financially with Daddy.

Monday 19

Daddy left, and I said goodbye to him. Took Toots, Doris and Margery into Canterbury in a taxi. Doris went to the dentist. Gave them all lunch. Took Doris and Margery to the cinema, and Jack and Jackie came. Toots went to see Margery Green. Said goodbye to Dolly and Mrs Drake. Had a lovely time with sweet little Doris at the cinema and in the motor. She came round to Quaives to say goodbye to Peggy. Mother told me, after, that she looked sweet. I am sure she is really fond of me and we are both sorry to lose each other. Took affectionate farewells from Westenhanger party, Rectory, Kelseys and Bob. Missed Dr and Jabez. Made up row with George.

Tuesday 20

Left home early by the 8.47 at Canterbury. Caught the 11am from Waterloo to Plymouth Millbay. Travelled with Hutchinson, Tottenham and O'Leary. Joined *Cornwall* alongside jetty at Devonport dockyard. Mother not very well when I left, although children flourishing. I had bad chilblains. Had a fearful job unpacking; found I had got much too many clothes. Found we had a nice cadet gunman. Did not feel so sorry as I might have been. Would have been quite happy had it not been for leaving Doris and not being skipper, which I daresay I shall get over.

Wednesday 21

My sub was duty sub and turned out early to assist in lashing and stowing hammocks. Had poor night; novelty of hammock, sentry above and cold. Lieut. Harris came to say goodbye. We were shown over part of the ship. Left Devonport about 11.30; left the Sound about 1, and made for Ushant at ten knots. Stowed gear away and settled down. Quite calm so far. Examined collision stations after evening quarters. Hutchinson and some others played bridge all day. Feeling quite well.

Thursday 22

Very rough indeed all day; nearly everyone sick, including self, although not badly. Intensely hot below. I keep quite fit on deck, but cannot stand heat and smell below. None of us feel well. Did a lot of physical training and listened to a seamanship résumé from Lieut. Colville, but was too ill to take in much. Started writing a letter home and wrote to Doris. Have seen no land all day. We passed Ushant at 2 this morning and are now in the thick of the Bay of Biscay. Hutchinson, Bury, Batson and I lounged together on the cadet deck in the waist, all of us feeling rotten. I loathe turning out so early. A game of hockey started, which very few partook in. Exercised fire stations after evening quarters.

Friday 23

Sick in the morning, but far better afterwards. The stink and heat below unbearable. Got out of Bay, but did not sight land all day. Exercised 'towing stations' after evening quarters. Got a dull wire message from a Cornish station to say the bank rate had fallen and a few other equally dull things managed to get in there. Still on 'A' instruction, that is to say seamanship and torpedo. Listened to the band in the evening.

Saturday 24

I am 'midshipman of the day'. Sighted land, Cape Roca, in the morning and Cape St Vincent in the afternoon. Quite good fun being snotty of the day. Mr Jeffreys had afternoon watch, and was very decent to me. Gloriously brilliant day and very warm. Wireless messages from Gibraltar. Sealed up my letters home. Got paid.

Sunday 25

Church on board. Reached Gibraltar at 3. Lovely Spanish scenery, saw across to Africa. Went ashore with Hutchinson and saw something of the town. Drove about in a sort of Hackney carriage.

Monday 26

Study in the morning and afternoon. Went ashore again in the evening. Saw Hunter-Blair and France-Hayhurst. Purchased ink and postcards. Gibraltar is very picturesque, but full of dirty Spanish pseudo Englishmen. Very cheap smoking articles. Very few nice girls, in which I was considerably disappointed. Sent a postcard to Auntie Ethel and Mother. Am settling down to life in a cruiser. It is not bad fun, but I think we shall have to work pretty hard.

Tuesday 27

Strong levanter continued.* Coaled ship in morning and took in 350 tons. Wrote eight postcards. I was midshipman of the steam pinnace, and consequently could not go on shore. Had very little to do and was bored to death. Some people went to Algeciras and some to Linea, the latter coming back with tales of elaborate whore shops. Everything very dirty with coaling. XI duty sub again.

Wednesday 28

PO Boat *Medina* came in for four hours, but I was unable to go on board owing to instruction. Porritt came on board; he was going to Egypt in the *Medina*. He told me that Mr and Mrs Drake were on board, but I was unable to see them. Had a long letter from Joko. Levanter continued. About ten of us went to Algeciras in the afternoon. A funny old Spanish town with an excellent hotel. Lost to Hutchinson one down on a funny course. O'Leary had a row with Caballero.

---

* A strong easterly wind in the Mediterranean region that can cause squalls in Gibraltar Bay.

Thursday 29

The beastly levanter continued. Wrote to Joko, Doris and Mother. Did a lot of torpedo study. I was actually 'midshipman of the steam pinnace' again, making twice in three days, which is a beastly nuisance. I took the captain on shore. Am feeling rather bored, and shall be glad to get to Las Palmas. I thoroughly enjoyed yesterday's expedition to Algeciras. The quaint old Spanish fashions rather fascinated me.

Friday 30

The levanter increased with strong rain. I felt very bilious in the morning, but got better as the day went on. I was midshipman of the boat before breakfast only. Went on shore in the afternoon; bought a few necessaries, and went for a walk around to the north of the Rock. Branson got cursed for faulty reporting. JWM very unpopular. Skippers seem to get a rotten time. Heard from home.

Saturday 31

A much nicer day at last. Ordinance studies in the morning. In the afternoon we had a half holiday. The 1st XI played the Royal Scots Fusiliers (who are quartered here) and won 3–1. The 2nd ship XI, for which I played, drew 2–2 with RGF. JWM is getting still more unpopular. I am looking forward to hearing from Doris, but she is slack in writing as usual.

FEBRUARY

Sunday 1

Went on shore with Bench. We climbed the Rock (north and middle peaks) and were very interested. Had tea at Risso's. Lovely view and scenery from top of Rock. Heard from old Lavers.

Monday 2

Left Gibraltar at 9.30. Shifted from A to C instruction, viz. from seamanship and torpedo to navigation and gunnery. Signalled Tangier about 12, and saw the wreck of the SS *Delhi* about four miles further south.* Snow in the distance on the Atlas Mountains. Left the Moroccan coast about 2. Practised 6-inch gun drill after lunch, and piped to general quarters at 4. Quite calm. Deck cricket in the evening.

Tuesday 3

A big swell; did not feel at all well. Got into a row for doing a bad rifle drill. Read *Dombey and Son*. Practised 6-inch BL gun drill again. Did not sight anything all day. No evolution after quarters. A lot of people slung hammocks on deck, but I slung below, and was very glad to turn in. Went to Spencer Cooper for pilotage.

Wednesday 4

Turned much calmer and a very nice day. Felt much better. Usual studies and routine. Took two sights of the sun and fixed the ship. Navigation and pilotage are both quite interesting, but Mr Andrew is rather dull. Exercised fine quarters. Had a chat with Mr Sinclair. Danced on QD. Slung on deck.

Thursday 5

Dropped anchor in Puerto de la Luz Bay, the port of Las Palmas in Grand Canary, at 9. Sighted Tenerife Peak, which is 12,150 ft high, fifty miles off. Very lovely, enveloped in clouds. Glorious morning, but changeable weather later. Fired salutes, twenty-one guns for Spain, and seven for consul. Landed in the afternoon and saw over the town of Las Palmas. Lovely cathedral, also fruit market, hotels, casino, wine shops, etc. Lovely scenery in Grand Canary.

---

* SS *Delhi* was a steamship of the Peninsular & Orient Line (P&O) that was lost off Cape Spartel, northern Morocco, on 12 December 1911.

Friday 6

Mountains covered with snow looked lovely in the early morning sun. Very gusty day. The bad weather seems to have followed us from England. The deputy governor and the deputy commandant came on board and were saluted. We were attempting to work out a day's work and were seriously interrupted. I did not go on shore, but stopped on board and wrote and read. Made a fool of myself in gunnery drill again.

Saturday 7

Nice weather. Navigation all the morning. Had a headache. My relations with Hutchinson improve, as they have been rather strained of late. A mail arrived, and I was very disappointed at not getting anything by it. Wrote to Daddy and Amy Drummond Hay. Several people played golf. The ship cricket XI played Las Palmas and won easily. Hutchinson and Fitzroy batted well, the rest failed. I went on shore in mufti and went about the town. I solaced myself with fem. for the first time.

Sunday 8

Ship's company beat Las Palmas at soccer 6–1. We all went for an expedition to Monte. Great fun. Lovely climate, although very rough motor ride. Had a huge meal there, seventy of us had fifty-one eggs and thirty-seven bananas, also figs, pears, etc.

Monday 9

Started engineering duty. Atmosphere unbearable. Weighed and left Las Palmas. 1st Lieutenant ran Clarke, Pearson and myself for drinking whisky and soda at Las Palmas. He was very angry, which riled me considerably, as when he caught us at Monte he pretended he would not do any more about it; I cannot see anything caddish in drinking W&S. This will effectively stop any chance I may have of being made a skipper again.

Tuesday 10

I am afraid the W&S row has made us very unpopular with the officers. No. 1 ran us in to the skipper. Continued engineering; was on third duty, the worst of the lot. Felt damned ill, and the heat and swell below is damnably execrable and appalling. Had the afternoon engine room dog watch from 4–6, and so have had a jolly stiff day. No. 1 fell us in and jawed us about the W&S incident. He finally let us off with a caution.

Wednesday 11

Engine room atmosphere still awful. Lost *Dombey and Son* from the library overboard. Had got to the return of Walter from his overseas voyage and his betrothal to Florence, and must remember to finish it when I go on leave. The cadets played the officers at deck cricket and won by six runs. The supply of fresh water for washing gave out, but was renewed towards evening. Captain swore at me for having my hair long.

Thursday 12

Arrived at Cape Verde islands, and anchored at St Vincent. Very misty. The Portuguese governor came aboard. Started harbour routine. Wonderful diving for coins in the harbour by the natives. Very disappointed to find no mail. Went ashore in mufti. Found the Portuguese towns less smelly and cleaner than the Spanish, but the people were just as dirty. Played golf with Tottenham and won easily; quite a nice little course. Had tea at the Hotel de Brazileiro. Met several good fellows from the Eastern Telegraph Company. Very tropical heat.

Friday 13

Extraordinarily hot. Bath supply gave out again. Cape Town mail boat arrived, but no good for us. I was steamboat engineering party in the morning. General drill 5.30am. Ship hockey team played Western

Telegraph Company and won 7–1. Scrum practice for us afterwards, a beastly sweat. Missed 6.00 boat. Donkey riding very popular.

Saturday 14

Tropical heat still. Three hours in the morning finished the week's engineering course, thank God. Mr Colville caught a shark and Armstrong nearly did so. Rugger pick-up in the afternoon; I played, after protests and a row, and got two tries. We won 27–6; Gardner did well. Had a long chat with Mr Meggs. The mail arrived from home, and I heard from Mother and Doris. The ship drew with WTC; we made 167–9 dec, they got 116 for 8 in reply. Bury failed again. We should have won. The officers gave a dinner party in return for the concert, which the captain refused for us, much like the Las Palmas dances.

Sunday 15

Several visitors to church. I did not go on shore, but stopped behind and wrote letters. The ship played golf against WTC and drew. Trollope and Bury won. Lost my seamanship book. Saw some flying fish. Got *Sketches by Boz* from the library.

Monday 16

Studied 'A' instruction again; was minus my seamanship notebook, and No. 1 made me copy it out again, which I just succeeded in doing in time to get on leave. Saw over the Portuguese prison, which was a disgusting sight. HMS *Cornwall* full strength beat WTC at rugger, 23–0. Very good game and win. Very windy. Hutchinson played OR first half; in second half he changed with Mr Whitehead to his old place and the change was a great success. Gardner, Bury, Hutchinson, Henderson and Tottenham played well. We gave a dance on board in the evening, which was a great success. Only fifteen of us went. I thoroughly enjoyed it, and was much taken with the three Misses Shoesmith and little Dinah Taylor, the consul's daughter. Was disappointed with the German governess.

Tuesday 17

By the way, the officers were very decent last night, and Cooper told me he had heard from Louis Greig.* My early watch this morning; woke up with a very thick head and a terrible stomach ache from eating and drinking too much last night at the dance. Managed to struggle through the early watch with Mr Sinclair, although de Wet was late in relieving me. Was sick four times and shat innumerable times. Murray made me go to the sick bay, where I slept all the morning. I was down to play cricket against the officers, at which I should have met Dinah, and was looking forward to, but felt too ill to land. Officers went to dance on shore.

Wednesday 18

Left St Vincent at 6am, and saw the last of the Cape Verde isles at about 8. For the first day since our arrival, San Antonio was plainly visible, and its towering mountains looked glorious in the rising sun. I was very sorry (and I fancy I was not the only person) to leave Dinah Taylor and Tommy Shoesmith, as they were very nice little girls, and it is topping to see an English girl after so many foreigners. Our fears of a rough voyage were unrealised. Went to sleep in torpedo lecture.

Thursday 19

Fine day. Quite well. Usual studies. Exercised evolution for towing ship astern after evening quarters. Found my keys that I had lost. Commenced copying in seamanship notes. Now I have been here a month I am beginning to form a tolerable opinion of all the officers' characters, and shall now begin to enter up these in my diary and see if I change my opinion later. Garside showed me some nice photos of Dinah.

---

* Louis Greig was a British naval surgeon, an international rugby union player for Scotland and the British Lions, a courtier, and a confidant of King George VI.

Friday 20

Dead calm day. Usual studies. Very hot spell in torpedo submerged
flat. Exercised general quarters in the evening. 1st Lieut. seemed rather
dissatisfied with the efficiency of casemates. My opinion of the captain:
a bluff, gruff, typical old sea dog. Hearty and sociable, but curt to his
friends; he looks what he is, is typically stout and weather beaten. He is a
good officer; is popular with the junior officers. I am not sure if he likes
the little commander too much.

Saturday 21

Arrived at Santa Cruz de Tenerife early in the morning; the mountains
look lovely. 'X' group on the casemate to witness process of anchoring.
A mail arrived. Posted letters to Mother, Doris, and heard from Amy,
Mrs Drake and Joko. Amy's letter was coupled with a pressing invitation
to stop the weekend there, with which I could not comply, but got
leave to spend the day there (at Puerto Orotava tomorrow). I was
midshipman of the day with Morley. Slung clean hammocks in the
evening. Showed some visitors round the ship in the afternoon.

Sunday 22

Trollope and I got leave to go over to Orotava, and left at 8.45. Got there
at about 11. We motored over about twenty-seven miles of glorious
scenery. The peak of Tenerife looked splendid. Saw Amy and Mabel
Drummond Hay and old Mr Price. They were very nice and I lunched
there. Went over to play tennis at the Cooper's (saw Spencer Cooper and
Murray), where Trollope and his aunt were staying. She (Miss Kennedy)
knew Sophie. We have just missed two jolly good dances. Thoroughly
enjoyed my day.

Monday 23

Half Holiday. Started 'C' instruction. Old Andrew taught us how to
work 'star sights'. Went on shore and called on the De Passes at the
Quisisana Hotel. They were very nice, and I took them over the ship.

The little boy, John, was very interested. They have another son, a lieut. in the *Indomitable*, and are first cousins of Chatty Salaman.

The commander (Commander HAB Wollaston) is a very nice little man, overawed by 1st lieut. rather, but a very keen, good and efficient officer, who should go far. He is unpopular with the men as he is strict.

Tuesday 24

Several of the officers came back very late from the Spanish ball on shore, so that we did not weigh until 9.30. Tenerife disappeared below the horizon at about 12.30. I was sick early on, but recovered later. I did an extra rifle drill (voluntary) in the afternoon, and played deck cricket afterwards on the QD. No evolution.

The eng.-commander (Eng.-Commander Leslie) is a quiet, unassuming sort of person, but quite energetic in his own deportment. Where he is a bit of a martinet, he strikes me as being rather common.

Wednesday 25

Quite a big swell. Garside gave me the photos of St Vincent. Had a very cold night last night. The captain judged a deserter after quarters. Usual routine.

The fleet paymaster (Fleet Paymaster Wilson) is a nice man, of whom we see very little. He has a nice open countenance, and is a good and keen golfer. Quite an ordinary sort of person. The fleet surgeon (Fleet Surgeon Cameron) is an extraordinary man; he wears a beard and very antiquated collars, and rather reminds me of Beans. He has absolutely nothing to do, and always pretends to be most solicitous after your health when you are quite well. He spends his time pacing the QD and bug hunting (he has sixty thousand bugs).

Thursday 26

Just managed to get off extra rifle drill, but practised in the afternoon. Took a whole crowd of star sights, sun sights, moon sights, etc. throughout the course of the day. Practised 'The Vicar of Bray' with O'Leary, Payne and Bury for Saturday's sing-song.

Lieut. J Wolfe-Murray is none too fond of me, I believe. No. 1 is the most discussed officer in the ship; loathed by some, loved by others. I cannot make up my mind as regards him. He is very strict and inclined to be rather unreasonable, and is a typical No. 1. He is a good officer and very keen, but I doubt whether he will get promoted. He has more bark than bite. A keen fisherman and shot.

Friday 27

On the bridge early for pilotage, lovely morning, several ships in the straits. A Spanish cruiser passed us. A TB brought the officer in charge of the harbour submarine flotilla to us as we were attacked by submarines. Steamed alongside commercial mole* at Gibraltar at 9.30, having finished the first part of our cruise. Received a huge mail from England, and wrote to Mother. Stopped on in the afternoon. Found the *Indomitable* had left, which was a disappointment as I had been looking forward to seeing Mr Knothe.

Saturday 28

Wrote to Louis Greig to congratulate him on his promotion to staff surgeon. Heard from Doris; quite an affectionate letter for her. I suppose I have tickled her up by not writing as often as I used to. The Kaiser's yacht *Hohenzollern* is also here on her way to Corfu. The officers beat cadets at hockey, 4–1. Ship's company played at soccer (by the way, they beat Tenerife 6–1 on Sunday last). We had quite a successful sing-song in the evening. Branson did well. I sung 'Vicar of Bray' in a quartet.

MARCH

Sunday 1

Hohenzollern left harbour. I went with about six others to the races. We all lost money except Bury.

---

* Breakwater that provides protection to Gibraltar harbour.

Monday 2

The guv'nor got himself very unpopular again for running people in
galore. Symonds in very hot water. Started engineering study again.
In the afternoon we cadets 1st XV played the officers (rather a weak
team) at rugger and won easily 24–3. The ground was in a terrible state.
Bearded No. 1 in his den of sanctity about seamanship notes. Russian
cruiser *Bogatyr* arrived. *Cornwallis* went out with *Blonde* to battle
practice.

Tuesday 3

Ship coaled (1100 tons). Whole holiday. We all went by boat to Algeciras
and then by train on to Ronda (two hours' journey). A most enjoyable
day. Glorious climate and wonderful scenery. Excellent lunch at the
Reina Victoria Hotel. Ronda quite an interesting old place. Thoroughly
enjoyed myself. Went with Hutchinson, Tottenham, Cockburn and
Johnstone. Had a long chat with No. 1 coming home. Bench and I
managed to have a ride on engine buffers.

Wednesday 4

No half holiday on account of yesterday's whole. *Cornwallis* and
Lord Nelson out firing again. In the afternoon the cadet XV played
the *Dreadnought* gunroom and won 58–0; a great and unexpected
victory. Great jubilation among all the officers, and sickness among the
defeated team. Hutchinson played a magnificent game, and so did Bury.
Henderson was rather off. I was quite ferocious and got a try. Heard that
Bombardier Wells had beaten Bandsman Blake by wireless.*

Thursday 5

My 17th birthday, heard from home. The Spanish fleet left for Cadiz
from Algeciras. The cruiser *Du Chayla* arrived, also German sloop

---

* Bandsman Jack Blake fought Bombardier Billy Wells for the British heavyweight
title. Wells won with a fourth-round knockout, inflicting the first defeat of Blake's
career.

Schwalbe and a Dutch (battleship?) *Jacob van Heemskerck*. Spent four-and-a-half hours in the ER and did not land. Full strength played 4th battle squadron at hockey (W 2–1). Ship's company played HMS *Cormorant* at soccer (W 3–2).

Lieut. (N) HEH Spencer-Cooper, the senior navigator and most popular officer in the ship with cadets, is a jolly good sort; very jovial and fond of the stick.* I thought I should loathe him as I did at Dartmouth, but I do not. He does himself jolly well and is rolling in dibs. Is very much in the king, as he looked after 'Bertie' for two years.

Friday 6

Fleet novice's boxing. Heard from Peggy and Amy Drummond Hay. Cadets' hockey team lost to the 'Gunrooms of Fourth Battle Squadron' (6–7). I stopped on board and did pilotage notes. Another long day in ER. The *Schwalbe* left. Listened to the sequence of national anthems at 8. The *Eclipse* came in convoying two submarines bound for Colombo. She brought back memories of Osborne days. Owing to general painting we were all forced to sleep below. I have a nasty cold. An epidemic of skin disease is going through the ship owing to faulty washing.

Saturday 7

Played the gunrooms of the fleet at rugger and won 11–3. Hard game but we did badly. Hutchinson hopelessly off his game. Several people went to Algeciras. Had a long chat with Meggs in the ER.

Lieut. Colville is quite a nice man, quite decent to talk to, but is rather inclined to be underhand in running you in to No. 1 without any warning. He is quite a senior lieut., but looks much younger. He has just been married. He never plays games and very seldom watches. He has an extraordinary habit of surprising us in the hammock flat.

---

* HEH Spencer-Cooper would go on to write a bestselling account of the Battle of the Falklands in 1919.

Sunday 8

Went on shore with Tweedy and had a 'fem. sol'. Nice girl. Smoked and drank like hell at the Grand. Very dissipated day. Found we shall miss the Second Battle Squadron by two days for the second time, which is a beastly nuisance as I know old Dalglish, the flag captain.

Monday 9

Cohen told me he knows Cecil Leveson-Gower quite well. A break in the lovely weather, which we have been enjoying lately. Heard from home of the decease of George Wilson's brother Douglas. Ship's XV minus Bench (who is crocked) played Fourth Battle Squadron and won 21–6. An exciting and fierce game. Mr Meggs crocked. Went boat sailing with Lt Colville. *Eclipse* and submarines left at 10pm. Several lines came in. Dutch warship *Jacob van Heemskerck* left.

Tuesday 10

I was 'mid of boat' in the early morning. Cruiser *Duke of Edinburgh* arrived from Portsmouth. Very wet weather. The band played a good tune called 'The Cotton March'. Ship's first rugger defeat by ETC 0–11; Bench and Mr Meggs away. Lt Whitehead, the substitute, did rottenly. Put in a lot of pilotage notes. Wrote to Culme. General searchlight practice throughout fleet at 8pm.

Wednesday 11

The cruiser *Du Chayla* left early, followed by British cruiser *Duke of Edinburgh*. We left at 9.30 from the mole, and Gibraltar was out of sight at 3. Dead calm day, but this served only to prove the old adage 'a calm before the storm'. About twelve of us turned in on the upper deck and found the wind to be getting up slightly. Nevertheless, I soon got to sleep until woken up by the ash party. At four bells, proving to be 2 o'clock, although I thought it 6 o'clock, we were all soaked and a terrific wind and heavy sea had got up, so we were all forced to go below. I went to sleep at 2.30am on the gunroom table.

Was woken up by No. 1 at 6, but he had compassion on us and we all slept on till 7. Most of the officers were washed out of their cabins and had no sleep.

Thursday 12

Still very windy and rough. We are making but little headway and shall probably be twelve hours late at Palma. Heard by wireless that the *Duke of Edinburgh* was making very heavy weather and had been obliged to heave to. Passed Cartagena at about 4pm.

Lieut. (T) Sinclair is my favourite officer in the ship and is very popular with 'X' group. He teaches very well and has a nice quiet, sympathetic manner. He is an excellent and clever officer and is jolly good at all games. I like him very much indeed.

Friday 13

Head from home and Doris. The sea calmed considerably. Sighted Ibiza and Formentera in the morning, and Majorca (or in Spanish Mallorca) at 2pm. Dropped anchor in Palma Bay and exchanged salutes at 4pm. I went on shore with Tweedy and had a look round the town. Palma is a very clean and nice-looking town, and although there is nothing to do, it is easily the most pleasant Spanish town we have been to. There is a very magnificent old cathedral.

Saturday 14

Lovely day. Stopped on board and did seamanship and pilotage notes. Wrote a postcard to Auntie Ethel and also wrote home.

Lieut. Jeffreys is a great big blustering, slack fellow. A jolly good sort and I learn quite a lot from him when on watch. Very unpopular with the men, as he curses them right and left. He has a bored, blasé sort of manner, but wakes up on the rugger field.

Lieut. Millar joined the ship a month late at Gibraltar. Is a smart-looking little man, but always in a hurry, always late, and always fussing. Quite a good athlete, but gives the impression of having too much side.

Seems quite strict, but is really very harmless, and I can't form an opinion as to whether he is a rotten officer or not. Has a very deep voice for his size.

Sunday 15

Lovely day. Most of us went for a sailing picnic over to San Lucano, the other side of Palma Bay. Not quite such a success as it might have been. Went with Mr Jeffreys and Hutchinson in the cutter. The English people came to church.

Monday 16

Lovely day. We did not leave Palma till 5.30pm. XI all got run in for a bad rifle drill before breakfast. No. 1, in a towering rage, used appalling language. I was also run in for leaving my paintbrush by the paintwork and got two hours' sentry. Misfortune never comes singly. XI did extra rifle drill after quarters. The boat hoist broke down and we had to pipe to clear the lower deck of all hands to hoist the heavy boom. No. 1 gave us a long pie jaw.

Tuesday 17

Very rough during the night. We on the upper deck were obliged to come down and sleep in the gunroom. A nasty gale blowing out of the Gulf of Lyon made things miserable all day. Nearly everyone sick. A vile state of things below, as we were battened down and the atmosphere was appalling. The lights kept going out and everything was wet, and people were being sick everywhere. Eat nothing but Bovril all day. Everyone very glad to turn in. Anchored at Villefranche at 11am.

Wednesday 18

Increased revolutions to seventy-two from sixty-five. The sea quite calm, a lovely morning; all our spirits revived. Passed Hyères (where the Walters are stopping) at 6; lovely views of the Maritime Alps and the Riviera coast. Passed Cannes at 8. Heard from Louis Greig and home.

Went with Hutchinson and Cobb to Menton. The Riviera is a gay place; went to Menton casino and then went on to Monte Carlo, but it started to rain, so did not get much of a time, and had no time to go to Monaco. Met George Graves, who had just won £600, and he stood us about six drinks.* Also met a very pretty cousin of young Fairlie's, just married to a dirty guardsman.

Everyone who went to Nice came back with glowing reports of the pretty girls and everything else. I can see I shall run through a lot of cash in this place with one thing and another. It will be the devil of a job to visit the Walters, who are at Hyères, as it is seventy miles off.

Thursday 19

Fine weather. Battle of Flowers of Nice, to which a lot of people went. I did not stop long, but as I managed to get late leave, went over to Cannes by train and called on Cag and Donah at the Beau Site Hotel. Had a lovely chat with them. Dined at Antibes. Saw a French squadron in Golfe-Juan. Several officers and cadets went to a dance at Monte Carlo; I arrived back too late to go. Managed to get over rifle drill all night.

Friday 20

A nasty SW gale got up which was most nasty and disappointing for the Riviera. The usual parties of gamblers went off to Nice, Monte Carlo, Monaco and Menton. I stopped on board and worked. The French admiral of the squadron in Golfe-Juan visited us, as did some Russian Grand Duke,† with his two daughters, the princesses Nada and Zia Torby. One of them was very pretty, and I had the pleasure of showing her round the ship. Wrote to Cag and Aunt Minnie.

---

* George Graves was an English comic actor who became a star in musical comedies in the West End in the early 1900s.

† Grand Duke Michael Mikhailovich of Russia, grandson of Tsar Nicholas I of Russia.

Saturday 21

Better weather today. Very disturbing news about the state of affairs in Ulster due to the Home Rule Bill.* Hutchinson and I went to Nice and had a very amusing afternoon. We went to the casino and gambled and drank the whole afternoon. I won a few francs, but Hutchinson lost heavily I am afraid. Thoroughly enjoyed the afternoon. Met an Irishman named Barrett, with whom we became very pally. He was a friend of Sinclair's and in the secret service. We missed the last boat on board and just got a shore boat.

Sunday 22

Rugger match v Nice today scratched. Bad weather in the morning. Went over to Cannes again to play golf with Cag and Donah. The course was too wet, so we went for a motor drive, saw lovely views, and then back to the casino for tea. Got back to ship late. Cag and Donah arranged to come to tea on Monday. Heard of Scotland's firm fight against England at rugger.†

Monday 23

Engineering again. Glorious day. Heard from Daddy and Bob. Extremely disturbing news from Ulster. We are under sealed orders by wireless (private code) in case of further eventualities. Arranged a fine tea and all sorts of things for Cag and Donah, but they did not turn up at all, although I waited for two hours. This was most annoying and disappointing. An aeroplane flew round the ship in the morning.

Tuesday 24

I am sorry not to have seen the aquarium at Monte Carlo, which is a very fine one. Have thoroughly enjoyed our stay at Villefranche,

---

* The Curragh Incident of 20 March 1914 saw dozens of Army officers stationed in Ireland offer their resignation or accept dismissal rather than enforce Home Rule on Ulster.

† England beat Scotland in a thriller in Edinburgh, winning 16–15 to carry off the Triple Crown and retain the Calcutta Cup.

as we have had a very gay time and I liked seeing Cag and Donah. Weighed and left for Genoa at 7am. Had a wireless message to prepare to return home at once if ordered. I suppose this is something to do with the affairs in Ulster, which are most critical. The band played 'The Girl on the Film' last night, a tune I love. We arrived at Genoa at 2.30pm. The weather was inclement or, to be less polite, damned awful, so very few landed. Genoa has a large statue of Christopher Columbus, whose birthplace it was; also a fine harbour.

Wednesday 25

Lovely day. A large party of officers and cadets went to a big dance given by the consul general at the Hotel de Bristol. There were about two hundred people there, including all the foreign elite of Genoa, as the dance was given in our honour, and several Italians, some of whom were exceedingly pretty and danced excellently. But however pretty a girl is and however well she dances, it is rather boring after a bit if you can't understand one another's language. There were some very nice American girls at the dance. Genoa itself is a fine town with some fine pictures and sculpture works, and a wonderful harbour.

Christie joined the ship from home, he having been put down a term through sickness. There are three large Italian Dreadnoughts in Genoa, where the famous Ansaldo dockyard is; they are more heavily armed than ours, but do not look so efficient.

Thursday 26

We had a most successful dance on board. Only fifteen cadets went. I was again a lucky one. I thoroughly enjoyed it, as there were several very nice girls, greatly superior to yesterday. I was very much struck by the three 'Amurrican' sisters, daughters of the USA consul, Mr Perkins. They were Jeanie, Argenta and Olive. Argenta quite knocked me 'all of a heap'. I tore my new coat to shreds to give her a button. I put several quotations in her book, and gave her my card. The Duchess of Mecklenburg-Schwerin and daughters were at the dance.*

Friday 27

Weighed anchor, cast off from the mole and left Genoa at 6am. Splendid scenery as usual of the snow-clad Apennines along the Italian coast. Reached Leghorn at 2pm. Unluckily it was very rough, and although we managed to get a mail boat onshore, it was too rough for anyone to land, which is a nuisance as I could not find out about the Florence trains. We had to lie at anchor outside the harbour. We received an invitation from the Italian Admiral to dine and go to the opera afterwards tomorrow. We can see the famous Isle of Elba in the distance.

Saturday 28

Quite a choppy sea, the pinnace was badly damaged while being hoisted out. Got leave to go to Florence tomorrow. I went with fifteen officers and cadets to a reception given by the consul, Mr Carmichael. There was roller skating, dancing and tea, but I did not enjoy it much – the girls weren't up to much. Met a great friend of Shaw's and Sir Francis Vane's, named Rich, hailing from Via Reggio. A large party of cadets went to dine with the Italian Admiral and cadets at the naval academy, and to the opera afterwards. They thoroughly enjoyed themselves. Other people visited the Leaning Tower of Pisa and also Lucca.

Sunday 29

Left at 6 from the ship and went up by train to Florence. Met a nice man named Carr in the train. Shifted into mufti at a German hotel near the station and went up to Villa Nuti, Bellosguardo, to visit Joko. She seemed very well and was with eight other girls (two quite pretty Americans). She introduced me to Emily White, Jack's cousin and

---

* Duchess Cecile of Mecklenburg-Schwerin was a German crown princess and wife of German Crown Prince Wilhelm, the son of Kaiser Wilhelm II.

old John Price's cousin. Joko took me to the Pitti gallery, the Uffizi gallery, the Duomo, etc., etc. The pictures were gorgeous, and so were the sculptures. We had a very expensive lunch at the Grand Hotel,* and then went to other galleries. Had tea at Villa Nuti, and thoroughly enjoyed my day. I hope Joko did also. Got back at 12.

Monday 30

Got up early to take early watch; very tired after my morning watch. Received a fiver from Daddy. I hear that yesterday we played the Italian cadets and won 2–1. Today all the Italian cadets came to see over the ship and we entertained them. Went to an amusing garden party at Mr and Mrs Fabricoli's, the great marble merchant. Took an affectionate farewell from Mr Carmichael, the consul. Had a successful dance on board in the evening. A fire broke out at 3am, but was soon put out.

Tuesday 31

Rich came on board to lunch and to say goodbye. An enquiry was held by the captain on last night's fire. Result not known yet. Weighed anchor and left Leghorn at 4pm. We are all in for a hard week's work now, as we have been having a jolly good time at Leghorn, Genoa and Villefranche. Anchor work after quarters; cleaned my sextant. Sighted Elba at 5pm and Corsica at 6pm.

APRIL

Wednesday 1

Passed the straits of Ajaccio at 6am and dropped anchor in Aranci Bay at 8am. Carried out multitudinous evolutions, such as 'mooring and unmooring', etc., etc. Pretty hard work. On watch in the afternoon. Heard from Aunt Do, wrote to Mother and HRB. A large party went off

---

* The Grand Hotel in Florence, now the St Regis Florence, is a former palace that was converted into a hotel in the second half of the eighteenth century.

after work for a fishing picnic. This is a deserted, lonely spot, miles from anywhere, with wild scenery. Weather ideal at present. Wireless reports improvement in Ulster.

Thursday 2

Several officers not concerned with the torpedo department went off on fishing and shooting expeditions, taking advantage of the wild country, some for one day and some for longer. Personally we were engaged in a long day's work running torpedoes and parting, from 6am to 3pm. We had seven runs with our 18-inch torpedoes, and one succession of quick time loading. Some difficulty in the picket boat in securing the fourth. Very interesting work and quite good fun, but jolly tiring. Got on shore in the evening and went fishing. We worked all our searchlights after dark. An Italian destroyer came to look at us in the afternoon. Heard from home.

Friday 3

12 par .303 tube, and 6-inch sub-calibre 1-inch firing practice most of the day, both for seamen and our gunnery group; most of the firing good. XI seamanship three-monthly test with the commander; I did badly. Five people attempted to swim on shore one-and-a-half miles in a choppy sea; three succeeded. Glorious weather continues.

Lieut. Whitehead, assistant navigator, usually known as 'Ally Sloper', is a sloppy, bow-legged man. Fairly good navigator in practice, but hopeless in theory and at teaching people. Is very slack, and has taken a violent dislike to Hutchinson. A fair athlete. I don't like him much.

Saturday 4

Italian battleship *Emanuele Filiberto* came in at 11 and went out to evolutions at 2. Came back later. 'X' boat sailing all the morning. Flashing Morse test, and No. 1 examined Z group in rifle drill. I was midshipman of the day. A large party went off to a picnic, and several other officers and cadets went fishing. Mr Colville and Dr Franklin went shooting. A strong breeze sprung up in the evening. Exercised night defence.

Sunday 5

Heard from Mother, Doris and Auntie Maud. Two picnic expeditions; one to the usual place in the bay, while ten adventurous spirits led by Mr Spencer-Cooper, who was awfully nice, went off on an expedition to Figarolo Isle, a wild, deserted and rocky islet at the harbour mouth. It was a difficult job landing the picnic party among the precipitous cliffs. I managed to light a fire and we all had a good meal. Spencer-Cooper, Davis and I went stalking mouflon, which are very rare. We had great fun, and some narrow escapes, but did not kill.

Monday 6

Gunnery exercises continued in the forenoon. We did a beastly 'day's work'; I worked out every sight wrong. X1 and X2 in trouble for bad gun drill. Did a pilotage test paper in the evening. In a very bad temper. Hard at it all day.

Lieut. Hammill, great friends with Jeffreys, is a large, loutish, clumsy fellow. Very red-haired and ugly. Rather uncouth, but a good officer. Kind-hearted and very keen in instructing us.

Tuesday 7

Sounding machine practice all the morning. Usual fishing parties. I walked up to the signal station, a 2000 ft climb. Went with the padre. The ship's company gave a successful concert in the evening, which we all attended. Some very good turns by the officers. Heard from Herbert Brown. Exercised night defence at 12, which meant no sleep. All torpedoes manned, night firing exercised and search light sweeping.

Wednesday 8

The commander woke us all up at 4am, and all steam boats went away on an imaginary torpedo attack. We unmoored and left Aranci Bay at

8.30. I have thoroughly enjoyed my stop here in the wilds. I am very tired, as we have all been at it since last night.

Thursday 9

Arrived in Castellammare Bay opposite Naples at 8.30. A big swell, so we had to 'up anchor' and remoor at 12. Trickish job landing, on account of sea. Faulkner had a narrow escape. No time to do much, as we were at work nearly all day. Castellammare is a dirty town. Heard from home, and received a nice letter and photo from Argenta Perkins.

Friday 10

Gorgeously hot boiling day. I was too lazy, and did a general slack on board for on account of Good Friday we had Sunday routine. Wrote letters to Argenta, H Brown, Uncle Jack, Gertrude and Phil. A few people roused energy to go over to Naples for the afternoon. I had arranged to climb Mt San Angelo, just above Castellammare di Stabia, with Tottenham, but we both felt too slack. Received some newspapers from home. Vesuvius looks very fine and is smoking.

Saturday 11

Another gorgeous day. Gunnery viva voce exam; I knew everything I was asked, but failed to do myself anything like justice. 'Y' group knocked spots out of 'X' group at seamanship, with the advantage of our experience. At present my exams are none too good. Some people went to Sorrento and some to Naples. Our expedition to the famous grotto caves of Capri was cancelled due to rough weather. I climbed part of Mt San Angelo with Tottenham. Tea at Hotel Weiss.

Sunday 12

Went to Naples with Branson and Tweedy. Visited all the decent hotels, and a very low haunt called 'The Glen House' from which we were very lucky to escape with our lives. Bury, Payne, Cookson and Bairstow gave an extempore performance at the local theatre.

Monday 13

YI, 2II and 2III in the soup. The cadets were given three days' leave.
Some people went to stop on shore at various hotels in Naples
and Castellammare. I elected to stop on board at nights and make
expeditions by day, with several others, as this is cheaper. About 30 of
us went up Vesuvius. We drove to Torre Annunziata, then to Pugliano,
lunched at Eremo, and then went up to the crater. Wonderful view of
country around, but sulphurous fumes very strong. Returned about 7.

Tuesday 14

Went for an expedition to Pompeii for the day. Left early. Lunched at the
'Suisse' Hotel. Spent the day among the ruins and in the museums. Was
very interesting. There is quite a good amphitheatre. A thunderstorm
late in the afternoon broke the spell of glorious weather. Had some fine
Italian music during lunch.

Eng.-Lieut. GD Campbell is an old Osborne acquaintance. Very nice
off duty to us, but sometimes rather treacherous. Has no instructions,
so we do not see much of him. The wag of the WR. A very fast three-
quarter, but inclined to funk.

Wednesday 15

Went off by the early train to Naples and visited the cathedral,
where there were some fine frescoes. Then to the museum, where
the sculptures were wonderful. The 'Fall of Rome' was quite up to its
reputation. Branson, Tweedy and I had a row with Colville and No. 1.
Lunched at the Café del Paoli, although not much of a lunch. Drove to
Pozzuoli afterwards to see the amphitheatre. Very hot so put away a lot
of German beer. Had a very musical journey home. I drove the frisco
through the streets to the quay at a furious pace. Very tired.

Thursday 16

Our leave is over and we commenced duty again today. Spencer-Cooper
collected our pilotage notebooks. Meggs lectured on the steering engine.

Weighed anchor and left Castellammare at 6pm. Passed in between Capri and the mainland. I am sorry we have not seen Capri during our stay here.

Eng.-Lieut. Moss is a red-haired, thin little Scotsman. An awful fool, who knows nothing whatsoever, and gets terribly ragged. His attempts to impress his juniors are quite ludicrous. Despite this, he is very kind-hearted and a good sport.

Friday 17

Got up early with O'Leary at 3.30 to see Stromboli. The glare of the volcano was distinctly fine. We were aboard at 7. Passed the straits of Messina from 10 to 11.30. Saluted an Italian battleship in Messina harbour. We went down the Calabrian coast close to Reggio. Messina shows no sign of the earthquake of a few years ago.* Etna was a fine sight covered with snow above the clouds with smoke coming out at the peak. Passed Catania and Syracuse, and left the Sicilian coast at about 6. I had ER dog watch. Engineering oral exams started, but not for me.

Saturday 18

Arrived Malta at 7am, where we found the Med. Squadron, and several old friends, including Knothe, Abercrombie and FS Collingwood. I had my oral practical exam with Eng.-Comm. I went ashore and saw something of the place. It is divided into three towns on three peninsulas, enclosing two fine inlets, which form the naval harbours, the dockyard being in the easterly. The island is barren, but the town is clean and contains many public gardens. Valletta is the largest of the three towns. The old capital, Città Vecchia, is connected by rail to Valletta. We met several midshipmen we have known before. We slung new hammocks.

---

* Then Messina earthquake on 28 December 1908 measured a moment magnitude of 7.1. The cities of Messina, Reggio and Calabria were almost completely destroyed, resulting in between seventy-five thousand and two hundred thousand people losing their lives.

Sunday 19

Worked all day. Went on shore at the invitation of the Rev. Vernon Hanson to church at the Barrakka garrison church and dine with him afterwards. He is an uncle of Murdoch's, and quite a good fellow. Our padre and Mr Andrew also there. Saw Duckworth (old St Vincent's) and TH Welsby.

Monday 20

Rev. and Mrs Hanson on board to tea with padre and Mr Andrew. Bought some silks. Heard from home. Received the Easter Dartmouth magazine. Some astounding news: Dickson received the King's Medal instead of Stromeyer. This was an extraordinarily surprising scandal, perhaps an aftermath of the Roxburgh affair. Working hard for exams.

Tuesday 21

Started half term exams. Coaled ship. Took in 850 tons; had to turn out early as they started coaling at 5. The First Cruiser Squadron went out to battle practice. I did a bad 'day's work' after a good start. But did a fair paper in the afternoon. Very hot and murky. Several people went up to practise at the nets on the Corradino cricket ground.

Wednesday 22

No half holiday. Pilotage exam. I did rottenly. Signals I did poorly. Seamanship I wasn't at all bad in. Torpedo I did pretty well and gunnery pretty well.

Eng.-Lieut. CJ Meggs is a self-made, hard-working north countryman, who has to live on his pay. Very energetic and plucky at rugger. Has played for the services. A keen photographer. An efficient officer, and although unpopular with some people, I like him very much.

Thursday 23

Heat and steam exam, and shipbuilding exam. I did well, I think, in both. This finishes half term exams. Very hot. Wrote letters and went ashore to do some shopping. Half holiday. Some people with relations went on leave until Monday. Ship painting started.

Surgeon CRM Baker is an old Dartmouth acquaintance. Nickname 'The Squire'. A quiet, unassuming fellow. Very good looking, but looks bad tempered; nevertheless, he isn't. Very kind when you are ill and I should imagine quite a good doctor. A good bat and a fair golfer.

Friday 24

Polo match Navy v Army won by Army 6–2. H.S. King invited six of us to dine in the *Indefatigable*, but I had to refuse. Whole holiday. Had a row with a Dghajsa man.* Lunched with the Hansons, and afterwards we went on an expedition to Notabile and the catacombs at Città Vecchia, with Symonds and Mr Marshall, and then to a picnic at Bocchetta. Thoroughly enjoyed myself. The ship's cricket XI licked HMS *Egmont*, the port admiral's flagship. No. 1, Sinclair and Fitzroy made a lot of runs. Hutchinson and Armstrong lunched with keynotes in the *Invincible*.

Saturday 25

A dance on board the *Inflexible* a great success. Only a few of us went, although I did not. Another whole holiday. A picnic, lunch and tea to Birzebbuga; very good bathing. Went to some caves in the afternoon. A sing-song on board in the evening; good songs by Mr Andrew, Bethel and others, and a good topical alphabet. Several visitors. Oppressively hot weather. Most of us longing to leave Malta, although it is quite a good place. The results of the majority of exams up; I have not done badly.

Sunday 26

The commander-in-chief in the Mediterranean, Admiral Sir Berkeley Milne, inspected us in the morning. In the afternoon Bethel, Ashworth

---

* A Maltese water taxi.

and I called on Mr Knothe and had tea with him in the *Indomitable*. He
seemed very fit. Also met Lieut. de Pass, whose parents I met at Tenerife.

Monday 27

Fleet staff race won by a *Cornwall* ship company crew. Malta Races
spring meeting. Nicholson has a mount. Garside made a lot of money.
Several people went to the Grand Opera. The Maltese have a very fine
opinion of their opera, and I believe it is quite good. Salvati, the tenor,
had a benefit on Saturday. I laid in a large stock of cigarettes to take
home. Boat sailing all morning. Visited several places of interest in the
Strada Reale.

Tuesday 28

Invited Knothe to tea, but unluckily he could not come. We gave an
afternoon reception and dance on board. Quite good fun. Some very
pretty girls, although none very French or American as they were
mostly connected with naval or military officers. The prettiest girl there
was Miss Scott, and other nice ones were Mrs Gilpin-Brown, Miss
Davidson, Miss Weston, Mrs Gordon and Miss Heather, who lives in
Kent. Also met Mrs Collingwood, an old Osborne friend, and Mrs
Cameron, whom I met in Scotland years ago. Very sorry not to meet
Mrs Abercrombie, who was there. Navy v Army cricket started. 'Push'
only made 2, but wonder of wonders, Whitehead made 137.

Wednesday 29

Navy v Army match scratched owing to army mobilisation. Very
bad luck on the Navy. Instead, we (HMS *Cornwall*) played the
Mediterranean fleet at Corradino. We made 169; I made 5 not out in
half an hour, and batted very soundly. They gave us an awful licking and
made 326 for 6. I took one wicket for nine runs. Very tired of leather
hunting. Went to the 'Frolies' in the evening, a jolly good amateur
variety show, burlesque revue, etc., put on by Lieut. Corbett of the
Indomitable. He must be a very clever man. Crowded with officers and

ladies. Said goodbye to Keynotes and Mrs Collingwood. Did not see Mr de Pass, who was there. Got to bed at 2am.

I have enjoyed the last few days here, although not the first. I am quite sorry to leave Malta, as I realise the importance of English people over foreigners, even though it is a garrison town pure and simple. Several very nice girls. Muriel Biddulph, although engaged, is damned hot stuff. I thoroughly agree with everybody else in Malta that Miss Scott is the prettiest girl in the place.

Thursday 30

Left Malta at 8.30; passed the *Black Prince* coming in from England. Mr Sinclair seems very cool to the cadets now; I am afraid he must have got wind of the shady methods of the cliques in the Y and Z groups in the torpedo exam. Two marines sentenced for attempted desertion. Exercised 'towing astern' after quarters. Received 'Cumberland' magazine. Quite a swell set in during the dog watches.

MAY

Friday 1

Thick fog in the morning, cleared off later. Dropped anchor off Cagliari at 2.30. Very hot weather. Cagliari is the capital of Sardinia. Rifle shooting on the QD. Mulcahy, Morgan and Armstrong on captain's report for insolence. The washing contractor is a sister of Charley Arbela, the Carozzi and Dghajsa proprietor at Valletta, Floriana and Marsa. Dancing the 'Pongo' in vogue after prep. Lots of visitors on board.

Saturday 2

Very hot again. I was midshipman of the day. Picnic in the afternoon in the sailing boats. I was on watch all afternoon. Some people went into the town, but were very bored. The place looks quite imposing from the ship. The prefect and consul came on board and were saluted. Rifle shooting again. Three Italian destroyers came in at 4 and we exchanged offers of guards. I made a faux pas hoisting the cutter and nearly killed three men. Lieut. Hammill very annoyed; so was I with myself.

Sunday 3

Italian battleships *Roma* and *Napoli* arrived. Sailing picnic in the afternoon. Mr McKew lectured on Hinduism in the evening.

Monday 4

Weighed and left Cagliari at 6.30. Saw the last of Sardinia, Cape Spartivento, at 11. Ran through a fog, but fine afternoon. Away both sea boats crews for exercise after quarters. All hands to bathe.* I got cursed for foolishly diving down to the 'A' bracket.

Paymaster Rogers is quite a good fellow. Very keen on the girls and goes the pace all round. Is perhaps rather conceited. Has a nasty knack of cutting other people out at dances, and consequently there is a general cadets dancing combine against him. Has an exaggerated opinion of his own boat sailing capabilities. I like him.

Tuesday 5

Sighted Algerian mountains about 6am and secured alongside mole at 11.30 in Algiers harbour. The Greek destroyer *Flotilla* came in later. I did not go onshore, but the people who did were very pleased with it and described it as a miniature Paris. Town very full of Greeks.

Gunner Stones is the senior executive warrant officer in the ship. A tin striper. Not a bad chap. Very unobtrusive; keen on rifle shooting. A very ordinary sort of fellow.

Wednesday 6

Accession Day; dressed ship and saluted at 12. French and Greek commanders came on board. Went on shore with Shaw. Went to a cinema and saw something of the town. In the better parts it certainly

---

* 'Hands to bathe' allows sailors to relax after operational demands.

resembles Paris, but in the lower quarters and docks it smells terribly and is crowded with Arabs, Greeks and Moors. It has a large quantity of pretty French girls and several nice cafés. Heard from home. Armstrong and Blood dined in the *Canopic*. Very hot day.

Had just heard that Joko has returned home, so the chocs I sent to Florence will have been wasted. She is stopping at Quaives at present. Doris tells me she is rather conceited.

Thursday 7

Mr Colville and thirty cadets, myself included, were inveigled into going to a dance given by a Greek lady on shore. The dance turned out to be an absolute frost, and was merely a concert and amateur theatrical show all in Greek and French. The only English people present being the consul and his daughter. I escaped with P Buchanan at the earliest opportunity, and we went to a nice little café. Discovered two lovely French girls, whom we stood a meal, and attempted to improve our French with but scant success.

Friday 8

Appallingly hot. The dry, dusty wind blew hard over from the Sahara, and the conditions were appalling, worse than St Vincent. Faulkner and I went to tea with Flt Surgeon and Mrs Cameron; we quite enjoyed it, as they are a funny old couple. They are stopping at the Hotel Excelsior. Pearson and Tweedy invited ten chic little French girls to tea on board and had a very gay time. The contrast between the pretty French dresses and the Arab women with their yashmaks is very marked. First lieut. gave X3 and 4 hell in the 6-inch heavy gun drills.

Saturday 9

Whole holiday. We all went to Blida by train. I went with Shaw. Very quaint Arab market, where I made some purchases. Visited the French army remount depot; saw some very fine Arab horses. Went on to the Sidi les Gorges afterwards; very fine scenery. Saw some eagles and lots of monkeys. Returned home about 6. Hutchinson's friend Angèle Siatelli came on board and caused a great sensation in the GR. I wish we were stopping here longer, as I should cut him out.

Sunday 10

Weather cooler. O'Leary and I visited Angèle Siatelli's (fem. sol). She is quite a nice little thing. We had tea at the Hotel de Regence.

Monday 11

Left Algiers at 9.30am. Passed the SS *Prinses Juliana*, of the Dutch East Indies line, just outside harbour. Faulkner just missed his sister, who was on board. I have thoroughly enjoyed our stay at Algiers. Stopping and starting in the afternoon watch in the ER. General quarters in the first dog watch. Aiming tube firing for the 6-inch guns; only poor results. This attributed to varying winds.

Tuesday 12

At sea all day. Left sight of African coast in the night (Cape Tenez), but sighted Cape de Gata in the morning, and kept about eighteen miles off Spanish coast. General quarters at 4.15, and 3-inch sub-calibre firing ten rounds per 6-inch guns afterwards. Better results. 1st lieut. gave the bosun a most amusing blowing up, and poor old Gearing was nearly worried out of his mind.

Mr Gearing, boatswain, is a dear bluff, fat, red-faced old sea dog. One of the old school, full of anecdotes and yarns, and almost totally illiterate. A jolly good sort, and a good seaman, but quite ignorant of all modern appliances. Very popular.

Wednesday 13

Arrived Gibraltar at 10am and secured to a buoy. The rock is quite an old friend now. Just our luck to find a filthy levanter blowing again. No half holiday. 6-inch BL gun drill instead of refitting LP crankhead in the afternoon. I did log books.

Mr Pearn, torpedo gunner, known as the 'Canary', is a very nice little man, and not a bit ashamed of his seaman days as some WOs are. Untiring in his efforts to explain the ins and outs of the Whitehead torpedo. Very keen on record making and breaking in submerged tube drills. Has a mania for asking and solving riddles. Great chums with Mr Edwards.

Mr Hall, gunner (for cadets instructional duties), commonly known as the 'Mole', is on the whole unpopular with cadets and officers. Has an extraordinary north country accent and is very conceited. Is mean and unreliable, although very kind to you when you are ill. He toadies to No. 1 and will tell any lie at your expense to save himself. He is a very nest of immorality in its basest forms. In spite of all this, he is an excellent and pleasant companion when off duty.

Thursday 14

Levanter dropped about 6pm. Coaled ship, took in 700 tons. I was up at 4am with XI getting up steam in the stern pinnace. Afterwards we did a five-hour job refitting in the funnel. Everything covered with coal dust and no water to wash it when we had finished. Fully realised the disadvantage of coaling in His Majesty's ships. I arranged to play tennis with Raynes, C Cohen and de Wet, but we were too tired, so I intended to shop, but No. 1 kept me on board, so I spent the afternoon cursing him and all his ancestors. Yesterday Z beat Y 4–3 at hockey.

Friday 15

Today Y beat us 3–0. Branson off his game, although I did fairly well. I did some shopping afterwards. There is an abundance of strawberries here at present, which is rather nice, and most of us take full advantage of it. Group cutter practice in the evening. Refitted fore starboard LP eccentric strap in the morning. Old Auntie and CERA Passmore in good form. We pulled Goddard's leg by having him called at 4am. Ship's company shooting match against the dockyard.

Saturday 16

Hockey X v Z, Z won 4–2. I shot one goal for X. Very strong
partisanship. Did a lot of shopping with Johnstone; bought several
kimonos and silk things, and bargained with several merchants.
Johnstone and I had tea at the Grand, and I drank a large amount, and
became rather cantankerous and had a row with the manager. Also
left all my purchases behind (about 25/- worth to my great chagrin,
and I don't know if I shall get them back). Had a row with Henderson
on board.

Sunday 17

Shaw and I, having uncovered my parcels, went to bathe at Rosia Bay.
Afterwards we went on to the King of Spain's birthday bullfight at Linea.
Four bulls, young toreadors and matadors, no horses. Most intensely
exciting, but terribly bloodthirsty! One man killed and two injured.
I thoroughly enjoyed it, but doubt if I shall go again.

   PO Williams, TGM and TI (a jolly good fellow) got long service and
GC medals.

Monday 18

Battle practice. For some unknown reason we only did forty-two rounds
of 6-inch guns and nothing else. This seems most inefficient. Rumour
has it that we fired two hundred rounds too many last year, and Lieut.
G is now trying to economise. I went away rake spotting in the target
towing tug *Crocodile* with the gunner. Left ship at 6am and returned
at 12 noon. Midshipman of the pinnace on my return. Swedish cruiser
Fylgia, French cruiser *Friant* and HMS *Vindictive* came in. Officers
beat cadets 5–3 at hockey. Old Mole up the pole with the ever unlucky
Branson.

Tuesday 19

Slipped from buoy and left Gibraltar at 9am. Last of the Mediterranean,
for which I am sorry, as we have all enjoyed our three-month stop there.

The usual sham submarine attack in the straits. All hands to bathe after evening quarters. The captain asked me some questions and I made a fool of myself. We were instructed in the mysteries of the heated torpedo. Shooting match: WOs and cadets v ship's company. We won 475–465. I did well, so did Mole, under very poor conditions.

Wednesday 20

At sea all day. Passed Cape St Vincent, Lisbon and Cape Roca, otherwise out of sight of land. No evolutions. Our match cadets v WOs scratched and instead No. 1 started a shooting competition. First round shot today; several people did well, myself included. Tested Very's pistol lights in the morning. Turned in early. The steaming light fused in the dog watch and we had to rig an oil light as a substitute.

Thursday 21

Passed Vigo in the morning and Pontevedra Bay later. Dropped anchor in Carril Bay, an inner arm of Arosa Bay, off Villajuan at 4pm. The boats have to go to Vilagarcia, about three miles off, which is rather a nuisance. There is a railway from Carril to Vigo, Lisbon and NE Galicia, and also to Santiago. Very few people landed, although the country around looks invitingly green and pretty. Daddy sent me some cash by the mail. Group cutter practice in the afternoon; no rifle shooting. Seamanship all day, chiefly log books. I must finish my log book this week, and my signal notebook wants overhauling.

Friday 22

Early watch in picket boat. Went to Vilagarcia to fetch stewards. Filled up 14-inch torpedoes all morning. TGM, the only exec CPO in the ship, had a nasty accident as the dropping gear blew out backwards through his hands and made a horrible wound. In the afternoon we ran the 14-inch torpedoes from the picket boat, dropping gear at twelve knots. I fired the first one and it was a great success, although fifteen yards out in nine hundred. Branson fired the next three and they all misfired, and then Gardner had a mediocre run. Dog watch cutter practice; landed and walked through woods with Colville and Cowpat – very fine trees. No. 1 fishing all day.

Saturday 23

Whole holiday. No. 1 and four cadets went fishing for the day. The rest of the cadets took part in a relay cross country race; boat pulling six hundred yards, three-mile run and sixty-yard swim. X group won easily. I was 1st, Stratford 2nd, and Hutchinson 3rd. Y and Z groups did not try very hard, and some officers were rather sick afterwards. Shaw and I went for a long walk to about sixteen miles across country; very hard-going – went up to the top of Serpent's Hill, about 1000 ft, and came back through Vilagarcia and Villajuan. Gorgeous scenery and very fine woods. The valleys are excellently cultivated. A very strenuous day.

Sunday 24

Decided to apply for the *Warrior* instead of the *King George V*, after a lot of thought. A stiff gale got up in the afternoon and a picnic was cancelled. I stopped on board as there is nothing to do in Vilagarcia. Several officers and cadets went fishing again. I wish I had some fishing gear. Wrote home.

Monday 25

Gale continued; weather cold. Y group cutter sailing, and got very wet. In spite of the weather, the monthly diving exercises continued under the direction of PO Oliver, captain of MT, as no officers could be spared from the ship. Rifle shooting comp in the afternoon; I did badly. 6-inch gun drill.

Mr Eggford, carpenter, is not at all a bad fellow, of whom we see very little. Is a sink of filthy language and always ready with a dirty yarn. A healthy red-faced fellow, and not bad at his job.

Tuesday 26

Weighed and left Arosa Bay at 6am. Passed Cape Finisterre at 8am and left Cape Ortegal, the last of Spain, at 10. Prepared for towing forward.

Chief Artificer Engineer Crabb is a big-bearded man, rather brusque, but very nice when you know him. A very keen rifle shot, who is always ready to yarn about rifle shooting. A good man at his job in the ER. Unpopular occasionally due to brusqueness, but generally liked. No relation to our Dartmouth friend of the same name.

Wednesday 27

At sea all day. Good weather. Exercised towing stations after evening quarters.

Chief Artificer Engineer EC Edwards, commonly known as Auntie, is very popular with everybody. Rather smug, but otherwise an excellent sort; a good tempered, kind-hearted old chap. Full of his reminiscences and very amusing, although he does not know it. Is not particularly good at his job, but the fatherly superiority with which he treats all his juniors is extremely funny. Is a great, big, fat man. Most of his weird expressions are bywords in the ship.

Thursday 28

Received result of the Derby.* Sighted Cape Kinsale about 6am, and dropped anchor off Haulbowline at Queenstown about 8am. In the British Isles once more after four months' absence. I have never been to Ireland before. We found the *Hindustan* in the anchorage, but she left at about 10. The training cruiser squadron, consisting of six cruisers, were inside the harbour. Several people went to play tennis at Admiralty House by invitation. Others landed in Queenstown and some went up to Cork. I stopped on board to work, being rather behindhand in pilotage. Got a huge mail from home. Have heard nothing about Phil and Theo being at Oban. By the way, Legge is in the *Crescent* here.

---

* The 1914 Epsom Derby was run on Wednesday 27 May 1914, and was won by an outsider called Durbar. It followed the 'Suffragette Derby' of 1913.

Friday 29

Last night we left our moorings and came in to inner anchorage. Eng.-Commander Leslie left the ship and was succeeded by Eng.-Commander Maconnachie. Mr Legge came on board. Gunboats *Gossamer* and *Skipjack* came in. I got in the consommé with No. 1 again and I got my leave stopped. Several people went to play tennis with the admiral at the Rushhooke club (of which we have been made honorary members, as well as the Royal Cork club). The Irish people all left on weekend leave, lucky dogs.

Saturday 30

Whole holiday. Heard of the disaster of the *Empress of Ireland*.* We all went on an expedition through Cork, Blarney and Mallow to Killarney. Visited the lakes, and the scenery is very pretty. Saw over Killarney House, which was burnt down last year, belonging to the Earl of Kenmare. Lunched at Ross Castle. We had a very merry time. Met a fair friend of Cowpat's and Dr Baker's. Several people fished and played golf. Old Mole went on leave to Castle Gregory. They coaled ship in our absence, 700 tons.

Sunday 31

Judging the state of things today, Temperley's method of coaling, which we used yesterday, is a very clean one. Several people went to play tennis as usual. I went with Trollope and Henderson to play golf at Little Island. A very nice course and good food at the club house. DKT and I halved in the morning and we won 2 and 1 in the afternoon. Thoroughly enjoyed the day. Mr Legge was playing with Mr Sinclair. It was nice seeing him again.

---

* RMS *Empress of Ireland* sank in the Saint Lawrence River following a collision with the Norwegian collier SS *Storstad* in the early hours of 29 May 1914. Of the 1477 people on board, 1012 died. It remains the largest number of deaths in any Canadian peacetime maritime accident.

JUNE

Monday 1

Went to tea at Admiralty House. Played croquet and three very good sets of tennis. I played well for me. AJCC and self beat Raynes and de Wet 6–2, then Raynes and I beat AJCC and de Wet 6–1, then AJCC and Raynes beat de Wet and self 6–1. Thoroughly enjoyed the afternoon. Heard from Roxburgh; this and the thought of meeting Stromeyer brings back unpleasant memories of the debacle at Dartmouth.

Tuesday 2

Vice-Admiral Coke and Rear-Admiral Pears came on board in the forenoon. Cadet Payne discharged to hospital with appendicitis. Articles of war after quarters, as several cases of drunkenness among ship's company reported. I did not land, but stopped on board to work. Keogh seems to have picked some very nice friends here of the opposite sex. Mr Hall rejoined ship. Weighed and left Queenstown at 7.30pm. The VA has been very good to us. Left Irish coast off Rosslare at 12. Sighted Carnarvon [Caernarfon today] at 3am.

Wednesday 3

At sea all day. Kept about thirty miles off the Irish coast, and sighted the Isle of Man in the first dog watch and ran through the straits of Galloway between Ireland (Co. Down) and Scotland later on. We are all very sorry to lose poor old Spiker Payne. 'Y' group twelve par firing, and three par firing for the training classes. Excellent results. Swung ship by the sun after firing. Had considerable trouble with our boilers, and reduced to eight knots. Worked up auxiliary steam, all connections. Bury returned to duty.

Artificer Engineer PS Walkey is a small, sharp Cockney. See very little of him. He is no gentleman, by however much we stretch the imagination. Unlike most of them that go down to the sea in ships, he has no ideas of dressing, and goes ashore in a green suit, check cap, blue tie, red socks and brown shoes.

Thursday 4

Passed Machrihanish and ran through the Sound of Islay early in the morning. Machrihanish brought back old memories. Rough weather experienced, so we did not arrive at Oban until 1pm. Did a two-hour stoking trial in the morning; pretty hot work. Played golf in the afternoon at Glencruitten. A very nice course. Garside and I beat Blood and Nicholson 3 and 2. Thoroughly enjoyed it. Received invitations for the weekend from Freda Stanhope and from the Elles. Accepted the first.

Friday 5

Had the night watch. Thick fog, extra lookouts. Turned out at 4am to look after lighting up of steamboat furnaces, so got little sleep. Cookson, O'Leary and Tweedy in the soup for being 'scuppered' last night; all our leave restricted in consequence. Stopped on board. Refitted main bearing, and had a scene in the ER office with Jimmy Moss, much to his disgust. Commodore Goodenough of the First Light Cruiser Squadron, who are here, came on board.

Saturday 6

HMS *Cumberland* with Blakes arrived. They get an awful time. We played and beat them 7–1 at golf. We had four men away – self included. Went on weekend leave with Portal after work. Lunched at Oban and then bicycled from there (where we met Mrs Bethell) on past Dunstaffnage, Connel Ferry, Benderloch, to the Stanhopes' place at Invercreran. Seventeen miles. Met Mrs Campbell and the McKay family. Freda Stanhope was very nice and most hospitable. Went fishing with Portal and Mr McKay, who is a Queenslander. Several reminiscences of the Forshalls stay here. Daddy stopped here in 1891 and had an affair with a certain Mrs Clark. Phil and Theo arrive here in July; am so sorry to miss them. Saw round the house and the old lead mines. Gorgeous scenery. Saw photos of Betty Stanhope, whom I met in Edinburgh two years ago.

Sunday 7

Went for a walk in the morning. In the afternoon Freda, Portal and I bicycled over to Ardchattan, where Lieut.-General Campbell-Preston lives, for tea. Very nice wife and children. I got a bad blister. RSP and I went on over to Connel Ferry and back to Oban, where we dined. Back to the ship at 9. Thoroughly enjoyed the weekend. Sorry to leave Scotland.

Monday 8

Chevallier came on board in the morning. Weighed and left Oban at 2pm, and went past the *Cumberland*, across the Firth of Lorne and up through the Sound of Mull. Mr Campbell's unaccountable reluctance in lighting enough boilers to get twelve knots gave us some hard work forcing and faulting ventilation, which in turn took all the paint of the forward funnel. Ran past Eigg, Rum and Muck, and up inside of Skye through the Sound of Sleat and out past the Kyles of Lochalsh and Akin. Grand scenery, and the best in my opinion we have seen this cruise, although very difficult navigation. Reduced to nine knots to economise coal at midnight.

Tuesday 9

At sea all day. Passed Cape Wrath at 6am and left Scotch coast. Sighted Hoy at 10. Saw Old Man and the well-known cliffs, and later on Stromness, Costa Head, Eynhallow, Rousay and Westray. Very nice seeing my old friends the Orkneys. Past Fair Isle about 5pm. Wrote to Phil and Freda Stanhope at Invercreran, and Aunt Do. Lost my engineering sketching book, which is a confounded nuisance as Meggs intends to stop my leave. Sighted Sumburgh Head about 8pm and kept Shetlands in sight about two hours. Sunset 9pm.

Wednesday 10

At sea all day, watch-keeping, etc. Sighted Norwegian coast about 4pm. Routine as usual.

Acting Artificer Engineer E Foster is a very nice little man and very popular with everyone. He wears a mournful look, and is not, I think, over in love with his job and wishes he were a CERA again. He is badly treated in the matter of watches, as he is nearly always on watch in dogs and middle and in harbour.

It is very funny turning in at nights with the sun shining brightly, as the sun sets here now about 10.15 and rises at 1.45. Light enough for golf or tennis all night.

Thursday 11

Arrived at mouth of Trondheim fjord midnight, and after some difficult navigation anchored off Trondheim at 8.30am. Gorgeous weather and pretty scenery; the girls are absolutely it here. I did not go on shore, but stopped on board to work. Half holiday. Cutter practice for X group after lunch. Several visitors to the ship. Trondheim is a most civilised city.

Friday 12

No. 1 up the pole very badly, punishing everybody wholesale. Gorgeous weather. Went on shore at 4 with Armstrong and had a good meal and did some shopping. The Norwegian girls are absolutely A1. Took two Norwegian fellows, who were on board, round the ship when I returned; very good fellows. Forgot to ask them their names. Sunset at 10.35pm. Towards evening, No. 1's temper became worse than ever.

Saturday 13

Usual work in the morning. About twelve people went off salmon and trout fishing. I wish I had a rod, as it is very good here. The consul gave a splendid dance to which nearly all the rest of us went. The best dance we have had this cruise; all the girls are gorgeous and we all fell in love heaps of times. My chief loves were Edel Böckman and Lygne Tharaldsen. Branson very much in love. Mr Colville, Mr Meggs and Mr Moss well to the fore. My opinion of Raynes' misogynist feelings is on the wane.

Sunday 14

A large number of officers went off in PB till tomorrow on a fishing picnic. A thousand visitors to the ship in the afternoon, everywhere there were people. Branson and I had two friends we met at the dance yesterday to tea. Edel Böckman and Agnes. They were both very pretty and most charming, and we were both rather mashed. Thoroughly enjoyed my day. Had tea in the small room.

Monday 15

Boat sailing all the morning. In the afternoon, Branson and I took Edel Böckman and Agnes out; they are both very sweet, and I am awfully in love with Edel – she is topping, and plays the piano divinely. We called on Dr Böckman, before we four motored up to the falls on the river. They are exceptionally fine. Then we had tea and several photos taken. Got late leave. An affectionate and touching farewell at quayside rather ruined by the appearance of Reidurn Möller, whom I had a flirtation with yesterday before the arrival of Edel. Reidurn very jealous, as I had promised to call today. Several other parties with girlfriends ashore, and some very successful fishing parties.

Tuesday 16

Weighed and left Trondheim at 6am. Saw the last of the town half an hour earlier, and thought of dear little Edel fast asleep. I am afraid I am a very susceptible person. Several other people in the dumps. The seventy-odd intact hearts which came here have been sadly injured. Left the Trondheim fjord about 12 noon, just after passing HMS *Natal* and *Achilles* going up for a week's stop, which made me mad with jealousy. Sorry I was unable to visit Auntie Jessie's friends at Trondheim. Pretty rough in the open sea. Torpedo work all day. The result of the shooting match at Trondheim: ship did very well but just lost. Mr Hall gained diploma.

Wednesday 17

Entered the fjord of Bergen at 9am, and after forty miles of steaming up the fjord we arrived at Bergen at noon. Found HMS *Shannon*, flagship of Rear-Admiral CE Madden, and HMS *Cochrane*, and also a small Norwegian gunboat in the harbour. I was midshipman of the watch and day. Glorious weather, although Bergen is not going to be nearly as popular as Trondheim. Water polo match v *Shannon*. By the way, Sub-Lieut. Blunt, whom I met last leave, is in the *Shannon*. Consul came aboard.

Eng.-Commander Maconnachie, who succeeded EC Leslie, is a rather gruff, grumpy sort of man, whom I do not like as much as his predecessor. I don't think he is a bad fellow really, but he looks an awful tick.

Thursday 18

Fine weather continued. The mail service from here is bad, and altogether this is a rather 'dead-alive' sort of place. It is funny that it should be so different from Trondheim. Torpedo work all afternoon, boat sailing all morning. 'Z' group visited the *Cochrane* to study her control system. 'X' group cutter practice. Had a chat with Mr Millar; he is an awful good sort. Cookson had a row with the gunroom. WSH brought some curaçao on board, and we had a jovial evening.

Friday 19

I was midshipman of the pinnace. Usual cutter practice. Bergen as dull as death, the only redeeming feature being the scenery. Ship beat Bergen at soccer 7–1. Skiff race v *Cochrane*, and a water polo match v *Shannon* again. Several fishing parties went away. Had a row with Bumaly. Mr Millar very keen on 'X' group winning this cutter match.

Saturday 20

Sailing all the morning. Went away with WSH after work at noon by train to Nesttun and on to Kalandseid fjord, a big piece of water with excellent trout. We did quite well. Three other officers and four cadets also there. We caught some quite nice ones. Mr Rogers did best. I got very wet. Did not get back until midnight. Several other fishing parties in different places. The wardroom officers gave a dinner party to WR officers of the *Shannon* and *Cochrane*.

Sunday 21

A party of seven went to picnic with the consul and his wife to meet seven flappers, but did not enjoy it much. As usual comparing the Bergen flappers unfavourably with Trondheim. Rear-Admiral Madden came on board and inspected us, accompanied by Admiral Fawkes unofficially, as he is on a holiday here. I stopped on board all day. Gorgeous weather still. Several people lunched and dined in *Shannon* gunroom.

Monday 22

Weather changed for the worse. Group cutter practice took place and won by Y, then X and last Z. Eight laps of two cables, making two miles alternate pulling and sailing. X pulled and did most work very well and led easily with Y last, but excellent sailing by Y brought them up and gave them a win. We were very disappointed, chiefly for Mr Millar's sake. Reception and dance on board flagship, to which all the rest went, lucky dogs, and did little dancing, but got tight in the GR. She is the slackest ship for snotties in the fleet. In the forenoon gunnery group visited and examined *Cochrane*'s 7.5 and 9.2 gunfire system.

Tuesday 23

Unmoored and left Bergen at 6am. *Shannon* and *Cochrane* also left for Trondheim, to change over with *Natal* and *Achilles*. We arrived at mouth of southern Bergen at 11am and went right out to sea on account of the weather, as a nasty gale got up and it rained very hard. X group extra gun drill. The first rough weather we have had for some time.

Wednesday 24

On the bridge in the morning. Entered Bohus Gulf about midday and the Kristiania fjord at about 2, and after six hours' steam through very pretty scenery up the fjord anchored at Kristiania at 8pm.* The commander lowered boats and got everything ready for harbour at once. I did pilotage notes all afternoon and got well up to date.

Had a sweet letter from Edel; Branson didn't and was very sick. She had a good time in the *Natal* and *Achilles*. Heard of the robbery at Peggy's school.

Thursday 25

Rifle drill in the morning. Weather not so nice. Went to a dance at the British Consulate; we all looked forward to it very much, but it was rather a frost, and not nearly so nice as Trondheim. Mr Grey, the consul, his wife and two little daughters were very nice, but there was little else exciting. Met an old school friend of Auntie Bella's, a Mrs Dick, née Naylor, who asked me to go yachting tomorrow. Had three letters from Mother telling me about Jimmy's sports wins.

Friday 26

Study all the morning. Blood and Trollope went yachting with the Dicks instead of me. Mr Chambers, the commander's brother-in-law, whom we met at Oban, took ten people to an oyster tea. I went on shore with Pearson; we went to the Norwegian jubilee exhibition, which was nothing wonderful, but we had an excellent meal, and going on into the town we ate two very good lobsters at Österskjaelderen and drank a lot of beer and vermouth.

---

* Kristiania is now Oslo.

Saturday 27

Norwegian flotilla of destroyers arrived in the morning. We gave a
big ball to all the youth and beauty of Kristiania on board, and it was
an enormous success. Ninety girls came and there was a huge crowd.
I danced every dance; liked Thordis Lülken and Kathleen Falsen. Some
of the girls were awfully sweet, but I was quite heart-whole at the end,
although I loved every minute of it. Received the photo of our group at
Trondheim from Edel; she looked very sweet, but Agnes did not come
out well. Navigation test paper all the morning.

Sunday 28

The ship crowded with officers. Worked instead of going to church.
1st lieut. gave two hours' extra general leave. I went onshore with
NBB and DKT; we went and had an oyster feast at Österskjaelderen.
The man tried to swindle us and we had a fearful row. Ship inundated
with visitors.

Monday 29

Very hot day. Russian yacht *Iolande* came in. Mrs Findlay invited us all
to a huge ball at the Legation. At the last minute it had to be cancelled
due to the news of the assassination of Grand Duke Francis, heir to the
Empire of Austria.* We were terribly disappointed. We went to a quiet
reception there instead, but it only enhanced our sorrow for there was
a gorgeous ballroom and the most exquisite garden for sitting out. We
were given a splendid tea, but the loss of the dance was very sad. Said
goodbye to all our friends, including the Greigs, Findlays, Dicks and all
the girls. Heard from Edel.

Tuesday 30

Unmoored and left Kristiania at 9am. Left with the band playing and
leaving many hearts behind. Passed Horten and left the Kristiania fjord

---

* Assassination of Archduke Franz Ferdinand of Austria.

at 2.30 and lost sight of Norway for good in the Gulf of Bohus at 4. Well out into the North Sea by night time. A terrible heart-rending leaving the country, where we have spent such a good time. Edel seems to be having a terrific time with the other ships at Trondheim. Had a dog watch in the engine room.

Result of shooting match v Kristiania: won easily, and result of soccer match – lost 2–4. Both matches v Bergen: won 7–1 and 9–1.

JULY

Wednesday 1

At sea all day. P Buchanan and Faulkner gave two excellent lectures; the first on the history of the development of the torpedo, the second on the organisation and importance of the practical gunnery drill and instinct in HM Navy. Both were very well prepared and delivered. They inaugurate the new scheme of periodical lectures by cadets on diverse subjects, and were a decided success. Messrs Meggs and Edwards in great form in the ER. Mr Whitehead got a faulty noon DRG to the great annoyance of the captain.

We had a great night last night. The wardroom dined the lodger, Mr Chambers, and afterwards we had a mob on the GD and continued rag, dancing until midnight.

Thursday 2

At sea all day. Usual studies. Thick, murky weather around the mouth of the Thames. Exercised towing stations forward after quarters. Thick fog in the straits made us go slow and unfortunately shut out the sight of land from us. Passed the Goodwin lights between 7 and 8.30pm. To think that I am only about fifteen miles from home, after having been thousands for so long. Passed close to the Dover lights. Passed Dungeness and Beachy Head during the night.

Friday 3

Passed Selsey Bill at 6am and anchored at Cowes at 8.15am. Had my shipbuilding and practical engineering exams. Landed in England for the first time for six months, and went up to the college* with Bench. Thoroughly enjoyed myself. Saw all my old friends again, and spent about 10/- treating Drakes at canteen. Thousands of happy meetings. Heard of poor Joseph Chamberlain's decease in London; the finest statesman since Dizzie's death,† and a great Imperialist.

Saturday 4

Cadets match v college scratched; a great disappointment. Officers beat Osborne A 238 to 207 for 3 dec. 'Z' beat 'Y' in a group match by 76 to 60. A lovely afternoon, so like the old times. All our old friends among the masters were about. Mr Broadbent was playing, but I had no opportunity of a chat with him. I had a long talk with Eng.-Commander Maconnachie. Eng.-Captain Williams thoroughly enjoyed ourselves. Mr Bates is away in Germany. Several of our officers dined at the college.

Sunday 5

Bumaly, Tottenham and I lunched with PMB, and afterwards Tottenham and I beat Bumaly and PMB 2 and 1 in 18 holes at Osborne House course. Very good game; thoroughly enjoyed day.

Monday 6

Seamanship and torpedo instruction all morning. HMS *Maidstone* passed towing a D class submarine at 4am, and later HMS *Dreadnought*. We sent the picket boat to Southsea for beef. I stopped on board in the afternoon to work. Most people went up to the Assault at Arms at Osborne, which was quite a success. Franklin refused Bosun's challenge to the GR at

---

* Osborne Naval College at Osborne House, East Cowes, Isle of Wight.
† Benjamin Disraeli (1804–81).

cricket tomorrow, on account of a group match, amidst great indignation. Gieve's representative came on board and I ordered all my uniform.

Tuesday 7

Half holiday. Group match X v Z won by Z, 98 to 87, and gave them the cup. Very little keenness shown and poor cricket; I made 4 not out, and went in at 30–1 and poked about for an hour. Wardroom v college boardroom won 240 to 75; No. 1, Franklin and Andrew made a lot of runs and Sinclair bowled in deadly form. Had a short chat with Beans and said goodbye to everyone. I have thoroughly enjoyed our visit to Osborne again, but am sorry that Bates was away in Germany.

Wednesday 8

Unmoored 6am, weighed and left Cowes at 8am and proceeded down the Solent (without the lodger, who left us two days ago). Dropped anchor off Swanage at midday. Several people went on shore and Branson went on night leave to Bournemouth. Two minesweepers came in at 7pm. I did not go on shore, but worked hard at torpedo all day in preparation for the exam. Very windy and threatening weather.

Thursday 9

I had the early morning watch; all hands to paint ship. Lovely weather. I am afraid I am too busy to land here at all, as I am in the thick of a terrific sweat for the exams. I think from what I hear Swanage is quite a good place, although most people who land go over to Bournemouth for the day. I gave a lecture in the morning on 'Engines suitable for propulsion of HM ships in future'. I was terribly nervous in front of all the officers, but it was quite a success, I think I may say, and was heavily applauded, especially the political allusions.

Friday 10

Weighed and left Swanage at 9am, the captain coming on board from two days' leave at 8.30. Z group twelve par firing, the result not as satisfactory as X and Y, but poor conditions as they had strong sun in their eyes. Arrived at Weymouth, and anchored in the harbour at midday. X group seamanship, practical torpedo, electricity and flashing exams. I did well in the first but poorly in the second. Fourteen battleships, several light cruisers and two flotillas of destroyers, all of the First Fleet are here.

Saturday 11

Several officers went on weekend leave. We are lying between *Bellerophon* and *King George V*, in which are VA Lavender, Capt. Baird, Mr Dalglish, and old C Browne. I was midshipman of the day; Mr Millar OOD. Hands to bathe at 4pm. Very hot. In the evening we gave a sing-song, which was a tremendous success and easily the best we have had. Several officers from the fleet came, including ERSD and the old 'Bugger'. No. 1 did not approve of our shady songs. I got in a row with Millar for shirking rounds. Moss and the commander in great form.

Sunday 12

No. 1 stopped our leave and no friends allowed on board for four days on account of the vulgar songs last night. Most inconvenient to everyone, especially to me and WSH as we had arranged to meet old 'Cubhorse' Browne and spend the evening with him. Fearfully boring on board.

Monday 13

Coaled ship at 7am and took in 300 tons. Cleared up rapidly afterwards and left Weymouth at 1pm, arrived Dartmouth at 6.30pm, and anchored outside the harbour. The officer of the guard came out to see us from the *Britannia*. We all had a jaw from the captain about the concert. I and four others got off (personally I was on watch), the rest all got dog watch extra drill in addition to leave stopped by No. 1 yesterday.

Tuesday 14

Found they had developed scarlet fever at the college, so we could not go up there. I got 9.30 leave and went to Torquay for the afternoon;

visited all my old friends and saw Amy again. She was looking very well.
Called on Mr Lavers on my return and had a long chat with him. Saw
Mr McKean and my old servant Clarke. Found Blagrove, Eng.-Lieut.
Morgan, Mr Brown and Martin on board when I returned. Mr Sinclair
and Mr Whitehead played for the college against Hampstead.

Wednesday 15

Did not land, but worked at pilotage and gunnery. No. 1 and Whitehead
motored up to Two Bridges beyond Widecombe to fish. Goddard went
up to play tennis with the Stanleys, and came back full of contemporary
college gossip. I hear Hussey is the latest rage and Johnstone and
Tottenham green with jealousy of RVG's opportunities. Eng.-Comm.
Leslie came on board. Powell dined with Mr Bairstow.

Thursday 16

Weighed and left Dartmouth and 7.30am XI rifle drill exam. I did poorly
in giving detail, but did not drill badly. Joined the flag of VA commanding
the Fifth Cruiser Squadron, of which we are a unit, with the *Carnarvon*,
and in company with the battleships *London* and *Exmouth* proceeded
to a rendezvous fifteen miles SW of the Needles, where most of the
Second Fleet were assembled, consisting of thirteen pre-Dreadnought
battleships, three cruisers and one light cruiser. Proceeded up the Solent
and anchored in our station at Spithead for the review.* All the latest
Dreadnoughts already there. We were just astern of the *Cumberland*.

Friday 17

Moved today to astern of the *Good Hope*. The Third Fleet came in about
4pm. The destroyer flotillas and minelayers and auxiliaries also came

---

* With war looking increasingly likely by July 1914, First Lord of the Admiralty
Winston Churchill ordered the gathering of the entire Royal Navy, under the auspices
of a test mobilisation. Subsequently, a Royal Fleet Review was held at Spithead where
the entire strength of the Royal Navy, featuring more than one hundred assorted
vessels including fifty-six battleships, was inspected by King George V.

in and the fleet should be at absolutely full strength, viz. every ship in the Home Fleet that can move, by 8am tomorrow. It is most imposing. Seaplanes and naval airships circled over the fleet all day. Several people went ashore and found naval officers swarming everywhere! They also saw 'The Man'. The WR officers dined the WO officers.

Saturday 18

X group gun drill exam. Winston Churchill, with the Sea Lords and Col. Seely,* came on board 10am. The Osborne and Dartmouth cadets joined the fleet. Aeroplanes and airships circling round the fleet all day. Several people went on shore. Fired twenty-one guns at 5pm to salute the King's arrival. We gave a small dance in the afternoon. Capt. Cantrell to dinner.

Sunday 19

Last night's theatre party, who missed the last boat, arrived on board at 6am, and got nothing worse than a good wigging from No. 1, as they were extremely contrite. Second Sea Lord and Fourth came on board. Royal yacht, with the King and the Prince of Wales, came round the fleet at noon. In the afternoon Donald Portway passed in a service cutter with AS Russell and a crowd of Dartmouth and Osborne cadets.

Monday 20

The fleet unmoored, weighted and left Spithead between 8am and 10am. We steamed out in two lines: First Fleet, Second Fleet and Third Fleet, past the Royal yacht, with seaplanes circling all round above. Gave three cheers and manned ship as we passed the King. It was a most imposing sight. Carried out P2 exercise: sort of sham manoeuvres, blue fleet against red fleet. They were extremely interesting and exciting and quite like the real thing, as we cleared for action and fired guns. Finished up at 6pm, 20 miles SE of the Isle of Wight, and steamed with the rest of the

---

* JEB Seely, 1st Baron Mottistone, was a British soldier and politician. He was a great friend of Winston Churchill's, and the only former cabinet minister to go to the Front in 1914 who remained there until the end of the war.

Second Fleet down to Torquay, anchoring with three ships of the Third Fleet at 1am, much to the disgust of No. 1.

Tuesday 21

The Third Fleet weighed and proceeded west for firing practice with the rest of their ships off Cornwall at 6am. We weighed with the rest of Second Fleet at 9am and proceeded to a rendezvous about sixty miles east where we met the First Fleet. P2 exercise again, very complicated manoeuvres, which very few people understood and can have been of little use. We did our 'day's work' and navigation exams, pretty good sweat. After P2s, we proceeded to Weymouth and anchored there at 7pm.

Wednesday 22

Weighed and left Weymouth at 4am. Tactical exercises with First and Second Fleets all day. Thick fog about midday seriously impaired the operations. Nothing very interesting. We did our pilotage and heat & steam exams, and an extra Morse flashing test in the evening. Anchored with the rest of the First and Second Fleet about five miles from Lyme Regis. Prepared for night attack by destroyers. Pretty strenuous work all this.

Thursday 23

Seamanship, signals and gunnery exams. Left Lyme Regis with the rest of the fleet at 6am. Final P2s all the morning. Owing to the blundering mistakes of a certain flag officer, we were two hours late. The fleets dispersed at midday, and we proceeded to Devonport at sixteen knots. The admiral sent us outside the breakwater for coming in without permission, and we had to anchor in Cawsand Bay for two hours. Went inside at 5.30 and steamed alongside dockyard at 6.15. Came up harbour with the band playing, and feeling much happier than when we left six months ago. Still, I shall be sorry to pay off in some ways. Torpedo and shipbuilding exams finished our course of instruction with HMS *Cornwall*.

Friday 24

I have done fairly well; am top in engineering. Pandemonium reigned supreme on the chest flat. Everyone packing. It took me all the afternoon and through the first dog watch as well. Terrible mess everywhere preparatory to paying off tomorrow. Thankful when it is over. Last sing-song given. Some good turns, but nothing startling. Mrs Wollaston and Mrs Ellerton present. Colville, Stumpy and Moss in great form after. Turned in about 1. No. 1 up the pole.

Saturday 25

Prize giving and term photo. Took affectionate farewells of all the staff. They are most of them jolly good sorts. Left the ship at midday, shifted into plain clothes at the station and caught the 12.30 Cornish Riviera express up to Paddington with Hutchinson, Cobb and Cookson. The famous Drake Term 1910–1914 finally dispersed. Reached Canterbury at 8 and motored home; found everyone flourishing. Distributed all my things, which I have bought during the cruise. Everyone very pleased with them, also by the photographs.

Sunday 26

Daddy in great form. Went round to the Rectory and Westenhanger. It is sickening that all the Kelseys are away from home. Daddy and I had four sets of tennis with Bob and George.

Monday 27

Daddy went to the city. Mother motored into Canterbury to shop and to have tea with Bernie and Mary Collard. I played golf with George against Col. Wemyss; we beat them 3 and 2. I played pretty well. Col. Wemyss came to tea. In the evening Dr Morris and I took on George and the colonel, and they beat us on the last green after a terrific struggle. All the Westenhanger crowd, Byron, and the Escombes went to Margate. Bob, George and I had a carousal, they quarrelled.

Above: Alexander's parents, Alexander Caron Scrimgeour and Helen Scrimgeour.

Left: The typical Edwardian boy: Alexander dressed in a sailor suit.

Above: The Scrimgeour family outside their home at Quaives Farm, Wickhambreaux.

Top: The Drawing Room.
Bottom: The family also had a London residence at Cumberland Terrace.

ALDRO SCHOOL, EASTBOURNE.
FIRST ELEVEN, 1909.

F. D. MOUL.   W. R. C. PRATT.   R. W. O. THURBURN.   A. J. BURGE.
E. W. CASLON.   G. F. R. HIRST.   N. GOODWIN (Capt.)   B. L. HOBROW.   F. E. HILL.
E. J. P. THURBURN.   "JOCK."   A. SCRIMGEOUR.

Aldro School, Eastbourne.
FIRST ELEVEN, 1909.

J. F. NORRIS.   R. G. PERCIVAL.   F. C. PILLEY.   E. W. CASLON.
C. H. D. ELLIOT.   A. E. WYNN.   A. SCRIMGEOUR (Capt.)   A. D. CUMMING.   W. A. FROY.
C. V. M. SMART.   E. J. P. THURBURN.

At Aldro School Alexander showed an enthusiasm and flair for team sports which continued into adulthood. Top: The Cricket Team First Eleven, 1909. Bottom: The Football Team First Eleven, also 1909 with Alexander in the centre as captain (Aldro School).

Naval cadet Alexander Scrimgeour.

Much of Alexander's social life revolved around the theatre. Top left: The Tivoli Theatre on The Strand, London, photographed in 1910 (Getty Images). Top right: The Savoy Theatre, photographed in 1906, with taxi cabs waiting outside (Getty Images).

Above: View down Princes Street in Edinburgh past the Waverley Hotel, 1903
(Getty Images).

Top: One of the most popular actresses of the age was Gertie Millar, photographed here in 1910 for her performance as Prudence in the musical play *The Quaker Girl* at the Adelphi, London. Alexander saw her in *The Country Girl* at Daly's Theatre in Leicester Square (Getty Images).

Bottom: Alex was a regular visitor to Joko's house at Westenhanger in Kent (James and Lindsay Dixey).

Tuesday 28

The Dr and I played four strenuous sets of tennis with Bob and George, which I thoroughly enjoyed. Ethel Escombe came round to call on Mother, and later Jeram Escombe and John Parish came in, after golf, for a drink. John seems awfully well, and is full of contemporary scandal, especially with regard to Dolly Kelsey and Harold Wacher. Byron motored over to Barton. I went round to Westenhanger to supper; they have a bevy of pretty girls stopping there.

Wednesday 29

The continual diplomatic situation is very bad. Austria is bullying Serbia, and Russia protests. I think it is all a German plot to test the Triple Entente. Jimmy and I lunched with the Morrises at Littlebourne, and then we went on to Lee Priory. I played cricket for Littlebourne against Wingham (young Petley is their captain), and we were beaten by seven runs after a very exciting match. I made some runs, but was badly out of practice. The Dr did well all round. In the evening we discussed traps to catch the poachers, who have been troubling George Goodson so much lately.

Thursday 30

Went up by the boat-train from Canterbury and down to the Surrey-Kent match at Blackheath. Surrey had bad luck in losing the toss, and did well to get Kent out for 349. I travelled up with Mr Furley, the hon. treasurer of the Kent County C.C. We ran over a soldier at Rochester Bridge. All the Reserves are mobilised. I intended to spend the night at Arthur Russell's flat, but Daddy rang me up on the telephone to say the Admiralty had wired for me to join RN Barracks, Portsmouth. So I met Daddy at the Automobile Club and said goodbye, and then left Waterloo for Portsmouth. Met WSH and O'Leary at the station by chance. After a visit to Gieve's, we joined the RN Barracks at 10pm. Everybody in a state of suppressed excitement.

The mobilisation of the Naval Reserve, Fleet Reserve and Naval Volunteer Reserve has already commenced. Found lots of other officers, summoned to the barracks. I am very annoyed at having my leave stopped, but pleased at the thought of the excitement of war.

Friday 31

Hard work drilling with the Reserves, etc., all day at the barracks; but they do us very well at the mess, which is a boon. My uniform arrived by train.

Several of the Osborne officers arrived for the mobilisation today. I am afraid we shall have damned little leave, and I shall miss Canterbury, Dover, and Orkney, which I have been looking forward to for months. Still, it is all for the sake of the country. International situation worse in France, Germany, and Russia, but the peace party in England seems extremely strong at present.

JULY 1914 NAVAL BARRACKS, PORTSMOUTH

Friday (morning),

Dear Daddy,

Please thank Mother for her letter. My clothes have not arrived yet (10am), but suppose they will get here some time today. Gieve's may be able to fit me out by midday. At present the lack of uniform is a boon, as all the others are with the Reservists at gun and signal drill, while I am doing nothing. I am afraid I can give you no information, and even if I could I should not, as all movements of ships and men, known to officers or men, are to be considered as strictly confidential.

We are all quartered at the barracks until further orders, and are doing duty in lieu of midshipmen with the Reservists. We are frightfully cramped for sleeping room, but they do us very well at the officers' mess, which is something. The whole town is in a hubbub of excitement, as the 'terriers' are out, and everything seems alive.

We travelled down last night with a Stock Exchange man named Thurston; he seemed quite a good sort, and consumed large quantities of W and S.

Give my best love to all at Wickhambreaux.

Hope to be home again before the end of August; damned nuisance missing cricket week!

Yours,

Toby

PS I will let you know what ship I go to as soon as I know, but we shan't go for two or three days. Please send my diary by post.

AUGUST

Saturday 1

Usual dull barrack drill all the morning, with Lieut.-Commanders Fenn, Robinson and Leach. Saw Sergeant O'Dwyer and CPO Woodcock.
A party of us got a box in the theatre in the afternoon to see the 'Clever Ones.' In the middle there was a general recall to all naval and military officers and men in Portsmouth, and we had to leave (amidst the cheers of the crowd), which was a damned nuisance. Made the acquaintance of several nice girls in Portsmouth.

War rumours rife all day, some true, some untrue. I had a very wet evening. Learnt we are to leave the barracks and join a ship tomorrow.

Sunday 2

Germany has attacked France, and even our peace party cannot prevent war without dishonour. Left the RN Barracks at 8am and bade farewell to the mate, Mr Macdonald, and other friends. Joined HMS *Crescent*, a fairly old cruiser, flagship of the Tenth Cruiser Squadron, under command of Rear-Admiral de Chair. I found myself senior acting midshipman, and consequently president of the gunroom mess. Found our old friend PO Croxford was chief gunner's mate. I was put in charge of picket boat. We shall have lots of hard work, but it will be very interesting. Hope war will be declared soon.

Monday 3

Assistant-Clerk Glanville joined the gunroom from HMS *Lion*. The other acting 'snotties' are Johnstone, Cobb, Robinson, Richardson, Henderson, Hutchinson and Tottenham. It is the irony of fate that I should be senior to them all. Weighed and left Portsmouth Harbour at 11am, proceeded down the Solent, and made for the Lizard under sealed orders. GQs fire stations and collision stations in the evening. The Captain gave us a harangue on the war. We have an extraordinary mixed assortment of men – CGs, RNR, RNVR, RFR men and boys under training, with a smattering of active service ratings. Not much of a crew, I am afraid, but we will get them into shape. The guns are inclined to be obsolete, and the control and ammunition supply systems hopelessly crude. Oh, to be in a First Fleet battleship! I attempted to repair the rate clock with the aid of the gunner, Mr Croughan. I had the early morning watch and the first night watch, and turned in at 12.15, absolutely dead with fatigue. The Captain's name is Trewby, and he is an excellent officer, but the RA is a bit of an old woman.

Tuesday 4

Passed Land's End and steered north at 6am. *Edgar* joined Flag at 8am; GQs after divisions. Lieutenant GA Wilson, Johnstone and I tried to arrange an efficient fire control system. *Grafton* joined Flag at 11am. Working control all the afternoon. I had the middle, and I am afraid the constant racket will begin to tell soon. Great Britain declared war on Germany at midnight. We are without any news except wireless. Sir John Jellicoe appointed Commander-in-Chief of Home Fleets in succession to Admiral Sir G Callaghan, and Earl Kitchener made

Secretary of State for War. Our course is due north, up the Irish Sea; we passed Isle of Man during the night. Some of our Service officers are Commander Wardle, Fleet Paymaster Lawford, Staff Paymaster Weston, Lieut.-Commanders Popham and Beasley, and Lieut.-Commander (Ret.) Kiddle.

Wednesday 5

Passed out of the Irish Sea; off Kintyre and Islay. War began in earnest; sighted a German steamer off Jura, and the RA sent the *Grafton* to capture her and take her into Belfast. Our small squadron is thus reduced to two ships, although at full strength it should consist of eight. Shaped a course up the west coast of Scotland, to make the Orkneys eventually, as for the present they are to be our base. We had GQs all the morning and got the fire control system as perfect as possible. Rough weather all day. The gunroom atmosphere is very bad, due to poor ventilation. There are rumours of a great battle in the North Sea, but do not believe them. Wrote a line home in the 'dogs'. The other executive officers are Lieutenant (G) Kenyon, Lieutenant (N) Clark, Lieutenant (T) Attwood, and Lieutenant Wilson. Do not know them yet.

5 AUGUST HMS *CRESCENT*, AT SEA

    Dear Daddy,

    We joined this ship on Sunday and left a few hours later. It is flagship of the Tenth Cruiser Squadron, which is supposed to consist of eight ships, but at present only three are with the Flag. Being a nucleus crew ship, we have completed our complement with reservists, coastguards, volunteers, and untrained boys; a pretty motley collection, I can tell you. But they are gradually shaking down, and I dare say we shall be able to make something of them. There are eight acting midshipmen in the ship and a few other clerks and people in the gunroom. I am senior gunroom officer. Things are none too comfortable, but no one minds that. It is a great strain, as we have a watch on the bridge (four hours) once every twenty-four hours, and also a gun watch in the battery (four hours), making eight hours' watch-keeping a day; we have general quarters for action about three times in twenty-four hours, each time taking roughly an hour; divisions and quarters take about an hour a day, and the general work of the ship getting everything ready and efficient about four hours a day; so that, allowing two hours for meals – pretty scratch ones at that (as we have run out of bread and all drinks) – we only get about eight hours a day off duty.

I was very sorry to miss the cricket week, as I had been looking forward to it for months, but am perfectly contented, as I have been looking forward to war ever since I was a baby, and considering there has been no naval warfare proper for over one hundred years, we ought to think ourselves very lucky that we have come in for it. We have no news at all, so I hope you will keep all the daily papers, so that I can follow the course of events if I get home soon. I wonder how long the war will last; it was declared at midnight last night, and we did not have to wait long, for we captured a German merchantman early this morning and sent her into a British port with a prize crew. We hear rumours of a big naval engagement in the North Sea, but can obtain no definite details, as all the wireless messages are in different codes. I am not allowed to give any information of our whereabouts, but if you received my last telegram some days ago, just before I left the Portsmouth barracks, you will, I dare say, make

a rough guess of our approximate station, where we are
protecting British vessels and intercepting all foreign
or hostile shipping.

Rear-Admiral de Chair is our flag officer and
Captain Trewby the captain. Many of the officers
are very antiquated specimens, called up after years
of retirement, and consequently a large amount of
responsibility rests with us midshipmen, who are well
up, of course, in all the modern methods of gunfire
control, etc. It is very rough at present and damned
unpleasant into the bargain.

Let's hope that the British Empire will give these
Germans hell.

Good luck to all at Wickhambreaux.

> Best love from
>
> Toby

PS If by any chance we, or I, get 'scuttled,' you may
find my diaries of interest; they are in different
drawers of my writing desk. Please see they are not
interfered with otherwise.

Thursday 6

I had the morning watch. We ran through the Minch and round Cape
Wrath along through the Pentland Firth and into Scapa Flow, passing
the First Battle Cruiser Squadron coming out. We anchored off Scapa
and coaled ship, taking in 350 tons. RNR Lieutenant Oxlade joined
the ship from the *Edgar*. We left most of our boats behind to avoid
splintering in action, and I was in charge of mooring them off the
pier – quite a tricky job. I then went on shore in the picket boat and
just missed Uncle John from Swanbister by five minutes; he had been
seeing somebody off in the *St Ola*. Very sorry to miss him. Sent a note
to Auntie Connie by the harbour master. After coaling we proceeded
with the rest of the squadron (three ships) round west of Orkneys,

intercepting all ships we met. We took in a big supply of stores and ammunition from the Scapa base, which is strongly protected by destroyers; also heard many vague war rumours. The First Fleet are due to arrive at Scapa on the 7th.

Friday 7

Proceeded round to Fair Isle, stopping and examining several ships, all British or neutral, thus gaining little information and no prizes. Exercised control at GQs. A long job getting Dumaresq and rate clock into the top. Cruised about on our patrol to the eastward of the Orkneys and Shetlands. Arrived at a rendezvous 4pm. *Theseus, Endymion, Gibraltar* joined the Flag, bringing strength of squadron up to six ships. *Royal Arthur* and *Hawke* still adrift. There is a rumour of the capture of the German battle cruiser *Goeben* in the Mediterranean. I had the middle gun watch with Mr Oxlade; he is an awful good sort. The engineer officers of the ship are Eng.-Lieut.-Commander Fletcher and Eng.-Lieutenant Sims. Rough night.

Saturday 8

Sighted and captured two German trawlers from Vegesack at 6am. They seemed quite harmless, but had some incriminating papers. I went on board both as interpreter. I began fully to realise the horrors of war when I saw the misery of the crews (whom we took on board) at leaving their ship, their only means of sustenance. It was most touching to all of us. GQs 8am. The squadron exercised battle practice, using the empty trawlers as targets, both being sunk. Firing very satisfactory. My services as German interpreter much in need with regard to the prisoners. I also got something out of sonic Norwegian messages we intercepted by wireless. My opinion of Mr Oxlade is still higher; he is a fine chap, keen on all sports, and has knocked about the world a bit. At 4pm squadron divided, four ships going north-east to patrol the Norwegian coast. Bad news of a submarine attack on Dreadnought *Monarch*. I had first gun watch. A very dirty night.

Sunday 9

No GQs, otherwise usual routine. Captain's rounds. War routine; short service on QD. Stopped and searched several neutral ships. The *Grafton* parted company to the eastward at 3pm, chasing a strange sail. Several Norwegian messages obtained. Bad news of the loss of the *Amphion* off the Thames, but the *Birmingham* destroyed a German submarine off Fair Isle. First Fleet left Scapa after coaling. Our squadron off east of Shetlands all day. We met the *Dryad* at a rendezvous; she gave us some stores, extra ratings and a few mails, and a new RNR, Lieutenant Bacon. She took our mails and the prisoners, to whom I bade farewell, and then proceeded to Scapa, the chief northern base.

Monday 10

We were patrolling to the north-east of the Shetlands all day.

The *Hawke* joined the Flag at 10am. GQs after divisions. News of German aircraft over the Shetlands. Personally I believe they have a secret base in the Danish Faroe Isles to the north-west. The *Royal Arthur* joined Flag at 4pm, bringing the squadron up to full strength, counting the three ships off Norway. At 0.30pm we detached the *Endymion* to Busta Voe, Swarbacks Minn, a deserted, out-of-the-way harbour in the west of the Shetlands, which is to be used as our new base (Tenth Cruiser Squadron only). Gunroom life is getting unbearable owing to bad atmosphere and food. A new cowl slightly improves the former. I wonder whether Lieutenant Tovey, an old Osborne friend,* was saved from the *Amphion*, of which he was first lieutenant.†

---

* Lieutenant John Tovey, later 1st Baron Tovey, would go on to become Admiral of the Fleet in 1943 during the Second World War.

† The HMS *Amphion* was sunk on 6 August 1914 after hitting a mine off the Thames Estuary; 151 lives were lost, plus 19 German sailors who were rescued from the *Königin Luise*, sunk by the *Amphion* a day earlier.

Tuesday 11

Very rough all day, with a high gale. GQs not a success in the morning.
The captain made a great joke at my expense on watch, but the
RA turned it on to the back of Lieut.-Commander Robinson, the
flag-lieutenant. Very little news, except of more German submarines
and aeroplanes. The German battleships proper are all bottled up in
Kiel, and I am afraid the mines will prevent their outward progress, even
if they wanted to come out, so the chances of a big naval battle are small.
This shows the unwillingness of the Germans to challenge our mastery
of the seas. On watch Mr Kiddle was very loquacious on the charms of
gay Paris. Joined the three ships from Norway during the night, but each
division returned to its original station after an exchange of signals.

Wednesday 12

The weather greatly improved. GQs as usual. I was made deputy or
assistant gunnery lieutenant and excused watch-keeping, so I shall never
have a minute to myself now. The stores are giving out, and none of the
luxuries of life are left. We boarded a Norwegian vessel in the afternoon
and obtained some Norwegian newspapers full of war news. I spent
three hours translating twenty-six pages of it, and the RA congratulated
me on my work. WT messages say our submarines have volunteered
to attack the Germans in Kiel, but Admiral Jellicoe will not allow them
to, stating it to be a useless risk to valuable British lives at this early
juncture. The *Drake* has been ordered to the Faroes to investigate them.
The other wardroom officers in the ship are Staff Surgeon WP Walker,
Acting Surgeon Maxwell, AP Cockrem and AP Egleton, RNR; AP
Gallichan, RNR; Chaplain, Rev. Shell.

Thursday 13

Usual war routine all day. Hard at work with gunnery-lieutenant at
our ammunition supply arrangements. Revolver shooting, drill and
practice on the QD for two hours in the morning. I shot very well,
so did Tottenham and Cobb. Rigged the coaling Asiatic stay in the

dog watches. Heavy firing was heard to the south-east at 4pm, and we proceeded on that bearing at full speed, but found it was only the *Theseus* gun firing on a deserted derelict. WT rumours that a secret German air base is in the Shetlands.

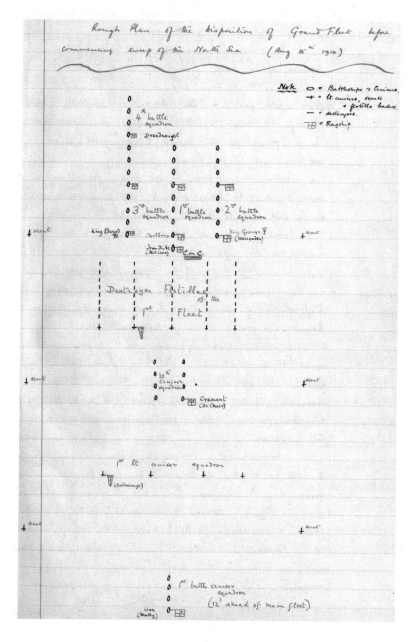

Friday 14

Usual war routine in the forenoon. Made Bussay Isle and anchored off Lerwick at 2pm. Obtained some very welcome newspapers, mails and stores, which cheered us up very much. A friend of old Shearer's at Kirkwall came on board. A collier came alongside at 3pm, and we commenced to coal, intending to take in 400 tons, and looking forward to twenty-four hours in harbour afterwards, but the C-in-C sent us a special WT message, and we had to sweat like niggers till 7.30, when we had 287 tons, then unrig collier and proceed to sea by 9.30 to join C-in-C at a rendezvous with the rest of our squadron. Our hold, the Fx, under the able guidance of Lieutenant Oxlade, Gunner Croughan, Robinson and myself, did exceedingly well, being well ahead in spite of disadvantages. I had second gun watch with Lieutenant Bacon, RNR, a most interesting fellow, who seems to have shot in every part of the world.

Saturday 15

Joined First Fleet at 7am, two hundred miles due north of Wick. I don't quite realise what he intended to use our Tenth Cruiser Squadron for. The First Fleet look a very grim sight, and inspire the utmost confidence. We all proceeded over towards the Norwegian coast, the battle cruisers leading, with the battleships four miles behind in three imposing lines, and light cruisers and destroyer flotillas scouring the seas all round on every quarter. There are no submarines, aircraft, minelayers or sweepers with us, however. WT messages say that aircraft bases have been found at Scapa and Thurso. We intercepted several insolent messages from German stations, obviously trying to induce us to appear off the German coast and probably entice us into a minefield. In spite of their taunts, the Germans remain securely mined in Wilhelmshaven and Kiel, although I believe they have defeated the Russians in the Baltic.

Sunday 16

Swept down off the Norwegian coast past the Skagerrak, down the Danish coast to within forty miles of Heligoland, but could approach no further owing to the German minefields. The Germans refused to come out. Glorious day. We left the First Fleet at 4pm, they steering south-west and we back to the Shetlands.

Monday 17

Joined *Dryad* at noon and obtained and despatched mails. I heard from Auntie Connie, answering by return and cadging for grouse, with which Uncle John seems to be supplying the Fleet. We arrived in Lerwick at 5pm with the remainder of the Tenth Cruiser Squadron, and prepared ship for coaling tomorrow. Harbour mouth patrolled by picket boats to insure against destroyers. I had charge of defence of the southern entrance from midnight till four – a great responsibility – but nothing untoward occurred. We landed several field-guns for harbour defence, and armed our steamboats.

Tuesday 18

Coaled ship in the morning and took in 275 tons; the Fx did not do so well as last time, owing to bad rigging of whip, but did well when once started. We all went on shore, after coaling, for a few hours, and did some shopping and had tea, also examined the local territorial foot. Fleet Paymaster Lawford stood Glanville and myself tea, the Captain also turning up. I like both these officers very much. Weighed and proceeded to sea on our patrol at 7.30pm, joining rest of squadron. Wrote to Auntie Connie.

Wednesday 19

On the usual patrol all day. Very little doing of any interest. But Mr Kenyon, myself and remainder of gunnery department were hard at work nearly all the day. Sighted Norwegian coast at 2pm, and ran up coast for a few hours. The Allan liner *Alsatian,* the first of a batch of four requisitioned for naval purposes in the squadron, joined the Flag at 6pm; her high speed will be of great use to us. A very dirty night, thick weather, Mr Bacon on with me. He was in great form.

Thursday 20

Usual war routine. Gunnery department had a very busy morning. First of all, group control practice for night defence, then loader drill and gun drill. The commander and 'Guns' do not get on well together. The former was a gunnery-lieutenant and thinks he still knows a lot about it, although he doesn't, and this annoys 'Guns' intensely. Received a big mail by the *Dryad,* including thirteen brace of grouse from Swanbister. Boarded SS *Bergensfjord,* Norwegian Amerika Line, and found papers correct, but captured two German reservists; the Norwegians were most hospitable, as they always are.

Friday 21

Boarded another Norwegian ship without result. Independent squadron GQs. Target practice with 1-inch aiming tube and 303. Did seven runs, four starboard side and three port side, most of which were exceedingly successful, and the Captain was quite satisfied. Stopped engines for some time while a chief stoker of the *Gibraltar* was buried, having died of pneumonia. The admiral thanked me for the Swanbister grouse, of which I gave him and the wardroom some.

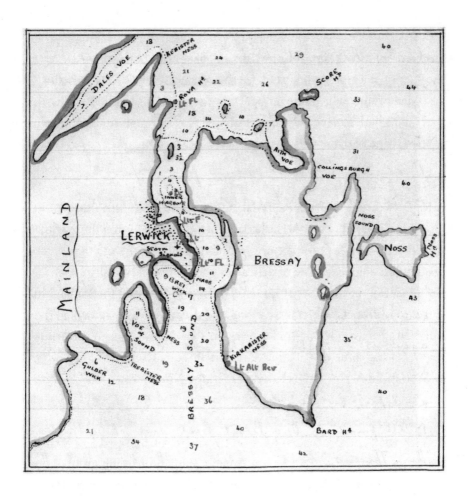

Saturday 22

A partial eclipse of the sun. Independent squadron target practice again
with 1-inch aiming tube and 303. We practised night defence stations
instead of GQs, with very pleasing results. The gunnery-lieutenant had
several small targets made representing TBDs, and we cruised round
about them, exercising first, middle and morning watch night-gun
defence stations. I had another exceedingly busy afternoon with the
gunnery department, making out five arc plans. Received a mail and some
more grouse in the *Dryad* at 7pm. All my cousins seem to be joining the
army and most of my friends as well. Rather bad news from the Front.

Sunday 23

Stopped engines at ten, and the captains of several of the other ships of the squadron came on board to see the admiral. Saw O'Kell, Dickson and Macfarlane, who came on board in their various sea boats. Heard that Japan had declared war on Germany. A very rough night. Rumours of the escape of some German ships.

Monday 24

A foggy morning. German submarines reported from Stromsay, Orkneys. Entered Lerwick Harbour at 11am and anchored there with the *Theseus*. Most people got on shore in the afternoon, and they brought off a goodly store of delicacies and stores. Personally I spent the afternoon in the store ship *Alcinous*, superintending the transfer of stores to our boats, which was a long and dreary job as it rained all the time. The *Forward* left at 2pm for Scapa. Two destroyers and the armed liner *Mantua* came in at 7pm. All our battle squadrons are off the west of Scotland now; only the cruisers are in the North Sea.

Tuesday 25

Left Lerwick and proceeded back on to our patrol. Stopped and boarded two ships during the day, one French and one Swedish, but gleaned but little information. All sorts of rumours of German naval activity, but the fact remains that the bulk of the German Navy remains skulking in harbour, their plan being to destroy our numerical superiority by submarine attacks, several foreign submarines having been seen in the Orkneys and Shetlands, and attempts to destroy them are at present unavailing. I had a hard day's work with the first lieutenant, Mr Popham, taking down and rearranging his 92-inch voice pipe fire control connections.

Wednesday 26

The rear-admiral invited me to breakfast, and I quite enjoyed it. He is an extremely nice, quiet man, a perfect gentleman, but is, in my opinion, rather oppressed and nervy, due to the responsibility of his command, and relies very largely on Captain Trewby for his initiative. The Secretary Fleet Paymaster Lawford is a very good sort and reminds me of Denniston; he has very little to do, as there is a most extensive Paymaster's staff on board. I had another hard day with Mr Popham, and in spite of much ridicule our efforts were crowned with some success. Received a signal from C-in-C to proceed to Scapa at full speed, but fog seriously retarded us. I was in very bad form in the evening. Wireless messages assure us that Namur has fallen. Bad news from the seat of war in Belgium. Heard that the *Highflyer* had sunk the German armed liner *Friedrich der Grosse*.* Rumours of an action off Cape Wrath between two armed liners unsubstantiated, though the *Blonde* left Scapa in that direction with sealed orders. British aeroplanes in evidence all round the Orkneys.

Thursday 27

Entered Scapa Flow at 5am, and at 6am we anchored with remainder of the Tenth Cruiser Squadron off Warkmill Bay. Found the majority of the First Fleet in harbour, with several depot ships, store ships and supply ships, and a whole legion of colliers and oilers. Coaled ship and took in 450 tons, not going nearly so fast as usual. I wanted to get on leave to Swanbister, but in the absence of the rear-admiral on a visit to the C-in-C the captain would not let me go. It was very sickening seeing the house and the tennis court and the pier and yachts, and knowing that although they were only two miles off they might as well have been two hundred. Went to Scapa Pier in charge of the beef party in the duty steamboat of the *Endymion,* as we had not lowered any boats. Made the acquaintance of Captain Hyde-Parker of the *Endymion.* All the captains of our squadron came on board to a conference with the admiral. First Fleet and destroyer flotillas put to sea at 7pm. The *Agincourt* arrived. Saw FF Turner and GAV Harrison during the course of the day.

---

* HMS *Highflyer* sank the SS *Kaiser Wilhelm der Grosse* rather than the armed liner *Friedrich der Grosse.*

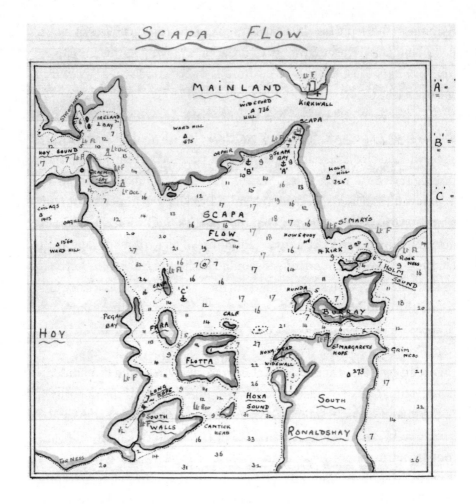

Friday 28

Weighed at 7am after losing our port bower anchor through cathead block carrying away. Five ships of the squadron – *Crescent* (flag), *Grafton*, *Royal Arthur*, *Hawke* and *Theseus* – put to sea and proceeded to our new patrol between Duncansby Head in Caithness to Buchan Ness in Aberdeen, thus protecting the entrance to the Moray Firth and the shores of E Caithness, E Sutherland, E Ross and Cromarty, E Inverness, Elgin, Nairn, Banff and North Aberdeenshire. We are to be based on

Cromarty. We left the *Edgar* and *Endymion* in Scapa and despatched the *Gibraltar* to Rosyth for refit. Our old patrol off the Shetlands across to Norway is to be taken over by the armed merchantmen *Alsatian, Mantua* and *Oceanic*.

Saturday 29

Despatched the *Theseus* to the White Sea to harass German trade there. There are no Russian warships there. Changed our patrol again to the east coast of Aberdeenshire and stretching about one-hundred-and-twenty miles out into the North Sea. Overhauled and examined several tramps during the course of the day. GQs at 10am. The commander sent Henderson during a watch to the masthead as a punishment. The yeoman of signals, PO Todhunter, also in the soup. Sighted the *Achilles* and the remainder of Second Cruiser Squadron in the afternoon proceeding from Cromarty to a patrol off Heligoland. Good news of a successful British naval action between two of our cruiser squadrons and some German cruisers attempting to leave the Ems River. Two German cruisers sunk by gunfire and one torpedoed. The *Arethusa* and *Laertes* received injuries on our side.* A large number of prisoners sent into Rosyth in the *Gloucester*.

Sunday 30

On our beat all day. Intercepted and searched several ships without result. Met the *Drake* at 6pm. She is now flagship of Sixth Cruiser Squadron. The *Latona* sighted two German destroyers off Kinnaird Head, and we went full speed to intercept them, but they were too fast for us. I hope the *Hawke* will intercept them. Two of our submarines which have entered Wilhelmshaven report that the harbour is devoid of German warships.

---

* The Battle of Heligoland Bight, a welcome victory for the Royal Navy against Germany.

Monday 31

On our patrol all day. Another German submarine reported from Linga Sound between Stromsay and Sanday in the Orkneys. Three-pounder shell firing practice in the morning; the first run a dismal failure, but things improved considerably later on; the captain rather cantankerous, and I got in a furious temper with Mr Coughlan, who was in charge of the cable deck guns, and he effectually smothered any spark of intelligence he ever possessed by stolidly refusing to open fire, and consequently I had to take the blame of his shortcomings. Boarded several Norwegian ships; the amount of Norwegian shipping in these seas is phenomenal. An urgent wireless message from C-in-C saying an attempt will be made tonight to lay mines between Pentland Firth and Rattray Head by a German minelaying squadron supported by cruisers; consequently we are to co-operate with the First Battle Cruiser Squadron and Second and Third Cruiser Squadrons to sweep the threatened area and destroy the Germans. Midshipman Cobb went sick with tonsillitis.

SEPTEMBER

Tuesday 1

After an exciting night's watching, at about 4am we sighted three strange vessels showing dimly in a cloud bank; we suspected them to be the enemy in question, and everything was prepared for action, but at the last moment they answered our challenge and eventually proved to be three pre-Dreadnought battleships of the Second Fleet belonging to the Fifth Battle Squadron, and were supported in a reconnaissance to be conducted along the Dutch coast by the eight First Fleet pre-Dreadnought battleships of the Third Battle Squadron and also a light cruiser squadron. Nevertheless, two hours later we sighted two German destroyers steering east-south-east at full speed in the horizon. They had eluded our blockade in the night and were being chased back to Cuxhaven or Emden by the *Boadicea*; we joined in the chase for one-and-a-half hours, but they were too fast for us, so we left them to the *Boadicea*, who, however, so we heard later, was unable to catch them. We had GQs at 10.30am, a very busy and productive morning for the gunnery department; loader drill, mantles put up, hand clock constructed, arcs painted, and shell-bag reversed system trials. Thick fog prevented us from meeting *Dryad* and so exchanging mails, which was rather disappointing.

1 September 1914   HMS *CRESCENT*, AT SEA

Dear Mother,

Many thanks for your letters, and please thank Peggy very much indeed for hers. Still all alive and kicking, but we are having a very trying time, as I have only been on shore for two hours since we left Portsmouth over a month ago, and we only get about five or six hours' rest in twenty-four hours. Also all the luxuries of life such as sugar and butter and bread are things of the past, except sometimes when we manage to obtain stores during coaling. The Swanbister grouse were a great boon after days of canned beef and salt fish; I divided them between the admiral, the wardroom, and the gunroom, and they were very much appreciated. I had breakfast with the admiral a few days ago; he is quite a nice old chap, and very like Norman Forbes-Robertson to look at.

We are having a certain amount of excitement, but all wish that the 'Grosse Deutsche Hochseeflotte' could be induced to come out and fight, instead of indulging in the glorious pursuit of sinking harmless neutral merchant and fishing vessels by mines.

I should be very pleased if you would start sending
some weekly papers again. The *Referee*, the *People*, and
every Monday's *Sportsman* would be very welcome; and,
by the way, a pair or two of these socks you are all
knitting would also be very welcome. Much as I enjoy
getting news from home, stupid sentimental twaddle from
Mrs Handfield Jones is not in great demand.

Has that renegade Canadian relative of yours decided
to do anything? His Christian name savours of a
better man.

If you do not burn this letter, see that it does
not leave your possession and is kept absolutely
confidential. Please give my love to Aunties Ethel, Ruth
and Maud, when you write.

Best love to all at home from

Toby

Wednesday 2

Met the *Dryad* and exchanged mails at 8am. Very foggy all day
again. Reports of a submarine attack on Scapa, but no details.
Received some grouse again from Swanbister. Met the Second and
Third Cruiser Squadrons with two destroyer flotillas at 4pm, and we
swept with them across to the Norwegian coast, and, although we
overhauled several neutrals, picked up no news. Chased and sank a
small German armed tramp just before midnight, all the crew lost.
Disquieting news from the French frontier, and also the Russians
have received a check in Eastern Prussia. Wireless messages tell us
that Kitchener is bringing home Gurkhas and Sikhs to fight, and
also forty thousand Russians have been taken round Norway and
landed in France. The Germans are trying to turn our flank and
are threatening Calais and Boulogne. No further Russian advance
in Prussia, but they have defeated the Austrians in Galicia, and the
Serbians have thrown back the Austrians in Bosnia.

Thursday 3

Thick fog all day necessitates extra gun watches. I had a very hard day's work, moving the loader, directing the construction of control instruments, examining night-sight switches, and was tired out. Had a long yarn with Lieutenant Bacon, Gunner Croughan, and PO Short. It is reported that four German cruisers and a bevy of submarines have eluded our blockade and are at large in the North Sea. Consequently we are making a big combined sweep to try and find them. I wish we could make more use of our sea-planes, as they would be very useful indeed as scouts. Deputy-Surgeon Buddle joined the ship temporary from an HMTB.

Friday 4

On our patrol and in the North Sea all day. GQs in the morning again a dismal failure. Mr Beasley and Mr Kiddle suggested sweeping changes in the control system, and after the usual wordy combat between the commander and 'Guns' it was decided to refer the matter to the captain. Heavy firing heard during the forenoon caused a sensation, but proved eventually to be the *Drake* and *Leviathan* of the Sixth Cruiser Squadron doing battle practice. The four German cruisers, reported to be in the North Sea, seem to have made themselves very scarce, as, in spite of extensive searching sweeps, nobody has seen anything of them. The first lieutenant has proposed that a mess committee should supersede the mess caterer, as the state of our messing is very poor under the present regime. Wireless messages report that the Germans are within forty miles of Paris, which is bad news. The French capital has been removed to Bordeaux for safety. Pray God the Allies may have the courage to continue this struggle to the bitter end.

Saturday 5

A German cruiser reported two hundred miles due east of the Pentland Firth by the *Thetis*. Four hours' chase at full speed proved her to be HM destroyer *Swift,* much to our chagrin, as we are all spoiling for a scrap. I hope we are not going to get nervy with this constant waiting, as German ships of mythical origin are continually being chased. Those lucky devils in the army are having all they want. The dastardly crimes of the Germans will commit them to everlasting damnation in the blackest depths of the nethermost hell. We met the *Dryad* at 4pm and obtained some welcome news. I got in a shindy with 'Guns' for not overhauling the fo'c'sle 6-inch gun night-sights correctly.

Sunday 6

Wireless news report the loss of HM ships *Pathfinder* and *Speedy,* blown up by German mines. This mine menace is becoming very serious indeed. I have devised a scheme for overcoming it, and shall lay it before the admiral. The British marines, with whom LLG went as surgeon, have been withdrawn from Ostend, and replaced by Russian troops which have been brought round from Archangel. The German advance on Paris is at least checked temporarily. A gorgeous day followed a still better night. Very busy with 'Guns' all day. Worked out some rather complicated deflection problems, and perfected the fire control system. Very bucked as 'Guns' complimented me on my work. Overhauled two ships without result.

6 September 1914   HMS *CRESCENT,* AT SEA

    Dear Mother,

    Many thanks for your letters. You have got to try to be a little less impatient and not draw so many odious comparisons with Captain Baird. A captain can take the time to write a letter whenever he pleases, even in wartime, while a junior officer has no time to spare. With luck I get from about four to six hours' sleep a night, and, with intervals for meals, am busy all day; I enjoy it, it is interesting, and it is in a good cause, but it is rather disheartening to be hauled over the coals by an exacting parent, for not wasting time writing continual letters when I am not allowed to give you any news. I have written three times to you and once or more to Daddy; perhaps you have not received the letters. Another small point: Battleships, like that of which Captain Baird is in command, are often in harbour and consequently have frequent chances of sending mails; cruisers are almost continually at sea, and on an average mails leave us for home about once a week, although local communications are more frequent. Anyhow, I will write whenever it is reasonably possible. Please thank Aunties Ethel and Ruth for their letters, and say I will write after the war.

By the way, who is young Anderson, whom you say is killed? I don't remember the name.

So glad to hear that all my friends are enlisting; splendid of Burberry. It is good that Malcolm and Gertrude's fiancé are going. Well done, Canon 'Stinkbreath'! He has lost a son in an excellent cause, and, I hope, is a proud man.

It is not so easy as it looks, this quashing Germany, as the Russians are deadly slow. I wish they would stop wasting time with the Austrians in Galicia and make a more determined advance in Prussia. There is a story being circulated that General Grierson, who is supposed to have died a natural death, was murdered by a German because of his extensive knowledge of the German Army and its methods.*

---

* It is still believed that Lieutenant-General James Grierson died of an aneurysm of the heart on a train near Amiens.

They seem to have no idea of the meaning of the
words honour and chivalry. The Hunnish strain,
which must have become ingrained in the German blood
during the raids of the Huns a thousand years ago, is
vindicating itself after ages of latency.

I wish these skulking brutes would come out of their
damned harbours, and we will soon increase the number
of the permanent German submarine fleet quartered
on the sand at the bottom of the North Sea. This
minelaying game is typical of the nation. I knew a man
who was saved from the *Amphion* very well; he was first
lieutenant.

A lot of frothy vapouring is being published in the
press about the Heligoland action. It was certainly
a most successful venture, as it is hoped all our
ventures will be. But to describe it as a great naval
victory is ridiculous, for there were only three
German small cruisers and a few torpedo boats present,
and they were easily outnumbered. There will be only
one great naval victory, and that will be accomplished
as soon as public opinion forces the Germans to put to
sea. Sinking unarmed trawlers and laying mines may
be a most amusing game, but it won't avail much in the
long run.

An interesting story is told of the Heligoland
affair. When the *Mainz* sank, a German officer was seen
to be struggling at his last gasp in the ditch. One of
our officers immediately jumped overboard and saved
him. When they were both standing on the deck once
more, the chivalrous (?) German showed his gratitude by
spitting in the face of the chap who had saved him. A
splendid nation of gentlemen! This story is absolutely
true, as I have it from an eye witness. The bottom of

the sea is the best place for people like this. Their
outrages on the Belgians make one livid with rage;
I should have considerable pleasure in gouging their
eyes out, I feel so angry when I read of them.

Tootsie no doubt thinks she is remarkably smart, but
it is very dangerous to mention the movements of any
ships even in private correspondence or conversation,
as things get round in an extraordinary fashion, and
there are plenty of friends to the Germans about. As
a matter of fact, although the *King George V* has been
there several times, it is quite incorrect to say she has
been there all the time.

Some of us would be rather pleased if this ship
was disabled or sunk by a mine, as in that case the
survivors would be transferred to one of the latest
ships, and would have a better chance of being in at the
death when the Germans put to sea.

What do Uncle Jack and Aunt Do think of the war?

There is one of the most gorgeous sunsets tonight
I have ever seen; I feel I must mention it; it is so
striking, the cloud effects being particularly fine.

No time for more now as I am very sleepy.

Best love to all from

Toby

PS Don't forget these socks you are knitting are just as
useful to me as to the soldiers, for all mine are rags.

Monday 7

Left our patrol at midnight and shaped a course for Cromarty. Entered
Moray Firth about 4am and made a landfall near Lybster, and then
steamed down the coast and entered Cromarty Firth at 8am, anchoring
between Cromarty and Invergordon at 8.45. Found the Second and
Third Cruiser Squadrons in harbour coaling, and also the *Edgar*, which

leaves tonight. Pearson came on board in picket boat from *Edgar,* and I sent them some grouse, as I have just received some more from Swanbister. This is first time we have anchored for eleven days, and we got some very welcome fresh provisions from Inverness and Cromarty. Coaled ship and took in 500 tons, a very tedious coaling. I hear some benevolent old gent has presented shoals of gramophones to the fleet; I hope we get one. Two German cruisers and some destroyers are at large in the North Sea and have sunk fifteen trawlers. Unluckily all our ships are coaling, or we would give them blue hell. A Wilson liner blown up by another damned mine off Hull.

Tuesday 8

Went on shore at 6am to superintend stores and ammunition being brought off from Invergordon Quay. Superintended the racers being painted in the forenoon. Landed in the afternoon and hired a motor with a warrant, in order to take despatches from the admiral to the naval victualling agent at Dingwall, and then had to go on through the Muir of Ord to Beauly to arrange about a trainload of new gun-fittings for our squadron to be sent on immediately to Invergordon. Got a square meal on my return to Dingwall. On the way home an aeroplane was seen to alight up in the deer forests above Alness. A sergeant of the Gordons stopped me and requested that I should lend him the motor to take his patrol up to investigate immediately, which I did. Unluckily I could not spare the time to go myself, so was obliged to charter a goods engine at Alness Station to take me back to Invergordon by rail at once. Heard on my return that the armed liner *Oceanic* had gone ashore in the Shetlands. A damned nuisance!

Wednesday 9

Oceanic became a total wreck. Good news from the Front in France. We weighed and left Cromarty at 10am, proceeding eastward out into the North Sea on to our own patrol. C-in-C forbids use of wireless between ten and three tonight. The whole of the First Fleet, battleships, cruisers and destroyers, are to go over to the German coast and try to force an action. Unluckily we and the rest of the Tenth (or Ragtime) Cruiser Squadron are to remain behind to sweep for minelayers. All very sick at it. *Royal Arthur* rammed and sank a Swedish ship in a fog. Government will have to apologise. I was superintending painter on 'bearing races' and very busy indeed all day long.

Thursday 10

No news of the First Fleet; they are lying in wait off Heligoland. The German advance on Paris has still been thoroughly checked, and our troops seem to be taking the offensive on the banks of the Maine. We continued on our patrol all day. I had a very busy day again, reconstructing 6-inch sights, in this case the gunlayer's range dials of A 1. The present state of affairs leaves me no time to get bored, which is a jolly good thing, and I am constantly employed. Mr Kiddle is setting up an agitation to reconstruct the control system, but at present he hasn't met with much success in any direction.

Friday 11

On our patrol all day. The Commander sprang a surprise GQs on us in the forenoon, much to the chagrin of 'Guns', and this was followed by group exercise and drill. Very dirty weather all the day. We had extraordinary luck in the evening, just missing a mine by a few yards, and if it hadn't been for the rough weather we should have been almost certain to have struck it. We stopped, and exploded it with rifle fire; it made a terrific din and sent up a huge column of water. Later we sighted another farther off and exploded it as before. No news from the Front or of the First Fleet.

Saturday 12

Destroyed two more mines by rifle fire. The *King Alfred* of the Sixth Cruiser Squadron joined us for two days at 4pm, while her flagship, the *Drake,* is in harbour. Usual routine all day. Good news from the Front, where the Germans have commenced to retreat. The report that the *Pathfinder* was sunk by a submarine, and not a mine, is completely untrue and a fabrication.* At 6pm the squadron captured a German sailing vessel, bound for Hamburg with beef and hide. We sent her into Scapa with a prize crew. Very rough all day, and the consequence was that we could not carry any gunroom scuttles.

Sunday 13

First Fleet returned, having made a complete sweep of North Sea and Heligoland Bight, and seen nothing at all of the German Fleet. Usual routine all day. Boarded two Danish steamers and got some Copenhagen news, but nothing that was of much interest. Still rough.

Monday 14

On our patrol all day. Heard that the *Vindictive* has made a valuable capture in the Atlantic. We sighted another mine at 7am and sent away the sea boat to examine it. They took it on board, and we are to land it when next we go into port, in order that the authorities may attempt to glean some information from it. 6-inch aiming tube firing at a target in the forenoon: three runs either side, and quite good results on the whole. A very dull, dreary, wet 'North Sea' day. Had a very jovial evening in the gunroom, and the commander sent down to request us not to make such a bloody din!

---

* HMS *Pathfinder* was sunk on Saturday, 5 September 1914 by the German *U-21*. The magazine exploded, causing the ship to sink within minutes, with the loss of two-hundred-and-fifty-nine men. There were eleven survivors.

1914

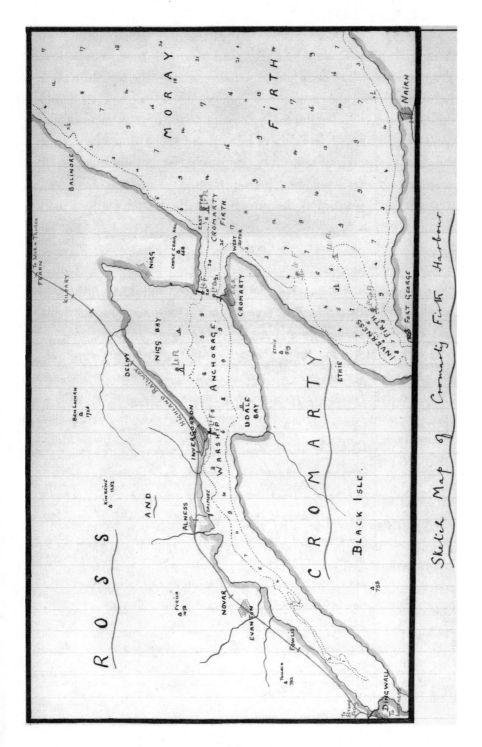

Sketch Map of Cromarty Firth Harbour

149

Tuesday 15

A big gale all day made things very uncomfortable. Those of us who
sleep on after shelter deck had to go below at 2am. The squadron at
full strength with the exception of the *Theseus* and *Edgar*. Considerable
difficulty in getting Poldhu through owing to the unfavourable weather
conditions. Although when we eventually did get it through it was very
satisfactory. Today our seniority as midshipmen commences, as we
are dated from 15 September. The captain told me we shall now have
to start keeping midshipmen's journals, and the staff paymaster will
demand them.

Wednesday 16

We communicated at 7am with rest of squadron and then left them
for Cromarty. Passed the *Roxburgh* at 10am. Divisional gunnery drills
and lectures in the forenoon. I got the old Dumaresq out of the top,
passed down the range dial, and got the painter on with his manifold
jobs. We entered the Moray Firth at 11am, Cromarty Firth at 3.45, and
anchored in between Invergordon and Cromarty at 4.30. The collier
came alongside, and we rigged for coaling preparatory to starting early
tomorrow morning. Found the *Hawke* and the *Edgar* and the Second
Cruiser Squadron in harbour.

Thursday 17

The ghastly and revolting atrocities of the German fiends on the
defenceless Belgians make me boil with rage. Rape, Ravage and
Rant are the German watchwords in this war. Right, Revenge and
Retrenchment shall be ours. God grant the defenceless may be avenged.
One of our submarines has sunk the German cruiser *Hela*.* German
submarines sighted in Moray Firth. Commenced to coal ship at 6am,

---

* On the morning of 13 September 1914, SMS *Hela* was torpedoed six miles
south-west of Heligoland by HMS *E9*.

and with a short interval for breakfast, continued until 10.40, taking
in 450 tons. The fo'c'sle and foretop holds were broken down most of
the time, due to broken slide rods. Watch-keeping officers excused,
and 'No. 1' took our hold instead of Mr Oxlade. Got on shore in
the afternoon for a few hours, went by train to get some stores from
Dingwall, and then came back to tea at Invergordon. Met several
gunroom officers from the Second Cruiser Squadron, including
Scrimgeour-Wedderburn and several friends of Edel's at Trondheim.
Received a welcome mail at last.

Friday 18

In harbour all day. Acting AP Cockerill, RNR, joined ship for passage
to HMS *Hawke*. The *Endymion* came in at 8am and began coaling
immediately. The *Dryad* left at noon with mails for our squadron out in
the North Sea. Leave to the POs and CPOs of the starboard watch for a
few hours in the afternoon. Most of them celebrated it by getting pretty
squiffy after six weeks consecutively on board. Most of the midshipmen
also on shore. I took a day on board to relieve the watch-keeper.
Large detachments of men from Second Cruiser Squadron went route
marching.

18 September 1914   HMS *CRESCENT*, Flagship, Tenth Cruiser
Squadron

Dear Mother,
Many thanks for letters and socks (not sox, I believe).
It was very kind to ask if I should like provisions
sent, but perishable goods would be no good, I am afraid,
as they might be a very long time in the post; still,
a few other sorts of things now and then would be
very welcome. The North Sea at its best is but a dull
place, and as winter begins to come on it is a most
God-forsaken hole, with continual rain, mist, fogs,

alternating with gales and rough weather. I believe the geography books call it the North Sea or German Ocean. 'What's in a name?'

At the beginning of the war I did not expect it to last long from a naval point of view, and consequently left most of my clothes with Gieve's in my big green trunk at Portsmouth.

At present, as we are evidently going to remain here for some time, I am badly in need of some, left in the trunk. I should be very much obliged if you would write to them and tell them to send the following things, which will be found somewhere in the trunk:

One pair boots, one pair sea-boots (important), half-dozen flannel shirts, and as many collars as there are, also handkerchiefs. The next time you are feeling energetic in the knitting line, woollen gloves and a scarf would be much appreciated.

By the way, the young Anderson killed at the Front, about whom I questioned you, is a brother-in-law of one of our midshipmen; it may be of interest that this fellow has nine brothers and three brothers-in-law – twelve in all; of these, three are in the Regular Army, one in the Navy, four in the Territorials, two have joined Kitchener's Army, and two have volunteered as temporary surgeons in the RN Volunteer Reserve. Two of the Army ones are dead, and the Navy one was saved from the *Amphion*. Our captain's secretary, Assistant Paymaster Cockrem, was at school with Harold Wacher.

Some old benevolent 'Johnny' has decided to present the Fleet with an innumerable supply of gramophones; we had already bought one, but his new records come in useful and help to amuse our gunroom, which is quite a cosy little hole when you get used to the thick

atmosphere. Please thank Mrs Drake very much for her
socks; which were hers? Please send George's address.
I hope the good folks at home won't forget that their
first duty is to the wives and children of bluejackets
and soldiers without support, even before the Belgian
refugees, and certainly before German prisoners.
Their atrocities in Belgium are too revolting. By the
way, in future you can address letters to Midshipman
Scrimgeour, Royal Navy, as the rank of acting
midshipman, held since the beginning of the war, has
now been confirmed.

Nearly everybody is growing beards and moustaches
now, as shaving water is a waste of precious coal to
work the fresh water distiller, and also shaving is an
unnecessary nuisance. If we stop here long enough, I
shall get quite a good beard.

Why does not Daddy get a rifle and practise firing
at birds from the roof? He might be quite useful if
the projected German attack on England ever comes off.
I hope Jimmy and Billy are being drilled, and Peggy
initiated in the mysteries of first-aid nursing.

How is our district doing in the recruiting line?

I have just remembered those lovely peaches I
was going to gorge before I went away; I feel more
incensed against the Germans than ever; the insolence
of preventing me eating my peaches is a far greater
offence than all the Belgian atrocities, I am sure.

The party leaving Swanbister deprived us of a
welcome change of diet (grouse) for a bit, but several
people in Scotland are sending consignments of game to
the Fleet, and we get some now and then. The Germans
have invented a splendid game, so our submarines tell
us. They come out of harbour a mile or two, well inside

their protecting minefields, under cover of night or
fog. They then fire off all their guns, a terrific
cannonade for hours; they knock a few spars, strays and
things about, possibly lowering a mast and dropping a
few boats overboard. Then they return to harbour and
report a huge naval victory over the British. This has
had to be given up, as the German officers and men, who
are really quite sound at heart and ready to come out
and fight, if they were allowed, gave the show away.

By the way, in addition to letters of news, if you
get any photos of things or people at home, I should
find them very interesting.

Stanley and Sophie are the last people I should have
expected to enjoy hop-picking; give them both my love.

I hear turkeys will be very scarce this year; Auntie
Maud should do well.

No more now.

Excuse this disjointed effusion, but I write a few
lines whenever the spirit moves me. Is Daddy very busy?
I should enjoy his opinions on the war, especially
his expert financial views. Very best love to all at
Wickhambreaux.

From

Toby

Saturday 19

RA Second Cruiser Squadron shifted his flag from the *Shannon* to the
Cochrane. *Shannon* went into the floating dock, stationed here, for
repairs; and rest of Second Cruiser Squadron put to sea at 9am. HMS
Sappho came in at 9.30am from Loch Ewe, and placed herself under
our orders as she is to join the Tenth Cruiser Squadron; she will put
to sea on Monday. Hands aired night clothing after divisions. Lieut.-
Commander Beasley relieved Lieutenant Wilson as officer (in lieu of

Sub-Lieutenant) for gunroom duties. Completed with stores during the afternoon. NC Day from *Sappho* (Exmouth term at Dartmouth) came on board with official papers and had a drink in the gunroom. We weighed and put to sea at 5.30 to return to our patrol. Received a broken thermos flask by post (I don't know who sent it) from Junior Army and Navy Stores.

Sunday 20

It is rumoured that Germany intends to attack London with a gigantic aerial fleet. I hope we are properly prepared. Bad news of the loss of the depot ship *Fisgard* off Portland in a gale comes through. She was bound with dockyard stores for Cromarty. A very rough night. We took several big seas in. Those sleeping on deck had to go below. Joined the squadron at 10am. The gale continued all day. Conditions most uncomfortable. The *Edgar* proceeded to Cromarty and then to Newcastle to dry dock. The routine with regard to ships of our squadron proceeding to Cromarty to coal will continue in turn as at present. The *Endymion* goes next.

Monday 21

On our patrol all day. The gale continued, and, although the barometer rose, got but little better. GQs in the forenoon. Rigged a net at loader to safeguard practice cartridges, and fitted a range dial on port side after-bridge. Exchanged stores with rest of squadron during the dog watches, although the lowering of sea boats was very difficult owing to the big sea running. Physical drill at 4.30. Wireless via Poldhu says Battle of the Aisne is still raging.

Tuesday 22

Better weather today. The *Sappho* joined Flag at 8am. Exercised after control starboard side firing all the forenoon 1-inch aiming tube and rifle. The first lieutenant was quite a success for the first attempt. Plenty doing all day. Received a weird collection of wireless fragments, the only intelligible news being that either the *Hogue* and *Aboukir* have been sunk or have sunk something. But we have no confirmation or repetition. Physical drill in the dog watches very amusing, as the old admiral, the secretary, and the captain joined in, and we had great fun wrestling, cock-fighting and jumping the horse. The Second Destroyer Flotilla, supported by Second Cruiser Squadron, will attack the German patrol at the mouth of the Ems tonight.

Wednesday 23

Loss of the *Hogue* confirmed, also *Cressy*; *Aboukir* uncertain. A great disaster, as they were excellent ships, just older than the Drake class. Most of the snotties were of the Grenville term, a year junior to us. Do not know whether they were all killed or not. Believe young Cameron was one of them. The Admiralty postponed the attack on the Ems patrol due to bad weather. All British warships withdrawn from North Sea temporarily, as it is infested with German submarines, except our squadron, the Tenth, or 'rag-time', who thus hold a very distinguished but dangerous position. Captain Hyde-Parker of the *Endymion* is making quite a name for himself by the stupid antics of his ship. They were in trouble as usual today. Squadron scattered for target practice. At 9am we lowered two targets, but both were destroyed by the choppy sea, and we had to give up the idea of firing, which was disappointing. Gym on quarterdeck in dog watches as usual. Most of wardroom and gunroom rolled up, had good fun with horses v. bucks, skipping, single-sticks, boxing, fencing, cock-fighting, etc.

Thursday 24

The Battle of the Aisne still continues – in point of view of duration, it easily beats the previous battles of this war *viz*. Haelen, Mons, Altkirch, Lunéville, Cambrai, Compiègne, and the Marne. The Russians have captured Jaroslav, and the Serbo-Montenegrin armies are all around Sarajevo, capital of Bosnia. It is reported that the

Breslau and *Goeben,* sold some weeks ago to Turkey, are being
remanned by Germans sent overland. I hope the Mediterranean
Squadron will not make a second mistake. On our patrol all day.
Usual routine. A great game of twos and threes on the QD in the dog
watches. It appears from wireless messages received that the *Aboukir,*
Hogue and *Cressy* were sunk between Rotterdam and Harwich by a
flotilla of four German submarines, two of which were sunk.* There is
some danger of hostile divers obtaining our secret signal codebooks,
so these are being removed. The Japanese have allowed the German
China Squadron to escape from Kiao-Chau, and they will be a great
nuisance. Submarine *AE* lost by an accident on patrol with thirty-five
lives off Sydney.

Friday 25

Patrolling as usual. Destroyed a mine by rifle fire. Light QF gunfiring
with night defence control stations in the forenoon. Poor firing,
although certainly the weather was bad. Skylarking as usual in the
dog watches. I had a row with Tottenham in the gunroom. A small
German squadron crept over to our coast to support submarine
attacks on Cromarty and Rosyth, but they were chased back to
the Ems; unluckily we were not fast enough to catch them. We are
still the only squadron at sea, a risky honour. Armed German liner
Spreewald captured by the *Berwick* in the North Sea. The German
cruiser *Emden* has bombarded Madras and badly damaged our Indian
Ocean trade.

Saturday 26

Patrolling as usual. Overhauled more ships than usual. News came
through that the Russian cruiser *Bayan* in the Baltic has sunk a
German cruiser and two German destroyers. Later the news that the

---

* It is believed that HMS *Hogue* was sunk with her sisters, HMS *Cressy* and HMS
Aboukir, by a single German U-boat, *U-9*. More than a thousand lives were lost.

whole German High Sea Fleet has put to sea in the Baltic, probably to attack the Russian coast. I wish we could get at them. There is a rumour of our sweeping either the Sound or the Great or Little Belt and so running through into the Baltic. This would be possible, as Denmark and Sweden are neutral. Lists of officers lost and saved from the *Hogue, Cressy* and *Aboukir* came through. Delmege, Corbyn, WAH Harrison and Froude are among those drowned. We captured a suspicious-looking trawler fitted with wireless, and though Dutch, with German papers.

26 September 1914   HMS *CRESCENT*

Dear Mother,

How are you all getting on at home? I am so glad Uncle John and Auntie Connie are going to Quaives. I hope they enjoy themselves. Very many thanks for the woollen goods you have sent. Daddy's vest and the socks are most useful, as it is exceedingly cold by night on watch even now, and in November and December and the early months of next year it will be far worse.

Among my books brought back from the Cornwall you will find a big brown leather book, *Inman's Nautical Tables*; also a green book, the *1914 Nautical Almanac*; I should like these sent as soon as possible; also, by the way, Sennett and Oram's *Marine Steam Engine*.

Have you got any walnuts this year? If you have plenty, I should love some; apples are another thing that would be much appreciated.

Do you mind getting me some more visiting cards printed when you have time? I will give you an example of what I want; no bigger, as that enclosed is just a convenient size. Did I ask you for George's address last time I wrote? Anyhow, will you send it me sometime? Thank Daddy for his splendid long letter.

I have noticed that several friends and relations are
rather apt to treat you as a sort of exchange for domestic
servants. I wonder if you could look out for a job for
me (not me personally). The man I recommend is aged
forty-five, a retired naval petty officer, a teetotaller,
guaranteed a very capable and reliable man, for whose
trustworthiness I will vouch. He is married, with no
children, and wants a job as caretaker or lodge keeper or
something in that line. Only a very moderate wage, as he
has a pension. I don't expect it is much good asking you,
only I thought you might possibly hear of something.

Daddy asks if I want any money. I do not at present,
unless it is with which to feed the fishes, as we have
nothing to spend it on, except messing, and my pay
just covers that. Still, I should like my allowance to
accumulate while I am away, as it will go pretty fast, I
imagine, after the war.

I am thinking of volunteering to go to the Front
with the Naval Brigade when they go, as this is such
dull, dry work till the Germans come out. But I am
afraid they won't let me go, as active service officers
are much needed afloat, and the Naval Brigade will be
officered chiefly by Reserve officers and Volunteer
officers who know very little about Service life afloat
and would be far more useful on shore.

I hope you are all on the lookout for spies. The
father of one of our officers arrested, or caused to be
arrested, his butler on suspicion, and he proved to be a
dangerous alien spy. (This has been passed by the Press
Bureau, I don't think!)

Is George only a private? I should have thought
that with his experience of the South African War they
would have made him a corporal.

```
     Is your camera in working order? If it is I could
take some snaps which would be very interesting when
the war is over and the censorship removed.
     Please don't send any clothes other than what I
ask for, as space is very limited for stowing surplus
clothes away. If you want to send things, send food of
sorts.
     No time for more now.
     Very best love to all.

                                              From
                                              Toby
```

Sunday 27

It is feared that the submarine *E4* has been lost off Heligoland. The Battle of the Aisne continues. The Germans reinforced by troops from East Prussia have regained ground lost on the right wing at St Quentin. Russian investment of Przemyśl. On our patrol as usual. The *Sappho* and *Dryad* were temporarily detached from squadron and sent to Scapa on special service. Captured a four-masted German barque three months from Brazil.

Monday 28

A filthy night, very big sea running this morning. We were going into harbour today, but cannot get there before nightfall, and as we are only allowed to enter by day, we shall have to wait until tomorrow. The officers' commissariat has given out, and we are living on salt pork and ship's biscuit. Conditions altogether most unpleasant. More submarines missing, but it is hoped they are sheltering from the storm in some of the more deserted of the Norwegian fjords. German submarines supposed to be sheltering on our coast. First Light Cruiser Squadron and two destroyer flotillas searching for them. Our battleships are now based at Poolewe.

Tuesday 29

Came up the Moray Fifth at full speed to lessen the danger of attacks by hostile submarines supposed to be sheltering here. Anchored in the Cromarty Firth at 7.30am. Three submarines and three sea-planes have been based here for defensive purposes within the last three days. Coaled ship, taking in 480 tons. It was a double-derrick collier, and we had a most efficient coaling. I had a row with 'Guns' over 'empties', always a source of trouble between fo'c'sle and foretop holds. The gunnery staff brought out a scheme for the modernisation and re-armament of HMS *Crescent*; personally I consider it not worthwhile. Other ships in harbour – Second Cruiser Squadron, *Endymion* of the Tenth, *Argyll* of the Third, and depot ships. Snow in the distance on Ben Wyvis; this helped to create gorgeous sunset.

Wednesday 30

Received good mail from home. The *Argyll* went into the floating dry dock. *Endymion* weighed and proceeded to sea 7am. *Royal Arthur* came in 10am. Route march for our starboard watch in the afternoon; very good exercise for them. The Second Cruiser Squadron have done it whenever in harbour for a long time. Eight miles stiff walk inland over the moors and two pints of beer at the end, then straight back to the ship. First lieutenant in charge, also lieutenant (G) and four midshipmen. A very humorous affair, but ship's band a great success. Old 'Pops' has but little idea of managing a large quantity of men, and 'Guns' was two cuts above helping him. Cobb motorbiked to Dingwall with despatches for the naval victualling agent. Ran over two hens, one dog and a sheep. Stood him a bottle of fizz to commemorate it. Gunroom wine store just received twelve-dozen fizz.

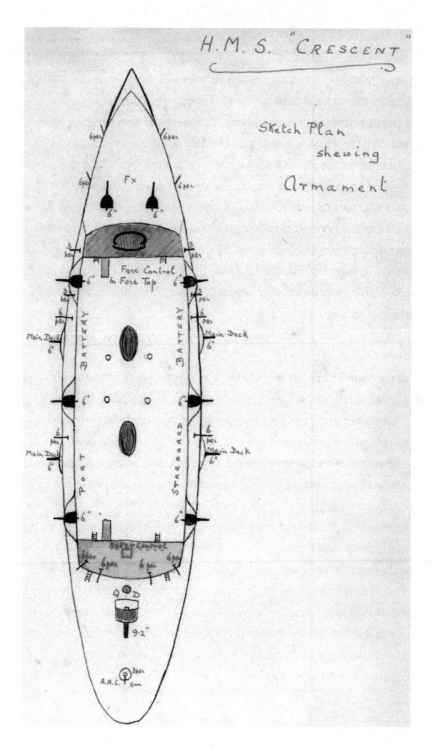

H.M.S. "CRESCENT"

Sketch Plan
shewing
Armament

30 September 1914   HMS *CRESCENT*

Dear Auntie Ethel,

Very many thanks for your letter and for Auntie Dora's
enclosed; I hope you will drive out of her head the
lingering idea of sympathy for the Germans, with which
her point of view seems stricken. The Kaiser is mad, but
that is no excuse for the appalling atrocities committed
in France and Belgium, quite apart from vandalism, such
as at Louvain and Rheims – the guilt for these crimes
is indelibly inscribed on the judgment hooks of the
impartial critic, against the German military officers
and NCOs who have instigated their men and have
themselves committed the ghastly orgies of drunkenness,
destruction, cruelty and rapine.

I am proud to belong to a nation whose bounden duty
it is to stamp out the military caucus and displace the
depraved dynasty who have caused these disasters to
civilisation.

Before the war I admired and respected the Germans
as an honourable and enterprising nation, although
quite realising their lack of scruples in international
affairs. Although our naval opponents have shown
considerable proof of that chivalry with which the
Franco-English encounters of the past were usually
tempered, yet the hypocritical behaviour of the military
forces of a nation professing culture makes one gasp at
the brazen audacity of the perpetrators in pursuing their
career of crime against humanity. Enough of hot air!

It is very kind of you to make woollen goods for us;
it certainly is very cold and unpleasant in the North
Sea, and will get far worse as the season advances, but
the Admiralty are showing better organisation than
in the past, and the men are getting plenty of warm

clothes. Personally I am quite well off for woollen clothes, as mother sent me a lot.

Daddy also keeps our gunroom supplied with papers. Eatables are really the most acceptable presents, as tinned meat and ship's biscuit and salt pork are our chief staples of diet, except for a few days after leaving harbour, when we go in periodically for a few hours to coal and reprovision.

Unluckily, being an old ship, we are not fitted with refrigerators, and nothing will keep very long.

We all love chocolate, which is very nice in the long night watches; but do not bother about us too much, as the Army are having a very severe time, I expect. We can do nothing until the Germans come out, except keep the seas clear for commerce, although, of course, there are plenty of submarine attacks and destroyer raids on both sides. In two years Percy Scott will be right – submarines and sea-planes will drive the battleships from the sea. Beresford was also right when he raised his cry of 'Speed!' unavailingly; if we had built more fast cruisers, the *Emden* could never have committed the depredations on our commerce in the Indian Ocean that she has done. The cry of 'if' leads one on to think of what might have been if Lord Roberts' ideas and warnings had been listened to, but 'ifs' are worthless things; our conduct has exceeded all my highest hopes; the government have done well because they are full of capable men (scoundrels if you will). The immediate appointment of Kitchener was remarkable, as if they realised, as we did, that he was essential to the War Office, why was he not sent there years before?

The war has made men out of thousands of monkeys, and is undoubtedly a much needed tonic to the

British Empire. I am afraid you anticipated matters
in addressing me as lieutenant; it is a rank which
cannot be attained in the Navy until long technical
courses have been gone through in the various subjects
of engineering, gunnery, navigation, seamanship and
torpedo; at present I am a midshipman. I expect you
were misled by the rank of lieutenant in the Army. I
will give you a list of equivalent naval and military
ranks, which may be of interest, and you will see that
a lieutenant in the Navy ranks with, but before (as the
Navy is the senior service), captains in the Army.

NAVY
Admiral of the Fleet
Admiral
Vice-Admiral
Rear-Admiral
Commodore
Captain
Commander
Lieutenant-Commander
Lieutenant
Sub-Lieutenant
Midshipman
Naval Cadet (sea-going)
Naval Cadet (Osborne and Dartmouth)
ARMY
Field-Marshal
General
Lieutenant-General
Major-General
Brigadier-General
Colonel
Lieutenant-Colonel

```
Major
Captain
Lieutenant (First)
Lieutenant (Second)
Subaltern
Military Cadet (Sandhurst and Woolwich)
```

I hear that all my friends at home are joining the Army. George Wilson was offered a commission after the South African War, but refused it, so it is very sporting of him to enlist as a private again. I volunteered for the Naval Brigade to go to the Front, but they are only sending Reserve and Volunteer officers who are of little or no use afloat, and as far as possible no active service naval officers are going, so that is off for me.

I'm afraid the German Fleet won't ever risk a fleet action, so it will be a matter of submarines, unless the unexpected occurs.

Now I must turn in and go to sleep, as sleep is a valuable commodity to us.

Don't suppose I shall get a chance to write again for some time. Very best love to all in your district, including Tentworth, etc.

From
Toby

OCTOBER

Thursday 1

The *Emden* is doing considerable damage to our trade in the Indian Ocean, and there are still several other cruisers at large. The *Cumberland* is doing excellent work off the Cameroons and has sunk a gunboat and captured nine large valuable German liners. The Canadian Expeditionary Force is due to leave in a few days. The Battle of the Aisne still continues with varying success. Von Kluck's army on the German right is their weak spot and is reported unofficially to be in a bad position. The fighting is fierce and continuous. The Germans in Belgium are operating with a view to the siege of Antwerp. The German army has advanced right into Russia and is attempting unsuccessfully so far to cross the Niemen. Meanwhile the main Russian Army threatens Breslau and Cracow, is besieging Przemyśl and finishing off Austrians. Main scheme is to advance simultaneously on Berlin and Vienna with 5,000,000 men while leaving a masking force in East Prussia. Another route march for port watch under Lieut.-Commander Beasley, Torps and four snotties. I went again. Got three hours' leave afterwards, and got introduced to a very nice little girl, Mina George. Also met an awful good subaltern in the Camerons, a real good sort. Midshipman Florence of Sturges' Exmouth Term came on shore from the *Drake*. She has two guns out of action from a collision with a Danish merchant vessel. Russell AS, Murdoch and P-Pinhey from *Royal Arthur* came to dinner in our gunroom, and we had a very festive evening. Drambuie much in evidence. Second Cruiser Squadron went to sea 6am. *Drake* came in 7am. The Third Cruiser Squadron came in 10am, and the *Devonshire* changed places with the *Argyll* in the floating dock.

Friday 2

Weighed and proceeded to sea at 7am. Went out through the Moray Firth at full speed. Joined the squadron at Rendezvous P3 at 5pm, and then continued our patrol work. The minelaying squadron – *Apollo, Andromache, Naiad,* etc. – have been put under the orders of our admiral; so that, in addition to the eight ships of the Tenth Cruiser Squadron proper, he now controls three armed liners on the Shetland–Norway patrol, eleven minelayers, and the *Dryad* and *Sappho.* We communicated and distributed mails when we met the squadron at 5pm. Very much improved weather, although there is a heavy swell.

Saturday 3

A big combined sweep from Scotch coast across to Norway for all cruisers in the North Sea and for Second and Third Battle Squadrons under Vice-Admiral Warrender, ships working in pairs. This is to prevent the escape of a German cruiser force, said to be going to attempt to escape into the Atlantic via the Norwegian coast, in order to attack the Canadian contingent, which is about to leave for Europe. The weather has taken a decided turn for the worse and is most unpleasant. The loss of submarine *E1* is now practically certain. The Battle of the Aisne continues, now having lasted three weeks. In many places the Allies have forced back the Germans to the Somme. The Russians are before Cracow, where the Germans and Austrians are under Hindenburg.

Sunday 4

The Battle of the Aisne, the Russian advance on the Cracow–Przemyśl district and the German siege of Antwerp continue. Russian troops have been landed to reinforce the Antwerp garrison, but the very heavy German siege guns are sure to be dangerous later on, although at present they have had no success. The First Cruiser Squadron in the Mediterranean has been disbanded. The *Black Prince* and *Duke of Edinburgh* have been dispatched to the Indian Ocean to help run down the *Emden* and the *Defence* has gone to join the *Leviathan, Cornwall, Hyacinth* and *Astraea* under Admiral King-Hall at the Cape, while only the *Warrior* remains in the Mediterranean. The big sweep of the North Sea continues without incident in very nasty weather. A German sea-plane sighted off the Dogger Bank, fired at by destroyers, and disappeared in a fog. It is a funny coincidence that the ill-fated *Cressy, Hogue* and *Aboukir* were all named after battles won against our allies the French.

Monday 5

Filthy day. Divisions on the cable deck. No GQs, much to the chagrin of 'Guns'. We were concerned in various operations in the North Sea, the exact nature and object of which is known alone to the rear-admiral, secretary, 'Flags' and the skipper. Exchanged signals with the *Russell* of the Third Battle Squadron at midday. The Admiralty have not yet confirmed the loss of *E1*, but all hope has been given up definitely. The *Emden* still at large.

Tuesday 6

We have gone on to another wireless wave in direct communication with the C-in-C, secret code, and are no longer on the commercial code, hence for the present we shall get no news of the war from the Poldhu station. The extensive operations continue. I think they are merely another method of sweeping. The first fruitful result is that a disguised German store ship with oil fuel and stores was captured off the Scotch coast. Bad weather continues as usual. The Germans are reported to be going to try and creep down the Dutch coast, up the Scheldt, and so attack Antwerp from the sea.

Wednesday 7

German destroyers sunk off Dutch coast. The sea went down, but a thick North Sea fog set in. The senior naval officer at Loch Ewe, which has been used as principal base for all our battle squadrons since they left Scapa to obviate the danger of submarine attacks, reports German submarines sighted in vicinity. Consequently all colliers, store ships, oil ships and depot ships have been ordered to leave, and a new battleship base will be chosen in a remote spot in the Hebrides. We were suddenly ordered to chase on a given course at 4pm, but after a quarter of an hour at full speed we received 'Negative chase'. Object of first signal unknown.

Thursday 8

Learnt from the *Albemarle* that the Russians under Rennenkampf have badly defeated the Germans and driven them back into Prussia. The Battle of the Aisne still continues. In the western end of the line, both sides are attempting to outflank the other. Thick fog made our operations hard to carry out, although occasional snatches of sunshine came through. Sea an oily calm. Owing to incorrect dead reckonings in both ships, we spoke to the *Albemarle,* now of the Third Battle Squadron, late Fifth, about midday and exchanged news. We attempted to communicate with the *Hawke* before she leaves for Invergordon, but failed. Had a wireless from the *Gibraltar,* who is retrieving her picket boat at Scapa, that she will rejoin tomorrow. *Dryad* sighted suspicious sailing craft, proving to be a disguised German minelayer from Brunsbüttel, and so sank her.

Friday 9

Fog became thicker than ever; you could not see fifty yards from the ship. We passed several tramps perilously close. The operations closed at 2pm, and we made back to our old patrol between Aberdeen and Denmark at six knots. Guns' crews stood by the guns all day. All signalling with rest of squadron, who rejoined, done by siren Morse. By luck we made the *Grafton* out from Cromarty and got a welcome mail. C-in-C asked our admiral for a reliable cruiser, fit for a long steam, and he selected the *Gibraltar,* which has been forthwith detached. Much conjecture as to what she is to do. Personally I think it is to relieve the *Theseus* at Archangel in the White Sea. The *Drake* has been sent to Spitzbergen to destroy the German fishing settlement there.

Saturday 10

On our patrol all day. Communicated with torpedo boat *No. 027* at 4pm; she is acting as Admiralty despatch vessel, and brought us out the new *Navy List.* Very disappointed to find that gunroom officers have already been appointed to most of the new ships due to commission this month, such as the *Queen Elizabeth* and the *Tiger;* many of the midshipmen are junior to us, and we are learning nothing but sea-going experience in these old ships. All the Dartmouth cadets who have been made midshipmen have gained from six months to two-and-a-half years, but

I suppose it will all be squared up after the war. My opinion is that the captain does not take nearly strict enough measures with regard to the boarding of neutral vessels.

Sunday 11

Very stringent regulations have been issued with regard to neutral shipping in the North Sea, all fishing craft being prohibited anywhere there; this is a good step to end minelaying. The Germans have started laying mines disguised as periscopes, to make us ram them and so hit the mines (this information gained by spies). On our patrol as usual. Nasty weather again. Met the *Liverpool* and *Southampton* with two destroyers chasing a German supposed to be in this area.

Monday 12

Came up the Moray Firth in the early morning and anchored in the Cromarty Firth 9am; found the *Hawke* and *Endymion* and Third Cruiser Squadron in harbour. Coaled ship 600 tons; fo'c'sle hold jolly good; a very dirty coal, owing to the high wind, which blew dust everywhere. We had a practical example of the German spy danger, as a large portion of the coal was soaked in benzine, and several detonator fuses were found, which, if successfully ignited, would soon have demolished both us and the collier; luckily they were detected. This must have been the work of German spies. A mishap to the whaler while being lowered; a rotten fall parted, and one man broke his arm and another his collarbone; both were disobeying regulations, and were before foremost fall. Received an excellent mail. News of the fall of Antwerp received with disappointment; jubilation at the exploits of the great Marine-Naval Brigade; sorry to hear some of them interned in Holland. A very jovial evening helped along by drambuie; Messrs. Bacon, Oxlade and Buddle and 'Flags' were gunroom guests, and damned good ones, too. Wrote a note to Mina. Midshipmen applied for appointments to a new battleship, but the captain refused to sanction application, as he could not spare us. This was disappointing, but nevertheless a compliment to the midshipmen, who undoubtedly have a large share in the responsibilities of the ship. Then I personally applied for an appointment to the Naval Brigade, but received the answer that no active service officers can be spared, only Reserve and Volunteer Reserve officers being sent. I thought that I might possibly see more service on land, but perhaps it will be better to go on with this job.

12 October 1914   HMS *CRESCENT*

Dear Mother,

Very many thanks for all letters and parcels. I returned the thermos (broken) to the stores, and received a communication some days later to the effect that it had not arrived, but will wait and see for the present. The things you have sent are most useful and welcome, but send no more clothes for the present, as I am full up in my sea-chest and no spare gear is needed. It was very kind indeed of Mrs Sillars to knit me the scarf; it will keep me wonderfully warm, and I am most grateful. Please thank her very much from me, and I will try and write myself if I can spare the time. Also do the same to Aunt Arabella; the sterling worth of her regard is more ethereal than worldly, as I am of agnostic tendencies and by no means a strict Christian, believing the Bible quite good enough without extracts in book form; nevertheless, she is a worthy soul, and I appreciate her point of view. Thank Bob very much for his letters, which interest me greatly, and tell him that as I now regard him as one of the family he must not expect regular answers (I am always rude to near relations), and he can demand to share the news (what little there is) in my effusions to you, should he be so inclined.

This letter must seem almost as mad as some of Auntie Ruth's (it must run in the family).

Give Jimmy and Peggy my very best love and thank them both many times for their letters, which are splendid, especially Peggy's.

Burbery must be a great loss; give him my good wishes when possible.

Owing to the burning of a naval mail waggon some days ago, I have probably lost some of your letters, but doubt if there was anything of importance, as I have noticed no great gap in the dates of those I have received.

Give everyone at home my love, and also Aunt Do and Uncle Jack, if you write to either. (I am afraid I am in Uncle Jack's black books, as I have not heard from him for a very long time.)

You seem to have been having a very gay time at home. Extraordinary how you manage to enjoy yourselves whenever I'm out of the house. We always get on so well by post; I seem to act like a wet blanket on all your ideas of enjoyment as soon as I come back – sack all the servants, all the children infectious, no guests, swollen livers and constipated stomachs. Directly I go, lurid letters of enjoyment, shooting house-parties, frivolous evenings, open bowels, etc. An Englishman is never happy without a 'grouse'. This is my grousy page. I enjoy the descriptions of your gay times.

What a pity Joko has not got longer hair; it is so very short. (Mum's the word.) (Not passed by the Censor.)

Who is the pretty girl you mentioned as having arrived at Wickhambreaux, possibly a Belgian. Details, please. This is more interesting to a naval officer aged seventeen than details of the milk-giving propensities of the new Jersey cow, or how many eggs the old hen has laid. The man I asked you to look out for a place

for is ineligible until after the war, as he is still on
active service. Will give you his address when needed;
at present he is chief gunner's mate of this ship (he was
petty officer of my term at Osborne).

Good luck to everyone. Excuse this extraordinarily
weird letter and weirder writing, but I feel in a
sketchy mood just now.

Germans!

Your dutiful son,
Alexander Scrimgeour

Tuesday 13

Route march for the starboard watch, eight miles stiff walking. Called
on Mina afterwards, found the whole family down with the measles.
Went on to the Royal Hotel, where the Cameron officers' mess is (the
Cameron Highlanders' recruiting base is here), and had several drinks
with Lieutenant McLeod, an awful good sort. The *Antrim* reports that
she was attacked by German submarines two-hundred-and-five miles
east of Rathsay Head three days ago, but their torpedoes missed. The
Germans are having a good time just at present, as a Boer rebellion has
broken out in Cape Colony, the Russian cruiser Pallada has been sunk
in the Baltic, although the *Bayan* and Admiral Makarov escaped, and
the Russians have abandoned the siege of Przemyśl, and spies are doing
good work at home. Received a fine consignment of goods from Daddy.
Bet LEJ £5 I am a skipper before he is.

Wednesday 14

The store ship *Alcinous* came alongside at 10am, and we took in a large
supply of paymaster's stores and other gear.

Tested the 9–2 sights. Route march for the port watch. I went to
have tea with Mina afterwards, and found her very sweet indeed, but
with a nasty attack of measles. I expect I shall catch them, too, now.
Several other people went out for trips on the local motorbikes. Found

two fellows in the local hotel talking suspiciously broad Scotch, and they tried to pump us carefully. So we told the police to shadow them. Two Zeppelins were reported over Fortrose last night, also at Delny. Personally I don't believe it. Tested the range-finder before sunset.

Thursday 15

The crying necessity of our Empire at present, more than twenty Dreadnoughts, fifty submarines, five hundred aeroplanes or fifty thousand men, is to stamp out the German spy peril now rampant in the British Isles, which is a continual source of great danger to the nation, both by information supplied to enemy and by damage done to us. Let's hope the government will soon realise this. Churchill has made an awful hash of the Antwerp show. His business is at the Admiralty and not dabbling about on land expeditions. If Kitchener needs any assistance, fully equipped naval brigades should be supplied him to do what he likes with, and not played about with by Winston Churchill. Anyhow, no skilled ratings should be wasted in naval brigades, owing to their value afloat. Landed for two hours at nine, and started riding a small 2½ hp Humber motorcycle and thoroughly enjoyed the first attempt. *Hawke* and *Endymion* put to sea, and the *Grafton* came in, both between 9 and 11am. Took in more ammunition and shell from the ammunition lighter. Weighed and left harbour at 4.30pm, the boom being specially opened for us to pass (the boom has been fitted while we were at sea last time). A gorgeous sunset – a fitting close to a glorious day like midsummer.

Proceeded to make our squadron out in the North Sea at fourteen knots through Moray Firth. I got in the soup with 'No. 1'. Panic caused on the bridge in the first watch by a trawler firing a signal rocket.

Friday 16

Theseus reports being unsuccessfully attacked by German submarine, which was observed by sea-planes later to be moving in direction of Cromarty. Nothing has been heard of the *Hawke* since she put to sea and parted company with *Endymion* (was escorting German steamer *Nordsee* into Lerwick). Either her wireless has broken down or else she has been sunk by submarines. We were to join the squadron at 11am, but this order was cancelled and we were told to proceed to a rendezvous fifty miles due east of Lerwick, a position back in the old Iceland patrol.

At midday we passed through a large number of pieces of wreckage and saw some lifebuoys floating about, so we stopped to examine, but could find no clue. The wreckage may be possibly that of the *Hawke,* or otherwise some steamer blown up by a mine. GQs in the morning. 'Guns' quarrelled with the captain, commander and 'No. 1' in turn, but received considerable moral support from the admiral. Joined squadron at 6pm. *Edgar* in the soup for using her searchlights.

Saturday 17

The object of our cruising up north is to form a complete cordon, from Shetland across to Norway, in company with Third Battle Squadron, Second Cruiser Squadron, Third Cruiser Squadron, and the armed liners attached to us. Thus the oil ships bound from the USA to Germany should be captured. Four of them already have been sent to Lerwick with prize crews. All hope of the *Hawke* has now been given up. It is reported that only four officers and sixty men were saved. German submarines are particularly active just now, as the *Antrim* was again unsuccessfully attacked today. At 4pm we sighted a big steamer and chased for three hours, when we overhauled her, and she proved to be the *Proper III*, a valuable prize with foodstuffs for Germany. We sent a prize crew of six ABs under Lieut.-Commander Bacon, RNR, and Mr McLachlan, the junior boatswain, on board her, with orders to take her into Lerwick; I should have loved to have gone. *Theseus* captured *U.S.A.* and let her go through ignorance and could not catch her again, so the armed liner *Alsatian* was sent in chase. During the day the new system of blockade has captured ten food ships.

Sunday 18

HMS *Crescent* was attacked by submarines. At 6.30am the bridge
lookouts reported an object on the water about five miles off. This was
made out by glasses to be a submarine on the surface. The day had
broken and light was getting strong, but the submarine had not sighted
us. The OOW woke the captain and the admiral, and we immediately
notified the C-in-C and our adjacent ships fifteen miles distant either
side – *viz.*, HM ships *Edgar* and *Endymion*. It was decided to attack
the submarine, and we altered course towards it, ringing down for
full speed, fourteen knots being almost immediately forthcoming.
'Repel torpedo attack' was sounded off (as night defence stations were
considered more suitable for action with submarines even in daytime),
and the guns' crews on watch closed up and loaded. About five minutes
later, when about eight thousand yards away, we were discovered, and
the submarine submerged. The order was given to fire, and the two
foc'sle guns opened at eight thousand yards, the shot going over. By this
time the gunnery-lieutenant had arrived on the foc'sle with myself and
his assistant, and he took over control from Lieut.-Commander Oxlade,
RNR, who was on gun watch at the time.

From the movement of the periscope of the submerged submarine
through the water, she appeared to be moving towards us with the
intention of attacking, but we were not caught napping, as the previous
ships who have fallen victims to submarines have been. The guns now
firing on her were the two foc'sle 6-inch (A1 and B1), also the two
forward battery 6-inch (A2 and B2) and the two forward cable-deck
six-pounders. The shot were falling about the periscope, the necessary
range having been attained (the rate of change was very high,
approximately twenty knots), but none hit. Suddenly a white streak
came at us broadside on, and passed fifty yards under our stern. It had
been fired from another submarine, which had been lying submerged
and had not been previously sighted by us. The port battery guns
opened fire on the new enemy, whose periscope was visible, but the first
salvo was badly short, showing that the torpedo must have been fired at

long range. Our first submarine was now getting so close (for we were still steaming towards her at full speed) that the fo'c'sle guns could not be depressed enough to bear. Realising that we intended to ram her, she submerged completely, and only just in time. She had been unable to fire a torpedo at us, owing to the fact that we never gave her time to turn broadside on, and the class of vessel to which she belongs is only fitted with broadside tubes. The port guns continued to fire, when suddenly the masthead lookout, who had gone aloft at daybreak, reported a third submarine on the starboard side. The starboard guns were slow in picking her up and never opened fire, as she soon submerged, and opinions differed as to whether she had ever fired a torpedo at us. All three submarines had now disappeared, and we steered S 72° W full speed (the engine room had now got us up to seventeen knots) to meet the *Edgar*. A wireless message was sent to Admiral Colville, commanding officer in charge of the Shetland defences, and two of the Scapa sea-planes, which by luck were at Lerwick, came out about two hours later to search for the submarines, while we warned all our ships in the vicinity of their presence. At midday they were sighted submerged steering S 37° E, and a destroyer flotilla was sent from Scapa in chase, but they were not seen again. The time from our first seeing the submarine to when the last one disappeared was twenty minutes, perhaps the most exciting I have ever spent. The men behaved well, and any excitement shown was due to over-keenness. The fo'c'sle guns and port battery fired well, the laying and training being good, but efficient spotting was impossible, due to the semi-daylight with the rising sun in our eyes and the minute size of the periscopes, which were an extremely small object and at first could scarcely be distinguished with the naked eye. The starboard battery were so engrossed in watching the firing of the port side that they were unable to open fire when the third submarine appeared on their side.

And this, and the fact that the 'Klaxon' alarms did not work, were the only incidents that could be found fault with. Contrary to my expectations, the officers all went to their groups without any of the muddle which the obstinacy of J Kiddle has so often caused in exercise actions. The captain made a speech after quarters, congratulating the ship's company on their prompt answer of the bugle when turned in, and their general behaviour. It was the most exciting incident I have experienced. Some people think we sank the submarine on the port side, but I am convinced we did not actually hit her at all; if we had done so, it would have been entirely due to luck. In consequence of this attack, the line of blockade was changed from the north of the Shetlands (Muckle Flugga), north-westerly across to the Faroes, and then across to the Norwegian coast. Only one ship captured today, and that by the battleship *Russell*. Details of the loss of *Hawke* received; seventy-five officers and men saved.

Wireless messages say that HMS *Undaunted* and a flotilla of destroyers destroyed four German destroyers at the mouth of the Scheldt. She was only commissioned two months ago. This is a pleasing set-off to recent losses. On our patrol all day; quite dirty weather.

NOTE ON THE LOSS OF HMS *HAWKE* (18 OCTOBER 1914, HMS *CRESCENT*)

Apropos of the loss of the *Hawke*, it is interesting to note that two hours before she went to sea on her last trip, Capt. Williams came on board to ask for two days extra in harbour to repair his engines. This was refused as he could still do ten knots. In order to obviate the danger of submarine attacks it is customary for all our warships to leave and enter Moray Firth at full speed, minimum speed seventeen knots. The *Hawke* could not possibly at forcing power do more than just over half this speed. Capt. Williams realised the extreme danger of this, hence his personal appeal to the admiral. His last words to the flag lieut. when leaving the QD of the *Crescent* were 'it is pure murder sending the ship with over five hundred officers and men on board to sea in this state'.

His words proved correct in a disastrously short space of time. The story of the *Hawke* being stopped for boarding a ship, when hit by the submarine, was invented by the Admiralty to prevent unpleasant questions and a public outcry. She was attacked going out of the Moray

Firth at maximum speed *viz.* ten knots, and an extra five knots would have probably saved her. Those five knots could have been attained by an extra two days in harbour.

The above is strictly confidential, and were it discovered at the present time would lead to my dismissal from the service, but it is a point that may be of interest in future years.

Monday 19

On our patrol all day between Muckle Flugga and Foula. None of the required submarine oil ships were met with, and none others were boarded, although I think we might have done so with advantage, as I am in favour of stricter measures. The captain evidently does not want to give submarines a chance of firing at us when stopped, although we probably shall not meet any here. Yesterday's affair proves [sic] the theory that the German submarines do not work singly, but in groups of three or more. The battleships of the First Fleet are now based jointly at Tobermory and Stornoway, but submarines are reported in the Minch, so they will probably move south to Greenock or somewhere in the Clyde. Reports say two Zeppelins and aeroplanes have been seen over the Moray Firth coming from the west of Scotland. Personally I don't believe them and think they are the imaginings of overwrought brains. Transferred two signalmen to the *Alsatian*.

Tuesday 20

Had a row with 'Torps'. Divisional drill, loader and deflection teacher in the forenoon. Fitted up the anti-aerial three-pounder on the QD capstan. The mounting has been built to the commander's design by the armourer and his crew. The *Dryad* is once more under our orders. She joined at noon and reports having sunk a submarine off Scapa southern entrance, which is excellent news. There is also a rumour that four other German submarines have been sunk. The destroyer *Hope* has been ashore off Mull, and is to be docked in the Clyde. German submarines reported off South Ronaldsay, Wick, Banff, Peterhead and Aberdeen.

We have abandoned the North Sea for big ships, and are only leaving destroyers, submarines and aircraft there. The German submarines are very daring; two German minelayers have laid mines in the Firth of Forth; it is to be hoped they will be caught. After quarters, firing tests were carried out with the anti-aerial three-pounder, which were most satisfactory, the mounting holding splendidly, in spite of the pessimism of 'Guns'. Maxim (anti-aircraft) drill after the three-pounder firing. The Northern Lights are very bright at night now, and so is the comet, which has an exceptionally fine tail.

Wednesday 21

Trafalgar Day anniversary. Very bad weather. *Endymion* captured grain ship. At 4pm we sighted a big petroleum ship with no colours, seventy-three miles NNW of Foula, and altered course to examine her. Suddenly several shells whistled over the masts. The apparently unarmed merchant ship was armed with three new 41-inch guns, and was evidently a commerce marauder and also a submarine oiling ship. We sounded off GQs at once, and 'Guns' decided to use the after-control, but before we were ready she had fired several rounds, but owing to the big swell her shooting was bad. One shot cut the port main shroud and passed through the maintop, and another cut the forestay. Then we opened fire at seven thousand yards, and more by good luck than good management hit her in the bows first time. This apparently set alight an oil pipe, for she burst into flames, and after we had fired another salvo, which went over and to the left, she hoisted a big white flag as a token of surrender. It was too rough to lower a boat, so we signalled to her in the international code to consider herself a prize. She managed to put out the fire in about twenty minutes, and then we convoyed her to five miles north of Muckle Flugga, where we told the *Dryad* to take her into Lerwick.

Thursday 22

The *Dryad* rejoined at 7am and reported the prize (now safe in Lerwick) to be a Norwegian steamer bought two months ago by Germany, to be used primarily as a long-distance submarine depot ship, and has very likely been used by those in the west of Scotland. She has been badly holed in the bows, and it is unlikely that it will be considered worthwhile repairing her. The loss of our forestay means that we shall have to remove one of our wireless aerials, as the strain on the foremast will otherwise be too great, and consequently our wireless range will be reduced from 1700 to 250 miles; this will mean less news and only transferred communication with the C-in-C. It was very exciting yesterday when we were fired on. None of us have been under gunfire before. I was in the gunroom having tea at the time, and was too busy to notice much else when the bugle sounded off GQs for action. Detached the *Dryad* again 11am, and in the evening she sent a message to say she was on shore at Offness Skerries; two destroyers were ordered from Lerwick to go to her assistance, but owing to the very big sea running nothing could be done; anyhow, with the rise of the tide she managed to get off at 4pm and is proceeding to Scapa to repair damages. A very nasty gale got up during the night, and yesterday's bad weather is really far worse today. Made an attempt to get a sight, but all efforts were absolutely futile. Two of the forward funnel guys carried away, and it is considered possible that the funnel may topple over, as the sea is so big, like those of the *Edgar* of this class did ten years ago in the Bay. Two stokers run in for gambling. AJSR in the soup for not discovering them during 'rounds'. John Kiddle very objectionable. Rigged a temporary forestay.

Friday 23

The sea got very big in the night, and when we altered course at 10.45 we heeled to about 45°. Everything got adrift; chairs, tables, chests and boxes went careering all over the place. In all the offices everything was chaos. In the gunroom the table was smashed in half. Two anchors broke loose on the booms and swept about the upper deck. All the guns on the starboard side under water. Fifteen casualties on deck and twenty-one in the engine room. Nine cases of concussion. All the gear in the gunroom smashed, including gramophone and records, and the majority of the crockery in the ship. The weather improved at daylight. GQs and shrapnel tests; three boxes did not explode, due either to damp, old age or faulty construction. They will be returned to the dockyard. A marine reservist got three days' cells for fooling the Censor.

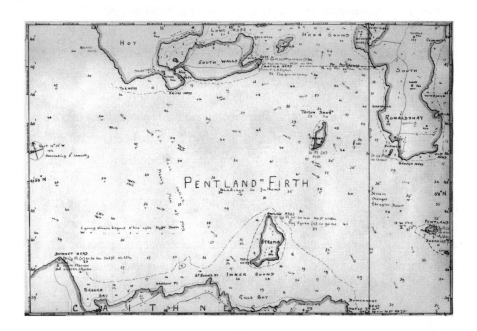

Saturday 24

At sea on our patrol as usual all day. Assistant-Paymaster Cockrem, clerk to the secretary, went sick for a day, and I took on his job, and so learnt all the most interesting confidential signals. Heard that the *Badger* has sunk a German submarine. Two more British submarines lost, the *E3* and another of B or C class, in the Pentland Firth. The Dover Patrol flotillas and monitors *Severn, Thames* and *Humber* are doing the most excellent work on the Belgian coast harassing the Germans' right wing, and have been unsuccessfully attacked by German submarines.

Boarded two steamers, but nothing of interest; one was Russian with rubber goods and stationery from Brindisi to Archangel, and the other Norwegian with fish from Newfoundland to Tromsø.

Sunday 25

Left the squadron at midnight and entered Busta Voe at 7am. Busta Voe is an inlet in the west of the Mainland of the Shetlands, a deserted spot that is being used as a naval base now for our squadron. It has a post office, a kirk and four houses. It is twenty-two miles north-east of Lerwick, but thirty miles by road. Very pretty scenery with the sun rising over the hills. Found the *Alcinous, Endymion, Theseus* and *Zealandia* in. Midshipmen are now going to take OOW in harbour to relieve the wardroom officers. The captain says it is a compliment to the efficiency of the midshipmen in this ship that they can be given this responsibility so soon. Captain of *Zealandia* came on board at 11am, and they put to sea at 1pm. Landed at two to climb a hill and examine the surrounding country. This is a very desolate corner of God's earth. Our picket boat to patrol harbour by night. Tottenham in charge for first watch, ran on shore three miles from his proper station, and the commander signalled him to stop there till he could get off, as a punishment for making a bloody fool of himself. He got off at 1am.

Monday 26

Started to coal ship at 6am in the dark, raining hard, strong wind and very cold. What a happy life! Seven hundred and fifteen tons the biggest coal we have had this commission. Still, in spite of adverse conditions, coal came in at an excellent rate, and by 3pm we had finished. An excellent performance, which left everyone dead to the world. The *Edgar* came in for two hours in the forenoon to land ten hospital cases, which are being sent to Lerwick by ambulance. *Theseus* left at 7pm. In addition to the picket boat by night, two armed trawlers patrol the mouth of the Voe by night and day. All luxuries have run out again, so we are once more on bare rations, and are likely to be so, as Lerwick is so far away. No mail.

Tuesday 27

All sorts of weird rumours floating round about Prince Louis of Battenberg being in the Tower with Mrs Cornwallis-West as a spy. If this is true it must be a terrible calamity in our midst, but I don't believe it. Also rumour that four German submarines were sunk in Scapa Flow. The patrols and monitors under Rear-Admiral Hood still doing excellent work on the Belgian coast. Mail arrived. First for a very long time. Very welcome provisions and letters. Heard that LLG is a prisoner in Germany. Much news of interest. I was employed all the morning constructing new charts of Lerwick, Kirkwall, Scalloway and Stromness harbours from the Admiralty originals for the use of officers taking prizes into these places. Landed with Tottenham in the afternoon and called on Mr Fairburn, the local UF padre. Found him and his wife to be most hospitable and the direct antithesis of the average Scotch 'meenister'. They lent us two rods, and we spent the afternoon fishing in the Delting Burn and had jolly good fun, catching eleven between us, some nearly half a pound. Brown trout, of course, are out of season, but there are sea-trout, the season for which in the Shetlands goes on till 16 November. Three suspicious men were seen up in the hills examining the harbour with spy-glasses, and although they were chased they made good their escape. The *Grafton* came in at midnight. We have established a signal station on shore to be manned by signalmen of the successive ships as they come in to coal. It is in direct communication with Lerwick by telegraph. A store depot is also being established in an old barn, and Mr White, the factor of the Busta estate, has been appointed naval store officer by the authorities at Lerwick.

Wednesday 28

Got on shore at 11am with Johnstone, Tottenham and Mr Kiddle. Johnstone motorbiked, Mr Kiddle rode, and DFCLT and I biked seven-and-a-half miles along the Hillswick Road to Johnny O'Mann's Loch and fished all the afternoon, but did not have much luck, only getting thirteen between us, all small. Got back to the ship at 6pm.

This part of Shetland must be one of the most deserted parts of the British Isles, as we sighted no human habitation the whole seven-and-a-half miles between Johnny O'Mann's Loch and Brae at the head of Busta Voe. The scenery among the hills and voes is very rugged, wild and fine indeed. No trees or vegetation, just rocks with a little smattering of grass, moss and thin heather. The first lieutenant and Mr Bacon went shooting all day and got some rabbits and a few snipe. The *Endymion* left at daylight. At 7am the whole of the Third Cruiser Squadron came in; a secret court-martial was held, sentence carried out, and the Cruiser squadron put to sea three hours later. They anchored in Olna Firth, the adjoining voe to Busta. The prisoner was a reserve paymaster who had been discovered to be a German spy, although an Englishman. He had attempted unsuccessfully to communicate with the Germans and was caught. He was proved guilty by naval court-martial, sentenced to death, and shot half an hour after. This is the way we do things in the service. His crime was a blot against the honour of all naval officers, but it must be remembered he was only temporarily entered for the war two months ago and was not a real NO at all. An attempt has been made to lay mines by trawlers off the west of the Shetlands, but owing to the vigilance of the trawler, motorboat and yacht volunteer patrols, the attempt has been most opportunely frustrated.

Thursday 29

Commander Startin, RNR (late Admiral, RN), motored over from Lerwick to see the admiral. It is very sporting of all these retired admirals to volunteer as lieutenants, lieutenant-commanders, and commanders for active service in the RNR and RN Volunteer Reserve. The *Royal Arthur* came in to coal at 10am. We shortened in to two cables. Raynes came on board (he is intelligence officer in the *Grafton*), and 'Guns' of the *Grafton* came over to see our 'Guns'. Weighed and proceeded out of Busta Voe through Swarbacks Minn to the open sea at 1pm. Made for our patrol off Muckle Flugga. Saw several suspicious trawlers, but took no notice, as the *Endymion* is chasing a suspicious steamer at full speed, and we hoped to cut her off, as she was outsteaming the *Endymion*. We thought her probably to be that ship reported to have been minelaying off the Shetlands. We got up to eighteen knots in an hour, which was a feather in the cap of the engine room.

Friday 30

The *Endymion* came up with the ship at 1am on the morning of the 30th, and shortly afterwards both we and the *Edgar* arrived. The ship proved to be the Norwegian liner *Bergensfjord*, which, by the way, we boarded some weeks ago. She had a cargo of contraband foodstuff on board for transference overland to Germany, so she was sent into Kirkwall as a prize under the convoy of the *Endymion*. A large number of German reservists were found on board from the United States, and the German consul-general of Seoul, the capital of Korea. The president of the Norwegian Parliament was also on board, and his detention may lead to trouble with Norway. Returned to the Muckle Flugga patrol at daybreak. GQs all the morning. Extremely cold weather. The flag-lieutenant and Lieut.-Commander Bacon, RNR, went sick with bad influenza.

Saturday 31

At sea on our patrol all day. Very bad weather as usual. Big sea running, squally and very cold. 'Guns' and Mr Beasley added to the influenza sick list. In his absence I had to do 'Guns' duties, and had a fearful row with Mr Lowman, who tried to be too officious, also with Mr Croughan. Wireless news reports that Lord Fisher has succeeded Prince Louis of Battenberg as First Lord of the Admiralty. Fisher is a strong man, though unpleasant and rather a cad; he won't be bossed by Winston as Prince Louis was. Heard that we had declared war on Turkey at 5pm. The Turkish Fleet with the *Goeben* and *Breslau* has bombarded the town of Odessa.

NOVEMBER

Sunday 1

On our patrol all day; filthy weather. Stopped the Danish liner
U.S., but let her go as she was outward bound. I relinquished my
duties as assistant gunnery officer and took up those of senior
watch-keeper, being relieved by WSH. We are all changing round as
three months is up.

Monday 2

The weather up here is so uniformly bad that in future I shall only
remark in my diary when it is good, which I expect it will be very
seldom, as the only variation to the prevailing south-west gales with rain
and big seas is a biting cold northerly wind coming straight down from
the Arctic Circle and Spitzbergen. No GQs. Thanks for small mercies!
Had a long chat with Bacon, who with 'Guns' and Beasley has returned
to duty from the sick list. Made up the row I had with Mr Lowman, the
gunner. The *Hermes*, old light cruiser, has been torpedoed and sunk by a
submarine off Dunkirk.*

Tuesday 3

Persistent rumours that four German submarines have been sunk in
Scapa Flow and that the Dreadnought *Audacious* has been torpedoed;
both are unconfirmed.† Left patrol at 4am and went into Busta Voe
at 8am to get mails and land a hospital case. Found Third Cruiser

---

* HMS *Hermes*, a sea-plane tender, was sunk by the German *U-27* while
transporting aircraft.

† Although only commissioned in 1912, HMS *Audacious* did not survive her first
conflict, and was sunk on 27 October 1914 after striking a mine off the northern
coast of Donegal, Ireland. Initially the Royal Navy tried to keep the loss a secret,
officially listing the ship as in service during the entire war, but in the end this
proved to be futile.

Squadron, *Edgar* and *Theseus* in harbour. In harbour two hours and then put to sea back to patrol. A sudden wireless signal recalled us to Busta to coal immediately when two hours from land. A German battle squadron has put to sea and everything is on the *qui vive*. Admiral Beatty despatched to warm the Deutsche Breeches. The whole seven ships of the Tenth Cruiser Squadron arrived before midnight and coaled rapidly, all except the *Grafton*, *Theseus* and *Crescent*, who are stopping in to repair small engine defects. The advent of 'Jackie Fisher' to the Admiralty in place of Prince Louis of Battenberg will probably put a stopper on Winnie's gambols. Fisher is a strong man, whatever else he may be, as is stated by those who are not in the 'fishpond'. Personally I know nothing of the split, and take no sides. I don't think anyone does in wartime. Very pleased to turn in at 11pm; been on duty since 3am. The secretary and a midshipman from the Gibraltar dined in the gunroom. The wardroom had a very merry evening.

Wednesday 4

No news from the scene of the German squadron's reconnaissance from Heligoland. The Turkish trouble looks embarrassing, as they are preaching a holy war. The *Cumberland*, *Duke of Edinburgh* and *Black Prince* have been ordered to Alexandria. The *Minerva* has done good work bombarding Turkish forts in the Red Sea, and a squadron of Turkish gunboats will be confronted there by the *Espiègle* and the *Odin*. I was very nearly sent to the *Minerva* at the outbreak of the war, and instead of freezing just outside the Arctic Circle, I should have been sweltering in the Red Sea. It is just about time some of these raiding cruisers were nipped in the bud. They have got plenty to 'veer and haul on', certainly, but we have stacks of ships after them, and they are doing a lot of damage to our trade. Coaled ship, commencing 8am. Took in 450 tons; finished midday; excellent work. The *Edgar*, *Gibraltar*, *Endymion* and *Royal Arthur* put to sea before 10am. Admiral Colville has transferred his headquarters from Lerwick to Kirkwall, and is now senior naval officer in chief command of the defences of the Orkneys and the Shetlands.

Thursday 5

German submarines are operating round Land's End. AP Gallichan, RNR, has been appointed to a shore billet under the admiral commanding at Rosyth, and his place will be taken by AP Cockerill, RNR, an old friend, who has come back from the *Royal Arthur*. Took in stores from the *Alcinous*. The *Grafton* left at 7am. It has been decided to erect a small fort on Muckle Roe, and an observation station with buzzer at the entrance of Swanbacks Minn, also a permanent harbour officer is to be appointed, so that Busta Voe will be quite a swagger naval base. Boom defence is also to be fitted if possible. All the postal authorities in the Shetlands have been arrested on charges of treachery, so for the present all mails are held up. Mr Wilson was arrested on shore as a spy, being an eccentric-looking fellow, so arrested the PC for impertinence in retaliation. Rear-Admiral Beatty failed to catch the squadron from Kiel, and they scuttled back to Heligoland after attacking the *Halcyon* and sinking a submarine. It is a long lane that has no turning. The hospital ship *Rohilla* has run on a rock and foundered off Newcastle. Things doing badly at present.

Friday 6

I took on the duties of navigator's assistant ('Tanky') in harbour, instead of harbour watch-keeping. Spent the day correcting charts from *Notices to Mariners*. Also put some gunnery entries in my journal. German cruiser *Yorck* sunk by a mine (one of their own) off Wilhelmshaven. Rumours of an unsuccessful naval engagement off the Chilean coast. The *Grafton* came in again 7am. Some of our old torpedo boats have been told off for patrol work round the Shetland coasts, scouring the numerous voes and sounds. It has now rained for nine consecutive days

without stopping. Mr Bacon and Dr Maxwell dined in the gunroom.
We celebrated Guy Fawkes Day a day late (as we were too busy
yesterday); four bottles fizz. Got up at midnight to assist intelligence
officer, owing to press of signals.

Saturday 7

HMS *Dryad* came in with mails and washing for Tenth Cruiser
Squadron at 10am, the first washing we have had back for ten weeks.
Went on shore with LEJ at nine and fished in Delting Burn all day.
Had a good day; caught eleven sea-trout, several about quarter of a
pound. Johnstone got a nice one of just a pound. We have had five
days in harbour in order that engine room defects may be made good.
The senior engineer says that we shall probably go to sea on Monday
morning. *Theseus* went to sea back to patrol at midnight. The battleships
of the First Fleet are once more back at Scapa Flow.

Sunday 8

Captain Gillespie, RMLI, joined ship for wireless and intelligence
duties. Officially confirmed that the *Audacious* was torpedoed sixteen
days ago. *Royal Arthur* came in at daylight. All the *Dryad*'s ship's
company came on board to church. Route march in the afternoon. Saw
Raynes, Pears and Lafitte from the *Grafton*. Hoisted in all the boom
boats before dark.

Monday 9

Weighed and left harbour 7.45am. A strong gale with unpleasantly big
sea from the south-west running outside the shelter of the land. We
get the full force of the Atlantic gales here. We have shifted our patrol
line to the westward considerably, and the armed liners have been
told off to patrol north of the Faroes to prevent ships passing between
the Faroes and Iceland. The Admiralty have sold off a large number
of the old pre-Dreadnought battleships for foreign service, and they
will be attached to the various cruiser forces abroad, to act as fortified

mobile bases for these cruisers. By the way, the battleship *Canopus* should have been with Rear-Admiral Craddock at Valparaiso, and this would have made a considerable difference.

After reading the treatises and observations of several prominent civilian so-called experts in naval matters on the naval situation at the present, it seems to them to be an established fact, of which they are all convinced, that our Fleet is conducting a close blockade of the Heligoland Bight and German North Sea coast. In fact, a blockade of the type that Nelson exercised before Toulon preceding the Trafalgar campaign.

It would surprise them to know that the blockade is of the 'open' type, advocated by Lord Howe; or, even more so, Lord Howe's reason for favouring this type was that the efficiency of his material might be kept up. Jellicoe's reason is a knowledge that in face of hostile submarines to keep capital ships before Heligoland would be sheer folly.

The aforesaid journalists prate of the impossibility of our abandoning the North Sea. It would surprise them to learn that the North Sea has, to all intents and purposes, been abandoned by our capital ships for weeks, except for a few patrol flotillas of old gunboats and older torpedo craft, helped by yachts and launches along the coast.

The naval disposition of the Grand Fleet at present is as follows:

Before Heligoland, in the Bight, there is a constant patrol of our most modern submarines, relieving each other in turn from Harwich. Otherwise there is not a British warship in the North Sea, except for the small coast patrols before mentioned. East coast naval bases and the mouth of the Thames are defended by port flotillas of submarines and small torpedo craft, assisted by sea-planes. The Straits of Dover are closely blockaded by swarms of small craft, French and English, submarines and torpedoes, but even these cannot prevent the occasional egress and ingress of German submarines. Off the Belgian coast there are three monitors and some pre-Dreadnought battleships, with gunboats and torpedo craft harassing the enemy's flank on shore.

The Second Fleet and older battleships are based at Portsmouth, Portland and Plymouth and, except for occasional excursions to the Belgian coast, are unoccupied.

The four battle squadrons of most modern battleships (about thirty-two) and the Second Battle Cruiser Squadron – the Grand Fleet proper – have for the past few weeks been stationed for safety in the Hebrides, but have now returned to Scapa. The passages between Shetland, Fair Isle, Orkney and the mainland are guarded by the First Fleet destroyers and light cruisers; while in Cromarty are the First Battle Cruiser Squadron under Beatty, ready to dash out directly the Heligoland submarines report by wireless of the Germans leaving port. The original Admiralty scheme was to blockade the Shetland–Norwegian passage, but owing to the danger of attack by submarines using the Norwegian fjords as a base, it was decided on 19 October to shift the line of blockade from the Shetlands to the Faroes, and this was to be carried out by the Second, Third and Tenth Cruiser Squadrons. Thus all ships, wishing to evade the British blockade, would have to pass north of the Faroes, and near to Iceland, then along a far northern parallel eastward, and then down, hugging the Norwegian coast. It was considered improbable that any ships would attempt or succeed in doing this.

The news of a naval battle off Valparaiso is now official. The armoured cruiser *Good Hope* (Rear-Admiral Craddock), with county-class armoured *Monmouth*, the light cruiser *Glasgow* and the armed liner *Otranto*, were defeated by the *Scharnhorst* and *Gneisenau*, armoured cruisers, *Nuremberg* and *Dresden*, light cruisers. The *Good Hope* and *Monmouth* were destroyed.* The result, though disappointing, is by no means disastrous, and should not be interpreted as such.

---

* The Battle of Coronel took place on 1 November 1914 off the coast of central Chile near the city of Coronel. This was Britain's first naval defeat since the Battle of Lake Champlain in the War of 1812.

Tuesday 10

Big gale blowing, with very large seas and squalls. I had a most
pleasant middle (I don't think!). Came down at 4am to find my
hammock sopping with water, a whole sea having come down the
hatch. Slept on the deck, and was again sopped with water. Excellent
news received from the Admiralty at noon, stating the light cruiser
Sydney has sunk the light cruiser *Emden* at Keeling, Cocos Isles;
and the light cruiser *Chatham* has run the *Königsberg* to earth in
German East Africa. At 4pm we heard that three German minelaying
cruisers will attempt to lay mines off Foula tonight, and we with
the *Edgar* and *Theseus* are to attempt to destroy them. Everyone
on tenterhooks and very excited. Too rough to eat ordinary meals;
everything a stand-up picnic.

Wednesday 11

A sensational night.* At twelve the commander sounded the alarm by
accident, and in two-and-a-half minutes every gun was manned and
everything ready for immediate action. Very disappointed that there
was nothing doing, but the test was most satisfactory. Two hours later
we heard that the minelayers had put back to Wilhelmshaven owing
to the heavy gale. During the night the gale increased in intensity,
accompanied by squalls of wind and hail. Big seas came in and swamped
everything.

At 4am a signal came from the C-in-C telling all ships to take shelter if
possible, but by that time we were forty miles WNW of Foula, and it was
impossible. With the gale increasing, the temperature and glass steadily
dropped.

---

* Admiral Sir Dudley de Chair later described this storm as 'the most appalling
gale I have ever experienced in all my years at sea, and we really did not think the
old ship would weather it'.

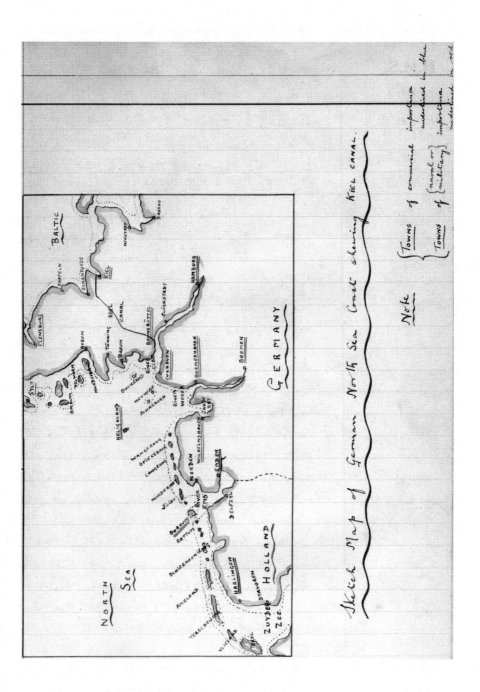

Sketch Map of German North Sea Coast shewing Kiel Canal.

Note { Towns of commercial importance underlined in blue
{ Towns of (naval or military) importance underlined in red

The gale now blowing started about 2am on Monday, 9 November, increasing gradually for fifty hours in intensity until it became a regular storm at 4am on Wednesday, the 11th. It raged with its maximum ferocity then for about eight hours till midday. During this period we waged a war against the elements of a most trying and arduous nature. For eight hours the wind was logged at 10–11, and the sea at 9–10 by the Beaufort standard. It was impossible to stand on deck against the raging wind, and huge seas swept over everything.

The storm came from the westward, and the seas were exceptionally steep and high, although uncommonly short for an Atlantic storm. This shortness made it most uncomfortable, as the ship had not time to rise to the seas, and consequently she took in tons of water, which swept over the decks.

The waves averaged, at the worst time, between forty and forty-five feet in height, and at times must have reached the phenomenal height of fifty feet; thus, considering the short length of the seas, it can be realised how steep the seas must have been. Squalls and gusts every ten minutes or so, accompanied by rain and hailstorms, increased the discomfort. The barometer dropped to about 281 inches, reaching its lowest at 7.30am, and fluctuating rapidly, and the cold was very noticeable.

Everything below was swimming in water, about four inches on the main deck, and regular streams through the hatchway cracks and gunport lids. All the flats and ammunition passages were also soaked. The admiral's quarters were drenched through and through, and he had to move into the captain's cabin. The wardroom was swamped. Everywhere a filthy smell prevailed. In the gunroom we got but little water, but being outboard the motion had its maximum effect. The ship rolled, tossed, and pitched tremendously, and everything was chucked about willy-nilly. Everything breakable like crockery was smashed, and chests, boxes, hammocks, etc., floated about from side to side, banging against everyone. When the signal came from the C-in-C at 4am for all ships to run for shelter, we were head-on to the gale, and after consulting the admiral and navigator, the captain decided that it would be impossible to turn and run before the gale for shelter, for fear of capsizing while broadside on, for even head-on we were rolling on an average 30°, sometimes going over as much as 40° either side. At 4.30am the starboard sea-boat (first cutter) was stove in, and half an hour later the port sea-boat (second cutter) was carried in and dumped on the booms, both davits carrying away. All the ready ammunition careered about the deck in most dangerous fashion. All the officers and ship's company were now roused, and the commander wanted to pass on extra lifeline to prevent the starboard sea-boat being lost altogether, as one of the gripes had carried away. The chief bosun's mate, the midshipman of the gun watch and myself, the midshipman of the watch (I had the morning watch), volunteered to get into the boat and pass the line. We managed to get into the boat after ten minutes' struggling with bowlines round us, but the commander could not get the sea-boat's crew on to the booms, so we were unable to get the line after all, and had to come back. Five minutes later the whole boat – davits and all was washed away by an extra big sea. Lucky we had left it before! Then two of the foremost cowls carried away, and all the others went later, except two, making an absolute shambles of the upper deck; a mass of ropes, wooden spars, bits of iron, cowls and projectiles rolling about in all directions, making it impossible to get about. Just before I went off watch at 6am the port sea-boat was smashed to atoms, and the fo'c'sle breakwater swept overboard. All such things as railings, etc., were swept away, and the quarterdeck and fo'c'sle were continually under the waves, and the batteries were knee-deep in water. I was thankful to get off watch, but rest or food were impossible, as all the galley fires were put out, and we munched chocolate and ship's biscuit, and then crowded into the decoding office and the after shelter deck, except when required for duties, such as clearing away wreckage, by the commander. The wireless aerials came untriced and streamed aft in the wind, thus cutting us off from communication. The dynamos were shut off and the ship lit by candles below. Owing to an accidental short circuit, you got a nasty shock whenever touching the metal round the wireless office. About nine a big sea took away the whaler, and it floated off most neatly into the sea, quite undamaged. Then the depression rails on the fo'c'sle were bent double, and then the biggest sea of all came. It smashed the fore bridge into smithereens, breaking all the glass and woodwork of the wheel house and chart room like paper. All the flags and signal books went by the board, but the signalman on watch escaped by a miracle. The quartermaster and helmsman were badly cut about the face and neck, and the officer of the watch and the midshipman and yeoman of the watch and messenger were isolated on 'Monkey's Island', and it was three hours before they were able to get down by climbing down the foremost mast ropes. All the gear in the chart house was smashed or lost, although luckily the deck log was saved. At the same time as this occurred the whole intelligence office was swept away from the fore shelter deck, with codebooks, signals and everything.

Captain Gillespie, RMLI, who joined last Monday, was inside it at the time, and everyone thought he was lost, but by an extraordinary piece of luck he clasped the starboard shrouds and did not go over the side.

The navigator and chief quartermaster now conned and steered the ship from the conning tower, as the officer of the watch was marooned on Monkey's Island, and the quartermaster and helmsman of the watch were injured. All watches were kept in the conning tower for the next twelve hours.

Everyone thought the foretop would carry away, and the after-funnel was very shaky, as two funnel guys snapped, but luckily both funnels and masts held, and except for the loss of the starboard fore range dial, nothing further was lost or destroyed of much importance.

During the worst of the storm we steamed eight knots (forty-two revolutions) in order to give steerage way, and could not go faster for fear of breaking the ship's back; even then we were making a leeway of about one knot.

About midday the glass began to rise, the squalls ceased, and the wind shifted to the north-west, we altering course accordingly. A watch of seamen was sent down to the stoke hold to relieve the wretched stokers a little, as the wretched men were having a slave's time of it.

The storm began now to gradually blow itself out, the wind shifting towards the northward, and becoming colder than ever, although not nearly so strong. At midnight things were far better, and at 2am on Thursday, the 12th, the wind dropped completely, the gale having lasted altogether three days. The sea was nearly as big as ever, but the captain decided to turn and run for port. There was one terrific roll when we turned, but once on our proper course we rattled off at fourteen knots for harbour and rest. A temporary wireless aerial was rigged up, and we learnt that the other ships in our squadron unable to shelter were the *Theseus* and *Edgar,* and both had been almost as badly treated as we had been, both losing several hands overboard, in which we were very lucky, as no one was lost, although several people were injured more or less.

The only other warships out were the battleship *Marlborough* and light cruisers *Nottingham* and *Falmouth,* but these managed to find shelter, before the worst came, behind Westray. The centre of the storm passed to the northward of us, and eventually must have vented itself on the Norwegian coast, while the southern limit of the storm must have been about Cape Wrath; thus luckily little damage should have been done along the Scotch and English coasts. At daylight on the 12th we sighted land and entered St Magnus Bay and steered for Swanbacks Minn, arriving at the entrance about 8.30am.

Thursday 12

Came up Swanbacks Minn and anchored in Busta Voe at 9am. In harbour for seven hours. Carried out as many temporary repairs as possible. Heard that even in harbour here they had a bad time, the *Alcinous* steamboat being sunk by the choppy sea. As we came to our anchor a heavy snowstorm broke out, and by nightfall all the surrounding country was white, being two or three inches deep in snow. Ronas Hill has been covered with snow for three days. An observation station with signal staff for communication with the harbour has now been constructed on Papa Little Island, commanding the anchorages in Busta Voe, Olna Firth and Aith Voe. Weighed and left for Scapa at 4pm. Big swell still running outside, and we had a most unpleasant time of it, as the ship rolled worse than ever, with the sea abeam from the NNW.

Friday 13

Reached Scapa at 7am and anchored off Weddell Sound to the southward of Cava Island. The whole of the First Fleet were at anchor off Flotta, and the Calf of Flotta, sheltering from the north-westerly wind. All the hills covered with snow. The admiral visited the C-in-C in the *Iron Duke*. A general signal from C-in-C congratulating the Tenth Cruiser Squadron on their successful patrol duties, which have been conducted in all weathers, and which he says are the most arduous being undertaken by any of our squadrons, but are nonetheless necessary, and their labours are fully appreciated by him although there may be no immediate recompense. All the First Fleet is pleased with our work. Everyone very pleased, as we thought the authorities might be apt to forget the poor old rag-time squadron away on its lonely northern patrol. We have been ordered to Greenock to overhaul after the storm. Snowing all day, very cold; all the hills several inches thick with snow. Had a gunroom row with the warrant officers. 'Torps' and Mr Bacon dined in the gunroom.

Saturday 14

Weighed and left Scapa Flow, going out through Hoxa Sound at 7.30am. Steered a course for Cape Wrath; encountered the usual bad weather, once outside the shelter of Hoy, big seas and frequent snowstorms. The Sutherland mountains looked gorgeous, the snow glistening in the occasional glimpses of sunshine. Went only eight knots so as not to reach the Minch before dark, as hostile submarines have been sighted again in the Minch, and we are to go through by dark. Rounded Cape Wrath 4pm and increased to fourteen knots after dark. Sighted three suspicious Swedish oilers off Stornoway; notified them to C-in-C, but did not stop. Ran through the Minch narrows between seven and eight and shaped a course through the Inner Hebrides for the Mull of Cantyre [Kintyre today].

Sunday 15

Passed Oversay Light at 2am, and then went over to the Irish coast to communicate by flags with a signal station there, as the Belfast wireless station has broken down, and we have a message for the SNO, Belfast. Then came across to the Mull of Cantyre, passed Sanda (where we saw Southend in the distance, and memories of old days came back), then on past Ailsa Craig and up the Firth of Clyde to the east of Arran Bute, and the districts round Rothesay, Dunoon and Wemyss looked very fine covered with snow. Ben Lomond, a great white mass towering away to the north, lost in the dark mists. Fearfully cold with a stiff south-east breeze and a choppy sea in the Firth. Came past Gourock and anchored off Greenock for the night at 4pm. Found the *Royal Arthur* and *Grafton* also at anchor, as they have been sent to refit also, leaving four ships up in patrol with Captain Thorpe of the *Edgar* as SNO. I hope we shall get some leave while the ship is in dock for her refit, and the sec seems fairly hopeful.

Monday 16

The pilot and tugs came alongside at 7.30am, and we proceeded up the Clyde. A lovely morning. Realised for the first time what a gigantic shipbuilding centre the long banks of the Clyde make. Just to mention a few of the biggest: London and Glasgow Shipbuilding Company at Govan, Beardmore's at Dalmuir, Fairfield Company, John Brown of Clydebank, Yarrow and the numerous yards at Glasgow, Scotstoun, Port Glasgow and Gourock. Passed several cruisers and destroyers building. Arrived off John Brown's yard at 8.45 and came alongside the basin jetty, preparatory to dry docking later on. All the dockyards are now under Admiralty superintendence, and all the authorities, with the captain of the dockyard, came on board to make out plans and lists for our repairs.

Leave for all the starboard watch and for officers. I went to Glasgow in attendance on the admiral to see the mail and store officers, but then he dismissed me, and I went off to call on Robert at his office. He gave me tea and was most hospitable in every way. Lieutenant Wilson dined in the gunroom. Learnt with the deepest regret of Lord Roberts' death.

Tuesday 17

Lieutenant GA Wilson appointed to battleship *King Edward VII.* The dockyard hands got well to work with our refit by midday, but no estimate can be made as to how long it will take. Leave in the afternoon; called on Robert Greig, Anna and Mrs Greig. Learnt that Mr Clarke, our navigator, is an old friend of the Sandhills people. The admiral and staff are going up to London for forty-eight hours with despatches, and on my arrival back at the ship he told me that I was to accompany him. Packed my bag at once. Left at seven, dined with the admiral and Mrs de Chair at their hotel, which was very kind of him. He also asked Johnstone, the second senior midshipman. Left St Enoch 11pm and travelled down to St Pancras, arriving the following morning. The admiral is accompanied by his flag-lieutenant, secretary and two clerks, and we had quite a good journey.

Wednesday 18

Arrived St Pancras 9am, and the admiral told me to be at the Admiralty by one. Went to 12, Cumberland Terrace, where Daddy and mother were staying. They were very pleased to see me. Went to the Admiralty at one. The clerk told me that the *Crescent* is going to be given a thorough refit and repair at John Brown's Clydebank yard, and the admiral very kindly told me to proceed on leave until receiving further orders, and said the refit would last about a fortnight. There is to be watch and watch leave for all officers and men during the refit, which will be very welcome after our strenuous job. The admiral is leaving for the north again immediately. Visited Aunt Do in the evening with Daddy and mother. She seemed very perky. Norman Forbes Robertson, whose house this is, dined at home. I have not seen him for years. His conversation is most amusing in its way! Norman Forbes Robertson is the brother of the famous actor Sir Johnstone and in the opinion of many is a more brilliant performer than his brother, and is certainly more versatile. He is a life-long friend of my fathers, and is intimately connected with several members of my family and is brother-in-law of my great friend George G Wilson. He is a remarkably clever man, and a thrilling conversationalist. He is a man full of emotion, and is always on the rattle. A long thin face, with a remarkably well marked and distinguished profile, he is undoubtedly handsome. He has had not the success of his more famous brother, and wears a worried expression. His acquaintances are remarkably varied and interesting and made up of all classes and professions. He married Louie, sister of GGW, and has five children.

Thursday 19

Got up late. Daddy and I called on Jack Russell and his wife, he is brother of my friend Arthur Russell. They have some sweet little children, two girls and two boys. Went in to the city with Daddy. Saw Jude Wise and Uncle John, had a very long chat with Uncle John. He seems in excellent form. Came home to dine after visiting Gieve, Matthews and Seagrove. My trunks and cases arrived from Portsmouth where they had now been stored. NFR dined at the Garrick with Claude Lowther;* he and Daddy wrote to the papers over the pension question. The Russian advance has been checked. There is a strong rumour in all quarters that the HMS *Audacious* has been sunk in Lough Swilly; I can hardly believe this, considering the signals we received with regard to the matter in the *Crescent.*

Friday 20

Lunched with Daddy and John Parish Robertson at the automobile club. Excellent lunch, and many cocktails before and after. JAR is now

---

* Claude Lowther was a well-known English Unionist politician and MP.

a 2nd Lt in the Hertfordshire Yeomanry, he was originally in the COL Yeomanry with GG Wilson, Arthur Grey, Arthur Russell, Ernest Baker, Bob Faber and Bob Kirby. EB has now also joined the ASC as 2nd Lt. Went down by the 4.15 to Canterbury, bought some oysters and supped at Westenhanger. All very surprised and pleased to see me. Mother visited P and J at Folkestone and came home later. I was also very late.

Saturday 21

Shot the Wickham Count shoot, very cold and windy. Shooting execrable. Five guns, Governor, Jack, Bing, Pongo, Baines and self. Hundreds of birds. Poor bag, six-and-a-half brace, three pheasants, I have three rabbits, two ducks, two pigeons. Lunched at the Rectory, tea at the Kelseys. Peg and Jim came home for a night at 3, and seemed very fit. I dined at home, and they thoroughly enjoyed the evening. Joko has got an awful 'pash' for me now (not permanent I expect), and fully lives up to her letters. She is a very pretty girl now, but her hair is still not quite it. I hope for some pleasant flirtations with her this drop of leave.

Sunday 22

Mr Oxlade wined about his bag again, what a damned nuisance he is. I hope the devil he gets his bag. Jimmy and I went around to Westenhanger to see Jackie who is not quite fit. In the evening I motored P and J back to their schools at Felixstowe. Miss White, Peg's headmistress, was very standoffish, but those at Jim's school were awfully nice. Joko came in the motor too and we had a great time together on the way home. Daddy had returned at midday, and he and mother dined at Westenhanger, Byron also there. Good evening I hope to God, the Germans have come out while the *Crescent* is in harbour.

Monday 23

Everyone here is in a state of unrest. A German aeroplane from Belgium is reported to have dropped a bomb in Canterbury and escaped unhurt. The news is strictly classified. Called on the Drakes, and had tea with Col., Mrs Baines and the boys. Little Andrew Baines is a splendid little chap. Byron had tea at Quaives. Mrs Drake talks Bertie's death wonderfully well. The Westenhanger crowd, Sophie and Byron came to dinner. Quite a good evening, all the girls being interested with my photographs of the *Cornwall*. HMS *Bulwark* blown up at Sheerness.*

Tuesday 24

Had tea at Westenhanger alone with Joko, and a very interesting flirtation as usual. We all dined at Westenhanger in the evening, but Daddy and I were rather tired. Olive is very anxious about Henry who is at Ypres. She leaves for Manchester tomorrow.

Wednesday 25

Mother and I went up to London in the morning; Uncle Jack and Cousin Sittie are stopping with Aunt Do at Kensington Grove, and I spent five hours there, lunch and tea. Uncle Jack seemed very well, and is rabid over the war. He and Cousin Sittie were very pleased to see me. Mother and I went down to Margate, and found the whole party over from Wickhambreaux. Norman is acting in a little piece over there, and we all went over to see him. Daddy was in poor form, and made me angry. Oysters, lobster and champagne on our return.

I went to bed early, but the others stopped up later till about 3.30! Joko has grown into a very pretty girl, but the old grumble remains, she has not got enough hair. What a pity it is. We are both rather taken with each other just at present. If I were four or five years older I might think of her seriously, but she is a few months older than I am, and will probably be married before I feel like settling down. She dreams of going on the stage, and might be a success as she acts well and has a nice voice.

---

* HMS *Bulwark* was reported to have been destroyed on 26 November 1914.

Thursday 26

Woke up late and had rather a rumpus with Daddy, and consequently stayed at home all day, wasting a precious day like an ass. Daddy went over to the shoot, taking Bing, Pongo, Baines and Gracie, Drake and the Dr. They got 15 oz pheasants, 6 oz partridges, three hares, seventeen rabbits, one pigeon, one duck, three woodcock, one moorhen. I wish I had gone as I should have thoroughly enjoyed it. What a fool I am to waste a day's shooting. Daddy came home in good form and we made it up.

Friday 27

Motored over to shoot again at Aldington. Daddy, myself, Jack, Pongo and Gracie, Baines, Drake and Selby Lowndes. Got nineteen brace 'pheasants', 3 oz partridges, I have five woodcock and twenty-four rabbits. Excellent lunch, thoroughly enjoyed the day. Shot Jack and old Pilcher, the farmer, by mistake. He was concealed behind a bush, still it was my fault. It did not really do him much harm. Had tea at Westenhanger. Uncle John, Aunty Connie and Capt. Orton-Palmer arrived for the weekend.

Sunday 29

Harold Wacher is a conceited swine and just now I loathe him. I suppose he is not really a bad fellow, a good doctor and a very clever amateur actor. His affair at present in full swing with Dolly. I make a point of blackguarding as he is a married man with children, but the real reason I dislike him now is that he is acting in a play with Joko and makes violent love to her. I, like an ass, am jealous.

Monday 30

Rather down in the mouth. Still, you can't really enjoy leave when you think of the trenches and the North Sea. Spent the day at Westenhanger with Joko. Went in to Canterbury in the evening for her rehearsals with the Wachers. Harold Wacher came out in the evening to rehearse with Joko, and I insulted him but he took it lying down. Dined at Westenhanger. Had a long chat with Joko. She is very discontented at home and she and Nita get on each others nerves dreadfully. She wants to leave home and go on the stage. She ought to get married as I think she would make a good wife and a sweet mother. If I were a few years older I am not so sure I might not. Told her some of my perplexities such as UJ and AC's ideas with regard to me and Esther. I also told Dora and her mother. No young man should marry under 30, but I am sure I shall fall.

DECEMBER

Tuesday 1

A much better day. Sophie left for London early. I motored to Folkestone with Joko, we had an excellent champagne lunch at the Metropole, which was terribly empty. Called on Peg and Jim at their schools and saw Jim playing football (by the way Miss White has humbly apologised for the contempt of last week). Took Doris out to Geronimo's and went with her, Joko and Jack whom we met in the cinema. Called on Miss Carey then motored home. Saw Frank Goodson (he should have gone to the Front). Said goodbyes all around, preparing for tomorrow's departure. Tootie arrived with Mother at Quaives. I am afraid I am rather neglecting darling Mother. I dined at Westenhanger. The Kelseys were there. Had a quiet evening with Joko. Very close together, but a tender farewell to all especially her. Long chat with Byron. All very depressed about old Henry at Ypres.

Wednesday 2

Left home at 9.15. Affectionate farewell to all at Westenhanger. Travelled up by the 10.40 to town with Mother. She tells me that the Robertsons are absolutely on the rocks again without a penny. I suppose Daddy will help them out. Mother is going to the manager of the 'palace' to try and get Jack a hearing. Joko cannot get on with Nita and thinks of going on the stage permanently. She is pretty sharp, but it is a hard life I am afraid. A huge family gathering at 12 Cumberland Terrace to bid me farewell. Besides Daddy, Mother, Aunt Adelaide, Billy and self, there was Norman Forbes Robertson, Uncle John, Auntie Connie, Esther, Aunt Maud, Bella Forshall, Auntie Ethel and Auntie Ruth. They all stopped to tea and Jack, Auntie's Maud and Ethel stopped the night. Esther looked extremely pretty. She has the most wonderful pink complexion I have ever seen. What an awful effort it will be having to marry anybody, as there are so many other nice girls left behind. I wish one could marry three or four wives. I left for Clydebank by the midnight from St Pancras.

Thursday 3

Arrived Glasgow St Enoch 9am and went straight down to Clydebank to join the *Crescent*. Found everything in pandemonium. She is to pay off tomorrow. The new Tenth Cruiser Squadron will consist of twenty-four armed liners, flagship the *Alsatian,* with Rear-Admiral de Chair still in command. All the gunroom officers of the *Crescent* are appointed to the *Alsatian,* and some of the wardroom officers as well. The *Alsatian* will be far more comfortable, as she is a fine liner, but it is the same miserable old patrol. Packed up everything of our belongings in the ship and left during the afternoon. Miserable wet weather. Went up to Glasgow again, after saying goodbye to all the officers who are going to other ships. Went to 18 Lynedock Crescent, to stop the night with Anna and Mrs Greig. Robert and Margaret came to dinner there, as they were going on to a lecture at the Royal Geographical Society afterwards. Anna and I went to the Glasgow Alhambra and saw Ethel Levey. Quite a good show, which I thoroughly enjoyed. Got to bed pretty early. Wrote to mother and Joko, Aunt Do and Christabel. I hear that Drs Buddle and Maxwell and Lieut.-Commander Oxlade and Bacon are not coming to the *Alsatian,* which is a pity.

3 December 1914   St Enoch, Glasgow

Dear Mother,

Arrived Clydebank early this morning, and found the
Crescent is paying off today for a long refit, which
will take some months; she is then going to be used as
an armed transport for troops during the war, and as
a training ship for boys afterwards, as her career of
active service is over. The admiral is shifting his
flag to the *Alsatian*. She was a liner before the war,
and is now armed as a cruiser; she is a fine big ship,
fast, and much more comfortable than the old *Crescent*,
though of course, as she was built for a liner, she has
no armour. I would rather have gone to one of the big
new battleships, but this is better than nothing, a
good deal. Nearly all the old cruisers of our original
squadron are now doing the same as the *Crescent*, and
are being supplanted by armed liners.

I am going to stop the night with Mrs Greig
tonight, and shall go down to Liverpool to join the
Alsatian tomorrow. Please tell anybody who is likely
to write to me that my address is now 'HMS *Alsatian*,
c/o GPO'.

I hope you got my wire in time not to send the keys
to the *Crescent*, as if you did it will be some time
before I get them. Have you found the card-case yet?

I hope the manager of the Palace will prove lenient
and lend you a gentle ear.

Very best love to all.

From

Toby

PS Please discourage people sending parcels, as the
Alsatian, having a far bigger coal capacity than my
last ship, only comes in to coal and get mails once a

```
month, and they say a chance of parcels being lost is
very large.
    The Alsatian is having more guns mounted, so I might
possibly get a few more days' leave before she goes
to sea.
```

Friday 4

Went to the Superintendent at the Central Station to try and get my lost warrant travelling money refunded. Then I went to call on Aunt Maggie Harvey. Robert's four daughters came to lunch – sweet little things. Left Glasgow at 2 by special train to Liverpool. Travelled via Carstairs, Carlisle and Preston. Arrived Lime Street Station at 9.30, and was then shunted round to Canada Dock. Arrived on board the *Alsatian* about 11 and found everything pandemonium. The staff confidential books arrived under the protection of a squad of marines with rifles and Glanvile with a loaded revolver, looking very fierce; he had slept all the way in the train, and any enterprising German could have snitched the lot. The *Alsatian* must be a palatial ship in peacetime. All is muddle now, as a large portion of the woodwork is being removed, and the most modern mark of 6-inch guns are being put in. Got an excellent meal on board and then turned in, in someone else's cabin – evidently having a night out. We shall be pretty comfortable here, I can see, but it will not do our training much good, as we ought to be in a battleship.

Saturday 5

Excellent breakfast. The captain came on board at 9am and gave us all leave again from noon until further orders when the ship is ready again for sea, which may be anything from three days to a fortnight.

Spent the morning trying to find my way about the ship; every luxury in peacetime – gymnasium, swimming baths, lovely suites of rooms, sitting rooms, lounges, saloons, etc. Much of this is being destroyed, but still even then she should be very comfortable. The ship is crowded with RNR officers, including eight RNR midshipmen. Lunched

on board and left Liverpool by the 2pm, arriving Euston at 6.10. Went
home to 12 Cumberland Terrace. Found them all at home, and 'Sweet
Alice,' as they call Lilian Hore. Very surprised to see me again so soon.
I am not any too keen on getting all this leave foxy, as I feel I ought
to be doing something more active. After the war, when I want leave,
I probably shan't be able to get it.

Sunday 6

Too lazy to get up early enough to go to Quaives. Spent most of the
day playing the pianola. In the evening we all went to a concert at the
Palladium; not much catch, but I quite enjoyed it.

Monday 7

Went down to Quaives by the 10.45 from Victoria to Bekesbourne.
Lilian Hore left early. Everyone very surprised to see me again so soon.
I feel quite hypocritical turning up again after all the loving farewells.
The Westenhanger crowd all in a ferment about the show they are giving
at the Canterbury Theatre, Thursday, Friday and Saturday, in order to
get funds for supplying tobacco to our troops at the Front. I think Joko
was really very pleased to see my ugly fizz again. We hit it off excellently
now. Saw Babs and Missie at the Kelseys. Supped *zu Hause* and went to
bed early.

Tuesday 8

Spent the day doing nothing. Bob turned up in the morning; he is on
sick leave from bad eyesight and expects to get invalided out. I advised
him to join the ASC, as Daddy will be furious if he does nothing. He
says George is very cantankerous and has been having the most awful
rows with everyone. I spent the afternoon at Westenhanger, Joko in a
rather bad mood. I pulled her up about her awful spelling. They have a
rehearsal on at Westenhanger tonight, and all the Wachers are motoring
over, so in the circumstances I refused their invitation to dine. Mother
came down.

Wednesday 9

Drove the pony into Canterbury in the morning and did some shopping, and went to have a tooth stopped by Westron, the dentist. Saw Nita; she had motored in with Byron to see about the dresses for their show, which they are all in an awful state about. Rehearsal at the theatre after tea. Joko and I supped together at the Rose grill room (lobsters and champagne) and then went on to see 'What-Ho Tango' at the theatre. Thoroughly enjoyed ourselves at supper. I am getting quite stupid about Joko just now. She is really quite pretty with cheeks and lips made to be kissed.

Thursday 10

Heard the news of the successful naval action off the Falklands.* I had heard rumours of this when in the *Alsatian* last week from the admiral's staff. Motored down to Ashford and picked up Daddy, Uncle John, Captain Orpen-Palmer (OK), and went to shoot at Smeeth; seven guns in addition to those above. Pelting rain all day ruined chances of good sport. Called on the theatrical brigade at the theatre, rehearsing in Canterbury, on the way home, and decided to come in and see the show tonight, which the Robertsons and Wachers and Kelseys are getting up to get money for a tobacco fund for the 'Buffs'. I have got the box tonight. So Daddy, mother and I motored in. The show consisted of three parts, first a play called 'The Patriots', then recitations by Harold Wacher, then songs and dances by the seven girls – three Kelseys, two Robertsons and two Champions. That little shit Crow, the manager, assisted by another crony, attempted to chuck me out for riotous behaviour, in giving tremendous applause; but, assisted by G Green, I crushed all opposition. We all supped on oysters and fizz at Harrison's afterwards. All the girls very tired. Margery Champion and Joko looked very pretty. I went and had a chat with Byron till 2am.

---

* Battle of the Falklands – after their loss at Coronel, this was a resounding victory for the Navy over Germany.

Friday 11

Had a wire telling me to rejoin noon Monday. A splendid morning.
Jack and I motored down with Drake to Cullen's cottage, where we met.
The others motored together. Auntie Connie and Lucy Godfrey, OK's
fiancée, motored from Godstone. Shot the Brabourne coverts. Seven
guns – Daddy, self, UJ, OK, Jack, Drake and Boosey, a friend of Jack's.
A very enjoyable morning's shoot, but in the afternoon it came on to
pelt, and we all got fearfully wet and cold. Found the girls very tired
still on arriving home and not keen on acting again. They hope to get
a better house tonight. I dined at home, and then when Daddy and
mother went to bed I went round to Westenhanger to meet them on
their return. Nita with a fearful headache. The show not a great success,
I am afraid.

Saturday 12

Started early and motored down to Smeeth. Met at Harringe Farm and
shot Birche's Huff in the morning and lunched at Smith's cottage. Shot
Rabbit Wood, Round Wood and Partridge Wood in the afternoon,
and also some partridge drives. A very amusing day, which we all
thoroughly enjoyed. Got fifteen brace pheasants, seven-and-a-half
brace partridges, four woodcock, eleven hares and seventy-six rabbits;
six guns: Daddy, self, Jack, Pilcher, Fuller (the estate agent) and Cullen,
Uncle J's keeper. All the three Pilchers are good chaps, the farmer being
most amusingly superior to his brothers. Motored home together. In
the evening Stanley and I went to Canterbury, supped at the Rose grill
room; he in excellent form as he thinks his khaki contract is coming off.
Then on to the theatre. I made it up with Crow. A very good house, and
easily the biggest success they have had. A collection amounted to £8.
We all went to the Kelseys at Wickham Court afterwards.

Sunday 13

Went round to Westenhanger early, found them all very exhausted
in bed. Daddy and mother went to London by the five. I spent the

day at Westenhanger with Joko. Olive returned. Said goodbye to the old people at the Rectory and to Stanley and Sophie, but owing to a mistake in the time could not go to the Kelseys. Very wet day. Bob lunched at Quaives. He is making desperate efforts to get into the ASC. I left by the 7.54 from Bekesbourne. Joko came to the station with me in the motor. I have gone the whole hog and am head over heels in love with her now. She is very sweet with me. The train was an hour late getting to London. Supped with Daddy at the Automobile Club, and got to bed about 1am.

Monday 14

Left for Liverpool by the 8.30 train, arriving 12.33. Rejoined the *Alsatian* in Canada Dock, found we are to sail tomorrow. Everything in a very muddled state on board, as they have not really finished fitting her out, but want to get us to sea quickly first. I spent a very dissipated day with WSH, JHC and LEJ, and spent the devil of a lot of money. Remembered to send Joko some nice chocolates. The Midland Adelphi Hotel is a gorgeous place, claiming to be the most luxurious in the world, including lounges, saloons, billiard rooms, tennis, racket, fives courts, American bars, swimming, Turkish and Russian baths, shooting ranges, etc. But it is damned expensive, as we found to our cost after various 'clover clubs', 'egg flips', Turkish baths, etc. Went to see 'My Harem' at the Olympia in the evening after a huge dinner, and then a sort of big public dance, in aid of some fund for Belgian relief. Arrived on board very late.

Tuesday 15

I turned out early at 5am to attend on the captain while we left harbour. Warped out of dock and made fast alongside Huskisson Wharf at 7am; left the Mersey at 8.30 and proceeded out into the Irish Sea for gun trials of the eight new 6-inch guns we have got. Some staff gunnery officers on board from Admiral Stileman's (SNO, Liverpool) staff. Anchored off the Mersey Bar at nightfall. We have eight RNR snotties.

I shall have a hard job as a senior snotty, with our eight active service fellows as well. The officers who have come on from the *Crescent* are Rear-Admiral de Chair, Captain Trewby, Lieut.-Commander Kiddle, Lieutenant Kenyon, Lieutenant Clarke, Lieut.-Commander Robinson, Eng.-Lieut.-Conimander Fletcher, Fleet Paymaster Lawford, AP Cockerill, RNR, Staff Surgeon Walker, Captain Gillespie, RMLI, all the midshipmen and no warrant officers.

15 December 1914   HMS *ALSATIAN* (AMC)

c/o GPO

Dear Mother,

Just a line while I can, as I may not have an
opportunity for some time of writing. I arrived here
all well yesterday with all my tins, etc., and spent
the day and most of the night on shore in Liverpool,
as they gave us further leave till 2am on rejoining.
We left Canada Dock at 5am, some of us a little sleepy,
as you may imagine, and have been testing our new guns
in the Irish Sea most of the day. The tests, we hear
whispers, are not considered entirely satisfactory,
and possibly we may have to return to dock again. So
it is just possible that I shall see Cumberland Terrace
before the North Sea, but it is unlikely; and we should
all be very disappointed to still further delay our
return to the rigorous patrol duties in the north. The
dockyard people had not nearly finished the ship, but
the Admiralty wish to get us to sea as soon as possible,
so everything on board is in a 'topsy-turvy' condition,
although nothing actually affecting the efficiency of
the ship is adrift. My job in this tub is one of four
decoding officers; one with plenty of responsibility,
as all the confidential codes and ciphers are in our
charge, and we have to code and decode all signals

received and sent by wireless. There is always one of us on duty, and frequently, when there is a press of signals, two, three or even all four are working together.

I do not like the job as much as the two I had in the *Crescent* (assistant gunnery officer and then assistant navigator), as although it is quite interesting being in possession of all the confidential news and secret signals, yet it is of no material help to me in gaining any technical experience and training in the various branches of the profession. We have got several RN Reserve midshipmen (apprentices in various liners in peacetime) on board, and they are rather uncouth in their manners and hardly what the world calls gentlemen, although I dare say most of them are all right really. However, they rub most of our active service people up the wrong way, and I shall have quite a nasty time preserving the peace in the gunroom, as I am still senior GR officer, there being no sub-lieutenants on board, worse luck.

By the way, in the cloak room at CT you will find an oilskin of mine, with a long gash in the skin. I should be obliged if you would mend it (the best way is with sticking plaster inside, or else like a puncture). You need not send it me, as I have another.

A merry Xmas to you all, in case I cannot write again. Please give Gertrude a wedding present from me, should she marry while I am away.

Very best love to Daddy, yourself, and all the family.

From

Toby

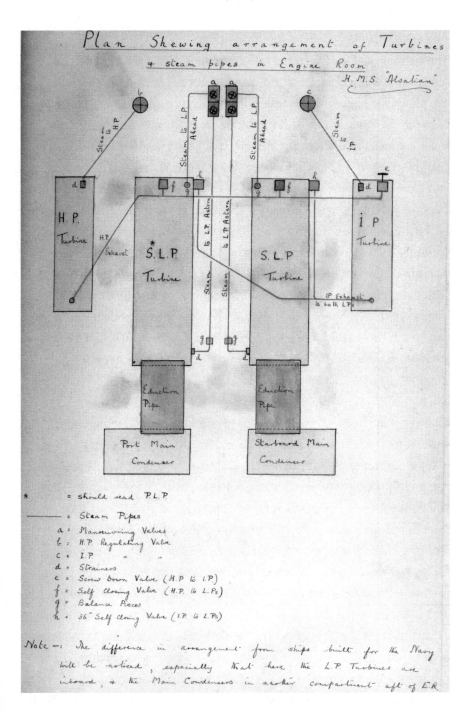

Plan Shewing arrangement of Turbines & steam pipes in Engine Room — H.M.S. "Alsatian"

* = should read P.L.P
——— = Steam Pipes
a = Manoeuvring Valves
b = H.P. Regulating Valve
c = I.P.   "   "
d = Strainers
e = Screw Down Valve (H.P. to I.P.)
f = Self closing Valve (H.P. to L.Ps)
g = Balance Pieces
h = 36" Self closing Valve (I.P. to L.Ps)

Note —: The difference in arrangement from ships built for the Navy will be noticed, especially that here the L.P. Turbines are inboard, & the Main Condensers in another compartment aft of E.R.

Wednesday 16

The gunnery trials of yesterday declared unsatisfactory, as much of
our framework was strained, so we shall not get back to our North
Sea patrol for some time. Came into the Mersey again and anchored
between the *Mauretania* and the *Lusitania,* with the giant *Aquitania*
towering away in dock in the direction of Seaforth. The dockyard people
and the gunnery experts had a confab, and it was decided the mountings
will have to be re-riveted, a job which will take about a week. The
Captain gave the ship's company a speech after quarters, and laid stress
on various points, complimenting the work of the *Crescent,* and saying
with pride she had done more sea time during the war than any other
warship of the British Navy. He realises he has a different crew to deal
with here, naval reservists instead of Fleet reservists (merchant sailors
instead of retired Navy men). At 8.30 we went into the basin leading to
Canada, Nelson and Huskisson Docks, and steamed alongside the outer
jetty, preparatory to the refitting of our gun-plates tomorrow.

Thursday 17

I believe that after all the *Audacious* was sunk in Lough Swilly, and
without loss of life; the Admiralty have done their best to keep it
quiet, even from the Navy themselves. I strongly deprecate this policy.
Apparently we have taken over two battleships building for Chile. They
will be renamed the *Audacious* and *Canada.* I hear that those lucky
dogs in the *Grafton* and *Royal Arthur* have gone to the *Marlborough*
and *Iron Duke*; perhaps we should be there were it not for the fact that
the rear-admiral and skipper seem to have taken such a fancy to us. At
present John Kiddle seems a great success in this ship as first lieutenant,
and is exhibiting qualities quite unknown in the *Crescent,* dormant,
evidently, since the days of youth. He has a very difficult job, as the reserve
commander does nothing, and Kiddle has to organise everything. At
present it appears 'Guns' is going to have a pretty slack time as gunnery
staff officer, not nearly so strenuous as gunnery-lieutenant of a ship. By a
funny coincidence, Roxburgh, my old Dartmouth friend, has a brother

on board as temporary surgeon. All the details of the bombardment came through. Scarborough, Whitby and Hartlepool were the towns to suffer.* The German naval force consisted of four battle cruisers, *Seydlitz, Moltke, Von der Tann* and *Blücher,* with some attendant destroyers. I am afraid that this raid will considerably shake public confidence in the Navy. I can quite understand their squadron getting here, but am very disappointed they were allowed to get back; and, in spite of the fog, I think they should have been caught. The action of the patrol destroyers, old as they were, was very plucky in attacking such a superior force, although, of course, it was bound to be unavailing. The dockyard people commenced work on our guns. Most of the people are having a pretty slack time in harbour, but our wireless is going all the time, so we coding officers have plenty to do, as signals are coming and going frequently.

Friday 18

It is rumoured that some German battle cruisers are going to try and escape, to carry on the work of Von Spee's squadron. The wireless petty officer is by repute a very clever operator. Apparently he discovered all the names of the German ships that were going to carry out the raid on Yarmouth, but was pooh-poohed by the flag-lieutenant, who did not send on the news to the C-in-C. Again on this occasion he found out the names of their ships, but not until after it was over. He does this by tapping their messages and then juggling with the numerous codebooks. The public seems to be very sick with the Navy. The dockyard authorities are still hard at work on our guns and deck plating.

Saturday 19

I got a touch of the flu. Decoding as usual. Lots of signals. I hear the *Karlsruhe* is coming north, and is to attempt to get back to Germany

---

* Targeting the munitions factories of northern England that were crucial to the war effort, the Germans initiated the first engagement of the First World War on British soil. The raid killed one hundred and twelve and wounded more than two hundred. Over three hundred and forty buildings were destroyed.

by going to the north of Iceland and then down the Norwegian coast;
so perhaps we shall fall in with her with luck. I went and did some
shopping in the town in the evening. We hope to get to sea by Tuesday.
Had some letters from mother, but several of our mails have gone adrift
by error to Inverness. I have not heard from Joko. I wonder if she has
written.

19 December 1914   HMS *ALSATIAN* (AMC)

c/o GPO

Dearest Mother,

I expect Peg and Jim are home by now. Wish them a happy
Xmas and give them my best love. I have not heard from
you yet, but all our letters were kept in London, as
they thought we had gone out for good, when really
we had to come back to dock to have our guns refitted
again; and we are going out for further gun trials
tomorrow.

The two parcels arrived this evening; I am returning
the oilskin for Daddy, and am also sending a sackful of
dirty clothes and linen, which, when washed, you might
keep at home. I have told you already it is no good
sending parcels now, as it is very unlikely I shall get
them (I only got those by luck). I am also sending a blue
Balaclava for Daddy.

The following articles I have left behind (it is no
good sending them now, but you might remind me to take
them next time I come):

My watch, some stiff white shirts (I don't seem to
have any here), and the shaving powder box.

Please thank Auntie Jessie for her letter; she wrote
me a very nice one.

A letter from you has just arrived. It is disgracefully
misspelt; why this lapse from your usual correctness?

You can pay the 20s. from Uncle Jack into my bank, if
you don't mind.

It is absolutely ridiculous of you to talk about
going as a nurse.

Your job is at home to look after the children, not to
go capering about making a damned nuisance of yourself.

Best love to you all, and a very happy Xmas.

From

Toby

Sunday 20

I have worked myself again up into a terrible state, because I have
not heard from Joko. I do not know whether she has written, or
whether her letter has been lost, but if I do not hear from her before
we sail on Tuesday, I shall never forgive her. Flu still most unpleasant.
Sunday divisions quite a funny experiment, none of the men being
very expert in 'dressing'. Had a long chat with old Kiddle. Dined with
Mrs Roxburgh and Dr Roxburgh at the Adelphi. She knows the Finnis
very well.

Monday 21

A large number of signals in the morning, so we had plenty to do. Went
on shore in the afternoon and called on Miss Housden, for want of
something better to do. I am not at all fond of Liverpool; it has rained
ever since I first came here! Miss Housden is a clerk in her father's office,
and looks fearfully ill. She was never a great friend of mine when at
Quaives, but she looked so miserable, and was in such a dingy office,
I took her out to tea. I had a chat and learnt some interesting details of
the Joko–Doris rivalry. What little cats women are. By the way I had my
long wished for letter from Joko this evening. It did not cheer me up so
much as I expected. They are going to do their entertainment again at
the Canterbury barracks. Perhaps the idea of the soldiers, Alan Hardy in
particular, gave me forebodings.

Tuesday 22

Heard from Byron. The much talked of gunroom pianola was hauled on board, after much swearing, gibbering and brain-waving during the morning. The staff gunnery commander came on board about midday, and at 1.30pm we left Huskisson Basin to go out to do fresh gun trials in the Irish Sea. But a thick 'home port' fog came down, so thick that we were obliged to anchor again in the Mersey between Birkenhead and New Brighton, and wait for it to clear a little. The tinkle of the fog anchor bells of the ships all around sounded very weird by night.

Tuesday evening, 22 December   HMS *ALSATIAN* (AMC)

c/o GPO

Dear Daddy,

Just a line to thank you very much for the gun and cartridges, which have arrived safely. I am afraid I shall be unable to ring you up, as I am very busy indeed. Everything is in a ferment, as we are feverishly trying to get to sea tomorrow. The weather outside is too gorgeous for words, and the sun makes our mouths water, but the docks are encased in an impenetrable fog of coal dust, sawdust, and every other sort of dust, also flour, paint, tar and every imaginable sort of filth. I shall be quite glad to get to sea again, away from it all. The dockyard people are still on board fitting up our new magazine protection and repairing the wireless gear, which is in a perpetual state of breakdown. To see us at present you would not think we could sail for a month, as none of the stores are stowed yet, and cases are lying helter-skelter everywhere. Still, the flag-captain has sworn to sail tomorrow, so I suppose we shall.

The other day, who should I see trailing across the docks but Ambrose, Mrs Preece and family, embarking in

a Yankee liner, the *Philadelphia*, for 'God's own country'.
Our letters have arrived at last, and I see in one of
mother's that May also sails by the *Philadelphia*. I was
too busy to speak to any of them. Please excuse the scrawl.

Very best love to all of you and good luck.

Toby

PS I may get some leave in June.

Wednesday 23

Left the Mersey 3.30am and anchored outside the Bar. The admiral and
staff dined with Admiral Stileman (SNO, Liverpool) and staff last night,
and then left overland for Scapa to confer with Jellicoe. We are going
to pick them up. Carried out our further gun trials in the forenoon,
and they were considered satisfactory, so dropped the gunnery staff
commander, and sent a mail ashore in the tug, and at 4.30pm got under
weigh for the north.

GQs for the first time in the afternoon. My GQ station is rate-keeper.
Very hard at work all day, as we had a tremendous number of code and
cipher signals all day. Did not turn in till past midnight.

Thursday 24

It seems awfully weird that this is Xmas Eve, and tomorrow is Xmas
Day – the first Xmas I have ever spent away from home. Good luck to
all at home! I hope they enjoy themselves. I cannot realise it is Xmas
myself. Still very busy, as the wireless gear was at it hard, and also fully
employed drilling the hands and instilling the warship feeling. Passed the
Mull of Galloway in the night, and ran out to the west of Oversay. Owing
to a mistake by the wireless operator, we narrowly missed running into
a minefield guarding the southern approaches to the Minch, and on
altering course ran right through another minefield two miles long,
without touching a mine. This is the second time this war I have been
in a ship which has come through a minefield unscathed. We passed
right to the west of St Kilda and the Flannan Isles to avoid further mines,

leaving the Hebrides far to the east. St Kilda looked very cold, dark, lonely and desolate. Altered course at about 11 to pass to the south of Rona, and steered to clear Cape Wrath and enter the Pentland Firth from the west. So far the weather has been very moderate but very cold.

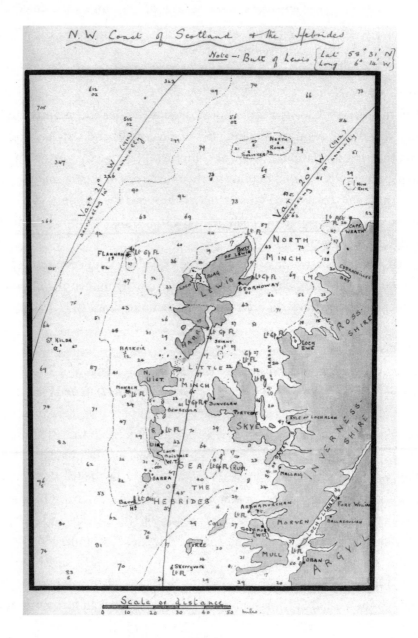

Friday 25

Came in through Hoxa Sound and anchored off Fara Island in Scapa Flow at 8.30am. The admiral and staff came on board immediately from the *Cyclops,* depot ship, in Long Hope. The First Fleet had already put to sea, except the dummy squadron of three ships, representing the *Audacious, Iron Duke* and the *Collingwood.* They are extraordinarily good models, made out of old tramps. Only a very experienced eye could distinguish them from the real thing; in fact, I don't believe I should have recognised them had I not been told. I don't quite know how they will be used, but there seem to be infinite possibilities. We left Scapa at 4pm and went out through Hoxa Sound and shaped a course for the Faroe Islands, which will be in the vicinity of our patrol. Very busy in the coding office all day. The Allan Line gave us an excellent Xmas dinner in the evening, and we had a musical time afterwards with the pianola and gramophone; and for the first time today I felt something like Xmas. Thank God the admiral let the Allan Line mess us after all, so the food is excellent.

Saturday 26

Boxing Day. Made the Faroes about midday. Our squadron consists of twenty-four armed liners, patrolling four patrols – A, B, C and D. A is between Iceland and the Faroes, B between Faroes and Shetlands, C between Shetlands and Orkneys, D off St Kilda. The *Alsatian* is in A. A nasty gale sprung up, and we had some very dirty weather, combined with extreme cold and interrupted our wireless. The admiral is living up to his nickname of 'Old Make-a-Signal', as he is making reams and reams of wireless messages to everybody. 'Flags' and Gillespie, the intelligence officer, at their wits' ends, as we cannot get any of the Admiralty messages through, and there is a congestion in the wireless office. All the coding officers working night and day.

Sunday 27

The admiral's signal craze continues, and we hardly get a minute's peace. The gale got far worse, and we were obliged to lie to in the shelter of the Faroes, off Strömsö. Thank God we are not still in the *Crescent*! The *Karlsruhe* is reported to be in the vicinity. The weather is so bad that I am afraid she may slip through. We are only getting five hours' daylight, and even that is pretty poor, dim sort of attempt. It gets light about 9.30 and dark at 2.30 in the afternoon again, and the sun is very rarely visible.

Monday 28

The weather moderated considerably. The precipitous snow-covered heights of the Faroes, terminating in the bold headland of the Mingganaes, looked most imposing. It is now considered a moral certainty that the *Karlsruhe* has managed to slip through in the long hours of darkness. There are twenty-four ships altogether in our squadron of armed liners. A patrol extends one thousand miles – forty miles a ship.

Tuesday 29

Forty miles a ship is a minimum, as six out of the twenty-four are always away coaling and reprovisioning, so it makes the patrol about fifty-five miles a ship, so it is easy in this weather for anything to slip through. Our coal will last about five weeks, so we ought to go back about the end of January. That is the advantage of this type of ship; a cruiser could never stop longer than a week for need of coal. Boarded a ship, a Danish vessel, outward bound, at 3pm, but let her go again. She had picked up a cargo of Faroe ponies at Vestmanna and was bound with mails for Reykjavík, Iceland, and Upernavik, Greenland. She is the first ship we have seen since we left Scapa five days ago, so that shows what a lonely spot this is. I spent all the day, when not on watch, in the engine room examining the engines. The admiral issued a set of war orders to the squadron which took three people five hours to code.

Wednesday 30

Gun drill 9am. A nasty dirty choppy sea, not big enough to affect a ship of our size much, but just enough to make boarding a very tricky process. Boarded another Danish ship, a trawler, and Ward, the midshipman of the boat, fell in the ditch and was nearly introduced to Davy Jones, but when nearly scuppered was hauled on board with a grapnel in the seat of his breeks, leaving a rent the size of a main topsail and more. He did not seem so grateful as he might have been. Wood managed to smash up the sounding machine very neatly, much to the navigator's joy. 'Guns' on the hop all day. Now that he is staff officer he has nothing divisionally to do with the ship, and is taking things easy, except for gunroom ferreting.

Thursday 31

GQs at 10am. Nothing occurred of any interest.

At midnight we observed the ancient Service custom, the youngest midshipman in the ship, Richardson, ringing sixteen bells in place of the customary eight, to ring the old year out and the new year in. All the officers in the ship turned up as usual, and the admiral shook hands all round, commencing with the captain and finishing with the junior head steward, RNR, the last officer in the ship. So ended the fateful year of AD 1914.

This completes the eighth consecutive year of my diary without a single day's gap. Of the eight years, I think that this just completed will be found to contain by far the most interesting reminiscences. For the first half of the year is taken up by my experiences during an extended cruise to various foreign ports in HMS *Cornwall* (with one exception I had never been abroad before); while the second half of the year is chiefly concerned with events occurring in and connected with my life, serving as a midshipman in HM ships *Crescent* and *Alsatian* in the Grand Fleet, operating in and around the North Sea during the opening months of the greatest international conflict the world has ever seen.

Several events of interest have occurred, and these I have recorded with as much accuracy as possible. Much of the knowledge contained herein is, at the time of writing, absolutely confidential, for it is strictly prohibited that officers or men of HM Navy on active service should keep diaries, which would in all probability give valuable information to the enemy should they fall in their hands. My opinions of various officers are also, of course, strictly private, and also will probably change, so they should not by any means be considered as permanent. I make no apology for the use of terms both technical and otherwise that are unintelligible to the uninitiated. This diary (although I hope that in future years it may be of a certain amount of interest to some of my friends and relations) is considered primarily for my own edification in times to come.

EXTRACTS FROM NOTES AT THE END OF THE 1914 DIARY

RA Dudley ft. Stratford de Chair

In command of the Tenth CS flagship HMS *Crescent*. I consider him as an officer to be rather a nervy, restless sort of man, and hardly the sort of fellow to inspire great confidence as a dashing commander. He almost gives the impression of weakness. He is nicknamed 'Old Make-a-Signal' owing to the large number of unnecessary signals he issues. He is very hard on Captain Hyde Parker of the *Endymion*, who, although a most eccentric man, appears at least to be a very thorough officer, laughed at as he is by other officers of the squadron. RA de Chair depends largely on the initiative of his flag-captain and flag-lieutenant for the orders he issues. As a man he is charming, a thorough gentleman, with perfect manners, and very kind-hearted. He is extremely solicitous for the personal comfort of all those under his command as far as is compatible with war routine, in direct contrast to the Spartan rigours of RA Pakenham of the Third CS. He is a tall, big man, but clumsy and unwieldy in appearance, and not very athletic. He is rather overcome by the responsibilities of his job, and, I should imagine, is better as a theoriser at the Admiralty than as a man of action.

Captain G Trewby
A capable officer, who has the knack of instilling the greatest confidence in his officers and men. He exercises great influence over the RA. He is a calm, self-possessed man, the direct antithesis of the admiral. Very reasonable. Is, perhaps, not quite so thorough as he might be, but this may be as he suffers terribly from lumbago. As a clean-shaven man he is good looking, but the beard he has grown has aged him considerably.

Fleet Paymaster Lawford
RA de Chair's secretary. An awfully nice little man. Very high spirited, always keen for a rag, and an excellent sort in every way, with a keen sense of humour. He must be quite forty, yet he always joins in the rags, games and exercises on the QD with the greatest energy. He reminds me both in looks and manner of AG Denniston, the Osborne master. His one *bête noire* is whistling, as tuneless whistling sets his teeth on edge, and puts him into a furious rage always. Very popular with everybody in all the officers messes.

AP Gallichan, RNR
(I mention him next as he is leaving the ship today.) Quite a good sort, he joined the reserve about nine months ago, and is a Jersey bank clerk in ordinary life, with a wife and child. He is, perhaps, a bit conceited now, as, being twenty-six years old, he is allowed in the wardroom, although as a one-stripe AP he should be in the gunroom. He is also rather an ass, and is probably too old to get it knocked out of him. Quite all right at heart all the same. A keen photographer, and has taken some excellent snaps lately.

Lieut.-Commander HB Robinson, Flag-Lieutenant
An excellent fellow. Very entertaining, tells jolly good stories, and sings well. He is rather short-tempered with the signal staff, but a flag-lieutenant's job in war is a very trying one. He is a married man and is always talking

about his wife. Has visited every corner of the earth. Was No. 1 of the Signal School, and a bit of a martinet before he came here.

Lieutenant GA Wilson, appointed to battleship *King Edward VII*
He is a weird man, fearfully wet, and very eccentric in every way, hopelessly incapable, and on the whole a thorough ass with his whims and stupid ways. Still, he is very harmless and kind-hearted. I don't think he is by any means fitted for his new position, or, indeed, for any other position of any responsibility. Spent many years in a West African gunboat. He is the captain's *bête noire.*

Captain Gillespie, RMLI
For WT and intelligence duties. A dark, middle-sized man. Very quiet and unassuming. See little of him.

Commander TF Wardle
In peacetime is acting captain of the ship. Not bad as commanders go, and reputed to be very clever, but has given no indications of this so far. At daggers drawn with the GL, as he was a GL before his promotion. A narrow-minded, fussy, stubby little man, always has a whine and no sense of humour at all. Not as popular or unpopular as he might conceivably be either way.

Lieut.-Commander AL Popham, First Lieutenant
A tall, fair-haired man, with a big bit of seniority in. He hardly looks his age, which must be at least thirty-seven. A good-natured, kind-hearted chap, although he gets very snappish at times. Very fond of his bunk, and difficult to rouse once he gets to sleep. Gets quite merry sometimes in the evenings. Very out of date and much at sea with modern appliances and inventions such as fire control, etc. Clever with his hands, and loves muddling about with some useless old VP and a hammer and chisel, knocking and filing. A keen sportsman with more zeal than skill. Married, with one child; has a penchant for nocturnal cocoa.

Lieut.-Commander FA Beasley
A very sound, steady, capable officer, not over-brilliant, but thoroughly reliable in every way. He is rather pious, and the more rowdy members of the WR think him a hypocrite, but I don't think he is. Keen on the fair sex; sings and plays well. He took the Prince of Wales' term, the old Exmouths, at Dartmouth, May 09–May 11. Has had interesting experiences in the *Drake* on the Australian station.

Lieut.-Commander J Kiddle, RN (Retired)
A thoroughly cantankerous, snappish, bad-tempered old idiot of a dug-out. He retired four or five years ago, and was then a very senior man. He is over forty now. Was considered a promising officer in his youth, but he had a row with the Fisher clique and was promptly shelved. He is now interested in several Stock Exchange concerns, and lives a gay life in Paris. Has had many interesting experiences, not all drawing room ones, in the Pacific and Australia, when in the mood to recount them, which is seldom. He is quite ignorant of all the modern requirements of a good NO, and, to add insult to injury, refuses to be told by his more efficient juniors, and his obstinate stupidity is a bugbear to the ship. A bad-tempered messmate, always grumbling and criticising the conditions in the WR. Nevertheless, at the bottom of his heart he is a kind-hearted old duffer.

Lieutenant GV Kenyon (G)
Very keen and clever at his job. In my opinion the most capable officer in the ship, and shall expect to see him go far in the Service. Had the pleasure of serving as his assistant for three months. He is a jolly good chap. Not at all frivolous, but quite good company. Has weird Socialistic ideas. Violent antipathy to the commander (who was a Lieut-G., and tries to interfere). His only fault is criticising his superior officers before their juniors.

Lieut. Marshal L Clarke (N)
A quiet, nice chap. Very steady (TT) and reliable at his job. Gets a bit short-tempered at sea, but his work is full of responsibility and very nervy.

Knows the Sandhills people and A and L Greig well. I am his assistant now, and he is very nice to me.

Lieutenant FN Attwood (T)

Reputed to be clever, and seems quite keen and good at his job. But is very objectionable at times. A tall, cadaverous, dirty-looking man. A fine bridge player. Not very well off, and is usually on the rocks and envious of other people's good fortune.

Lieut.-Commander CH Oxlade, RNR

One of the very best chaps I have ever met. An awful good sort in every way. He is aged about thirty-nine, but does not look it, and is very comfortably off, only doing this job as a hobby. He has knocked about in every corner of the globe, shot grizzlies in the Rockies, duck on the Yangtze, elephants and lions in Africa, and tigers in India. He was in the South African War, has been chief officer of a CPR liner on Japan–Frisco service, also captain of a cross-Channel boat. As a naval officer he is not much catch, as he is totally ignorant of any of the modern contrivances of gunnery, torpedo, etc., and is very deaf. Is rather liable to moods, and, I think, is a little bit balmy. Lives near Bexhill; is a great sportsman, of course. He is a tall, lanky devil.

Lieut.-Commander SK Bacon, RNR

Another awfully nice man of whom I am very fond. If all RNR officers were as nice as Oxlade and Bacon, what a damned good lot they would be! Bacon is a little bit unsophisticated. Aged about forty, is youngest son of a Hants JP, and lives near Hindhead. Desperately keen on hunting, fishing and shooting. Has been in the PO line all his life until three years ago, since when he has been captain of an Egyptian coastguard ship in the Red Sea. Knows Egypt, India, China, Japan and the East Indies very well. He is a short, stout, stumpy man. Excellent company, and has a bevy of most excellent stories, risqué, worse, and otherwise. Some of his reminiscences of early days in the PO Co. are excellent. Has a mania for hot cocoa in night watches and for cheap cigarettes, of which he smokes from fifty to sixty a day.

Eng.-Lieut.-Commander Fletcher

A big, well-proportioned, red-faced, jovial-looking chap, but thoroughly morbid and morose, especially in his ideas about the war. Very old womanish, although he is by repute a good engineer. A terrible pessimist. Nearly due for promotion to engineer-commander.

Eng.-Lieutenant Sims

A little meek, thin man. He used to be in the *Cornwall* years ago, and knows Meggs quite well. I should not think he is any earthly use at his job, as he spends most of his time fooling about with Cockrem on deck.

Staff Surgeon WP Walker

A tall, pleasant-looking man, but very unpopular, as he is an awful bore and gas-bag and no good at his job. Always spouting his opinions about the war and laying down the law. Loves buttonholing the admiral about it and worrying him to death. Has just married a very pretty girl.

Chaplain, the Rev Alfred Shell

In my opinion, a mealy mouthed bugger. Extremely unpopular with everybody. He is a terrible hypocrite and very mean and miserly. He swizzles everybody. We all feel sure he appropriates the men's funds to his own ends.

Surgeon Joseph A Maxwell

A very nice man, quite young, as he has only just left Dublin University, where he earned a valuable reputation on the rugger field, but did very little doctoring, I am afraid. Inclined to be quiet and is reticent on occasions, but still waters run deep, and Joe Maxwell never misses a real opportunity for a good rag.

Temporary Surgeon Roger Buddle
A New Zealander, a jolly good sort. Knows as little of doctoring as Maxwell, with whom he is great pals. Gets very tight every now and again, and is jolly good company. A very good bridge player when sober, they tell me. He has met Daddy's friend Acland at Christchurch in New Zealand.

Staff Paymaster Weston
A nasty little man, very objectionable and bad-tempered. A close friend of the padre and of SS Walker. Nothing really wrong with him except that he is one of those alternately surly and over-pleasant people who always grate up the wrong way.

Assistant-Paymaster Cockrem
A two-striper of about twenty-nine years of age, although he looks seventeen. Is senior clerk to secretary on the admiral's staff. A quiet, unassuming chap, although he has 'nights' occasionally. He made a ridiculous attempt to grow a beard.

Assistant-Clerk Glanvile
A young officer of seven months' seniority, junior clerk to secretary on the admiral's staff, and junior GR officer. On the whole quite a good little chap; we all like him. He was in the *Lion* before the war started, and is full of Beatty-isms and the tour to Russia. There is not much of him, but he has got a will of his own.

Assistant-Paymaster Egleton, RNR
Captain's clerk. A terrible fool who knows nothing, and does nothing right, and rubs everyone up the wrong way, and with so meek and innocent a countenance that I am constrained to pity him, though most folks ignore and despise him. An ugly man, who looks almost as big a fool as he is.

Assistant-Paymaster GTE Cockerill, RNR

A tall, spectacled, fair-haired youth of about nineteen. Took on his present job in August, as owing to his defective eyesight he could not get into any military force. Quite a nice chap; a bit green at first, but he will soon settle down into the Service way of things.

Ch Sig Bosun Mr Champion

A jolly, red-faced old chap of about fifty. A thoroughly good sort, Senior WO in the squadron. Has always got some moan, but this is only a sort of hobby. Very respectful to his superiors, in antithesis to some of the younger WOs of more modern date.

Gunner Mr FE Lowman

Not a bad chap, although a bit short-tempered. He suffers badly from gout, and spends most of his time in his bunk, otherwise quite a good officer. Loves relating dull yarns about his family.

Bosun Mr G Ford

A typical old bosun of the Mr Gearing class; wears the most extraordinary, antique, picturesque old uniforms. He is not so loquacious as Mr Gearing, or so energetic, and he does very little work, and I really believe knows but little of his job. A queer old cuss altogether.

Bosun Mr McLachlan

A small, insignificant young man, quite a nonentity; very seldom seen, and does nothing, except very occasionally when he has fits of cantankerousness. Tries to ape the 'knut' when on shore.

Acting-Gunner Mr Croughan

A young chap, not at all bad at heart. Very talkative. Most abominably familiar, which is a great drawback, I am afraid. Quite a capable man if he was not so full of gas, and even might be quite interesting if he would only stop talking a minute to let you digest what he says.

Torpedo-Gunner Mr King
A very nice man, quiet, and good at his job. Prematurely white hair makes him look twenty years older than he is. Very interested in the development of Canada, especially British Columbia, as he did three commissions in the *Rainbow* based on Esquimalt.

Carpenter Mr Lane
A thorough old tartar, with a red bearded face, and hot stuff in every way. Always very busy, but you can never get his staff to do anything; they are always so fully occupied tinkering about doing nothing. Mr Lane is a tremendous character, a good supply of language, and plenty of tall yarns, he would bamboozle Lord Fisher, if you gave him half a chance.

Artificer-Engineer Botling
A dark-eyed, morose man of forbidding aspect. Looks on life with a dark eye.

Warrant-Engineer French, RNR
Quite a good, stout old chap. From the Union Castle Line. Lives at Cowes. Very anxious to rise into higher society, and is always pleased and eager for a chat.

With regard to the eight midshipmen of the ship, I shall not indite separate notes on my seven colleagues and myself. We have all come through the training together in the same term, and have known each other intimately for nearly five years. In this ship, for various reasons, such as the partial inefficiency and ignorance of a large number of the officers of the ship, or rather the lack of *very* efficient officers, for with one exception none are really hopeless idiots; and as the war entails far heavier work being thrown on the willing back of the NO in consequence, the midshipmen of this ship have been entrusted with far greater responsibilities than we should have in most ships. I think I can say without exaggeration or conceit that the midshipmen have acquitted themselves well, and, without thinking that they absolutely run the ship, they certainly have a good share in it. I will not discriminate between my colleagues except to say that Tottenham is far less efficient than the others; this is as he is so terribly eccentric and mad (as I believe he has plenty of latent ability somewhere). Unluckily he doesn't realise his shortcomings.

1915

JANUARY

Friday 1

This time last year Bench and I were at the New Year Covent Garden Ball. I remember vividly how we enjoyed it, and what thick heads we had next morning. What a change of surroundings a year later! And what funny things that year has brought us!

Got the Admiralty's new year promotion list by WT; unluckily several interruptions occurred, so we did not get the complete list, but Mr Wolfe-Murray, the First Lieutenant of the *Cornwall,* was among the promotions to commander. The Germans made determined efforts all day to make our wireless useless by making continuous signals of absolute gibberish in English, French, German, Russian and Norwegian. Gun drill at 11.30. I have taken a great liking to Mr Macintyre, one of the RNR engineers. He is a very nice man. Also a great dislike to that fat swine, Jack Barton, the RNR one-stripe AP; his manner is intolerable.

Saturday 2

We had a sing-song and quite a jovial evening last night, after a very good dinner. The Allan Line messing is excellent after the *Crescent.* The only trouble about the ship is that, practically speaking, I never get any fresh air, and the coding office is a stuffy place, as the ports can seldom be opened, the seas coming in usually during the scanty hours of daylight, and 'darken ship' enforcing them being shut by night. Also the admiral keeps us on the hop so with his signals that we are too tired to take any exercise when off watch. Henderson has got a very nasty attack of flu. The captain examined our journals; judgment deferred. The *Hilary*'s barque she was towing to Kirkwall sprang a leak and sank. One sub-lieutenant, RNR, and one signalman drowned. Received news of the loss of the battleship *Formidable*.*

Sunday 3

Received supplement to promotions list.

Among the new commanders of interest are: Sneyd, First Lieutenant HMS *Cumberland*; our old friend Mr Dalglish; Holbrook of *B2*; Horton of *E9*; Burgess-Watson, Uncle John's friend; and two cousins of Hutchinson's. The Norwegian liners *Kristianiafjord* and *Bergensfjord*, old acquaintances, passed close to us in the night, as we heard them talking by WT at a range of less than twenty miles, but we sighted neither. I got in the soup for omitting Admiralty reference serial numbers in decoded messages.

Monday 4

Several German submarines reported off the Shetlands. A new dodge of theirs has been discovered. Apparently oil tanks have been sunk in the open sea, either before the war or since by neutrals, in a given position, and their submarines use these as fuel bases, hence their big ranges of action. We detached *Teutonic, Mantua, Virginian* to watch Trondheim, whence contraband running is reported. All the midshipmen in the *consommé* with Kiddle for not reporting their divisions at evening quarters. Record day for signal section; no rest, enormous number of signals. Thankful to turn in soon after midnight, dead to the world.

Tuesday 5

Nasty gale blowing. Not quite so busy as yesterday. Hands painting ship. Gun drill 11.30am. The *Otway* and *Cedric's* operators both in Captain

---

* HMS *Formidable* was sunk off Portland Bill by torpedoes from the German submarine *U-24*. She was the first battleship serving with the Royal Navy to be sunk during the First World War. Five-hundred-and-forty-seven men lost their lives.

Gillespie's (squadron WT and intelligence officer) bad books. 'Flags' in a hilarious mood. The Staff Eng.-Lieut.-Commander (Mr Fletcher) drivelled for several hours on gun mountings, about which he knows nix. Still, it amuses him, I suppose. The new German submarine bases are known to be in the vicinity of the Orkneys and Shetlands. Confidential Admiralty reports state the Germans intend to try and rush a battle cruiser squadron up this way. Of course, this would annihilate us, but we ought to get Beatty well on their track first, which is the chief thing. The *Karlsruhe* is reported as not yet having reached Germany, so perhaps she turned back after all.

Wednesday 6

It is reported an attempt will be made to smuggle a lot of German reservists over in the *Bergensfjord,* next trip from New York to Norway, and thence to Germany. So she is to be intercepted and searched. I took some sights in the afternoon, but the sun was refractory, and a heavy ground swell made sextant work difficult. Pretty busy all day. The *Warrior* carried out firing practice near our patrol. She is just home from the Mediterranean, where she was originally in the First Cruiser Squadron under Rear-Admiral Troubridge. She is the ship to which I was to have gone probably had there been no war.

Thursday 7

Took up a position considerably to the southward of our regular patrol, sighting St Kilda in the afternoon. Control practice, using a trawler as dummy target in the morning. I distinguished myself afterwards by dropping the Dumaresq down the fore A deck hatch and badly damaging it. It is a big one of the latest mark, and will cost about £25 (pay stopped for several months) unless I can get the chief armourer to repair it. The ship was rolling heavily, so it was not altogether my fault. Had a long chat with 'Guns'. Considerable excitement caused after dark by flashes of heavy gunfire, but proved to only be the Sixth Cruiser Squadron night firing.

Friday 8

The WT department have fitted up a small sending and receiving apparatus in the motorboat detailed as the admiral's barge. I don't know what it is for, as she hasn't dipped this commission yet, but it is quite a neat little installation. Communicated with the *Cedric* off Foula, where we had come from St Kilda. Sent despatches on board for the SNO, Liverpool, as the *Cedric* returns to Liverpool in a few days to coal. Practised both after groups, 1-inch aiming tube firing in the afternoon; not bad results for first attempt. I, in my capacity as rate-keeper in the principal control, had plenty to do, as my trainer was away, and I had to train myself. The captain very liverish and critical. Urgent signals from C-in-C to say *Bergensfjord* must be caught at all costs.

Saturday 9

'Guns' lectured on the theory of fire control to all the control officers and all the gunroom officers; quite an interesting lecture despite the interruptions of Mr Schlosser. I got in the soup with Gillespie for muddling call signs and calling up the *London* off the Belgian coast, instead of the *Patuca*. At 4.30pm stopped engines and buried a fireman who had died of double pneumonia. The captain conducted the service, as we have no padre on board. It is the first sea funeral I have ever witnessed. All over very quickly. A few prayers, then the body sewn in a Union Jack and weighted with a shell, committed to the deep, three volleys by the marines, and the 'Last Post' to mark that Nature had reclaimed one of her living creatures from this troubled world.

Sunday 10

Boarded a Swedish oil steamer; all correct, so allowed her to proceed. German submarines reported off Lerwick, Stromness, Aberdeen and Flamborough Head. Either submarines or else disguised neutral ships have managed to lay mines between Sulisker and Sule Skerry. At 4pm we heard the *Bergensfjord* calling up SS *Bergen,* about seventy-five miles away. I hope she won't get through in the night.

Monday 11

At 7.30am the *Viknor* intercepted and captured the *Bergensfjord* to the north-east of the Faeroes; she had, as anticipated, been trying to slip through to the northward under cover of darkness.* The C-in-C made a signal 'Well done!' to our admiral and to the *Viknor* on hearing the news. The admiral is not such a fool as he appears, and the disposition of our patrols to effect this capture was most skilful. Detached the *Eskimo* for special duty off the Norwegian coast. Very cold; the ships looked like great white icicles, all glistening with frost. On hearing of the capture of the *Bergensfjord,* we communicated visually with the *Teutonic* and *Orotava,* and proceeded to rendezvous the *Viknor* and her prize at full speed, coming up with them at 1pm. The man Spero, with the Mexican passport, was arrested with seven German stowaways, but no signs of the numerous reservists were found, although of course it would have been easy to disguise them among the eight hundred passengers. Spero is supposed to be the famous Baron von Wedel, referred to in the spy Karl Graves' book, the chief of the German spying bureau. What his mission in America was is unknown, but it is of little doubt that only a tremendous bribe would have induced the captain of the *Bergensfjord* to risk his all by contravening international law so flagrantly as to bring a man like von Wedel across the ditch. The great importance the Admiralty attached to his capture is indicated by the fact that no less than twenty ships, the whole of our squadron not coaling, and available, were detailed to capture the ship at all costs. The fact that we knew

---

* The supposedly neutral *Bergensfjord* would trouble the Navy on at least three separate occasions during the war. On the first, she was found to be harbouring a known German propagandist, Dr Durnberg, and on another the German consul from Korea, the Norwegian prime minister as well as numerous German reservists.

he was coming in her shows our secret service to be by no means a minus quantity. Immediately on being boarded by the *Viknor*, Spero, alias von Wedel, was arrested. He was found burning incriminating papers. He was taken unawares, as he did not expect us to know of his disguise. The *Bergensfjord's* wireless was taken over and a prize crew put on board to await the arrival of the rear-admiral in the *Alsatian*. When we got there at 1pm the *Viknor* was ordered to take Spero and the German stowaways on board and to escort the prize to Kirkwall for examination, as either the German reservists, reported to have embarked at New York, were hidden on board, or else they must have been transferred to other ships in the Atlantic. The Norwegian skipper cut up nasty, and the incident will probably lead to all sorts of complications with Norway. They proceeded in company for Kirkwall at 6pm. We left for the south of the Faroes immediately, and boarded two Danish vessels at 10pm. Apparently a company has been promoted in the USA for running the blockade with food and reservists for Germany at all costs – of course, being very highly paid by the German government. Our squadron are after several suspicious ships just now, and we are fearfully busy with signals in the flagship, of course.

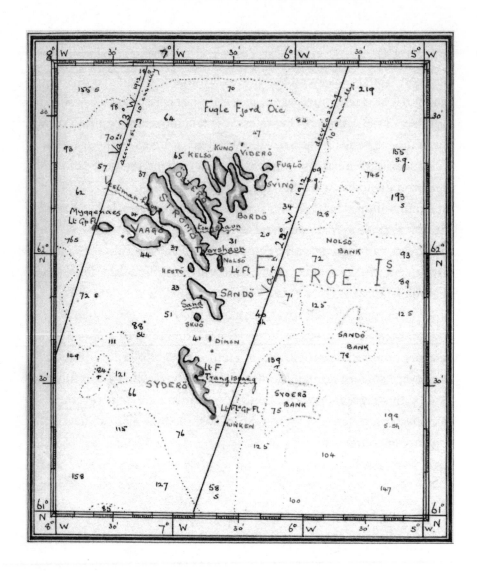

Tuesday 12

Back to our old patrol off the Faroes. Still very cold. Snow in the morning, turning into sleet, hail, and then rain in the afternoon, as the wind backed from NNW to SSW. General quarters all the morning. Remarkably good work by the fire control. I got congratulated by the skipper for keeping an excellent rate, my rate giving clock ranges which coincided with range-finder ranges for two whole runs. One-inch aiming tube firing for all guns. After control and local control poor, owing to inefficiency of auxiliary communications.

Wednesday 13

A variety of signals full of useless bunkum came through, and muddled us considerably, due to careless decoding in other ships. Sir George Warrender is having a most unlucky time with his Second Battle Squadron. In addition to the loss of the *Audacious,* the *Monarch* is at Plymouth disabled with serious turbine defects, and now the *Conqueror* has suffered serious damage, and has left for Liverpool to be docked. Some of us would have been pleased if it had been the *Thunderer* instead, as, by the amount of balderdash she sends out, her wireless staff ought to be throttled or worse!

Thursday 14

Received orders to detach the *Ambrose* to rendezvous the *Conqueror* off Stornoway. Much speculation as to the nature of her damage. Admiralty (to all ships) signal reported considerable activity among the German Fleet at Kiel, apparently preparing for sea. All First Fleet ships ordered by C-in-C to prepare for all eventualities. *Alsatian* patrolling off the Faroes as usual. Intercepted a Danish steamer, *Spigerborg,* from New York with oil cake for Germany. Sent a prize crew on board under Midshipman Adams, RNR, with orders to take her into Kirkwall. Much wrangling in the gunroom, chiefly over the question of McNaught, his airs and manners. The captain of the *Otway* made a bigger BF of himself than usual.

Friday 15

Big gale, high wind and heavy swell from the NNE. I got in the soup badly for faulty coding, although, as a matter of fact, Captain Gillespie was entirely to blame. Received information to the effect that A code has somehow fallen into German hands, probably through spies at the Admiralty. They have now got A and C of our numerous codes and ciphers. C-in-C reported that a cruiser raid is anticipated against our patrol tomorrow night, and ordered us to shift patrol line one hundred miles to the west; thus the Germans will find, instead of several moderately weak armed merchant cruisers, two strong cruiser squadrons, with Beatty's battle cruiser squadron in reserve.

Saturday 16

During the night the Germans tried without success, by making *en clair* signals for help, to induce us to betray our position. 'Guns' settled the RNR dispute satisfactorily. He gave a further lecture on fire control, which unluckily I was too busy in the coding office to attend. Still a nasty gale from the NNE, although the swell diminished somewhat. Frequent snow storms. The *Viknor,* with von Wedel and the German prisoners on board, is now three days overdue at Liverpool; grave fears are expressed as to whether she has been blown up by a mine. It is inconceivable that Wedel has managed with the other prisoners to overcome his guard. German cruiser raid came off, but weather was so bad that no one saw them, and they saw nobody, so nothing occurred.

Sunday 17

Gale abated somewhat. Sighted and spoke to the *Patia* at 4pm. Very cold. Argued learnedly about advantages of range-finder control.

Monday 18

Last night after I had turned in the gunroom held a rowdy sing-song to celebrate Cobb's birthday, and the promotion of Glanvile from assistant-clerk to clerk. The admiral objected to the din as it was Sunday, and I got scrubbed this morning in consequence. The joys of being senior midshipman are not unalloyed. The *Digby* reported a steamer she could not catch at midnight, so we shaped a course to intercept her and did so at 3.30am, the *Digby* coming up half an hour later; but she proved to be only a Russian carrying volunteers from the USA to Archangel. Our senior wireless officer, Captain Gillespie, RMLI, in the soup with the Fleet wireless officer of the *Iron Duke.*

Tuesday 19

Learnt that a German submarine expedition has just left to operate against our armed merchant cruiser squadron, and so, if possible, to relieve the blockade. A great compliment to the efficacy of our patrol. It is said that the exports of copper and food from America to Germany via Scandinavia have dropped enormously since the armed merchant cruiser squadron started its duties properly last December, and in consequence the Germans are beginning to feel the pinch. Detached three ships for a patrol of the Romsdalsfjord on the Norwegian coast, as the ships coming round the north of Iceland are said to enter the fjords here and work their way south, thus evading the examination of our blockade. The C-in-C reported that bodies and wreckage, presumably of the *Viknor,* had been washed ashore at Portrush, so all hope has been given up. She had von Wedel on board and all the prisoners. I hope von Wedel did not escape. The disaster is the irony of fate, after their success, and the commander was practically sure of promotion. By a funny coincidence we were the last ship to sight the *Viknor,* as was the *Crescent* with the *Hawke.* Whether the *Viknor* was mined, or foundered in a gale, is still a complete matter of conjecture.

Wednesday 20

Heard through the British Minister at Kristiania (my old friend Mr Findlay) that a big German steamer, the *Marie* from Apenrade, had arrived at Frederikstad; she will attempt to reach Thamshavn near Trondheim to bring back a cargo of copper. She intends, apparently, to work her way up inside the fjords via Vobervig, Haugesund, Alesund, etc. We warned the Norwegian patrol to look out for her. Received news of the German Zeppelin air raid over the Norfolk coast. I expect the Hemsby people had some excitement.*

---

* On the night of 19 January 1915, the first airship raid on Britain took place. Zeppelins of the Imperial German Navy Airship Division dropped bombs on Great Yarmouth and King's Lynn, killing five people.

Thursday 21

Continuous snow storm all day. Intensely cold, thermometer below freezing point; the ship looked like a great white iceberg. A strong wind drove the snow down at a great pace, and a very nasty sea got up. One of the after wireless aerial braces carried away, but did not interfere with our signalling. The Yankees have been making all sorts of complaints about their ensign being hauled down when sent into Kirkwall for examination, and the captain of the *Cedric* is going to get it in the neck.

DESCRIPTION OF THE TENTH CRUISER SQUADRON PATROL WORK

21 January 1915

The primary object of the Tenth Cruiser Squadron (cruiser force B) patrol is to stop the traffic in contraband of war, intended eventually for Germany, and shipped from America to Scandinavian ports. A similar patrol is being maintained at the entrance to the English Channel in the south by other cruiser forces. In the north twenty-four armed merchant cruisers under the command of RA De Chair (HMS *Alsatian*) have superseded the seven old cruisers of the *Crescent* type which were carrying out the patrol duties previously. The advantages of the new patrol are manifold, the ships being more numerous, better able to keep the sea in any weather, and having coal capacity for considerably longer periods, which in many cases the ships are newer and faster; the conditions of living for officers and men are also considerably improved.

It is the duty of the patrol to intercept all ships passing to the north of Scotland or between Orkneys, Shetlands, Faroes or Iceland. In view of the order closing the North Sea and various arrangements, described later, made with neutrals, all neutral vessels whose arrival has not been notified should be regarded with suspicion. Thus all eastward-bound vessels should be sent in with prize crews to Kirkwall for examination by the customs authorities. These ships should not be treated as prizes, but with courtesy, being allowed to fly their own colours, in order not to offend the susceptibilities of neutrals. If, however, contraband is found on board, the authorities will exercise the right of confiscation. Certain vessels of neutral shipping lines, have been granted special permits to use the northabout route, provided they call at Kirkwall, and it is unlikely the privilege will be abused, as this would entail the withdrawal of the permit. It is also possible to obtain clearances from other British ports. British and allied vessels may use the northabout route, but if from foreign to Scandinavian ports must call at Kirkwall.

The present regulations with regard to westbound ships are that they should be advised in their own interests to go to Kirkwall for examination, but force must not be used to turn them back. Few vessels take this advice, however, and it is probable that in the near future stricter measures will be taken, as it is easy at present for these vessels to escape examination of any kind, especially when bad weather prohibits boarding, and so to slip through the blockade. Thus mines can be easily got through, concealed under a cargo of salt or some other such commodity. Vessels westward bound are directed to Lat 60°N Long 3°W, whence they should keep to northward of 60° parallel until they reach 3°W, and then to Kirkwall. Eastward-bound sailing ships should make Faroes, and then keep 50° north of the Shetlands. Stornoway has been suggested as an examination port for westbound ships to reduce the amount of ships going to Kirkwall. Kirkwall and Fair Isle passage should be made by day, as there are no lights by night. The Pentland Firth passage is prohibited at all times.

It is probable that as the pressure of the patrol is increasingly felt in Germany, bigger commercial inducements will be offered to smuggle through copper and other contraband. In consequence, the duties of the patrol are likely to become harder rather than lighter.

Friday 22

On patrol as usual today. Snow storm continued unceasingly, and thermometer lower than ever – several degrees below freezing point. Intercepted some signals from the *Minotaur* and *Hampshire*, so discovered they have returned from China; thus the old 'Bird'

(CT Wilson) is knocking about near home again. This means Kenneth is home also, I suppose, unless he remained at Hong Kong in the *Triumph*. McWilliams on the sick list with influenza.

Saturday 23

Left patrol off the Faroes and proceeded to Rockall for firing practice. Rockall is a conical rock eighty feet long by about fifty feet high, sticking straight up out of four hundred fathoms of water, in the middle of the Atlantic, about the most desolate place in God's earth; it is four times as far west from the Hebrides as St Kilda, and St Kilda is considered about the loneliest habitable spot in the British Isles. Firing practice; fire control, seven rounds' practice each side, with two rounds common. Results satisfactory, but nothing to enthuse over, as several things went wrong. Afterwards proceeded for Barra Head.

Sunday 24

Proceeding to Liverpool to coal. Made Barra Head 8am. All lookouts double-banked, as these waters are mine-infested. Much better weather. First sun for some weeks. The extra daylight down south here is most welcome. Passed the *Calyx, Clan MacNaughton, Otway* and destroyer *Swift*. The captain of *Otway* is taking charge in our absence. Passed Oversay and Dubh Artach, making Mull of Cantyre 3.30pm. Great excitement in the evening. I did eight hours' consecutive watch-keeping. The *Hibernia* reported hostile submarines off Larne, though how they got there the Lord only knows! Later they were reported on our starboard beam, about three miles off, but immediately we increased to twenty-two knots – full speed – and escaped.

Monday 25

Anchored off Mersey Bar at midnight. Too foggy to go up the river before 10am. Docked in the evening. Very exciting day. Intercepted all sorts of wireless news; apparently the First Battle Cruiser Squadron with some destroyers engaged the German battle cruiser squadron which had

ventured out of Wilhelmshaven.* We sunk the *Blücher* and sent them
scuttling back to port, with the *Seydlitz* and *Lützow* badly damaged. On
our side the *Lion* was damaged, and so were the destroyers *Liberty* and
Meteor. I celebrated five weeks' abstinence by drinking more than was good
for me and getting a head like a hen. It is quite funny being in port again,
after five weeks continuously at sea. Received a bumper mail, also first for
five weeks. Some very interesting letters. The majority of the officers went
on leave, but they kept some of us on board, self included, to run the ship
while she is being coaled. Shut up the wireless office at twelve noon; they
are going to fit a new set. We are going to change duties next month. Four
other midshipmen are going to take on coding officer. I am going to be
navigator's assistant again, as I was in the last month in the *Crescent.*

Tuesday 26

Took over my duties as 'Tanky'. Cobb is going to be my extra assistant
in harbour. Spent most of the day correcting charts and winding
chronometers. Most people have a pretty slack time in harbour, but I
seem to have more to do than ever. There is simply heaps to be done.
All the sailing corrections to light lists from N to Ms, etc., with several
clocks and chronometers to look after. Went ashore in the afternoon, did
some shopping, and called on Miss Amy Soderströme, a Norwegian girl
I met in Norway, and then had tea with Mrs Roxburgh at the Adelphi.
Worked up till midnight at chart correcting.

26 January 1915   HMS *ALSATIAN*

Dear Daddy,

Best love to you and mother and the rest of the family;
please thank mother for all her letters. We arrived

---

* Battle of Dogger Bank. Buoyed by the success of the raid on the factory towns of
northern England and the subsequent public and political outcry, Admiral Hipper
decided to repeat the exercise by attacking the British fishing fleet at Dogger Bank.
However, he was intercepted by Admiral Beatty and the British Grand Fleet before
the raid.

in port to coal yesterday and anchored for the first
time for five weeks; we have not seen any terra firma,
except occasional glimpses in the distance, since 23
December. Christmas and New Year at sea. So you can
imagine we were pretty pleased to be at anchor again,
especially as we have had no news or mails whatever
since we left, except occasional fragments intercepted
by wireless. I don't think we have ever appreciated
letters so much before. We are going to sea again at
the end of the week. Nearly all the officers have gone
on a few days' leave, but about six of us are left on
board doing the work of the other fifty. I have got
two hundred charts to correct, all the chronometers
to overhaul, and a hundred and one other things to
do, as the navigator has gone, so I don't expect to see
much of the shore. One of our midshipmen has just been
appointed to the battle cruiser *Australia*, and I should
not be surprised if we all get to battleships and battle
cruisers before long. If all goes well, and I am still
in the *Alsatian*, I hope to get down to London for a few
days next time we come in, which will be roughly about
6–12 March.

We are far more comfortable than in the old *Crescent*,
but are kept a good deal busier, for as there are
twenty-four (now twenty-three) ships in the squadron,
there is the devil of a lot of staff squadron work to
get through, in addition to the ordinary watch-keeping
and work of the ship.

I should be very much obliged if you would tell
the people at the bank to send me some sort of account
occasionally. I should have thought the beginning
of the year would have been a suitable time. Mother
should have paid £1 for me, which Auntie Enid sent as

a Christmas present, but either she forgot or else she omitted to inform me that my request had been carried out. I am sending them £12 of my pay by post, and if they don't acknowledge it they will lose my custom. It won't make much difference when my pay is £31 a year, but when it is £5000 a year for First Sea Lord, perhaps they will buck up a bit.

We have had quite an interesting time, though a bit monotonous at times. It has been bitingly cold where I have been, with snow the rule rather than the exception. I expect you read of the *Viknor*'s loss; she belonged to our squadron. 'A tale hangs thereby' of remarkable interest, which makes the old saying that truth is stranger than fiction appear remarkably true. The whole affair is shrouded in mystery. After the war, when censorship is dead, I think the loss of the *Viknor* and the events leading up to it will be found to be one of the most dramatic stories of the struggle, on the naval side at all events.

Best love to all.

From
Toby

Wednesday 27

The navigator, Mr Clarke, the captain and the commander went on leave. So I am senior navigating officer on board. Still more work to do. I am no shirker, but I can't possibly get everything done in three days. Robinson got an appointment to the battle cruiser *Australia,* so our gunroom mess was broken up. He is very pleased, naturally. Johnstone went to London on thirty-six hours' leave. The captain of the *Caribbean,* a commander, RN, and Commander Wardle, captain of the *Calyx,* came on board. Mr Croughan, another old *Crescent* friend, also of the *Calyx,* whose gunner he is, also on board.

Dined in Birkenhead with Tottenham and a Reserve AP from the *Orotava,* and then went to the Argyle Theatre. Returned to ship at midnight.

The mystery of the *Viknor*'s loss, with the fate of von Wedel, and the events transpiring on the capture of the *Bergensfjord,* seem likely to remain unsolved. Whether the ill-fated vessel foundered in a gale, ran ashore, struck a mine, or was destroyed by the agency of the German prisoners on board, it will probably never be ascertained. There is considerable pathos attached to the event, as the *Viknor* was coming into harbour after a long and weary sojourn on patrol, and her officers and men were looking forward to a rest in port, and leave to their homes for many. She had, by intercepting the *Bergensfjord,* scored a notable success and been congratulated by the C-in-C. Thus Commander Ballantyne, her captain, must have felt sure of accelerated promotion to the rank of Captain. Then when almost in safety she was swallowed up, and another record imprinted in the vast list of unsolved mysteries of the ocean. It is a point of some satisfaction to feel that in all probability Baron von Wedel (alias Spero), the arch spy and schemer of the German secret service, with his fellow prisoners, perished with his captors. True, the foreign newspapers report the arrival of Baron Wedel in Rome with important documents; but this is almost certainly a blind to mislead the ignorant on the part of the German authorities, chagrined and frightened at the loss of their chief spy. Nevertheless, the report has given rise to a theory that von Wedel actually escaped, either by bribing a neutral in the *Bergensfjord* to impersonate him, and so escaping to Norway, or else as a lone survivor of the *Viknor.* The first idea is remarkably improbable, owing to the fact that however large the bribe offered, the man must have known that he was taking in exchange death or at least imprisonment for life; while the likelihood of the well-guarded and valuable prisoner being the sole survivor of the doomed ship is practically nil; for even had he escaped the wreck, how could he have landed and fled the country, unnoticed and unthought of.

No! There can be but little doubt that though in the loss of the *Viknor* we suffered a sad loss of valuable lives of officers and men, yet the blow to the German spy system, in the almost certain death of its prime mover, cannot be overestimated in its importance.

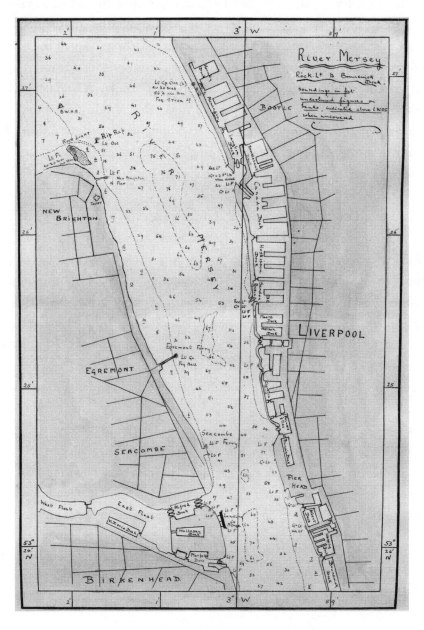

Thursday 28

A day of catastrophes. The auxiliary steam pipe burst in the engine room, and we were in complete darkness for half an hour, as the dynamos stopped, and no one could find any candles. No hot water, and a cold dinner, the worst we have had in the ship, because we had a guest, I suppose. HMS *Natal* came in for a refit in the morning and secured astern of the cargo liner *Hesperian*. I did not go ashore. I spent most of the forenoon with Cobb wrestling with the chronometers. Corrected a large number of charts. Went on board the *Natal* and had some drinks in the gunroom. They are to be in a fortnight, and hope for five days' leave each. The AP came on board and had five cocktails, and Greenland came to dinner. A pretty rowdy evening, liquid flowing freely.

Friday 29

The captain and navigator returned from leave. Three hostile submarines reported off Bardsey Island. HMS *Natal* went into dry dock, in place of the SS *St Paul*, a Yankee liner. Two stokers broke out of the ship and deserted. More charts arrived for correction. Submarines reported off the Bar at midday, probably the same as those seen earlier at Bardsey. The brutes seem to be everywhere. One actually fired at the Barrow forts. It will be pretty dangerous work getting in and out of the Mersey now. How I envy those devils in the battle cruisers! Everyone does. They get all the fighting, and not nearly such hard work as we do.

Saturday 30

Hawkins and Martin came on board from the *Natal*. Met old 'Tweedledum', our signal instructor at Dartmouth three years ago; he is in the *Caribbean*, in which ship is also CPO Lobb. Went to the Adelphi in the afternoon, after working all the morning. Spent most of the afternoon imbibing cocktails, also had a shooting pool with Bench and Ikey, and took 5s. off each of them. Met old Hole, who was surgeon at Dartmouth with us; he is now senior medical officer of the *Bayano*. Pleasant reminiscences of old days. Dined with the captain and AP Cockerill (his secretary) at the Adelphi. Tottenham was also invited, but couldn't come. We had a box at the Empire and several drinks afterwards. The skipper behaved like a brick, and the dinner was excellent, so was the wine. I went on a tour with Cockerill afterwards – he is not nearly so wet as he appears – and did not get back on board till 2am. The German submarines, of which one is *U-21*, sank three merchantmen off the Bar.

Sunday 31

Eleven more merchant ships sunk; the matter is getting very serious. All sailings of HM ships cancelled, so we shall not leave tonight. Ships of the Tenth Cruiser Squadron coming in to coal are being diverted by wireless to the Clyde, and all the big liners to Southampton. The enforced inaction of several ships in Liverpool will weaken our patrol badly. Later news states that the authorities have declared the port of Liverpool closed to all shipping. This will seriously damage trade. We are under sailing orders, but shall not leave for two or three days, when we shall probably try and slip out in the dark, which will be very exciting, especially as we know three submarines are waiting for us.

FEBRUARY

Monday 1

The despatch of a torpedo boat flotilla from Pembroke to attempt to waylay the submarines is anticipated. All officers and men returned from leave except the captain and the admiral. I worked all the morning and afternoon. Several trawlers, yachts, motorboats and fast Isle of Man packet-boats have been commandeered by the authorities, and are being sent out armed with six-pounders to hunt down the submarines. There is little doubt they are oiling from neutral vessels, which have previously received British clearances under false pretences. The *Natal's* picket boat also went after the raiders. I went on shore in the evening, did some shopping, dined with Johnstone, met old Hole. Then went to the 'Whirl of the Town' at the Olympia with Ward and Learmont. An excellent show; Wilkie Bard, Daisy Wood very good, and a very pretty chorus. Daisy Wood sang recruiting songs exuberantly, with a very naughty twinkle. House crowded with naval officers. Got back on board midnight.

Tuesday 2

Working all day as usual. Broke leave in the evening. Went on shore with Ward to the Olympia again. Havers and Rae from the *Natal* both there. The 'Whirl of the Town' is the best show I have ever seen out of London. Supped with Olive Russell and Ninon Oste afterwards, two very nice and chic little girls. Ninon Oste has got about the second most important part. Got back at 2am. I am beginning to feel rather a wreck with this enforced inactivity in harbour working all the day, and on the spree all the night, no sleep.

Wednesday 3

Usual routine, worked all day. Heard from Joko; not much of a letter. 'Drippie' P Porritt with a friend, and Little from the *Natal* to lunch. Porritt is now in the King's Liverpools and leaves for Canterbury shortly; I must inform the people at home. Went on shore with Ward and took Olive and Ninon out to tea. Came back to the ship to dine. The *Calyx* took fire at anchor – cause unknown; still burning at midnight. On shore again after dinner, and to the second house of the Olympia. Havers and Rae there as usual. Took Olive and Ninon to supper at the 'Exchange'. Very hilarious.

3 February 1915   HMS *ALSATIAN*

    Dearest Mother,

    We are still in harbour, a week extra owing to the fact that there are some submarines waiting for us outside, so I am taking this opportunity of writing. We hope to slip out on a dark night and so get back to our patrol,

which will be quite exciting. The devils would have had
an excellent chance of bagging us, but for the fact that
they were foolish enough to betray their presence, of
which we were unaware, by sinking some merchantmen,
as I dare say you have read in the papers. I was very
busy the first few days in harbour, but finished all
the work on hand by attacking it ferociously until
midnight two or three times. Since then I have been
very nice and lazy, and have spent most of my spare
time pleasantly, but not too wisely, with more amusing
objects than charts. There is an excellent revue with
a first-class chorus (for looks) at one of the theatres
here; so possibly you can guess our amusements. A large
number of us will go to sea 'broke', so perhaps certain
members of the cast or company or whatever it is of the
revue will have heavier purses.

Prospects of leave in the immediate future – that is,
for a month or so – are nil, but I will write again as
soon as we return to harbour in a few weeks' time. Best
love to all.

From

Toby

Thursday 4

Last night, at the Olympia stage door, whom should I meet but old
Dean, eng.-lieut.-commander of a destroyer refitting in Albert Dock.
I have not seen him since Osborne days. He was not waiting for a
fairy, but for Wilkie Bard, whom he knows. The 'Whirl of the Town' is
practically entirely monopolised by the Services now. HMS *Macedonian,*
armoured merchant cruiser on foreign service, proceeded to Sandon
for half-tide basin. At 10.40 we slipped and proceeded in charge of
pilot and tugs also to Sandon half-tide basin; this is a sign that we
shall sail soon, submarines or no submarines. Secured alongside the

Cunard liner *Mauretania* in Sandon basin at 11.40. I spent the day
on board, recuperating and doing a little work. Left the Olympia girls
to themselves for a change. By the way, there is a big dance on at the
Adelphi, but I am too much of a wreck to go.

Friday 5

Usual work in the morning. Since the submarine scare, the remainder
of our ships (Tenth Cruiser Squadron) have been using Loch Ewe
and Glasgow as coaling bases instead of Belfast and Liverpool. Went
on shore in the afternoon and up to the Adelphi. Ran across Olive
and Ninon, and had tea with them under the disapproving glances of
Commander Wardle of the *Calyx*. Met their friend, Mrs Carmichael, a
jolly good sort, and also the stage manager; several cocktails with him,
and he said if I came tonight he would put me up to all the best of the
charms, behind the scenes, I don't already know. So I determined to
break leave and have the time of my life. Tottenham and Glanvile dined
with the captain, and Richardson with the admiral. Wood and Learmont
had three girls on board to tea, and McNaught one to dinner. But bad
luck dogged me; just as I was leaving the ship bound for Olympia,
looking forward to a tremendous night with the girls, I ran right into
Lieutenant Kenyon's arms, and he nailed me and stopped my leave, of
course. I expect I shall catch it tomorrow. A damned nuisance! I was
very disappointed, but put the best face on it and did some more work
instead. It was a proper walk-over. If Jellicoe catches Tirpitz as well as
Kenyon did me, he will do well.

Saturday 6

Cast off and left Sandon basin at 2.35pm.

Found the *Lusitania* and HM ships *Calyx*, *Caribbean*, *Orotava* and
Bayano in the river. Anchored for an hour off New Brighton, after
passing the *Aquitania* in dry dock. Weighed later and proceeded to sea.
Dropped the pilot off the Bar Light and proceeded at eighteen knots.
Much speculation as to whether we shall evade the numerous mines and

submarines and get back to our patrol. Ran past the Mull of Galloway and out of the Irish Sea during the night.

Sunday 7

A fire broke out during the night in the fore starboard fan room, but was easily extinguished. Passed Oversay at 6am. Very dirty weather, and thick, consequently came in unpleasantly close to Skerryvore and had to alter quickly to clear the reefs. Shortly before noon a mine was sighted. The starboard six-pounder was manned and a firing party of marines got up to sink it. But there was a very high wind blowing, and owing to the bad weather we lost sight of it. Cruised about for half an hour or so, but failed to find it again, so continued our course. Passed Bana Head and outside St Kilda. *Bayana* reported more mines off Skerryvore.

Monday 8

Arrived back on patrol, and took over command once more, after fifteen days' absence. Dirty weather. Spoke the *Bayano* in the forenoon. Went to GQs, and spotting table practice afterwards. No sun, but just managed to snap a time azimuth to get a deviation. I like my job as assistant-navigator (Tanky). Sighted Sydero at 5pm and altered course to the south-west. No news has been heard of the *Clan MacNaughton* since the 2nd instant, and bodies are said to have been washed up.* She is the second ship of our squadron to be lost. With her goes Commander Jeffreys, her skipper – he is our *Cornwall* Jeffreys' cousin – and dear old Lieut.-Commander Popham, our first lieutenant in the *Crescent*. Very bad luck, as he was an awful good sort; married, with one child, to whom he was absolutely devoted.

Tuesday 9

Very busy all day. There is heaps to do in this job, but it is excellent experience, and I get good sleep, as night hours are fairly slack. Swung

---

* It is believed that HMS *Clan MacNaughton* was sunk off the north coast of Ireland on 3 February 1915 after striking a mine during a storm.

ship roughly in the forenoon and compared the four compasses.
Mr Green issued a large number of Service text- and work-books,
etc., to the gunroom. The loss of the *Clan MacNaughton* is now to all
intents and purposes certain, but whether she was blown up by a mine,
torpedoed by a submarine, ran ashore and broke up or foundered in a
gale, remains a mystery, as with the *Viknor*. Wreckage has been found
far out from land, presumably hers. Communicated visually with the
Hildebrand in the afternoon. Fine, sunny day, very nice after Liverpool
fog; still a big swell, and gale got up again after dark. I have got into
the admiral's and skipper's bad books just lately. Stopped up late and
finished correcting charts. Great game of deck hockey in the 'dogs'.

Wednesday 10

Took advantage of moderate weather to play more deck hockey on
the lee side. It is very nice to be able to do this, after the cramped
decks of the *Crescent*. Intercepted a Danish barquentine bound for
Troon with timber; she proved to be the *Esther* of Marshal. Let her
proceed. Had a long chat with old Outram. He is a dear old chap, and
talks in a gruff old voice; very interesting some of his anecdotes are.
It must be rather unpleasant for him, as the commodore of the Allan
Line, now being only a commander, RNR, and junior to our skipper
and the rear-admiral, and treated as practically a nobody. He is a fine
old seaman.

Thursday 11

The armed boarding vessel *Caesarea* has been detached for service with
Tenth Cruiser Squadron, for bringing out prize crews to their ships. I
like Lieutenant Clarke, the navigator, my chief, very much. He is a quiet,
methodical sort of devil, a great favourite of the skipper's. Reputed very
good at games. Rather apt to be a bit short-tempered, but on the whole a
damned good sort. Very fair weather on patrol. Worked both sounding
machines forward, also the *Empress* after one, in the forenoon. The
Cedric reported unsuccessfully chasing a big steamer at dawn, which

drew away from her at sixteen-and-a-half knots. We told off all our
patrol to intercept her and went south ourselves. She was intercepted
in the afternoon and proved to be the *Frederick VIII*, a Danish liner;
examined and allowed to proceed. Several Scandinavian liners are
suspected of smuggling Germans across from the USA. Took an Eiffel
Tower time signal at 11.45pm. A great game of deck hockey in the dogs.
Very ferocious play.

Friday 12

Very wet and unpleasant all day, although the sea and wind kept down
fairly well. GQs in the forenoon, 1-inch aiming tube firing, with the
starboard guns, the proper guns' crews closing up first, and then the
corresponding part guns' crews taking their places. The firing was fairly
good considering the blinding rain. The skipper had a row with 'Guns',
much to that individual's annoyance. The imperturbable Clarke was
nearly drawn in, and, of course, old JK had to have a jolly good gas
about it.

Saturday 13

The *Otway* intercepted the Norwegian America liner *Trondhjemsfjord*
during the forenoon and sent her into Kirkwall with a prize crew.
A close watch is being kept for the *Oscar II*, which is supposed to be
carrying German officers and men of the reserve to Copenhagen. The
captain inspected our journals; only very cursorily, however, and made
but few remarks. Apparently he didn't see my plans of the steering
arrangements, which would, I think, have interested him. Tottenham
very much to the fore; could not understand why his noon sight was
three hundred miles out, having used a 1914 *Nautical Almanac*.

Sunday 14

Evidence now obtained seems to show that the *Clan MacNaughton*
was very probably torpedoed by *IT21* returning from her raid on the
Mersey shipping. The *Cedric* reported intercepting the *Oscar II* and

sending her into Kirkwall with a prize crew. We stopped the Norwegian sailing ship *Olav*, cleared from Falmouth with bran; very probably intended for Germany; sent her into Kirkwall with a prize crew under Midshipman Evans, RNR. Stopped a trawler after dark, but let her go after examination. All the RN snotties in the soup. Had a long chat with Clarke about game, the Greigs, etc.

Monday 15

Suspicion has fallen on the Falmouth customs authorities, who are said to be giving neutral ships false clearances with contraband, intended ostensibly for neutrals, but in reality for Germany. Submarines sighted off Loch Ewe and Stornoway. They are reported to have unsuccessfully attacked the store ship at the Stornoway naval base. More wreckage of the *Clan MacNaughton* discovered. Sighted HMS *Digby* in the forenoon. She was 'told off' by the admiral for having bungled his instructions *re* the prize crews at Stornoway. Germans are said to have lain mines off Lerwick, which the *Benbow* narrowly escaped. One trawler patrol ship sunk by them. Sighted the battle cruiser *Australia* doing night firing. I wonder how 'Fober' Robinson likes his new ship.

Tuesday 16

The *Caribbean*'s urgent demands for coal resulted yesterday in her being sent to Loch Ewe to coal, instead of Liverpool, much to her disgust. Very cold day, a snow blizzard in the morning watch, but it cleared up beautifully in the forenoon, and we had some gorgeous and most welcome sunshine. How we value the sun now, when a year ago it was nothing! Communicated with the *Cedric II,* visually, and sent a mail by her into Liverpool, as she is off to coal. 'Guns' got his leg badly pulled, trying to read the *Cedric*'s semaphore. 'Guns' trousers are quite a by-word now in the gunroom. GQs and rate of change practice in the forenoon. Passed the Second Light Cruiser Squadron under Rear-Admiral Napier coming back from firing practice. HMS *Glasgow,* of Valparaiso and Falkland fame, among them. They looked like great long greyhounds, but were making very heavy weather in a sea which didn't even the move us.

Wednesday 17

The battle cruiser *Tiger* and light cruiser *Active* passed the patrol for firing practice. During the night there was a sudden change for the worse in the weather. The glass dropped steadily all day, and the wind blew a full gale from the south-east, backing gradually. A very big sea by noon. By dark there was a regular storm, the worst we have experienced since I was in the *Crescent*. The *Alsatian* is an excellent sea-boat, but nevertheless we were none too comfortable, and all the smaller ships must be having an appalling time. The admiral heard by wireless that information concerning our patrol is leaking out, consequently he is thinking of stopping all leave next time we go to coal, and anyhow the strictest reticence must be observed. He issued a memorandum to the commanding officers of the squadron *re* this.

Thursday 18

Germany's threat to torpedo all merchant shipping in British waters, regardless of loss of life, comes into action today. I am afraid the effect will be more serious than is generally anticipated. As a forerunner of what is to come, five German submarines were sighted at noon yesterday off Cape Wrath, proceeding to the south-west, probably bound for the Irish Sea. Thirty trawlers are reported to have left the Kattegat full of German mines, and the First Light Cruiser Squadron and some destroyers have been sent to look for them. An oil ship has escaped unexamined from the Manchester Ship Canal, and it is feared she will oil the submarines. Considering the Russian military situation, things are looking rather black in general just at present. Weather moderated a little, but still very bad, high wind and very big sea running. All the RN snotties in the soup with JK again. He is getting very bumptious now as acting commander; very different from the

devil-may-care sort of chap that he was when a mere watch-keeper in
the *Crescent*. Stopped and boarded the Norwegian steamer *Sisland* from
Kristiansand to Baltimore at 11pm. Allowed her to proceed.

Friday 19

Sighted two more steamers during the middle watch, but weather
prohibited boarding. Gale continued all day, getting considerably worse
towards nightfall, and we hove to. Went to GQs in the forenoon. Very cold,
and a very high wind from the ENE to NNE. The Second Light Cruiser
Squadron have been sent to support the First Light Cruiser Squadron and
destroyers, sweeping down to the Kattegat for the minelayers, but little can
be done in this weather. The First Cruiser Squadron, composed of some
of the China and Mediterranean ships home from foreign service with
'B' patrol of the Tenth Cruiser Squadron, will sweep east on a line north
from Muckle Flugga, and so catch the minelayers if they have not already
escaped up the Norwegian coast.

Saturday 20

Gale still blowing in all its fury; seas mountainous, running right down
unchecked from the North Cape and off Spitzbergen. Miserable day.
The signal bosun sounded off the alarm by mistake after breakfast, and
we all rushed to our action stations, thinking a scrap was in sight at
last, and were very sick to find it a false alarm. It reminded me of the
false alarm on the *Crescent* when Commander Wardle sounded off by
mistake. The old man gave the signal bosun what for. He has a nasty
liver this morning. Merchantmen and trawlers report submarines off
the Faroes; they are probably after us, but they won't like this weather.
We are shifting temporarily from the south-west to the south-east of the
Faroes, about halfway to the Shetlands, to support 'B' patrol.

Sunday 21

Two German disguised minelayers will leave the Norwegian port of
Bergen tonight. Owing to the submarine menace, all our patrols are to

be moved about a hundred miles to the westward by noon tomorrow. Gale continued without abating one jot. Communicated with the *Digby*, who reported sinking mines off Sydero. Sighted two trawlers, apparently British; too rough to board.

Monday 22

Gale went on like blue hell, but continuous snow supplanted the rain squalls we have had previously. Wind shifted to of the northward. Very big sea running. Cold intense; the coldest weather I have yet experienced since I joined the ship; average height of thermometer 16°F, 16° below freezing point, although at times it has dropped considerably lower. The spray flying over the bows froze before it reached the bridge, and cut your face with the force of the impact. All the decks not actually awash were as slippery as ice. Intercepted and examined the SSF *Heredik* of Hangesund for the second time in a fortnight. She is bound from Goole to Reykjavík, and appears to be taking her time over it.

Tuesday 23

A great controversy – Lieutenant Kenyon and the gunroom officers, RN, *versus* Lieut.-Commander Kiddle and the gunroom officers, RNR. Result, a draw in their favour. Woke up and turned out on deck to find the decks covered in snow, inches deep. The gale abated, and sea went down a little. Snow storms all day, and still fearfully cold. Made Sydero early, luckily near Sunbö Light, otherwise we might have fetched the Munken. Stopped and examined a trawler from Iceland to Sorvaag. She looked more like the icing off a wedding cake than a real live ship. Went to GQs in the forenoon, but too cold for target practice and too rough to lower target.

Wednesday 24

Not quite so cold and weather better. Fears expressed for the safety of the *Patia* and *Orotava*; they have not been heard of for three days. We met the *Changuinola* and *Columbella* at a rendezvous in the forenoon, and got back our prize crew with Midshipman Evans, which took in the *Olav* ten days ago. They spent three days in Kirkwall, and went to St Kilda in the *Caesarea,* and finally went on board the *Changuinola* and so back here. Ben Evans brought back some messages from old Shearer at Kirkwall. The *Digby* and *Hilary* both reported sinking mines.

Thursday 25

McNaught's twenty-first birthday celebrated in great style. The famous *Dacia,* which has been taking such a front seat in the newspapers of late, is reported to be in wireless touch with Valentia. Whether she will try the north- or southabout route seems uncertain. The *Ambrose* has three prize crews away and cannot send any more. We are leaving our patrol off the Faroes and coming south for a bit. Several changes are now being made in the constitution of the various patrols. The *Changuinola* has been despatched to the Flannan Isles. The safety of the *Patia* has been ascertained. We intercepted a Norwegian sailing vessel, the *Glen Lora,* and sent her into Kirkwall for examination with a prize crew under Midshipman Renfree, RNR. Also we stopped the Swedish steamer *Drottning Sophia,* but allowed her to proceed. I was employed superintending fitting out of after-control.

Friday 26

More bad weather experienced. Stopped and boarded the SS *Overdia,* bound from Baltimore to Malmö in Sweden, and sent her into Kirkwall for examination with a prize crew under Midshipman Elliott, RNR. The *Dacia* has been heard calling by wireless, but her route is still uncertain. We altered course to the north-east to stop a ship, making for the Shetlands, that the *Digby* had failed to catch. Took an Eiffel Tower wireless time signal at 11.45pm. 'Little things annoy great minds' – the amended proverb. The admiral searched for a stump of pencil the flag captain had lost for three-quarters of an hour; accused everyone of stealing or hiding it, and finally found it in his pocket.

Saturday 27

Very cold again, snowing all day. No news of the *Dacia*. I hope she hasn't got through, though it is quite possible, as the snow storms prevent us seeing more than a few cables from the ship, and she might slip through unobserved. Sighted Sydero early, and spoke the *Hilary* and *Digby* later. I had a row with Henderson over physical training. Tottenham logged our course S 84° W instead of N 84° W, and put our 8pm DR twelve miles out. He got scrubbed by all four OOWs, and was very anxious that the navigator and skipper should not know, as (he said) it would affect his certificate, which, however, in our opinion, must be already so bad that it can't be worse.

Sunday 28

Heard by wireless that the *Dacia* had been captured in the Channel by a French patrol. Mustered the hands by Open List. Big gale blowing, usual weather, heavy snow, large seas and very cold. Still to the south-west of the Faroes.

MARCH

Monday 1

Weather as per routine, glass well below freezing again. An American ship refused to be boarded by the *Ambrose,* who thereupon applied to the *Patuca,* the senior officer of her patrol, for instructions. Shots were fired across the Yankee ship's bow (the *Navahoe* her name was), and she then hove to. A boarding party from the *Patuca,* who had come up, was sent under our old *Crescent* friend, Lieut.-Commander Bacon, RNR, and she was taken into Kirkwall as a prize for examination, in spite of the vehement protests of her captain and crew.

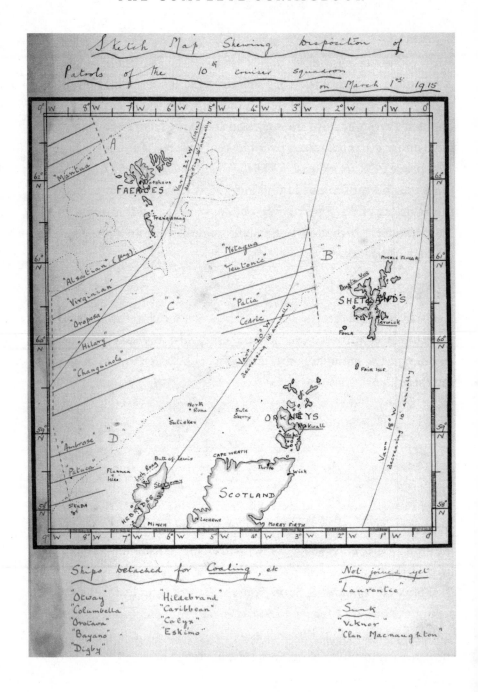

Sketch Map Shewing disposition of Patrols of the 10th cruiser Squadron on March 1st 1915

Ships detached for Coaling, etc

"Otway" "Hildebrand"
"Columbella" "Caribbean"
"Orotava" "Calyx"
"Bayano" "Eskimo"
"Digby"

Not joined yet
"Laurentic"

Sunk
"Viknor"
"Clan Macnaughton"

Tuesday 2

Heavy snowfall all the forenoon; better weather in the afternoon.
Went quite close to Sydero, the black heights of Sunbö Head, topped
with the glistening snow-white hills behind, looked very fine.
Sighted HMS *Cedric* at noon and cruised in company during the
afternoon; communicated by boat and exchanged several signals.
She proceeded south-east to her patrol at 4pm, and we went back to
ours to the south-west of the Faroes, from ten miles to two hundred
miles distant from Sydero. The *Patuca* reports the death of her
commander. I had a row with Clarke; he accused me of being abrupt,
and we argued thereon.

Wednesday 3

Sea and wind moderated, but steady rain and thick fog all day. Went to
spotting table in the forenoon. 'Pompous Percy' in his element. John
Kiddle ranting about the gunroom doing 6-inch loader, but no one
listened. The wardroom started a backgammon competition, and the
secretary tried to arrange a concert for Saturday night; success patchy.
Sighted a steamship, the *Jemtland,* at 9pm, examined her, and allowed
her to proceed; then went full speed ahead to deceive her, altered course,
and came around astern unobserved, and followed her throughout the
night to find out if her intentions were genuine.

Thursday 4

Neutral vessels are now taking the precaution of having their name and
national flag and port of register painted on their sides. In spite of the
unfavourable predictions of 'Guns', the secretary's concert is advancing
apace. The ship's company have several turns, and a gunroom septet
are singing 'Old Uncle Tom Cobleigh'. The gunroom will also provide
'When Irish Eyes Are Smiling' and 'A Capital Ship', and McNaught is
going to give a piano solo.

    Boarded the *Jemtland* at 7.15am, and as everything was found
all right she was allowed to proceed, as she promised to call at

Kirkwall for full examination. Personally I think she should have been sent in with a prize crew. Came up to the east of the Faroes to act in conjunction with A and B patrols, in order to catch a Danish ship laden with whale oil, trying to get through from the Faroes to Germany. Sighted HMS *Martial* 5.30pm, and at eight boarded and examined an Aberdeen trawler.

Friday 5

Boarded, examined, and allowed to proceed, the Norwegian steamer *King Haakon*. Went back again to the south-west of the Faroes. Heard that a Yankee ship with foodstuffs for Germany has succeeded in slipping through down the Norwegian coast. Carried out rate of change practice in the forenoon, and target firing practice in the afternoon. The firing was quite good, especially with the 6-inch guns; although the six-pounders were not so good, we did not manage to damage the target much, but succeeded in deafening everybody, which always seems a great objective of gunnery experts. Tottenham and the signal bosun had a long argument over a pair of spotting glasses. They were so surprised by hearing the first gun go off that they dropped the glasses and smashed the prisms, 25s. each; language unprintable.

Saturday 6

Worked the after sounding machine successfully. Had a last rehearsal of the concert in the afternoon. Weather fair, but very cold indeed. The concert came off at six. Rather early, but if it had been later it would have disturbed the night watch-keepers. A great success. About fifteen turns, all the gunroom ones being excellent, especially 'A Capital Ship' and 'Widecombe Fair'. The admiral seemed very pleased, and the skipper expressed approbation in his usual philosophical manner. With the exception of the secretary and Staff Surgeon Walker, the wardroom did nothing, which was awfully flat of them. Individually they are a very nice set of chaps, but as a mess they are the dullest I have ever served with; no go or guts at all. It is the same in everything. Very busy all day clearing up generally, preparatory to going into harbour early next week.

Sunday 7

Left patrol for the south to go to Liverpool to coal. Stopped a Danish steamer with cotton from Galveston to Göteborg, and sent her into Kirkwall with a prize crew under Midshipman Wood, RNR. Communicated with HMS *Patuca* visually and by boat. Examined another sailing vessel in the evening.

Monday 8

Passed Barra Head at 8am. Later Skerryvore, then Oversay, and then across to the Irish coast. Turned all our boats out and kept a very close lookout for mines and submarines, with which these waters seem infested. Passed between Rathlin Island and Portrush, then rounded Fair Head and ran down into the Irish Sea.

A whole network of trawlers minesweeping between the Mull of Cantyre and Larne, also the gunboat *Skipjack* and patrol despatch vessel *Tara*. The longer light and extra warmth down south again most welcome. Arrived off the Bar at 12.30. A very busy and exciting time. On the bridge all night. Coincident with our return the German submarines have arrived again, and two ships were sunk tonight within three miles of us, although fog prevented us rendering any assistance. All hands drowned.

Tuesday 9

Anchored in the Mersey off Pier Head at 2am. A very welcome mail came off at six. Stacks of letters for me, and, tired as I was, I waded through them, taking about two-and-a-half hours. A wasted day spent dawdling about in the Mersey, as the docks are so full of shipping. Very busy clearing up in the chart house, although feeling dog-tired from want of sleep. Secured alongside in Canada Dock at 8pm. HMS

Columbella, the only other ship of our squadron in, leaves at dark. Another submarine victim just outside Bar. Passed HMS *Devonshire* in dock. Landed 8pm. Had some cocktails at the Adelphi and proceeded on leave by the 10.45pm train.

Wednesday 10

Arrived London 4am, went to Cumberland Terrace, and turned in. Claude Lowther and Jack Russell dined here last night. Spent the forenoon in bed, then went to call on Aunt Do after lunch with Norman. Daddy, Uncle John, Auntie Connie and Esther also there. Went to call on Sophie; met Fanny Hallowes and Olive. Went home in a fearful hurry, stopping at Gieve's for a cap on the way, when I saw dear old Humphrey Legge for a minute. Rushed off, dined with Olive at the Tiv., then on to 'Peg o' My Heart' at the Globe. Rotten play, but Peg excellent. Norman and Claude Lowther there. Took Olive to sup at the Cri.,* and then home about midnight. Old Norman has been to see 'Peg o' My Heart' nearly twenty times.

Thursday 11

Got up late, went and shopped most of the forenoon in Bond Street, also went to my bank in Russell Square. Norman accompanied me at first. Came home to lunch. Olive to lunch. Gertrude and Aunt Amy arrived about three, but I had to leave directly afterwards to go to Victoria to catch a train to Canterbury East, arriving 6.10. Got some oysters at Harrison's, and then went to Quaives to get some fizz. Loved being home. Stopped the night Westenhanger. The oysters and fizz a great success. Poor old Jack arrived very late, about twelve. Toots in bed with a breakdown; she has been doing too much. I had a long nocturnal chat with Joko from our bedroom windows. I find myself worse than ever over her.

---

* The Criterion Restaurant in London's Piccadilly.

Friday 12

Got up late, went round with Jack and Joko to see Grannie at the Rectory; saw Byron, Dolly and Gwen Cohen, who is stopping with the Kelseys, and has developed into a very pretty girl now. After lunch called on Mrs Kelsey and had several drinks with Bob, the Doc, Jabez and Frank Goodson at the Tank, then went on to Quaives to get some gear. Left at four, motored to Ashford with Joko. Gone over her completely again, and very jealous as she is very keen on two damned carabineers, Dent and Charlesworth. How I long for the dear, safe, dull old Buffs again! Went by train to Godstone. Met Malky and Miss Judd at the station. Stopped night at Godstone with Uncle John. Auntie Connie, Grannie Greig, Malky and old Uncle John Thomson also there.

Saturday 13

Hunted; met at Oxted with the Old Surrey. Cecil Leveson-Gower out and in great form. Not much of a day; killed a lame fox early on, and then did rottenly. May Gould out; a very nice girl, and quite pretty, or rather picturesque; Malky raves about her. Uncle John Thomson left, and Mike, Mog and Beg arrived in the evening. Old 'Doc' Paterson came in with Cecil to tea. A tremendous game of billiard bowls in the evening after dinner; Malky tremendous fun. I sat up very late swigging whisky and sodas and talking to Mike, and as I did a bottle of fizz for dinner, felt quite happy. Old Grannie Greig not at all well.

Sunday 14

Went up by the 11.10 train to town. In the afternoon Daddy, Jack and Mrs Russell, with their children and Billy and Donald Hugh and I all went to the zoo. Donald Hugh Ellis is a little boy of Billy's age, who is living with us during his parents' absence in India. He is a grandson of Admiral Finnis, my old friend. Jack R invited me to dine at the Berkeley with him, but I could not go, as Joko came to town and I met her.

We dined at the 'Troc', then to a concert at the Palladium, and then home to Sophie's. Poor old Stanley laid up with a broken ankle. On my return home at one, found a wired leave extending Tuesday till Saturday.

Monday 15

Got up late, went to meet Joko at Down Street Station, and then we shopped together in Regent Street, Oxford Street and Bond Street. Lunched at the Café Royal.* Then called on Aunt Do and had tea. Then went to see Henry, who is wounded in hospital and looking awful. Olive was with him. Also called on the Buchanans, but they were out. Then Joko went home to dress, ditto me. Met her at Piccadilly Station, and we dined at the Savoy. Then went to 'The Country Girl' at Daly's. Excellent show; Gertie Millar† and WH Berry excellent. Mabel Sealby, the girl JPR was engaged to, was acting. Went back to the Savoy for supper and stopped for two or three hours' dancing. Thoroughly enjoyed every minute of it. Went home madly in love.

Tuesday 16

Got up late again. Joko came to lunch. Then she and I went to Madame Tussaud's and called on the Phelps and Woodwards. Then we both went home our ways. Izzie Phelps to tea at home. Joko and I dined with Johnstone at Prince's. Then went on to 'Kings and Queens' at the St James's Theatre. Marie Löhr‡ acted wonderfully well, but the play was rather too tense. Afterwards we met Florence Lomax, and then went to supper, the four of us at the Piccadilly Restaurant. Then on to dance at the '400'. I was very disappointed with the '400', as were Joko and Johnnie, although we all enjoyed ourselves. Got home about 3am. Mother and Daddy dined with the Finchs. These days with Joko are a beautiful dream, I am madly

---

* Café Royal restaurant on Regent Street, today part of the Hotel Café Royal.

† Gertie Millar was one of the most famous stage actresses of the era, renowned for her performances in musicals.

‡ The actress Marie Lohr would later go on to have a long and distinguished film career in Britain.

in love with her. I wonder if I shall ever get over it. She is very fond of me, but I am afraid would not marry me anytime for many years. I fear people will begin to talk about us being so much together soon.

Wednesday 17

Got up late again, and Joko came to lunch again. Then in the afternoon we went to the 'Flag-Lieutenant' at the Haymarket, which she thoroughly enjoyed. Queen Alexandra there. In the evening Daddy, mother, Joko and I dined with Mr and Mrs Russell at the Bath Club, and then went on to 'Business as Usual' at the Hippodrome; Harry Tate* very funny, and quite a good show. I took Joko home afterwards. Heard that Henry is very serious now. I told Joko that although I have enjoyed these days with her more than anything on earth, I don't think they ought to be repeated, as people are beginning to talk about us. Oh, that I was a few years older and could ask her to marry me, as I am sure we should hit it off well together. I think Joko is fond of me, but not enough to promise anything at present, so I shan't ask her. I feel helplessly miserable as I shall hardly see any more of her. Oh why at eighteen must I suffer the troubles of men five years more my senior.

Thursday 18

Joko rang up about 11am to say she would come round in the afternoon to see Norman about getting a job. So I was looking forward to seeing her for the last time, when imagine my chagrin to find she rang up again to say she could not come as she must stop with Olive as Henry was undergoing a very serious operation. She even let me know what train she was going home by with Jack, consequently I felt absolutely miserable and wretched at not seeing her again. I learnt too late from Sophie that she had gone down by the 7.45 with Jack. I was nearly off

---

* Harry Tate was a Scottish comedian who performed in musical halls and later in films. He died in 1940 as a result of the injuries he sustained during the London Blitz in the Second World War.

my head with misery. Norman, Louie and the two little girls, Olivia and Jill, arrived home from Torquay from stopping with the Blackers. Daddy and mother persuaded me to go and dine with them with Dr and Mrs Handfield-Jones, but I was too miserable to enjoy it.

Friday 19

Went to the Automobile Club, met Daddy, and went to call on Admiral Finnis at the Naval and Military Club, but he was out. Then went up to see Daddy's searchlight position on top of Oceanic House. Saw the model of the *Alsatian* in Trafalgar Square. Went on to the city, called on old Alex Thompson, saw Jack Russell and his Uncle Jeph, saw Blunt and Uncle John and Charley Tatham. Lunched with Daddy at the City Canton, then went to see Aunt Do, and on to Sophie's at Earl's Court. Unluckily Stanley and Olive out, but Sophie said Henry was better. Muriel Stubbs and Miss Fell called. Went home. Little Olivia, Norman's eldest girl, is a wonderful character, years older than she really is, and an awful flirt. She quite fascinates me. Dined with Daddy and mother at Gennaro's. Then went on to see 'The Man Who Stopped at Home'; quite good. Denis Eadie very clever, and Isobel Elsom* very pretty. I wish Joko had seen it.

Saturday 20

Daddy got a bad cold. Packed, wrote letters, etc., and settled up my affairs generally. I am leaving my diary at home for safety, and shall write it up on my return. Left for Liverpool 6pm. Said goodbye to little Olivia and went up to Liverpool; travelled with Johnstone. Arrived on board about 11pm. Lots of interesting chatter. Rumours of an attack on Heligoland in the future. HMS *Calyx* and *Eskimo* of our squadron have been paid off, being too small for the work. During my absence the prize crews had joined up. Elliott had had

---

* Isobel Elsom was a notable actress of stage and screen, and would later go on to enjoy a long and illustrious career in Hollywood.

an interesting experience, being chased by a submarine off Westray. A drastic blockade policy, which has been decided on by government as retaliation against German submarine policy, has resulted in one hundred and twenty being stopped and sent in during our absence from patrol.

Sunday 21

Found HM ships *Devonshire, Virginian* and *Victorian* in harbour. The latter may join our squadron later on. A gorgeous day. Wrote to mother, Aunt Do and Joko. We went out into the river at 1pm and left the Mersey at 11.30. A submarine reported right ahead off the 'Chickens', and we made a detour south-west and saw nothing; Micky Freer looking very ferocious with a huge cutlass and two revolvers.

21 March 1915 HMS *ALSATIAN*

Dear Mother,

Just a line in a hurry, before we sail, which will be soon, I expect. It is a gorgeous day here, quite hot and bright sunshine. I hope Daddy's cold is better; don't let him go back to duty until he has got rid of it. When he is up again, please remind him to leave a card at Admiral Finnis's club.

No news; give my best love to all, and a kiss for Olivia.

Toby

PS We sail at midnight tonight (Sunday). This will be delayed two days in transit.

Monday 22

My job this trip is gunfire control officer. There are four of us aft and four forward, each in four watches. Dropped the pilot at Formby, and left the Bar Light Vessel at 1am convoyed by HM destroyer *Dove*. Strict lookout night and day owing to submarine and mine menace. Boats turned out in case of accident. Hostile submarine reported off Corsewall Point. Went to general quarters in the forenoon. Got safely out of the Irish Sea without mishap. The *Dove* left us at Oversay, and by evening we were past Barra Head and out of the danger area. On passage back to patrol. Had a long chat with 'Pompous' Williams.

Tuesday 23

Back on patrol south-west of the Faroes. The fine weather we have experienced down south still continues, but the drop in the temperature is very noticeable. Rendezvous with HMS *Cedric* at 4pm, and took over charge of Tenth Cruiser Squadron from Captain Benson. She reports having experienced the coldest weather of the whole winter in our absence. I had a row with Lance-Sergeant Powell, RMLI, and told him off. John Kiddle is said to have suffered serious financial losses lately owing to the war; hence his temper, which is phenomenally bad.

Wednesday 24

Two prizes sent in during the day, both Norwegian, one Galveston to Stavanger, and the other Norfolk Island to Aalborg. Midshipman McNaught, RNR, in charge of the first, and Midshipman Ward, RNR, of the second. Very cold still, glass below freezing point. A strenuous game of deck hockey in the dog watches. In the first watch 'Pompous' Williams continued the story of his multitudinous experiences in Yankee-land.

24-27 March *Midshipmen's Journal* Daily Log
On Patrol
Rough extent of patrol ground {Lat 60°–62°N}
{Long 10°–13°W}
On 25th sent in Swedish SS *Centric* to Kirkwall with prize crew under Midshipman Adams, RNR.

APRIL

28 March-3 April *Midshipmen's Journal* Daily Log
On Patrol
On Sunday, 28th, shifted our patrol position to 'A' between the Faroes and Iceland. Sighted the Icelandic coast at 10am. The great snowy mass of Öræfajökull (6900 ft) appeared most imposing.

The captain read letters of congratulations, to the ship's company, from the Lords of the Admiralty and from the C-in-C, Admiral Jellicoe, to Rear-Admiral De Chair, on the work of the Tenth Cruiser Patrols.

A large number of fishing ketches are met with in these waters, returning from and going to the Icelandic fisheries. On the 28th we challenged in error the small Danish fishing gunboat *Islands Falk*; but on discovering her identity, apologised, and allowed her to proceed. The Norwegian SS *Bergensfjord* has again been caught with several German reservists on board, and she has been sent to Kirkwall by HMS *Otway*.

On Friday, 2 April, we regained our three prize crews from HMS *Digby*, whence they had been transferred from HMS *Patia*, who brought them out from Stornoway. They were conveyed from Scapa to Stornoway in the armed boarding vessel *Duke of Cornwall*, which has succeeded the *Anglia* and *Caesarea* on Tenth Cruiser Squadron prize crew duty. While at Scapa the prize crews were accommodated in the *Cambria*, lying at Long Hope. The officers in charge of the prize crews report that the major part of the Grand Fleet is lying at Scapa. While in the *Duke of Cornwall* they were fired on by the armed yacht *Vanessa* off Cape Wrath, owing to an error in the challenges.

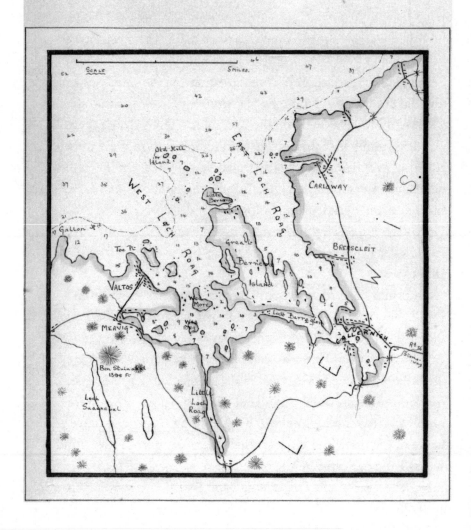

THE LOCHS ROAG

4 April *Midshipmen's Journal* Daily Log

After receiving our prize crews, we did not return to 'A' patrol, but remained on 'C' patrol west and SW of the Faroes.

We escorted an eastward-bound American SS towards Muckle Flugga. About noon we turned her over to HMS *Motagna*, it being too rough to board; and then altered course to the SW to make Butt of Lewis.

Suggested new base for Tenth Cruiser Squadron

The Admiralty have suggested a new base for the Tenth Cruiser Squadron at West Loch Roag on Lewis on the NW coast. The object of this new base would be to minimise submarine danger, and to save time taken by ships proceeding from and to patrol while using the Mersey and Clyde as bases.

In consequence we decided to visit West Loch Roag in order that the rear-admiral commanding the Tenth Cruiser Squadron might report personally on its suitability for a base, after examining it himself.

5 April *Midshipmen's Journal* Daily Log

We passed Sulisker Rock and North Rona in the forenoon, and later the Butt of Lewis. Gun control watches were set, owing to the submarine menace, a submarine having been lately sighted off St Kilda. At 1.30pm, being about midway between Gallan Head and Old Hill Island, we altered course into West Loch Roag to the SE.

At 3pm, after passing through Vuia Sound, we anchored SSE of Vuia Mor Island, in the inner part of the loch. The steam and motorboats were immediately lowered from the davits, the motorboat being told off as ship's duty boat, while the steam boat did duty as admiral's barge.

A boat was sent off to Meavaig, about three miles away, in the western portion of the loch, to bring off Rear-Admiral Tupper (SNO Stornoway) and his secretary, in order to confer with Rear-Admiral De Chair. Rear-Admiral Tupper went ashore again at 6pm, and motored back from Meavaig to Stornoway.

During the evening two patrolling trawlers came in and anchored close to the *Alsatian*. We sent the duty boat away with the navigator in order to mark the position of a dangerous submerged rock in the Sound of Vuia, by laying down a 'Reindeer' buoy, after fixing the position by sextant angles of the cairns on top of the Vuia Mor Island, Vuia Beg Island, and the south and north extremities of Vuia Mor.

S. 519.—Revised, May, 1914.

JOURNAL

FOR THE USE OF

MIDSHIPMEN.

Mr. *A. Scrimgeour.*

H.M.S.^{hips} "Crescent" + "Alsatian"

From Aug 2nd 1914

To

LONDON :
PRINTED FOR H.M. STATIONERY OFFICE BY WATERLOW & SONS LIMITED.

1914.

OW 13762.
11.

Sta. 45/14.

6 April *Midshipmen's Journal* Daily Log

A strong breeze from the mainland caused the ship to 'sheer'
considerably at single anchor, and as our stern was in close proximity
to the lee shore of Bernera Island, we let go a second anchor, which
steadied her considerably. We sent a mail ashore at Meavaig, and at 6pm
weighed both anchors and proceeded out of harbour back to patrol
again.

8 April *Midshipmen's Journal* Daily Log

Sighted a large number of ships during the day, and intercepted and
boarded the majority. The steam ships *Lapland* and *Zamora* with
one sailing barque were sent into Kirkwall with prize crews under
Midshipmen Renfree, Elliott and JG Wood, RNR.

Received information that HMS *Teutonic*, who is detached for
duty off the Norwegian coast and has effected some valuable captures
including that of the *Sir Ernest Cassel*, was chased last night by a ship
with strange lights. The captain of the *Teutonic* surmised that she was
a German cruiser, and attempted to draw her towards Muckle Flugga
to engage her in daylight. The *Teutonic* omitted to challenge her. On
receipt of the news the C-in-C despatched two light cruisers to look for
the vessel.

9 April *Midshipmen's Journal* Daily Log

Considerable alterations in the patrols of the Tenth Cruiser Squadron
are under consideration, owing to the shorter periods of darkness now
being experienced with the approach of the summer. The alterations
include a patrol north of Iceland, one between Iceland and the Faroes,
reduction to single line patrol between Sydero and Cape Wrath, and a
patrol east of the Shetlands off the Norwegian coast. Several more ships
will be required.

Details will be given later.

10-18 April *Midshipmen's Journal* Daily Log

On the 12th we communicated with HMS *Cedric*, just out from
Liverpool, and on the following day with HMS *Teutonic*, from whom
we received two of our prize crews under Midshipmen Elliott and
Renfree, RNR.

Prize crew procedure

East-bound prize crews take their ships to Kirkwall, except in some
cases of sailing ships, which are obliged to make Lerwick. West-bound
vessels, when sent in, go to Stornoway. The prize crews making Kirkwall
are accommodated in the *Cambria* at Long Hope. At intervals of about
a week, the *Duke of Cornwall* conveys them all to Stornoway, where
they are transported to a ship of the Tenth Cruiser Squadron, which
distributes them to their various patrols. Lerwick crews go to Kirkwall
in a drifter, then as above.

Midshipman Wood, RNR, who took in a sailing ship on the 8th
was obliged to make Lerwick, and here assisted with his prize crew
in putting out a fire, caused by a serious explosion in an ammunition
shed.

On the 14th we went up north of the Faroes to patrol in latitudes
64°N and 65°N, and extremely cold weather was experienced. On the
18th, however, we came down south again, preparatory to leaving patrol
to coal.

19 April *Midshipmen's Journal* Daily Log

Finally left patrol to go in to coal, leaving HMS *Cedric* as SO Tenth
Cruiser Squadron, in the absence of the rear-admiral. HMS *Digby* is to
be despatched to Reykjavík, the capital of Iceland, to deliver despatches
to the British vice-consul, and to ascertain the probable limits of ice in
the Icelandic districts this season.

We passed Barra Head sixty miles to the westward at noon. Received
news that HMS *Oropesa* had been attacked by a submarine further to
the south, consequently a vigilant lookout was kept.

HMS *Oropesa's* action with submarine

The *Oropesa* (Commander Stanley, RN) was returning to patrol after coaling in the Clyde. When off Oversay a submarine appeared astern and chased. The RA *Alsatian* and SNO Larne were immediately informed, and fire was opened with the after guns. After a time several shells exploded close to the submarine, which disappeared. Consequently the *Garry* and *Tara*, which had been sent to the assistance of the *Oropesa*, were recalled by the SNO Larne.

The *Alsatian* passed the *Oropesa* at 2pm and later in the dog watches, large patches of oil were sighted, when off Oversay. Thus the *Oropesa* may have sunk her adversary.

20 April *Midshipmen's Journal* Daily Log

A new route was followed, and instead of going over inside Rathlin Island, the Scotch coast was hugged, and we passed the Mull of Cantyre light abeam at 9pm.

We arrived off the Mersey Bar Light Vessel at 6am, and picked up Mr Trenter, the Allan Line pilot, from the tug *Bison*. At 7am we dropped anchor off the Pier Head, Liverpool, in the Mersey.

21 April *Midshipmen's Journal* Daily Log

Three gangways rigged, and the coal lighters came alongside, coaling commencing at 7am with shore labour.

When the coal lighters amidships between the ship and jetty were emptied and required to be shifted to give place to full ones, it was necessary to start the ship out from the jetty a little. To do this an eight-inch hemp, secured to the *Scandinavian* on the opposite side of the dock and lying on the bottom so as to avoid impeding the fairway, was brought to the capstan on the port side of the *Alsatian* and tautened up; the strain, this brought on the hemp, being sufficient to start the ship out enough to let the lighters pass, without it being necessary to interfere with the wires securing her to the jetty; these not being taut enough to oppose the motion. When the lighters were shifted, the hemp was slacked off again to the bottom, and the wind carried the ship back to her old position.

JOURNAL FOR THE USE OF MIDSHIPMEN.

1. The Journal is to be kept during the whole of a Midshipman's sea time. A second volume may be issued if required.

2. The **Officer** detailed to supervise the Midshipmen's instruction is to see that the journal is properly kept in accordance with the following instructions. He should initial the midshipmen's journals at least once a month, but should see that they are written up from time to time during the month and not immediately before they are called in for inspection.

The **Captain** is to have the journals produced for his inspection from time to time, and should initial them at each inspection.

The **Midshipman** on leaving a ship should get the Captain to initial his journal.

The following remarks indicate the main lines to be followed in keeping the journal.

Midshipmen should record in their own language their observations about all things of interest and matters of importance in the work that is carried on, on their Station, in their Fleet, or in their ship. They may insert descriptions of places visited and of the people with whom they come in contact, harbours and anchorages, fortifications; they may write notes on coaling facilities, landing places, abnormal weather, prevailing winds and currents, salvage operations, Foreign ships met with, and the manner in which Foreign Fleets are handled, Battle practices, Gunlayer's test, actions in manœuvres, remarks on P.Z. exercises. On the ship making a passage of sufficient interest, they should note the weather and noon position.

Separate entries need not necessarily be made for each separate day, but full accounts should be given of any events of interest.

Midshipmen should understand that the main object of keeping the journal is to train (a) the power of observation, (b) the power of expression, (c) the habit of orderliness.

Midshipmen should illustrate the letter-press with plans and sketches pasted into the pages of the journal, namely :—

Track Charts.

Plans of Anchorages. (These should show the berths occupied by the Squadron or ship, and if a Fleet was anchored the courses steered by the Fleet up to the anchorage).

Sketches of places visited, of coast line, of headlands, of leading marks into Harbours, of ships British and Foreign, of parts or fittings of ships, or any other objects of interest.

4. The Journal is to be produced at the examination in Seamanship for the rank of Lieutenant, when marks to a maximum of 50 will be awarded for it. (K.R. Appendix X. Part II. (13).

21-28 April *Midshipmen's Journal* Daily Log

In Liverpool, alongside No. 1 Canada Dock coaling, provisioning ship, making good minor defects and receiving various new fittings.

Six days' leave to one watch. Received on board various RFR ratings (chiefly stokers) for exclusive duty with prize crews.

Six officers with three prize crews joined the ship for passage to HMS *Cedric* on patrol.

Repairs and alterations

While in harbour, several minor defects were made good, and small alterations made. The wireless set, always a source of trouble, was repaired; the dynamo armature having been burnt out some days before entering harbour, this necessitating the use of the emergency set. A new main dynamo armature was fitted; and also a 'direction finder', the extra aerials being supported by spars above the boat deck. This contrivance should be of great use in approximately locating ships to be intercepted, when they can be heard using wireless.

The most important of all items however, was the *new magazine protection* fitting. In several cases of ships being torpedoed, it has been found that their magazines have exploded, thus extra protection has become a dire necessity. Up to the present a torpedo striking the ship abreast the magazines, would only have had a narrow and thin plate to pierce after destroying the side plating; thus magazine protection was to all intents and purposes nil. The cartridges are stowed against the port side of the magazine and the projectiles the starboard side, and only the thin plating and ships side separated them from the water. The new system of protection, however, is as follows:

The deck has been slightly armoured both above and below the magazine. In the case of the fore magazine, two stiff fore and aft plates have been substituted for one thin one. They are joined at the fore end to a stiff transverse plate, and at the after end to the ordinary ship's bulkhead. The space between the outer of the two transverse plates and the ship's side has been fitted with *sandbags*.

In the case of the after magazine, the beam limits of which are considerably further from the ship's side than in the fore magazine, only one fore and aft plate was fitted, and was secured fore and aft to the transverse bulkheads, no extra transverse plate being considered necessary. Sandbags were packed as before between the side plating and side of the ship.

It is hoped that this will prove an efficient protection against mines, or submarines firing torpedoes, and exploding either magazine.

While in harbour, a system of electric clocks was fitted up in the ship, the 'master' clock being situated in the chart house.

25 April 1915 HMS *ALSATIAN*

Dear Mother,

How are you all at home? We got back into harbour on Thursday, after quite an exciting four-and-a-half weeks at sea. I was laid up for about a fortnight owing to a small accident, but am quite well again now. We were very disappointed on arriving in, to find no mails waiting; apparently they had been sent to Inverness by mistake, and we are still awaiting them, as so far we have had no news. Everything is chaotic on board; most of the officers are on leave, and ourselves, the unlucky remnant, are living in a seething mass of coal dust, wet paint, and filthy rubbish of every description. Dockyard 'mateys' all over the ship, as we are having special magazine protection fitted. On Saturday (yesterday) I had to accompany the admiral's secretary up to London with despatches for the Admiralty, being in charge of his escort. We started at 4am and got up at 8.30, and I had to spend the morning and afternoon at the Admiralty, but managed to get off for a few hours in the evening, and went to meet Daddy at the Automobile Club. We dined with Mr and Mrs Jack Russell

at the Berkeley Grill Room, and I had to catch the
midnight train back to Liverpool, arriving at 5am,
pretty tired, as you can imagine, and found myself with
a 'day on'.

The chaos seems to have increased, but we are supposed
to be sailing on Tuesday, although I don't see how we
can sail for at least a week.

I got some of the news from Daddy that you had left
Cumberland Terrace, Grannie Greig's death, etc. How are
Peg, Jim and Bill?

Best love to all of you.

Toby

HMS *ALSATIAN*, FLAGSHIP, TENTH CRUISER SQUADRON: A DAY ON BOARD AS OOD

At Liverpool, Canada Dock, April 1915

Four am turned out with a very thick head after five hours' sleep, threw on some clothes, and relieved Midshipman Cobb, RN, as OOD, who retired with unholy glee to his bunk. Went the rounds with the corporal of watch; everything quiet and correct and remarkably dirty, coal dust, sawdust, straw, packing cases, etc., lying everywhere. At 4.30 the shore gangs of dockers began to arrive, and the foreman asked permission to commence coaling at 4.45, and soon the ceaseless bang, squeak and whine of the steam winches started, accompanied by the roar of the coal rushing down the shoots. At 5.30 they asked me to shift the ship a little to allow the coal lighter to be changed, so I called the duty part of watch on board and mooched aft with the QM to haul her out by tautening our after eight-inch hemp, bringing it to the port capstan and taking the slack out of the wires. Tried to look happy with a pipe of ship's in the pouring rain, but my oilskin was leaking, and I have lost my sea-boots, so I am afraid I failed dismally. Called the hands at six, and was much refreshed by a boiling cup of ship's cocoa. After a stormy interview with a sleepy and bad-tempered CO (Lieut.-Commander Edwards, RNR),

I turned the hands to getting on board stores, under the auspices of Lieutenant Freer, RNR, who came out of his bunk like a rag-time ballet girl, I don't think! Then the short-leave night liberty men began to arrive. With much difficulty I assured the MAA that it was tomorrow morning, and then he, I and the corporal OW, with the assistance, more or less unwilling, of several marine and seamen sentries, began dealing with the streams of shore-goers. The marines came off, spic and span, smarter than when they left; seamen roll off in an eminently seamanlike fashion, the regular nautical roll, so that you can't tell whether they're drunk or sober; in this, however, there is no difficulty with the firemen, whose sobriety or otherwise is quite apparent, usually otherwise. The MAA discovered multitudinous bottles of gin, auntie's joy, etc., smuggled in trouser legs, scarves, caps, etc.; he is a genius at hide-and-seek. Put two men on commander's report for insolence, under the influence of drink. At seven the bugler woke up and blew the reveille, one hour late. It brought back pleasant memories of Osborne baby days, but I refused to allow his tender years to bias me, so gave him a dose of No. 10A to refresh his memory.

The clank of the steam hammers of the party fitting up the new magazine now added to the din, and the blue ether was quite indistinguishable amidst clouds of coal dust. At 7.45 an orderly arrived from Admiral Stileman, the SNO, Liverpool, and I made out the daily harbour leave report for him. At 8am sounded off 'Stand easy' and piped hands to breakfast. Attempted to have a wash and shave, but the water was thick with coal dust and quite tepid, so after cutting my fizz several times with a razor, and reducing myself to a frenzy of rage and despair, I eventually gave it up as a bad job, and went off to mess. A steward, obviously suffering from 'the morning after-itis', advanced after ten minutes' wait and brought me some stewed prunes, one dish I abhor, so determined to risk the eggs. The first two were past the age limit, and I had just started on the third, which showed signs of comparative youth, when a messenger arrived saying the commanding officer wished to see the officer of the day.

After struggling with my sword belt, I found Mr Edwards, the CO, and he introduced me to a Mr McWhirter, the contractor's agent, who had come to see about the fitting up of the new magazine protection; I spent the remainder of the breakfast hour grovelling in the magazines and ammunition hoists, and attempting to prove to Mr McWhirter, a ubiquitous Scotsman, that the primary duty of ammunition is to be fired from a gun, and the requirements of safety, however important, should not be allowed to block the passage of ammunition to the guns on deck. Nine o'clock 'Divisions' at length relieved me of Mr McWhirter, and, assisted by Midshipman Cobb, the stand-by officer, and one or two other unfortunates, inspected the various divisions and reported them to the CO.

Marched on the QD, and the CO read prayers, briefly and in a great hurry, finishing up the last prayer as follows: 'For Jesus Christ's sake – On caps' with no pause between the two sentences. Marched off the QD, and hands fell in. Told off the various parties for getting in stores, etc., and retired to the GR for a welcome smoke and a cocktail. Five minutes later a ship's corporal arrived, with a gleam as of a lion who scents his prey, to say that a stoker, obviously under the influence of drink, had assaulted Eng.-Lieutenant Fortay, the EO of the day, in the engine room, and could I come to investigate the case? A pleasant party assembled on the QD, the prisoner, a ferrety-faced-looking individual, between two huge marines, also Eng.-Lieut.-Commander Jackson, known on the lower deck as the 'slave driver', Mr Fortay, the MAA, a ship's corporal, the corporal on duty and sundry messengers, etc. Heard the evidence on both sides, and although strongly in favour of prisoner, obliged to refer matter to CO as charge was brought by an officer. The CO was sent for, and arrived in about twenty minutes, and, after asking twenty or thirty useless questions, put the prisoner on the captain's report.

At 10.30 the captain arrived on board from shore leave; the bosun's mate, of course, was adrift with his piping, and I got scrubbed by the CO. The skipper sent for me later and asked me to dine with him that night; hearing that I should be on duty, he very kindly asked me to come tomorrow. He seemed very chatty and pleasant. On arriving back at the gangway, the captain of Marines arrived in a fearful fury, shouting for the officer OD. On seeing me, however, he calmed down, and demanded an escort to be sent immediately to Lime Street Station to fetch some very valuable wireless machinery which had arrived there. I told him that there were absolutely no hands available, and advised him to go to the Naval Base Office in Water Street and apply for an escort there. He went off mumbling to himself, with one moustache bristling and the other drooping almost to the deck.

The remainder of the forenoon passed without incident, except for a few minor offenders, whom I dealt with as necessary. Sounded off 'Cooks' at 11.45 and attended the issue of rum to the men, the MAA with an eagle eye there to prevent any man having one drop more than his proper tot. At noon piped hands to dinner and went off to mess. A most appetising menu, rather marred by coal dust, sauce and questionable cooking, but things looked up after a glass of port and a cigar. Cobb relieved me very kindly for two hours in the afternoon, and I had a doze in my bunk. Woke up at three, and, after dipping my head in a basin of water, went back to the gangway. I found Cobb, his lanky six feet three inches of bone shivering with rage, 'putting the sergeant-major of marines in his place', as he called it (to me it sounded like a costermonger reviling a much-loathed rival). Apparently the postman, a newly fledged corporal of marines, had left the ship, reporting to the SM, who was complaining to the OOD in disparaging tones which did not please his lordship, Mr Cobb. Cobb left on my arrival, and the sergeant-major retired disconsolately to his mess.

Sounded the 'Cease fire' at 3.30, and piped liberty men to clean and shift, and then went and had a cup of tea. At four sounded off 'Evening quarters', inspected the men, reported to the CO, and then piped hands to tea. At 4.20 inspected the liberty men and marched them over the side. A few minutes later the defaulting postman arrived with the mail, and as he had some interesting letters for me I decided not to punish him, and handed him over to the tender care of the sergeant-major.

Then Hutchinson, who is now temporarily running the gunnery department, arrived with a heart-stirring appeal. He apparently wants to get one of our after 6-inch guns stripped down by tonight, and, not knowing how to do it himself, was depending on my help. The armourers are pensioners, and have never had anything to do with guns of this pattern, so this complicated matters. Rummaged in my sea-chest, and eventually found a gunnery notebook, written during my 'G' course in the *Cornwall*, with the help of which I managed to show the armourers how to get to work on the gun, after smearing my best coat in oil and grease. Then left the armourers and WSH struggling with the gun, and returned to the gangway.

Found three ladies, apparently a sort of governess person and two girls, one about twenty-two and the other about sixteen, a flapper. They are cousins of Fleet Paymaster Lawford, the admiral's secretary, who is away in London on duty with the admiral. They seemed very keen on seeing over the ship, which I had to refuse, the regulations prohibiting this in wartime. However, they came and had tea in the GR. Both girls were quite good sorts, and the elder very pretty, but the governess was rather a stumer. Their names were Miss Sybil and Dorothy Grant, and they lived near Chester, where they had motored from. They asked me very kindly to go over and play tennis if I can ever get away.

The remainder of the dog watches passed without incident till dinnertime, which was half an hour early for some obscure reason, causing me to be three-quarters of an hour late. Quite a good dinner. What a contrast to the food in a real battleship in the Grand Fleet or at the Dardanelles! But it was spoilt by Athenry, who persisted in smoking cheap cigarettes throughout the meal, in spite of my pointed remarks that nowadays noblemen were no nearer always gentlemen, and in that a title did not entitle him to inconvenience everyone else in the mess.

He continued, however, with his usual silly jokes, far-fetched humour, and everlastingly grinning face.

After dinner spent half an hour with Lieutenant Freer overhauling bosun's stores, stoppers, nippers, hawsers, blocks, etc. At 9.45 went rounds with the CO, and at ten the hands piped down and turned in. Feeling very sleepy, as I usually do at this time, after a day on, but managed to keep myself awake with frequent pipes and by chatting to the QM, a hoary old individual, who told me stirring yarns of events in the Egyptian Wars of '82, in which he apparently had played a part which should have entitled him to at least a VC and immediate promotion. At 11.30 went rounds again with the corporal of the watch, then signed up the rounds book, and sent the messenger to call Hutchinson, my relief, and waited in patience for 12. Midnight arrived, but no Hutchinson; however, at ten past he slouched up; gave him my belt as a badge of office, turned over the various details in about five seconds, and went off to bed, tore off my clothes, and was asleep in half a minute.

28 April *Midshipmen's Journal* Daily Log
Left Canada Dock at 6am; cast off and proceeded in charge of pilot and tugs; warped through Sandon half-tide basin gates and anchored off Pier Head.

29 April *Midshipmen's Journal* Daily Log
Sailed at 8pm; dropped the pilot off at the Bar Light Vessel, and shaped a course to pass to the south of the Chickens Rock Light, to the west of which we met the destroyer *Dove* which convoyed us through the chief submarine danger area. Passed the Mull of Galloway, thence shaped a course to pass Fair Head (Co. Antrim) and inside Rathlin Island. Altacarry Lighthouse abeam 1pm. The *Dove* parted company off Oversay. Speed throughout the day eighteen knots, zigzag. Strict look out kept for submarines, as many have recently been sighted in the

waters passed through, and only yesterday a fleet collier was sunk off the Butt of Lewis by a large German submarine. Their latest type from all accounts is of considerable size.

30 April *Midshipmen's Journal* Daily Log

Rendezvoused HM armed merchant cruisers *Cedric* and *India* fifty miles WNW of St Kilda. Took over charge of Tenth Cruiser Squadron patrols from Captain Benson of the *Cedric*, who has been senior officer in the absence of Rear-Admiral De Chair. Transferred her three prize crews to the *Cedric*. The *India* has just joined the squadron, having recently fitted out in the Thames as an armed merchant cruiser. She is very short of the necessary code books for WT signalling.

Proceeded at 10pm to the northward to pass to the westward of the Faroes and back to patrol.

1 May *Midshipmen's Journal* Daily Log

Arrived on patrol to the north of Faroes, this is now 'A' patrol. Communicated with HM ships *Otway* and *Digby*. The *Digby* has lately returned from Reykjavík, the capital of Iceland, where she proceeded with despatches for the British consul.

During our last period at sea, the following ships were intercepted by the Tenth Cruiser Squadron:

Ships intercepted, 8 March – 19 April

Norwegian	106
Danish	97
British	82
Swedish	53
USA	14
Russian	1
Finnish	1
Not ascertained	3
TOTAL	357

West-bound	95
East-bound	167
Trawlers, locals, etc.	94
Not ascertained	1
TOTAL	357

Of these 129 were sent in:

To Kirkwall	115
To Stornoway	10
To Lerwick	4
TOTAL	129

Disposition of the patrols of the reinforced Tenth Cruiser Squadron as rearranged

'A' *Alsatian* (flag), *Otway, Orcoma, Mantua, Alcantara, Teutonic*

'C' *Cedric, Patia, Orotava, Oropesa, Changuinola, Motagua, Digby, Patuca*

'E' *Virginian, Columbella, Andes, Arlanza*

'F' *Hildebrand, India, Ebro, Hilary*

'G' *Caribbean, Ambrose, X*

'B' and 'D' patrols have been discontinued.

Ship 'X', in 'G' patrol, is a cruiser to be detailed by C-in-C.

'A' patrol must always have a minimum of four ships on patrol, and is to extend from the north of the Faroes.

'C' patrol must always have a minimum of five ships on patrol, and is to extend between Cape Wrath and Sydero Island.

'E' patrol to the north of Iceland spreads north from Latitude 67°N along the meridian of 15°W.

'F' patrol to the south of Iceland spreads at 150° from a position 63°20'N 15°W.

'G' patrol must have at least one armed merchant cruiser on patrol, extending on the meridian of 3°E from Lat 62°N to Lat 63½°N.

2-3 May *Midshipmen's Journal* Daily Log

On patrol between Iceland and the Faroes. Stopped, boarded and allowed to proceed two vessels. Communicated with HMS *Hildebrand* on the 3rd.

4 May *Midshipmen's Journal* Daily Log

Proceeded from the north of the Faroes to the SE to Busta Voe in the Shetlands.

Went to general quarters in the forenoon, and picked up some fishing buoys and jettisoned spars.

5 May *Midshipmen's Journal* Daily Log

Arrived in St Magnus Bay in the NW of the Shetlands at 3am, and at 4am came to with port anchor in Busta Voe. Found a squadron of three auxiliary armed patrol trawlers there. Received a visit from the SNO Lerwick. HMS *Duke of Cornwall*, armed boarding vessel, came to anchor at 5pm, and sailed at 9.30pm after discharging prize crews for the *Patia* and *Virginian* to *Alsatian* for passage.

Day spent in examining the anchorage and considering its suitability as a coaling base for the Tenth Cruiser Squadron.

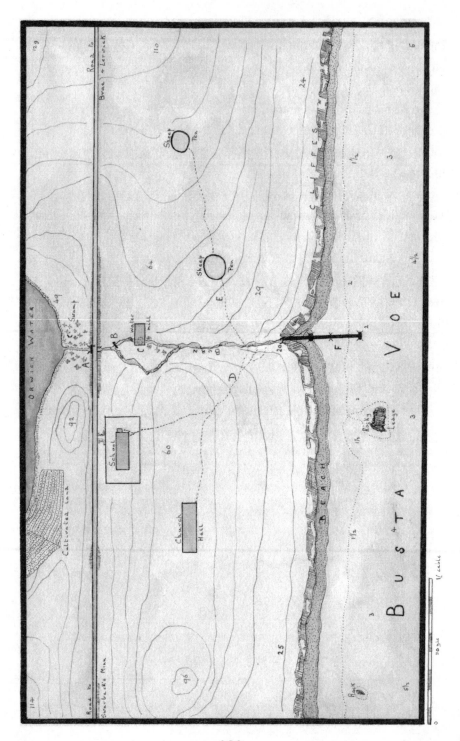

Busta Voe has already been used as a base by the old Tenth Cruiser Squadron, when formed by the Crescent class. It is proposed to use Busta Voe in conjunction with the adjoining water of Aith Voe and Olma Firth.

An important item of the question is the water supply, a plentiful and pure local source being necessary. In the forenoon an expedition consisting of the Staff Surgeon, Lt Kenyon (squadron gunnery officer) and one midshipman went in the motorboat to examine the supply of a small burn in the Muckle Roe Island to the south of the Busta Peninsula. An aqueduct had been constructed here in November last, but was wrecked by the winter gales.

6 May *Midshipmen's Journal* Daily Log

It was intended to go round and examine Olna Firth today, but receipt of the news that an east-bound oiler had eluded patrols, necessitated a change in plans; so we weighed and proceeded to the northward of Muckle Flugga, to intercept her.

At 3.30pm we came up with the oiler, about fifteen miles NNW of Muckle Flugga, and she proved to be the SS *Petrolyte* of American nationality with a large cargo of oil for Copenhagen, probably intended eventually for Germany. She was sent in for investigation to Kirkwall with a prize crew under Midshipman Learmont, RNR.

7 May *Midshipmen's Journal* Daily Log

Discharged their prize crews to the *Virginian* and *Patia*, also communicated visually with HM ships *Patuca* and *Hilary*, all of 'C' patrol at present. Sighted battleship *Orion* returning to Scapa Flow, after a refit at Plymouth.

8-9 May *Midshipmen's Journal* Daily Log

On patrol north and west of the Faroes.

On the 8th we communicated with HM ships *Digby* and *Teutonic*, and on the next day we intercepted the Swedish SS *Kronprinzessin*

Margaret bound for Rio de Janeiro and Santos, with German exports on board. She was sent in with a prize crew under Midshipman Ward, RNR.

Loss of RMS Lusitania

In the Poldhu WT news of the 9th we received regrettable news of the loss of the mammoth Cunard liner *Lusitania*, torpedoed by a German submarine off the Old Head of Kinsale, while homeward-bound. Nearly one-thousand-four-hundred lives were lost, including that of many well-known passengers. A great outburst of indignation is reported from the USA, as many Americans were lost. The loss of life rivals that of the *Titanic* disaster of 1912. The Cunard Company had not previously lost a passenger's life for eighty years, and it is suggested that at the successful end of the war, they shall be compensated with the Hamburg Amerika liners *Imperator* and *Vaterland*.

MAY

A DAY AT SEA ON PATROL

By an officer in HMS Alsatian, 28 May 1915, west of the Faroe Islands

Turned out at midnight to take the 'middle' watch as Midn. OW on the bridge. The usual 'dead dog' sort of feeling was slightly lessened as I met the gun-watch officers of the 'middle' going to their various stations, feeling and looking more miserable than myself. Relieved McNaught on the bridge, and he wasted no time disappearing into the bowels of the ship. 'Lieutenant Chester' was OOW, and as he seemed in no mood for telling any of his yarns, I sent the messenger below to fetch some cocoa, and then retired to the chart house to examine our position on patrol and news in general.

It was a miserable night, a cold north-easter blowing, temperature 30°F, certainly better than recently off Iceland, but not much to boast of, as there were frequent snow and sleet squalls, and the ship was making heavy weather of a nasty sea, rolling and pitching like a cockleshell. Luckily the barometer was rising, so there were hopes of a change for the better. Cocoa and ship's biscuit were most refreshing, and, having finished my shave, I relieved Chester on 'Monkey's Island' while he got his. Not all my oilskins, woollies, etc., could keep out the cold, and my hands and feet were like blocks of ice. The four hours of a middle watch always seem like twenty-four of any other watch, and at 1am I felt as if I had been on watch for hours; the weather was worse, the wind having increased to force seven or eight, and the sea being about six or seven by the Beaufort scale.

Soon after 1am I went below to go rounds with the corporal of the watch – a long job in a ship of this size. First of all visited all the offices, ship's, admiral's, captain's, etc., to see them all properly locked up. Then looked round the various cabins and officers' messes, and passed down to the seamen's mess decks below the Fx, groped my way along beneath dozens of hammocks emitting loud snores, with the Corporal OW in front with his lantern. Visited all the forward store rooms, and tested the WT doors. Returned to the cells, and the sentry reported the cell prisoners correct; next visited the ER office, and rang up the engineer in charge in the ER and stoke hold, who reported all correct below.

Then through the marines', boys', stewards' and stokers' messes and flats. Found four stokers playing cards outside the chronometer room. Obliged to run them in. What extraordinary people these stokers are! They work frightfully hard and yet, instead of getting a little sleep at night, they must get in the rattle for gambling. All the after store rooms and magazines correct. So went the rounds of the guns and upper decks.

Found the various gun-watch officers more disconsolate than ever, cursing the weather, the ship, the war and everything else in general. Looked in at the wireless office to pick up any scrap of news from the Grand Fleet, but heard nothing much of interest except the multitudinous reports of submarines from all quarters of the British Isles. Bill Adams in the coding office, struggling with a signal in an abstruse cipher, miles long, from the C-in-C, all hot air. At 1.40 returned to the bridge and reported rounds correct to the OOW.

The worst of night rounds is the filthy smell below, which is most nauseating. Chester, a little more communicative now, came out with his usual story about the Odessa girls and the sentry boxes. About 2.15 the clouds cleared a little, and I managed to snap a sight of Arcturus, which should gladden the navigator's heart, as we have not had a sight for two days. Soon after the crow's nest lookout reported a light on the starboard bow. I went below and called the captain, and we altered course to close the light. It proved to be a small trawler, flying the British colour, steering north-west, apparently for Iceland. The sea being considerably too high to board, we allowed her to proceed.

I then worked out my sight of Arcturus, which gave a position line eleven miles away from our estimated DR position. Dawn now began to break in the east, and just before 4am we fell out the night defence guns' crews and their officers. At 4am Lieutenant Chester and I were relieved by Lieutenant Oram and Midshipman Learmont, and cold and wet and tired I rushed off to my bunk. Turned out at 7.30am and attempted a bath, but the ship was rolling badly, and the water flatly refused to stop in it. Went into the mess for breakfast and succeeded in getting a certain amount of food down, in spite of the cups, plates, etc., doing a highland charge continually up and down the table.

Quite a fine morning, except for the heavy sea and the cold north-east wind, but the sun was very cheery. Got in a hasty smoke, and then went to 'divisions', followed by prayers. Then took my division at Swedish drill. I am getting quite an expert instructor at nutty exercises now, and the men, I really believe, think I know something about it, which certainly shows their lack of intelligence.

The commander, as usual, had a frightful early-morning 'liver', and scrubbed poor old Ben Evans for about ten minutes for some trivial matter. At 9am HMS *Cedric* (Commander Benson) had been sighted, and we now went to general quarters to exercise action with dummy firing, using the *Cedric* as target. The captain got very excited with 'Guns' and Williams, when they pointed out the limitations of our guns. But we continued steadily for nearly two hours till 11am, and the exercise should certainly have increased our fighting efficiency, although I doubt if it did.

General quarters affords excellent voice practice for control officers, at all events. The 'Luny' worked his rate of change clock much to his own satisfaction, but not to everybody else's, while Glanvile and I struggled with the Dumaresq, and McNaught sat in silent glory at the range-finder. Having sunk the *Cedric* at least three times, we at length sounded the 'Cease fire' and the 'Secure' at 11am, and I went off to help 'Guns' test the sights of the fore starboard battery guns until noon, when we struggled off to get pot-luck lunch.

During the afternoon the sea went down considerably, and we were much more comfortable. Directly after lunch the signal bosun gave all the midshipmen off watch a semaphore and Morse test, the flag-lieutenant-commander making caustic remarks the whole time. At 2pm the divisions went to rifle drill, followed by squad and company drill. I shouted myself hoarse trying to instil into the wooden heads of the RNR seamen from Newfoundland, etc., the elementary motions of the rifle, turning, marching. This game continued most of the afternoon, until the commander, repenting of his decision (having been woken up by the din from his afternoon nap), gave the order for us to knock off.

I managed to swallow a cup of tea before going on watch again at 4pm, when we went to 'evening quarters'. The captain now decided to close HMS *Cedric,* which we did, and I went away in charge of the sea-boat with despatches for her, and also for her to transmit to Captain EL Boty, MVO, of the *Otway.* Came off watch from the first dog at six, shifted in haste, and managed to get in half-hour's strenuous deck hockey, and got really warm for the first time since yesterday.

Then shifted again and had dinner, after which 'Guns' announced his intention of giving a lecture to any officers who felt inclined to attend, on 'Lessons in tactics learned from the Falkland Action'. I was too lazy to go, as the commander, now being in an excellent after-dinner mood, asked me into the wardroom for a chat. At 9pm we sighted a steamer eastward-bound, and she proved later to be a big Dane. I went away in the boarding boat with Lieutenant Williams and AP Barton, as the Mid. OW was busy aft with the patent log. Got on board after a struggle and getting sopped through. She proved to be the SS *Escalonia* of Copenhagen, bound from Boston, USA, to Aarhus with a cargo of wheat and oil cake, ostensibly for Denmark, but intended, no doubt, for Germany. We morsed this information to the *Alsatian,* and then were told to return to fetch off a prize crew, as the RA had decided to send her to Kirkwall to be dealt with by the customs authorities.

Pulled back to the ship, and after much cursing and swearing got Mr Barton on board, although he nearly dropped all the ship's papers into the ditch. A drizzling rain had now come on, which did not add to our comfort, and Midshipman Wood, RNR, who was to take the *Escalonia* into harbour, incurred everybody's wrath by taking about ten times as long as necessary to get ready, collecting his revolver, oilskin, love letters for the post on shore, etc. At last he arrived, and we pulled over to the *Escalonia* and put Mr Wood and the prize crew on board, and ordered them to proceed in execution of their orders.

Then went back to the ship, and the sea-boat was hoisted. I wasted no time getting down to my bunk and turning in for a few more hours' sleep; but a quarter of an hour later was woken up to hear that I was wanted to take charge of the marine firing party on the Fx, as we had sighted a mine, and were going to sink it. Apparently the OOW by, after much thought, putting the helm over the wrong way, had narrowly missed ramming it and sending us all to perdition; he forgot it was not a submarine. A few rounds water-logged the mine, which luckily was an electrical contact one, and so sank quietly without exploding. Then at last, it being now 11.30pm, I really got off to sleep until 4am the next morning, when it was my turn to go on watch again.

JUNE

Thursday 3

Left by the 10.09 train from Haslemere with Jack, after thoroughly enjoying my visit. Called on Denniston at the Admiralty and had a chat and drink at his club, the Junior Army and Navy. Lunched with Aunt Do, Uncle Jack and Cittie at Kensington Gore. Travelled home as far as Sittingbourne with old Edwards, who is leaving the *Alsatian*, and has got command of the armed yacht *Wildfowl*, and is off to take her over at Sheerness. Mother met me at the station, full of news, but I was rather liverish. The garden exquisite. Daddy was playing tennis at Westenhanger, but I did not go round as I have resolved not to chase Joko, unless I can possibly help it. I do not trust myself much, however.

Friday 4

Tea and tennis at Westenhanger. Harry Baird there. Byron, Nita, Toots, Joko and I went to 'The Count of Luxembourg' at the Canterbury theatre, and supper afterwards at Byron's club. Went to the Fifth Liverpool's Officers' Mess to see 'Drippie' Porritt, but he was out. 'The Count of Luxembourg' was very good for Canterbury, but I did not enjoy the evening much. I am an ass, an ass, an ass. Joko kept on harping on about those damned carabineers, Dent, Charlesworth, etc. Whether she really cares for one of them or not I don't know, but she acts quite well if not. I loathe them. She looks awfully nice! Auntie Connie's scheme for a Robertson pension seems a great success, as both girls have got new dresses. I was in a rotten mood, and made all sorts of arrangements so as not to see Joko before I go, so I suppose I shall make myself absolutely hopelessly miserable.

Saturday 5

Went in to Canterbury in the morning and saw heaps of friends, both Goodsons, old Hobbs, old John Robinson, Mac Hilton and Blake

Wacher. Lunched at the Officers' Mess of the Fifth Liverpool's, with quite a nice chap called Keet, home wounded from the Front. Afterwards, 'Drippie' Porritt and I went up the town and had some drinks etc., and a long chat about the old days; he seems to be doing rather well. Another Zeppelin raid over Sittingbourne. Harry Baird motored Tootie and Joko over to Margate to see Henry and Olive. I played tennis with Daddy at Westenhanger till tea, then we went round to Seaton and played with the Drakes, Miss Page, and a capt. of the Third Dgs. Went round to Westenhanger after supper and had a long chat with Nita. Joko there, of course. I now feel convinced that she is very much in with some of the carabineers and I am quite cut out. She is a fickle creature, as I am sure she used to be fond of me. But now all is UP. I should love to snub her, perhaps someday the wind will change.

Sunday 6

'Drippie' Porritt motored over, and we all lunched at the Drakes. Colonel Clarke (who got on VG with mother) and Major Scott, both over from the Marine Depot. JTP and I then motored to Dover to see Keigwein, who is a Lieutenant, RNVR, and Admiral Bacon's flag-lieutenant. Unluckily we missed RPK and went to Folkestone to find him, but he was not there. Came home and found some frightful old bores there, Colonel Lushington and another soldier. We all played tennis and then the Robertsons, Harry Baird and JTP came to supper at Quaives. JTP is commissioned by me to try and flirt with Joko, whom I snubbed assiduously and who seems inclined to thaw a little. Later on I went and had a chat with the Kelseys. I got a wired extension of leave till Thursday.

Monday 7

Played tennis all morning with Joko at Westenhanger, and then lunched with her alone in the garden, an idyllic scene. But so short-lived, and I am sure she is in love with Charlesworth. I think now he is the one. He is very wealthy, and I believe a good fellow, although of course I loathe him with the most unspeakable loathing. Frightfully hot all day. Went up to London, dined at the Trocadero with Cobb and a friend, a man named Gass of the RFA. An excellent sort. Then went out to 'Betty' at Daly's. An excellent show. Bench joined us and we had a first-class box. Took Cobb's cousin Doris Preston and a friend out to supper at the Savoy. Winnie Barnes of 'Betty' was there, very sweet; Mabel Sealby, JPR's old flame fainted during the performance.

Tuesday 8

Went home by the 10.45. Another sweltering hot day. Lunched at Westenhanger; in the afternoon motored Nita and Joko over to Margate to see Henry, Olive and Toots. Found Daddy and Harry Baird already there. I was fool to take Nita as well, as I might have pumped Joko about Charlesworth, if we had some tête-à-tête. We dined with Olive and then all went on to quite a good revue at the Margate Hippodrome. A nice drive home – but two's company, three's a crowd; I wonder if Joko is really in love with Charlesworth. He wrote her a very long letter today.

10 June 1915   HMS *ALSATIAN*

Dear 'Papa',

Just a line in haste before we sail tonight. There seems at last some slight chance of getting a different job, as the skipper has at last consented to forward my application for the submarine service or RNAS. However, there is a lot of red tape to get over first, and it will be necessary for me to produce a certificate from my responsible parent or guardian saying he has no objection to my being employed on either of the above services.

I have written out the necessary wording and should be pleased if you would copy it, sign and post to me.

My very best love to mother, and thank her for putting up with all my whims and making such an excellent valet.

Good luck and a speedy recovery from your dire
disease.

Toby

PS Excuse dirt, but ship is smothered in coal dust.

SIR,

I beg to state that I am willing for my son,
Midshipman Alexander Scrimgeour, Royal Navy (being
under the age of 21), to be employed on any special
service, e.g. submarine or that may be considered
suitable; and I should raise no objections to any such
appointment that he might receive.

Signature

6 July 1915   HMS *ALSATIAN*

Dearest Mother,

We shall be in harbour again for a few days on 10 July,
but I doubt if it will be much of a rest, as it seems
probable that all spare time is to be taken up with
exercising landing operations, route marches and field
work. This points to the fact that as much experience as
possible is to be gained in shore operations, evidently
with an eye to eventualities that may crop up in the
future. The last fortnight at sea has produced more
interest and excitement than we have had for some
months, due to various reasons which cannot be safely
stated on paper.* But anyhow, we hope that possibly
our work in the immediate future (that is to say,
until the winter weather starts again in October)

---

* The interception of the Norwegian steamer *Kristianiafjord*. She slipped through
the blockade and evaded capture, and in trying to avoid the *Alsatian*, ran into
the other ships of the patrol. *Kristianiafjord* was eventually seized, and with the
five-hundred-and-forty-four people on board was sent into Stornaway with an
armed guard.

Midshipman Alexander Scrimgeour – a photograph taken of the portrait that graced the hall at Thorncombe House in Surrey.

Above: Alexander began the war in the armed cruiser HMS *Crescent*, flagship of the Tenth Cruiser Squadron under Admiral de Chair (IWM Q 21126).

Left: Admiral Dudley de Chair (1864–1958), photographed in 1924 at Government House just after he became Governor of New South Wales, Australia. According to Alexander he earned himself the nickname 'Old Make-a-Signal', 'owing to the large number of unnecessary signals he issues' (State Library of New South Wales, Australia).

R.M.S. Alsatian.

Tonnage
18,000.

Dimensions.
Length........600 Ft.
Beam........72 Ft.
Depth (to C deck)....45 Ft.

Top: *Alsatian* of the Allen Line before and after she was converted into an Armed Merchant Cruiser. Alexander transferred into her after the Crescent was severely damaged in a storm (Bottom image IWM SP 2082).

GOULDEN'S
SMALL
SCRIBBLING
DIARY,
WITH ALMANACK.
INTERLEAVED WITH BLOTTING PAPER.

1915.

PRICE ONE SHILLING.

Canterbury:
H. J. GOULDEN,
39 & 40 HIGH STREET

GOULDEN & WIND, 35, BANK STREET, ASHFORD.
GOULDEN & CURRY, 61, HIGH STREET,
TUNBRIDGE WELLS.

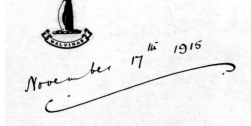

November 17ᵗʰ 1915

Dear Daddy & Mother,

I have no time at present to write two letters, so you must rest content with one between you. I am returning Mother's letters, which she asked for; Very sorry to hear she has not been up to the mark, & glad to hear that her inane scheme of secreting this indisposition from the old man has fallen through.

Winter has set in with a will, and it is jolly cold; we have had a lot of snow and hard frost. Luckily there are excellent skating facilities in the vicinity which is great fun. In addition we are not dependant

Above: Alexander writes to his parents from Invincible on headed notepaper.

Opposite top: The front cover of Alexander's 1915 diary. He used a Goulden's Small Scribbling Diary for every year of his diary.

Opposite: HMS *Invincible*, flagship of the Third Battle Cruiser Squadron. (Conway)

Rear Admiral Horace Hood (1870–1916) commander of HMS *Invincible*.
Alexander had already encountered him at Osbourne College before he was
transferred to the battle cruiser under Hood's command (Conway).

Right: Admiral Sir David Beatty (1871–1936), Commander of the battle Cruiser Fleet, pictured here on the deck of HMS *Queen Elizabeth* in 1917 with Rear-Admiral Hugh Evan-Thomas (1862–1928), who was in command of the Fifth Battle Squadron at Jutland (Conway).

Left: Admiral Sir John Jellicoe (1859–1935), Commander-in-Chief of the Grand Fleet during the First World War (Conway).

Top: HMS *Invincible* explodes at 6.34 pm on 31 May 1916 (Conway).

Right: The Portsmouth Naval Memorial at Southsea seafront includes a host of familiar names.

SUB LIEUTENA
BARLOW A. H. C.
BRIGGS G. L. C.
CAMPBELL-COOKE
COBB T. H.
GIBSON-CARMICHAE
HENDERSON R.
HUTCHINSON W. S.
JOHNSTONE L. E.
KIRKLAND J. S.
KITCHIN G. G.
PAUL H. B.
PORTAL R. S.
RICHARDSON A. J. S.
RIDER C. H.
ROBERTSON T. A. W.
SCRIMGEOUR A.
SEYMOUR N.
TATHAM W. I.
TOTTENHAM D. F. C.
VANCE P. H. G. I.

will not be quite so dull as heretofore. The poor old
Russians appear to be getting it in the neck in Poland
and Galicia; I suppose it is owing to the shortage in
ammunition; or possibly it may be all bluff.

Give my love to all the various relations as you see
them; and tell Aunt Do when next you meet that I have
not heard from her for ages, and should love to have a
line if convenient.

Please send me four or five white cap covers from
Quaives, without delay, as I want to get them before we
sail again; also some thin pants if you can find any.
I am running rather short of woollen gloves, and have
worn out my favourite pair. I think they are possibly
past darning, but will send them to you, so that you may
be able to patch them up, and anyhow will realise the
type I like – *viz.*, with long cuffs.

Have all reasonable efforts been made to recover
my watch and to find the pipe? You have not so far
informed me. Except for the first page this is not
necessarily private, but I am afraid contains but little
news of interest.

My very best love to all.

From
Toby

Thursday HMS *ALSATIAN*

Darling Mother,
Just a line to tell you that my sojourn in this tin
castle is at an end, and I have been warned to pack my
things to be ready to leave for anywhere at half an
hour's notice. I have not had my new appointment yet,
but am expecting it very soon. You will probably see it
in the paper (*Morning Post*, etc.) under the heading of

naval appointments, in a few days' time, or perhaps it
will be out by the time you get this.

I hear on excellent authority that I am almost
certain to go to the *Invincible*, a battle cruiser of
17,250 tons. She went through the Falkland action, when
von Spee's force was annihilated, and has seen service
elsewhere abroad since the war started. A short time
ago she joined the Battle Cruiser Squadron in the North
Sea, and is now flagship of the Third Division of the
Battle Cruiser Fleet, flying the flag of Rear-Admiral
Hood, or Rear-Admiral Hon. Horace LA Hood, CB, MVO,
DSO, RN, as he is with all the etceteras. As I dare say
you remember, he was captain (before his promotion) at
Osborne, when I was there, for one year. Up till April
this year he was in command of the Dover patrols,
and distinguished himself as chief of the squadron
operating on the Belgian coast against Zeebrugge,
Nieuwpoort, etc. He is directly descended from the
famous Admiral Hood of Nelson's time, one of the three
brothers, all Admirals, Lord Hood, Lord Bridport, and
Sir Alexander Hood; a nephew, son of a fourth brother,
Sir Samuel Hood, was also a well-known admiral. Thus
they are about the most famous of all naval families.
The member in question is reputed to be about the
most brilliant of the younger school of flag officers,
and is simply bulging with brains, so he is a pretty
distinguished man to serve under. I expect you remember
my telling you when at Osborne, that he is thoroughly
Americanised, talking with a distinct Yankee twang,
and having married an American millionairess. With
the single exception of Beatty, he was promoted to flag
rank at an earlier age than any other captain in the
last fifty years.

If I go to the *Invincible* my appointment will be due almost entirely to old 'Duds' putting in a good word at the Admiralty. He has been very kind to all of us snotties.

I may not have time to write again, but I will try and let you know where I do go. At present I am in the throes of packing, and as we are coaling, and coal dust rules supreme everywhere, the result is unenviable.

I am afraid that there will be no time to write to Jim, but give him my love, and good luck with the tonsils.

You can make use of any information in this letter that you require, but it rather loses its point if the *Invincible* does not mature.

By the way, wherever I go, please inform everyone likely to write to me ever of the change of address, as I shall not have time to do it myself.

Best love to you and Daddy.

From
Toby

23 July 1915 *HMS INVINCIBLE*

Dearest Mother,

Many thanks for your many and interesting letters. I am sorry not to have written before, but have had no time until now. We left several good friends behind in the *Alsatian*, but are all jolly glad to come here. It is absolutely different, of course, from any previous ship I have served in, but it does not take long to settle down. I am still senior midshipman, as the seven snotties already here are all junior to us. It is rather an extraordinary experience having been senior midshipman in three successive flagships.

As far as I can judge, we seem to have a very nice lot of officers. It is excellent being in company with a lot of other ships, as I have already met shoals of old friends, contemporary officers and cadets at Osborne and Dartmouth, and shipmates of *Cornwall* and *Crescent* days.

This ship has already been in three actions this war: the Heligoland Bight early in the war, the Falkland Isles and at the Dardanelles. Some of the reminiscences of those who have been here all along are most thrilling. For example, in the 12-inch twin turret, in which I am stationed for action, a heavy shell from the *Gneisenau* actually penetrated the armour and entered the turret without exploding, during the Falkland action; and there are dozens of other interesting yarns.

The officer of the watch, when I joined the ship, was a certain Lieutenant Stewart, lately promoted from sub-lieutenant; he tells me that his father is in J and A's office. Apparently he lunched with Daddy not long ago, and he tells me Daddy was wearing a most eccentric hat. Verily are the sins of the father visited upon the children! He was very amused by Daddy telling him that I disapproved of the hat in question.

Yesterday I went to tea with Mrs Hood and family; they have a house on shore near our base, with a tennis court and some excellent strawberry beds. As there are two A1 daughters of seventeen and nineteen, you can bet their hospitality is fully appreciated. There are also two sweet little boys of six and two.

Most of the married officers have imported their wives and families up here, as we are by no means constantly at sea. It is a pleasant change after the weary four or five weeks at sea on end in the *Alsatian*.

On the other hand, leave is far more limited, as of
course we are always ready to sail at very short notice,
and you can only get on shore for a few hours in the
afternoon when not too busy.

The Beattys are very much in evidence here; they
have taken a huge place on shore in the vicinity, and
the anchorage simply stinks of Lady Beatty's hospital
ships, yachts, motorboats, etc.

Our captain is named Cay, and he seems a very good
sort; he is considerably older than the admiral, who is
and looks extraordinarily young and is most energetic.
We swarm with commanders, having no less than five, an
executive commander, a navigating commander, a gunnery
commander, and at present two engineer commanders,
although one is leaving shortly. There are also two
lieutenant-commanders.

The flag-lieutenant-commander is an extraordinary
man. He enjoys the unique distinction of being the only
RNR flag-lieutenant afloat, but is quite different
from most of the typical merchant service RNR lot. He
accompanied Scott and Shackleton on their Antarctic
expeditions, and is a most versatile personage, as before
the war he had just been appointed president of the
Labour Exchanges, and was apparently going to instil
some life into those lukewarm institutions when the
outbreak of war prematurely interrupted his labours.
His full name is Bill Adams; very democratic and quite
the antithesis of his 'boss', the "onorable 'orace' as he is
known on the lower deck.

One of the peculiarities of this class of ship is that
the men live aft, and the officers amidships, while
the quarterdeck, instead of being in its time-honoured
position abaft the mainmast, is also amidships.

The battle cruisers correspond in most ways to, and are usually known as, the 'cavalry' of the Navy. Not an unmixed blessing, as living in this ship, even in wartime, is twice or three times as expensive as the *Alsatian*. Still, in peace we have a reputation for setting the pace, so if we are still afloat then we shall no doubt have a good time.

Now I must 'pipe down'.

Give my best love to all and sundry.

This need not be private if of interest to anyone.

From

Toby

PS Please post one pair white flannel trousers, two pairs grey flannel trousers.

Did my washing ever arrive?

24 July 1915   HMS *INVINCIBLE*

Dear Mother,

Just a line to ask for the following gear to be sent in addition to the trousers. The revised list is as follows: Two pairs grey flannel trousers, two pairs white flannel trousers, one pair tennis shoes, one pair nailed shoes, two pairs white socks, my tennis racket and golf clubs (also my greeny-bluey woollen waistcoat).

The last two articles should be carefully packed.

My postal address is:

HMS *Invincible*,

c/o GPO

If it is impossible to send tennis racket or golf clubs by post, they should be sent by rail.

Rail address:

Midn Alexander Scrimgeour, RN,

Dalmeny Station,

North British Rl.

To wait until called for.

Under no circumstances must the words 'Invincible' and 'Dalmeny' appear in the same address.

I am very sorry to give all this trouble, and hope you won't mind. All the gear in question is at Quaives.

Long leave is, of course, a far more valuable and rare article now than hitherto, and is only likely to occur at fairly long intervals.

There is, however, a distinct chance of getting some shortly. In which case I shall probably go to Quaives for two days, and spend the rest in London.

I will wire Daddy when I am coming if I do come. Best love to all.

Toby

AUGUST

3 August 1915   HMS *INVINCIBLE*

Dearest Mother,

Many thanks for letters and all the gear, which arrived safely. I am so glad to hear you are having a good time at Thorney. How long will it be before you return to Quaives? I expect to get a week's leave very shortly; I shall not visit Thorney, in spite of the glowing pen-pictures you draw, artfully interweaving descriptions of an idyllic mode of life with less inanimate attractions, apparently with a view of enticing me there. It rests entirely with you and the children whether I shall see you or not. I wonder whether your maternal instinct or obstinate pride (hacked up by Aunt Crab, doubtless) will prove stronger.

I am still waging a war of silence with her, which
will last to eternity unless she considers my ultra-
reasonable proposals.

Please thank Daddy for his long and interesting
letter (?). The excuse of 'being so busy' on the Stock
Exchange is rather flat just at present. Thank him
for his news – is doubtless a very good man at his job
– *viz.*, stockbroking, and is also probably a fairly
well-read and well-informed man (like most Stock
Exchange products I have met). But apparently the war
has affected him like the vast majority of people,
naturally sane under ordinary conditions; they
either become morbidly pessimistic or else confidently
optimistic, due, not to quiet and determined confidence
that by a continuous sequence of energetic and sensible
progressions we shall gradually overcome all obstacles
and stumble home winners, but due to a laughably absurd
and childishly superstitious faith in the interference
of some master-factor in the art of war (this being or
thing varies from God to Lord Kitchener and Mr Li G,
and from high explosives to conscription), which will
finish the war at one fell swoop.

These bubbles are continually pricked, but new
fantasies are born in the brains of these people, and
they are never tired of proclaiming, like Mr –, that
some dramatic and sudden event will shortly spring up
and devour the enemy.

I am getting on pretty well, but absolutely dread
coming on leave, when we are due for our refit. There is
a most persistent rumour that the Germans are coming to
sea this month, and if they choose the time when we are
refitting, I shall never forgive myself – or them.

We are a very cheery crowd; everybody is in the

Battle Cruiser Fleet, and money goes like water. All the 'nibs' of the Service from every point of view seem to collect here.

My very best love to everyone.

Toby

29 August 1915   HMS *INVINCIBLE*

Dearest Mother,

Thank you for your letters. As I write I hear that there is just a chance of my getting some leave in September after all, but it is very remote. By all means send Burberry my periscope; it is of no use to me. Aunt Do has just sent me a life-saving belt, which is very kind of her. Another Mrs Duguid, Aunt Jessie, has written to me asking if I would visit her at Edinburgh, which I may do, although how she guessed my whereabouts I cannot think. I suppose you are the culprit, you naughty old thing.

It would interest me to hear what old – blithered about, so you might tell me in your next letter, otherwise I am sure you will forget. Smith-Osborne I have got to know better lately, and he seems an A1 chap. He dined in the gunroom with us last night.

Amy Drummond Hay wrote to me from Orotava a short time ago; will you please thank her very much and send her my love.

I have called on Mrs Roxburgh (the mother of two great friends of mine, one a surgeon in the *Alsatian*, and another a snotty in the *Indefatigable*); she knows Mrs Finnis and the Elles very well.

I enclose a letter from Captain Trewby, my late flag-captain in the *Alsatian*, which I thought might interest you; it struck me as being very nice of him.

He got the DSO about a fortnight ago, as I dare say you saw in the papers.

I am getting on pretty well on the whole. It is an enormous advantage being able to get on shore occasionally and get some tennis and golf, instead of the long weary weeks up in the Arctic Circle. Life is pretty strenuous; I spend most of my time in a picket boat, as I dare say I have told you before.

Please don't lose Captain Trewby's letter. My very best love to everybody.

Yours,

Toby

PS If Johnny is still at Newcastle, please find out his address.

23 August 1915   HMS *ALSATIAN*

Dear Scrimgeour,

Very many thanks for your letter of congratulations; of course, it is an honour for the Tenth Cruiser Squadron, and I have done no more than any other captain. I suppose you are all green with envy of the mids. in Dardanelles and their DSCs, but your turn will come one of these fine days, and all our talent is in the Grand Fleet, and you are in one of the best ships if there is any fighting. I showed your letter to the admiral, and he wishes you all the best of luck. I expect at sea you have a strenuous time, but you make up for it by good long spells in harbour and shore leave. We are back at the same old port covered with coal dust; a batch of new RNR mids. have just joined straight from the *Worcester*, I believe, in your place. I expect Glanvile finds it dull in the GR now. I see your notepaper has the Spanish name for Falkland

Islands and a penguin; I spent many an hour among the
penguins down there about thirteen years ago. With all
good wishes to you all, and may you smash up the German
Fleet this side of Xmas.

Yours very sincerely,

George Trewby

OCTOBER

Friday 1

Arrived London 9am after a filthy journey, most of which was spent
scrapping with Stewart. Went to the flat and found Jack Russell, Daddy
and Mother. Did some shopping and then went along to the office and
saw Uncle John, Blunt, old Stewart (RR's father) and Stanby. Had an 'A1'
lunch with Daddy. Things are in rather low water just at present, and we
are trying to economise. I went home by the 5.10, and spent the evening
with Mother at Quaives, successfully resisting the temptation to go
round to Westenhanger.

Saturday 2

Went round in the morning and saw them all. Drove Joko into
Canterbury and did some shopping; lunched with Cag and Mrs
O'Callaghan. Cag is now stationed here with his yeomanry. On our
arrival home we were just in time to meet Lady Maud Warrender,* who
is stopping the weekend at Westenhanger. Daddy loathes her, but she is
a friend of Norman's, and I took to her exceedingly. Joko came round
to tea at Quaives, and I dined at Westenhanger. Poor old Mother is very
funny, I believe she is jealous of my fondness for Joko.

---

* Friends with novelist EF Benson, Lady Warrender's house in Rye would provide
the backdrop for two of his novels, *Colin* and *Colin II*.

Sunday 3

Slacked in the morning, a lovely day. In the afternoon went up to the Rectory and saw Sophie 'Wasabelle', Kitty Mackintosh and the old people. Went to the afternoon service at the church to hear the singing, which was magnificent, especially that of Lady Maud Warrender and Jack. Tea fight at the Rectory afterwards.

Monday 4

Motored Joko over to Folkestone and had lunch at the Grand, lobster and fizz. Then we went on and took Peggy out from Miss White's; she seemed very well. Then on home. Florence Lomax arrived to stay. She is a funny girl, quite a good sort, very fast, but absolutely heartless and a bad influence on Joko, I think. Joko very uppish, making £5 bets with remarkable freedom. She wanted to go off in the dark on Byron's motorbike by herself, but got a bit frightened of Harold West's ghost, so funked it. I adore the little minx, but I am afraid I am just as big a flirt as she is. Had a long chat with Mother, she was very interested by my descriptions of Stroma.

Tuesday 5

Neville Handfield-Jones killed, also Cecil Gedge, who died a most glorious death, and whose soul shall float on in glory through Valhalla to all eternity. Went round saying goodbyes to everyone; old Baird seems very well disposed towards me just at present. Sorry to leave, as my visits home are always so short, but perhaps it is for the best. Joko looked too fascinating in the morning. I am sure she is a naughty wee thing, there is not much she does not know. As I have said before, Florence is inclined to hold out glimpses of London life, which are not good for Joko's imagination. Said goodbye to dear old mother, and went up to London by the 2.28 from Bekesbourne. Joko came to the station with me as usual, and was sweet as an angel, and drove me into ecstasies of adoration alas as usual. It is extraordinary what a change their Scrimgeour allowance makes to the Westenhanger family, relieved of their financial difficulties. The parents look years younger, and there are all sorts of little extra comforts in the home. It must be very nice for the girls having a dressing allowance etc., although Joko has not appeared in anything new to me. Perhaps she keeps them for the soldiers! Dined with WSH and Daddy at Simpson's,* then off from Euston by the 8pm express.

Wednesday 6

Arrived Stranraer 5.30am after a good journey; went across to Larne and rejoined the *Invincible* in Harland and Wolff's yard at Belfast at 9am. Everyone rejoined the ship. All the dockyard work complete, and we are ready to sail. The gunroom has been enlarged and improved during our absence, which is a mercy. Some people went ashore in the afternoon. I spent it rambling round the dockyard, a perfect beehive of shipbuilding industry. Went over the monitor *Earl of Peterborough* and the gigantic monster the *Britannic*; quite interesting. Wrote some letters. During our absence Mr M has been promoted to mate; he is a good chap, but hardly the sort for commissioned rank. Proceeded out of dock at 8am, met an escort of two destroyers off Carrickfergus, and proceeded out of Belfast Lough, and shaped a course for Mull of Cantyre and Oversay.

Thursday 7

I kept the morning watch, proceeded past Dubh Artach, Skerryvore, Barra Head, and through the Minch and round Cape Wrath. GQs in the forenoon. Everything pretty efficient in 'A' turret. The men hardly seem to have got as much benefit from their leave as I hoped. I think forty-eight hours, considering the time they spend travelling and the long periods elapsing between their leave, is too short, as they have a very monotonous time otherwise. Personally I should try and give seven days on end every nine months to all the ship's company, but I suppose

---

* The famous Simpon's-in-the-Strand restaurant.

that is impossible. It is my ambition to get into touch with the feelings of my men as far as possible. I am sure all officers should do this. Ran the Pentland Firth at 2pm and joined up with the Second Battle Cruiser Squadron north-east of Duncansby Head, then altered course SSE and made for Rosyth. I kept the first watch.

Friday 8

Arrived in the Forth at 8am, anchored, and the collier (SS *Camerata*, good derricks, narrow-mouthed holds) came alongside immediately. A terrific 'coalship', 1400 tons, the biggest we have had, lasting until 4pm. Very tedious and hard work. Coaling is an evil no landsman, not even the hardest worked soldier, has experienced. The fo'c'sle hold swept the board; I worked the in-board winch fairly satisfactorily, and de Lisle seemed very pleased as he stood me two sherries afterwards. Felt really done up at the end. The commander does not encourage the men as much as he really should, although, of course, I should not criticise my superiors. Mr Martin left the ship for the *Whaley*, and Surgeon McEwan for the monitor *Marshal Soult*. I am very sorry both are leaving – Martin as I hoped to learn a lot of gunnery from him, and Mac as he is a damned good fellow. I lost £2 of my pay two minutes after being paid by old Mainprice; most annoying, as finances are rather on the 'slump' at present, due to one thing and another. We are moored just astern of the *Canada*, who has just finished her trials. She is a magnificent ship; old Dalglish is commander, and Stromeyer one of the 'snots'.

8 October 1915   HMS *INVINCIBLE*

Dearest Mammy,

How are you all up at the cottage? I hope the move went off all well. I dined with Daddy and Hutchinson before leaving on Tuesday night. The old ship was not quite ready when we rejoined, and I spent the day wandering round the shipyard and exploring the new 'freak'

monitors they are building, and went over the monster
new White Star liner *Britannic*, which is also building
here.

I hope you have quite recovered from the evil effects
of my stay at home.

Give Daddy my love when you see him, and say I
thoroughly enjoyed my dinner, although not quite so
much as the lunch in the City. I shall live for another
such as that.

I hear that the Alexander-Sinclair family have left
their Edinburgh house and migrated into the wilds of
the northern Highlands until Xmas, so I shall not see
Stroma again for the present.

'Sammy', the admiral's little boy, is five on the
15th, and I had been commissioned to buy the gunroom
birthday present, a silver egg cup and spoon. Of course,
I forgot, so we are now in a panic.

I hope you won't forget all my wants, photos, washing,
shoes mending, messages, etc., ad lib. I believe I left
the copy of the six-hour concert in the *Alsatian* in one
of my mufti coat pockets, so please don't lose it.

My very best love to all.

Heaps of kisses.

Toby

Saturday 9

We have shifted our naval instructor from the *Indefatigable* to the *New Zealand,* which is rather a jar. I ran the first picket boat all day, pretty busy. Arranged Portal's stations after much cagging with old Borrett. Provisioned ship in the afternoon. The Third Battle Squadron went to sea at 4pm. The old 'wobbly' Third are a damned useful lot, in spite of the universal contempt in which they are held by most Battle Cruiser Fleet officers. Three stripes night in the gunroom; guests, Commander

Townsend (G) Dannreuther, Shore, Eng.-Commander Weekes, Major
Colquhoun, Fleet Pay Mainprice, and Fleet Surgeon Bearblock and
the Chaplain. Quite a success; most of the SOBs thoroughly enjoyed
themselves. I looked after old Bearblock, an ancient but dear old chap.
An excellent dinner, and we filled them all up. Afterwards two bridge
fours, and the remainder became young again with 'Up Jenkins'. Then
some songs, 'Recky' at the piano, and so at twelve to bed.

Sunday 10

Usual Sunday routine. Went up to Admiralty House in the afternoon
with SO Fisher, 'Flags' and WSH. Old Robin and Mrs Campsie Dalglish
there; she is very nice, and they seem very fond of each other; he is
commander of the *Canada*. Commodore and Mrs Goodenough also
looked in. Got in four sets of tennis; I played very well for me. It is
rather funny playing tennis up here in the middle of October, but very
convenient. The weather is getting cold, but quite dry at present.

Monday 11

'Out nets' evolution all the forenoon; port fore working guy parted,
much to Borrett's annoyance. The skipper got very excited and strafed
signal officer. In the gunnery-commander's section (incidentally mine as
well) all went without a hitch, except that I repeatedly forgot to exhibit
the 'all-well' flag. Went over the *Canada* in the afternoon, examined her
turrets, magazines, shell room, bridge, fire control and general gunnery
arrangements. Had a fearful cag with old Ferrugia the messman. He is
trying to do me for several quid with my mess bill. Mr Hunt, gunner of
the ship, promoted to chief gunner.

Tuesday 12

Working for the naval instructor of the *New Zealand* in the forenoon.
Accompanied Mr Cameron refitting the director training gear of 'P'
turret in the afternoon; spent the day on board. I am very keen indeed
to get five first-class certificates in my exam for lieutenant next year,

but I am afraid it will be almost impossible, as a whole year was wasted in the *Crescent* and *Alsatian,* and the gunnery-commander and the torpedo-lieutenant do not take very much interest in our instruction here, although old Dan is a ripper.

Wednesday 13

Third Battle Squadron returned. I ran the second duty steamboat (our first picket boat) all day. Mr Ferrugia, our gunroom messman, developed serious fever and was sent off to hospital, leaving us in the lurch. After much discussion and argument, the question was got down to the basis that either Powell should mess us, or else Logan, the wine steward, should do it. No other officer except Powell volunteered for the job. A silver egg cup and spoon arrived as the gunroom present for Sammy's fifth birthday on Friday. I was busy with ammunition work most of the day when not away in my boat.

Thursday 14

Robert Ross amused us with a navigation lecture in the forenoon. In the afternoon I had intended to go up to Edinburgh, go to the dentist and to Gieve's, and to tea with Stroma. Of course, just to spite me, we had to prepare for sea and all leave cancelled, although we did not go to sea till 10pm. I spent another afternoon at ammunition. Had a long chat with de Lisle; he, like me, strongly disapproves of the mate 'ranker' scheme, and thinks it will ruin the Service. He has just had a great quarrel with Cory.

Friday 15

Sammy's birthday. The gunroom have given him a silver egg cup and spoon, chosen by Daddy. GQs in the forenoon. Went up north of the Moray Firth minefield, then ran down the Sutherlandshire coast and into the Cromarty Firth, anchoring between Cromarty and Invergordon at 4pm. Commenced to coal at 7pm and took in 420 tons from the collier *Kilsyth* (single derrick); finished 10.30pm. Very uncomfortable and tricky work coaling in the dark. The *Indomitable* and *Inflexible* both got good colliers. We don't 'trade on our flag' like some flagships do, as we seldom get the best collier and never shirk duty steamboat. Other squadrons in harbour: First Battle Squadron, Second Cruiser Squadron, several minesweepers, and auxiliary.

Saturday 16

Weighed at 8am and went out to do full charge heavy gunfiring in the Moray Firth. A cinema of the firing taken from the light cruiser *Active*. We fired with the *Indom,* and the *Inflex* fired with the *Vanguard* of the First Battle Squadron. Firing medium only, but all the loading went off swimmingly in 'A' turret, much to the delight of de Lisle and myself. All glass in the ship broken by the firing and all small fittings dislodged. A gorgeous day. Left the Fifth and proceeded into the North Sea, going over towards the Norwegian coast in the afternoon, and in the evening we ran into a thick fog.

Sunday 17

Joko has not answered my lovely long letter nor has Byron acknowledged my cheque. I wonder if they received the letters. I kept the morning watch. Entered the Firth of Forth and anchored in our usual billet at 9am. Coaled ship from the collier *Slav,* 800 tons in very nearly record time. A beautiful collier, and everything went swimmingly except Campbell got jammed by a hoist of empties and twisted his hip very badly and is going on the sick list. I ran the first picket boat. A fine day, but the nip of winter returning in the air. Old Harold Begbie paid us a visit from the *Antrim* after dinner.

17 October 1915   HMS *INVINCIBLE*

Dearest Mother,
Many thanks for all your letters, which I fully appreciate; Peg's and Jim's are quite good, especially the former. All the clothes have arrived safely.

Now as to this matter of Spicer's bill. I have gone
into it thoroughly, and I find from my diary and my
accounts that the following took place:

On June the 8th and 9th I made use of Spicer's motor
to go to Margate and to go to Canterbury.

Re the Margate expedition, it took place on the day
that Harry Baird motored Daddy over to Margate to see
Henry; I took Nita and Joko. I directed Spicer to give
me his bill, which he did. Before leaving I gave you the
bill and also a £1 note with which to pay the majority
of it. I did not think it necessary to ask you for a
receipt. On the following day I used Spicer's motor to
take me to Canterbury on my way back to Liverpool to
join the *Alsatian*.

By comparison with your own accounts you should
be able to find out whether the bill has already been
paid or not; I expect you have already paid it. In any
case, it seems most unbusinesslike to send in a bill in
October for services rendered in June. Please let me
know the result of your investigations.

Now for more jobs for you, provided you are willing.

On 6 October I sent Byron a cheque for £2 for
the golf club, as he told me they were very short of
funds. He has not acknowledged the receipt of this
cheque. Would you mind asking him whether he got it?
If he did not, it would save time if you wrote to the
bank and asked them to stop it for me if it is not
too late.

The address is:

London Joint Stock Bank, Ltd,

Russell Square Branch,

1 Woburn Place,

London, WC

The number of the cheque to be stopped was 'A 158689', and was made out and endorsed by me (Alexander Scrimgeour is my signature) and payable to E Byron Kelsey. If he has not already got it, it has probably been stolen in the post.

Item No. 2:

I left all my snapshots of the *Alsatian*, *Crescent*, etc., at Westenhanger, with solemn promises of their being sent on. If you are in that direction, please walk boldly into the drawing room, procure the photos and send them on to me, otherwise I shall never get them.

If I have the time and inclination ever, I may call on Jim in Edinburgh, but I see no opportunity at present.

Winter is beginning to close in, and although the weather is still pretty fair, the cold is noticeable, and I am afraid we are into the thick of it for another six months.

No more now.

Very best love to all at home.

Toby

Monday 18

I am afraid all the letters I wrote in Belfast must have been lost, as neither Byron, Joko, nor Mrs Gedge have answered. Thick fog all day and very cold. 'Out nets' evolution in the forenoon. Everything fairly satisfactory. Dear old signal officer is a ripping fellow in every way, but he is a damned bad officer. Sammy's and the admiral's birthday celebrations. Several of us landed and went up to Admiralty House to a tea-party, which was quite fun, games, etc. Gunroom guest night; unluckily the First Battle Cruiser Squadron and *Lion* sailed at dark, so we only had one guest, the captain's clerk from the *Commonwealth*. I would have had Findlay from the *Princess Royal*.

Tuesday 19

A miserable, wet, mucky, cold day. We had the duty steamboat in the
first picket boat, and a most unpleasant job it was too. Big changes
made in the routine to cope with the long hours of darkness; they
seem most satisfactory. Heard from Byron at last, also Cockerill. Poor
Allan Hardy has been killed. Sent a small party of seamen to help run
the *Prince Charles,* a tramp commandeered by the Admiralty for the
anti-submarine service. She is one of quite a large number of tramps,
manned by naval officers and men, dressed as ordinary merchant
seamen, and disguised in every way. They have concealed guns, and
have proved (and are still doing so) most successful.

Wednesday 20

Went to the *New Zealand* naval instructor in the forenoon. Hydraulic
work with old Nixon in the afternoon. Feeling very mouldy all day.
Pessimistic due to the Service news, and bored with life and generally fed
up with things in general. Still, I must fight against these fits of depression
and their causes and conquer them. Determination and will-power can do
anything. I wish Joko would write, it would cheer me up immensely. I am
going to write my impressions of all the officers in the ship, as I did in the
Cornwall and *Crescent,* but neglected to do in the *Alsatian.*

Thursday 21

Poor young Blacker (who is in the Coldstreams) and John Kipling in
the Irish Guards are both missing. Temporary Surgeon Jones joined
the ship vice old McEwan, who has gone to a monitor. Rugger match,
Invincible officers *v. Indomitable* officers, at South Queensferry; we were
short of AJSR Unsworth, Franklin, Campbell and O'Reilly, but we wiped
the board with them 35–0; we should have a pretty useful three-quarter
line, WS Hutchinson, Morse, Portal and de Lisle. I managed to get two
tries, but was very blown at the end, feeling like death. O'Reilly, who
runs the ship rugger, refused to play at the last minute, as he wanted to
go up to Edinburgh to meet his fiancée; very slack of him. I am sure she

would have been just as pleased to watch him play rugger. By the way, poor young Campbell has fractured his hip, and he may be permanently incapacitated; now we have only four junior midshipmen, which is most annoying for the senior members of the mess. Young Campbell was a promising young officer, although a bit slow.

Friday 22

The *Lion* and rest of First Battle Cruiser Squadron, except the *Queen Mary*, returned to harbour and commenced to coal at 8am. Third Battle Cruiser Squadron picket boat manoeuvres all the forenoon. We went to GQs and exercised auxiliary loading for the right gun in 'A' turret, then to 'Abandon ship' stations, and finished up with 'Out nets'. I went ashore and up to Edinburgh in the afternoon, saw 'Keynotes', then went to Nicholson the dentist for an hour. Shopped, and then had tea with Scott, Bowlby, Annesley, Battenberg and Burghersh. Gunroom guest night; I asked Hall from our wardroom, whence came also Macmullen and Cory.

Saturday 23

A miserable swine of a day, pelting with rain from morn till eve. I ran the first picket boat and got stopped several times, doing all the routine trips, while 'Recky' Portal in the second picket boat did the odd work and thought he had a soft job, but I drew fires and moored up at seven, and he had all the night work, much to his chagrin. More hydraulics with Mr Nixon in the forenoon; he has gone through a complete hydraulic course and knows a lot of bookwork, but as far as this ship goes he doesn't know a thing. The ship played *Inflexible* at soccer and won 3–2. The 'Bloke' is in very good spirits just now; his wife and children have now got a house up here; he is devoted to them (very much married) and haunts the beach.

Sunday 24

Joko's birthday present arrived, a waist belt with a naval crown as clasp. I sent it off. All squadrons in the Forth went to one hour's notice; all leave cancelled, etc.; no one knew why, as there were no developments. Bill Adams, the flag-lieutenant, went off to London on three days' leave. It is rumoured that he is going to return to his old pre-war job of harbour work in connection with munitions, where he is a very valuable man; but we shall all be frightfully sorry to lose him. I supped with old 'Puroj', the gunnery-commander, in the wardroom. He is a dear old chap, and we had a long chat in his cabin after. He is a bit too prone to talking shop.

24 October 1915   HMS *INVINCIBLE*

Dear Daddy,

I enclose a guinea for the egg cup and spoon, and have posted the soup ladle back to Quaives, where I imagined it would be best to send it. Thank you very much indeed for your trouble. The present was an enormous success; the ladle was very sweet, but hardly so appropriate as the egg cup. The birthday party had to be postponed owing to unforeseen circumstances, but was a great rag when it came off.

Did you send the gun off, as it has not yet arrived at Dalmeny Station? I hope it has not gone astray. I hear from Mother you have had a day at Aldington with the new tenant. Please thank mother for her regular letters, and say I have heard from Byron, but have not yet received my snapshots from Westenhanger.

I have discovered a damnable abscess under the stump of the broken tooth, and am paying periodical visits to a dentist when I get the chance.

Give my love to Jack and Arthur Russell and to GGW when he returns.

                                        Best love from
                                                Toby

Monday 25

I ran the first picket boat. Quite an easy day, but very cold. 'Fire stations' and then 'Out nets' after divisions. More hydraulic work with old Nixon. AB Bird is leaving the ship with a draft for depot tomorrow. This notorious bad sheep of the fo'c'sle division will not be much missed by most people, but I am sorry he is going, as it was my ambition to strike the right note in his character (I am sure it exists somewhere) and try and reform him. Among the others leaving are CPO Goldring, a very good man, and AB Satchell, an inveterate rotter.

Tuesday 26

Usual routine all day. The aeroplane ship *Engadine* came in, and the sea-planes showed great activity all day. Stewart's brother in the RAMC, on five days' leave from the Front, arrived last night from London and spent the night on board, sleeping in Fisher's cabin; we had a great rag last night before turning in, turning the chest flat into an absolute shambles. Landed in the afternoon, and our gunroom team played the *Indomitables* at rugger, winning 9–3; quite good, but we should have done much better if only the forwards would heel, and the outsides take their passes. I got a try and played pretty well, but my language rather disgusted old Mrs Weekes who was watching, I am afraid. A very heated argument in the gunroom over respective officers' principles of work; I got very excited.

Wednesday 27

The hydraulics craze with old Nixon, the gay and debonair marine gunner at the head, continued apace, although many metaphysical pinpricks were required to get 'Labbie' and into a state of energy, much less enthusiasm. The 'Johnnie' de Lisle affair continues without break and with increasing vigour, in spite of the gibes and causticism of the wardroom three-stripe officers, and the vulgar jeers of the lesser gunroom fry. A rugger craze has arisen in this ship, and Service rugger, once it gets a hold on a community of

Service people, is quite irresistible. Today we landed for one hour's scrum practice at South Queensferry. O'Reilly came and ran the show; he is a fine player, but not much of a coach. It is a great pity old McEwan has left the ship. The Cory controversy has subsided somewhat, but the general unpopularity of the mate system is still more pronounced. Met Sophie Molyneux in her motor on shore with Battenberg, Burghersh, and Captain Pelly; being covered with mud and in footer rig, I did not expect to be very impressing, but she was most gracious.

Thursday 28

Terrible 'Buff' casualty list. D Lambert and Birkett, the Harlequin rugger men, Allan Hardy and poor dear old Kit Davidson have been killed in France. May the fury of all the eternal devils be called down on the fiendish, unspeakable Huns who have caused all our most gallant and best to lose their valuable lives! Poor old Kit, he was one of the very best. May every British subject arise in righteous wrath and never rest until each British life is avenged tenfold; I wish the glorious example of the heroic Serbians would rouse this befogged and lethargic nation to a realisation of its responsibilities. We chafe at our powerlessness to do more good. Went to the naval instructor in the *New Zealand* in the forenoon and did a good morning's work. A miserable wet day. Landed and went up to the dentist in Edinburgh in the afternoon, then went to call on Jim Robertson's family at 30 Inverleith Place; all of them immensely grown and changed, but still under the iron discipline and rule of Miss Shorediche, who showed such extraordinary appreciation of the senior Service that I believe she must be a German spy. Elspeth and Agnes have their hair up, the latter quite a good sort. Billy is at Edinburgh Academy and very keen on rugger, and Babs is a good sort. A joy party headed by Percy in the *Queen Mary*. Johnnie Cobb, the Nickersens, Portal and sister, and others went to the Haymarket Ice Rink and pronounced it a great success, the rink being, so they said, even better than Prince's.

Friday 29

By the way, of all the awful snobs I have ever met, Wilton of the *Queen Mary* and Bowlby of the *New Zealand* are about the most supreme. HMS *Argyll,* of the Third Cruiser Squadron, went ashore off Bell Rock; a nasty swell, and there seems little chance of getting her off; a flotilla of destroyers went out and took off her ship's company. I am afraid she will become a total wreck. GQs in the forenoon. I went round all the turrets with Mr Nixon; 'A' and 'X', the two Vickers turrets, are infinitely superior to 'P' and 'Q', the two Armstrong turrets, although the details of Vickers' work is rotten. Landed in the afternoon and played the *Hibernia* at rugger, full-strength match, at South Queensferry. After a strenuous and muddy game we won 30–0. We played very well. A huge tea afterwards at Queensferry Arms. Gunroom guest night. Humphrey Legge (flag-lieutenant of the *Princess Royal*), Tollemache, and Borrett guests; a very good night. We had a terrific gamble, and Tollemache swept the board, winning the hell of a lot, and we all lost very heavily.

Saturday 30

I ran the first picket boat for the last time, I believe, as I am starting three months' engineering duty on Monday.

Salvage work on the *Argyll* continued all day; pretty hard job. The big crane and pontoon came alongside at 11.30am, and the two 4-inch guns on 'P' turret were hoisted out of the ship, as we are getting rid of the 4-inch guns on 'P' and 'Q' turrets. Fellowes-Gordon came over from the *Indefatigable* in the afternoon with rifle drill party and had some tea with us. Owing to a general misunderstanding between the commander, commander (G), commander (N), signal officer, Stewart, Portal and myself, there was a frightful 'straf', and after various vows of vengeance against Portal and myself for misinterpreting the commander's orders, Portal got watch and watch for three days. Most unjust. Borrett stood up for me like mad, chiefly owing to his violent antagonism to the commander.

Sunday 31

Bill Adams returned to the ship to get his gear, and left at 6 to return to London. He is leaving us for good, worse luck. His new job is naval adviser to Lloyd George on the Munitions Committee. O'Reilly is now acting as flag-lieutenant, but he will be unable to do the job as well as signal officer. There is talk of Stewart getting the post, which would be about the limit in the way of good luck for that extremely lucky young officer. There is also talk of old Begbie coming back. Some of the Wobbly Eight went to sea, and consequently we all went to short notice. I stood all the first picket boat's crew a bottle of beer apiece to celebrate the successful conclusion of my three months in charge of the boat. Rae asked me to dine in the *New Zealand,* but I refused. A rotten foggy day. Heard from Joko at last.

NOVEMBER

Monday 1

Started three months' engineering duty. My day on as junior engineer officer of the day; not very strenuous, as I spent most of the time finding my way about below and tracing main steam. It will be nice getting my engineering time over in the winter months, as it would be damned cold in a picket boat. Heard from Harry Baird. I wish to goodness I had the strength of mind to absolutely dismiss Joko from my thoughts and dreams. I am sure she treats me as a sort of toy. I do not say she is not fond of me, but I don't believe she would dream of marrying me, which is after all very sensible of her and lucky for both of us. Still, I think she might not play with heartstrings so; although of course if I said so to her she would say she had no idea I was really in love with her. I cannot make up my mind whether to give up my affair with her altogether and write to tell her so, or to let things dangle on as they are at present, which is not very good for my peace of mind, although I still have a fleeting hope that some day she will marry me. I wish things would come to a head. Even if she was in love with me and would marry me, it would be damned silly of me to marry her so young. Again she is very lazy, indolent and a dreadful flirt, although she does have some very good points.

Tuesday 2

Last night Cobb and I had a long yarn with the padre in his cabin *re* the morals of the gunroom officers. The old boy is very sensible and not a bit of a prude, while the state of the gunroom would certainly rival the lowest haunts of the Stock Exchange. Coaled ship at 5.45am, taking in 375 tons. We had a big deficiency, this leading to a great cag between the captain, commander and engineer-commander. De Lisle was blamed for swinging in his hoists and so making the bags light, instead of dropping them plumb. LEJ's day on, he relieving me at 9am. Spent most of the day pipe tracing in the boiler rooms. Payne asked me to dine in the *Lion*, but I refused. 'Out nets' after quarters.

Wednesday 3

Pipe tracing in the forenoon down below. I had a very busy afternoon mapped out, but after our match with the *New Zealand* was scratched Scott arranged a match with the *Princess Royal*. A frightful cag took place, and eventually we agreed to play, but it rained like hell, and they did not turn up, so the whole afternoon was wasted, which was most annoying. Saw Dora and Kathleen Mackintosh in Queensferry.

Thursday 4

Eleana and Katherine asked Bench and me to go to the skating rink today, with a party including Stroma. Unluckily I had a previous engagement, and Bench a 'day on'. Spent the forenoon in the engine room. Landed in the afternoon and went up to Edinburgh with Scott, had a 'spot' at the Waverley,* where Payne and Troubridge rolled up; the latter is now in the *Comus*. Also saw old John Tovey and Begbie.

---

* The Old Waverley Hotel on Princes Street.

We went on and played golf at Milebank with two friends of Scott's, I playing with a Mrs Hill against Scott and Mrs Crabbie; we won 3 and 2. Both quite nice and knowing Louis Greig well. Jack Crabbie, her husband, and Phipps-Turnbull, her brother, both played for Scotland with Louis, and Major Hill, Mrs Hill's husband, captained England for several years; altogether a very 'ruggery' crowd. On our arrival back in the ship a bomb fell. Scott has been appointed away and is to go up to the Admiralty to report. He is being relieved by Campbell-Cooke, late of the *Collingwood* and *Argyll*. We shall be very sorry to lose Scott. He is an exceptionally nice fellow, very tactful and intellectual, though perhaps a trifle weak. I like him very much indeed.

Friday 5

GQs in the forenoon, nothing much doing. De Lisle, Richardson and I examined the director training clock in 'A' space, and then the 'A' magazines. My engineering 'day on', but managed to get ashore in the afternoon. We played the *Queen Mary* Portal away (leave stopped) and Cobb (crocked) – we won rather unexpectedly 25–9. Hutchinson crocked when we were down 6–9, so we did jolly well. A fierce game; Stevens, the constructor, playing a very questionable game. I managed to get two tries. Saw Mrs Richardson and the two young 'Shishlets' on shore. The Milebank crowd came over to watch us play. Betty Molyneux and Sibyl rather surprised by the language in the scrum. O'Reilly said I was the worst offender, but all signal officers are alike. Very busy in the evening with the main and auxiliary steam system.

Saturday 6

Turned out at five and went round the engine rooms. At 5.45am we got orders to light up all boilers and get ready for sea. Rather a nuisance, as I wanted to go up to Edinburgh and finish off the dentist and also call on Stroma and ring up Aunt Jessie. Sub-Lieutenant Campbell-Cooke, Scott's relief, joined the ship at 10am from the ill-fated *Argyll*. Rather wet, but seems quite a good sort. We unmoored, weighed, and proceeded to sea at noon in company with the *Lion,* First Battle Cruiser Squadron, and rest of Third Battle Cruiser Squadron. Carried out 1-inch aiming tube firing at splash targets towed by our opposite numbers off May Island. Then parted company with the *Lion* and First Battle Cruiser Squadron and proceeded east for the Skagerrak. The Germans have set a line of armed trawlers across to prevent the ingress of our submarines into the Baltic. Two light cruisers are going over to do a little 'strafing' on the aforesaid trawlers, and we are supporting them in case of eventualities. The second division of the Third Battle Squadron (Wobbly Eight), under 'my boy Sid', sailed from the Forth with us, and then proceeded south; it is rumoured they are off to the Mediterranean. I kept the first dog watch below in the engine room and boiler rooms with Macmullen. The boilers are in such excellent trim that it is very hard to keep the steam down to the necessary pressure.

Sunday 7

Kept the middle watch down below with old Bull, who was in a very surly mood. Very hot. Turned in at four and slept like a log. At six the light cruisers should have been in position for the 'straf'. At eight we rejoined the *Lion* and First Battle Cruiser Squadron and still proceeded east until noon, then ran down Danish coast for one hour and altered course for the Scotch coast. The result of the stunt has not been divulged. I kept the afternoon and first watches below with Macmullen and Bull respectively, and was damned glad to finish a very long day at midnight. It is very strenuous being in three engine room watches, as Hutchinson is *hors de combat* with a dislocated shoulder. A nasty sea in the evening, and we rolled heavily. The starboard torpedo boom heads got adrift and made enough clanking noise to drive anyone off their head, banging against the ship's side just outside gunroom.

Monday 8

Entered the Forth and anchored at 8.45am in company with the other ships. Started to coal immediately. My 'day on', as Bench is sick; spent most of the forenoon in boiler rooms superintending dying out, blowing down, and cleaning of boilers. Coming into harbour, one of the light cruisers rammed and sank a collier in the middle of the fairway. Finished coaling at 2pm, having taken in 850 tons with a very fair average, although the fo'c'sle men were not up to scratch. We finished cleaning the tubes, etc., in the boiler rooms by about 4pm, and I then had a most enjoyable bath and felt clean for the first time for some hours. Old Scott went ashore and left us at 5.30pm; off to the Admiralty. It is sickening, his going. Went the rounds of the deckplates, etc., and engine room rounds with old Fry, and then turned in early.

8 November 1915   HMS *INVINCIBLE*

Dearest Mother,

Many thanks for your letters (rather infrequent of late).

I am returning the ones you ask for; you seem to be carrying on a very violent correspondence with Harry Baird; I shall have to send his letters to 'papa' if it continues.

Please send me the square-toed pair of boots I left at home to be mended. Also I should like you to have a look for a cheap black tin box of paints and brushes I left at Quaives. Try my room, and the chest of drawers in it, and, if that fails, a very modified search in my writing desk. It is quite a cheap affair with about twenty squares of paint in two rows, and three or four brushes. I want it for colouring diagrams and charts.

Yours in haste,

Toby

Tuesday 9

I took Bench's 'day on', as he is still *hors de combat*. Spent most of the day looking after work on the oil fuel supply system. The engineer-commander had a frightful 'straf' on the last engineering section's notebooks. A very nasty day, blowing like a Dutchman from the south-west. We had to let go our sheet anchor, and set an anchor watch; also raised steam in eight boilers in case of emergency; several ships dragged badly. The picket boats had an awful time. Hoisting in our second at dark, the steadying line parted and the stern was dashed against the side of the ship. Old Tom Cobb and the boat's crew looked a bit green, as the slings were only hooked on forward, and she was making water heavily. The first lieutenant sent for the 'Bloke', who in his turn sent for the skipper, whose cap went soaring away in the gale on his arrival on deck. Poor Featherston, ordinary seaman, had a bad fall from the fore superstructure, and his state is critical. The picket boat at length arrived on the booms, rudder smashed to atoms.

Wednesday 10

Heard that WR Kennedy ('Calipers'), who left our term at Osborne owing to defective eyesight, and now of Argyll and Sutherland Highlanders, had been killed. Usual boiler room work in the forenoon. Gale still blowing like blazes; the officers of the watches kept their watch on the bridge, and five of the boat snotties kept watch to run the routine as additional officers of the watch down on deck. A heavy fall of snow; all the mountains away beyond Alloa towards Stirlingshire in the north-west thickly covered, but it did not last long down by the sea. We kept steam up all day, and shifted billet owing to the wind with the rest of the Fleet at 4pm. Old Begbie came on board again and moaned about our inability to finish the fire control communication diagrams he commenced.

Thursday 11

Lieutenant Murray joined the ship to relieve Stewart, the latter commencing his duties as flag-lieutenant, lucky young cub. Spent the forenoon making diagrams of the steam connections in the boiler rooms and engine room. 'Young Yonnie' in the soup – fire mains out of order at 7.30am. Landed at 11am and went to Edinburgh; saw Mrs Hood and Sammy, Mrs Alexander-Sinclair, and Stroma (who have returned from Dunbeath Castle) shopping in Princes Street. I had a spot with Morse at the Waverley, and then went off to lunch with Aunt Jessie at Merchiston Park. Quite a nice girl called Sheila McDougall, whom I met at Cannes before the war, there. Then went on to the skating rink at the Haymarket. It is a fine rink, larger than Prince's. Crowds there, including Mrs Crabbie, Roxburgh and his people, Percy, etc. A ship's company concert run by the padre in the evening; not a bad show. De Lisle and 'Young Yonnie' shot with Lord Linlithgow at Hopetoun.

Friday 12

Heavy snowfall in the forenoon. Usual boiler room work. In the afternoon our hockey team, about ten of the best away, beat the *Antrim* 10–5. The newly fledged 'Flags', O'Reilly, THC, LEJ, RSP, myself and Birch went to a show at the YMCA house at Rosyth dockyard, entertainment by Ellaline Terriss and Seymour Hicks and some others. A jolly good show. She is very nice. One hundred men from each ship, parties from the smaller ships attended, and heaps of officers. Mark II's birthday; all the admirals and their families attended, also the old Duke of Leeds, an RNR commander, whose patrol yacht was sunk the other day, and he is now living in the *Australia* with Rear-Admiral Pakenham. Sir David Beatty made a fine speech after the show; he speaks very well. We all went up to a birthday party at Northcliffe House afterwards; quite amusing. Stroma was there, and we had a long chat; she is off back to the Highlands again till April on Monday, which is rather sad. Gunroom guest night. I had old Commander 'Pwoj', who talked shop twenty-five to the dozen till 11pm.

Saturday 13

One of the Scapa light cruiser squadrons, *Calliope*, *Comus*, etc., arrived, making a total of sixteen light cruisers here now. Heard from Joko. My engineer 'day on'. Worked very hard all the forenoon and afternoon making diagrams of the boiler room auxiliary exhaust system, etc. Gave young Birch a stiff dozen, as he is getting much too slack and impudent. Lieutenant Murray, Stewart's relief, is a wonderful linguist. He is Macmullen's term – *viz.*, Grenville. He speaks seven foreign languages – French, German, Italian, Spanish, Portuguese, modern Greek and Russian, both the latter fluently. He served the first part of the war attached as staff interpreter to the Russian cruiser *Askold* at the Dardanelles ('Packet of Woodbines'), and lately he has been on Vice-Admiral de Robeck's staff. He came home on account of ill health, but some people think it means we are off to the Dardanelles, which I don't believe.

Sunday 14

Very cold indeed. On board all day and hard at work with Macmullen and the boiler party. Heavy fall of snow in the afternoon.

Monday 15

I am changing over from boiler room duty to engine room duty this week. Spent the forenoon in the engine room. Very cold again and more snow. Went ashore at 2.30 and went for a stiff hour and three-quarters' walk past Hopetoun Castle, and then straight back to the ship. A very hilarious dinner in the evening; old Macmullen came in and swigged cocktails by the dozen before.

Tuesday 16

On board all day. Engineering work of various sorts kept me pretty busy. Had a long letter from Mother, with reference to 'the chit of a girl', which sent thrills through me, which it should not have done. Try as I will, I can't help thinking about her, and the more I think, the more I love her. The commander very sour-tempered just at present. Another row with his stern and muscular missus, I suppose.

Wednesday 17

Still colder than ever; all the ponds and lakes, etc., in the vicinity are frozen, and several people went up to Dundas Castle to skate. My 'day on'. Nothing very strenuous. Worked chiefly in the engine room, where the distillers are being refitted and circulating crankheads adjusted. Macmullen ran two stokers in for mutinous behaviour towards a chief stoker. B was in the row; he is very tactless with the men, and in some ways he has no originality, as he copies my methods assiduously; the best of them, I must say, so I ought to take it as flattery instead of being annoyed.

17 November 1915   HMS *INVINCIBLE*

Dearest Daddy and Mother,

I have no time at present to write two letters, so you must rest content with one between you. I am returning Mother's letters which she asked for.

Very sorry to hear she has not been up to the mark, and glad to hear that her inane scheme of secreting this indisposition from the old man has fallen through.

Winter has set in with a will, and it is jolly cold; we have had a lot of snow and hard frost. Luckily there are excellent skating facilities in the vicinity, which is great fun. In addition, we are not dependent entirely on the elements for skating, as there is a very good artificial rink in Edinburgh, said by those who know to be the superior of 'Prince's', and it is 'the' thing to go there when the occasion offers.

I paid old Aunt Jessie Duguid another visit the other day, and she seems very keen that if ever mother comes north she should pay her a call. She is quite an amusing old 'bird'.

Young Stewart has got his appointment as flag-lieutenant. You might congratulate the parent on having produced a phenomenal son. His watch-keeping successor, also a youngster of twenty-one, one Lieutenant Murray, has had the most extraordinary

experiences this war, before coming here the other day.
It may almost be worthwhile giving you an outline, as I
think they are probably without an equal for variety.
So here goes.

The beginning of the war found this young officer
an unknown sub-lieutenant in a small cruiser on the
Mediterranean Station. On the outbreak of hostilities
the ship proceeded to W Africa, and he took part in
the operations against German Togoland, where he
was wounded and sent to Cape Town. He there joined a
transport as assistant navigating officer, and saw some
fighting in E Africa, and eventually arrived in the
Mediterranean again about the time of Vice-Admiral
Carden's first attack on the Dardanelles.

I should have told you that Murray's father was
Consul-General at Warsaw years ago, he himself being
born there. Also he is a brilliant linguist, speaking
seven languages in addition to English – *viz.*, Russian,
Turkish and modern Greek fluently, also German, French,
Italian and Spanish.

Consequently he applied for a job as interpreter, and
was appointed to the Russian cruiser *Askold*, in which
ship he saw all the preliminary Dardanelles fighting.

The Russians soon realised the value of such a
linguistic gem, and he was sent with despatches to St
Petersburg from the British C-in-C, travelling via
Salonika, Bulgaria (before her entry into the war, of
course) and Romania. His adventures on this expedition
were too numerous to recite.

He now returned to the Balkans, visiting the
British Naval Expedition defending Belgrade, under
Rear-Admiral Troubridge, and eventually joined
Vice-Admiral de Robeck's staff at the Dardanelles, where

he remained until September, when he was invalided home
with dysentery. The appointment of such a wonderful
interpreter to this ship naturally raises the hopes of
the optimists that we shall not spend the rest of our
lives in the 'Germined' Ocean (please excuse the coined
word). Personally, however, I am not so sanguine, and
am afraid that as soon as he is quite fit he will leave
us. But what a fairy story! It makes my mouth water to
compare his experiences of the war with mine, and even
mine are better than many other poor unfortunates in
the finest battleships in the world, who have never
even so much as smelt a German.

Don't forget the above story is not to be spouted
wholesale to all your Stock Exchange cronies and wine
merchants. 'Beg parding, guv'ner.'

The Balkan outlook does not seem too bright. Greece
is in between the Devil (the Kaiser) and the deep sea
(the Allied fleets). What a magnificent fight the
wretched heroic Serbians appear to have made, and what
disgraceful efforts we have made to help them!

Think of me wallowing in the bowels of the ship,
surrounded day and night by roaring furnaces and
hissing steam pipes; and although I am terrified by it
all, yet it is just as safe, I fear, as the AAC.

Good-bye and best love to both of you dear old
things.

Toby

Thursday 18

I have conceived a grand strategic scheme, in which by abandoning
serious participants in the Balkan struggle, we should land a large
expeditionary force at Alexandretta and invade Syria, joining with the
Persian Gulf force on the Euphrates above Baghdad and eventually with

the Russian Caucasian Army thus effectually blocking the
Turco-German designs in the east, safeguard Egypt and Persia, and
convince the Oriental world of our resource and invincibility. This
would for once give us the initiative. Examined the air-pump suctions
and discharges and engine room feed suctions in forenoon. Very cold
still and foggy. Landed at eleven and went up to Edinburgh in 'Recky'
Portal's sidecar. Portal, Hutchinson, Reid and I had a stupendous mixed
grill gorge, which developed into a vile debauch at the Waverley. Then,
life having a pleasant aspect, we lurched along to the skating rink at
Haymarket and skated for the rest of the afternoon. Great fun. I am
not much good, but thoroughly enjoyed it, and it is a magnificent rink.
Lots of naval and military officers and fair young things there, Selby
and Farquhar being particularly happy. Murray, who is a fine skater (he
was born at Warsaw, where his father was Consul-General), in great
demand, with his yarns of his experiences in East and West Africa,
Mediterranean, Russia, etc. The two Miss Inverarietys skate damned
well. A large party went over with the admiral to skate with the Beattys
at Aberdour; others went to Dundas Castle. Payne, Burghersh and two
wonks shot at Dundas and had good fun with the duck. When we got
back to the ship, received signals to say a German cruiser squadron with
destroyers have come through the Kattegat heading for the North Sea.
Lit up all boilers and went to immediate notice, and the Fourth Light
Cruiser Squadron and destroyers went off to investigate and 'straf' if
necessary at once. Started watch-keeping in three watches again, RH
being crocked now. A damned nuisance. The Serbian situation looks
exceedingly black, and all the pessimists are wallowing in their element.

Friday 19
Thick, dense and impenetrable fog all day; in the circumstances our
going to sea out of the question, but we remained at immediate notice
with steam for full speed in case the weather should change and the fog
clear. No further news of the Boches; the elements appear to be with
them. Tested both steering engines with all the steering positions and

controlling shafting in the ship in the afternoon. Everything satisfactory. I kept the middle and afternoon watches. Gunroom guest night; owing to the situation, no guests from other ships were available, so de Lisle from the wardroom was the only one. Campbell-Cooke on watch, so, as Terence Unsworth has gone to the wardroom, I officiated as president, and everything went well.

Saturday 20

Fog worse if anything; intended to coal ship at 6.45am, but the collier failed to come alongside until noon owing to the fog. We commenced then and took in 600 tons, finishing just before 3pm. I had already kept the forenoon watch down below, and coaling on top of it without any lunch made it pretty strenuous. I tipped with old Fisher in the starboard waist. Kept the first watch as well, and turned into my hammock at midnight with a pleasant thrill. The continuance of the fog forbids any operations, the ships at sea having to remain there, and those in harbour being unable to get out. Apparently several German squadrons are flitting about round the Danish coast, but it is impossible to get any authentic news.

Sunday 21

Fog as per routine. The Deutsche, finding that we are not asleep, decided to return to Kiel, without venturing out, so the 'flap' subsided at last, and we relaxed to the usual routine. My 'day on'. Blew down and cleaned boilers as far as possible.

Monday 22

The *Warspite* arrived after her docking early in the morning. Went to GQs after divisions, and then exercised 'Abandon ship' stations. Afterwards I examined our oil fuel sprayers. Landed at 2.30 with some others and went up to kick about and get some exercise on the rugger ground; very hard, but greasy on top. Had tea at Queensferry Arms. Payne came to dinner from the *Lion,* and SPEG Turner came over afterwards, and, as might be expected, a large amount of liquor disappeared. Very cold again, but the fog was not nearly so thick.

Tuesday 23

Warspite left for Scapa at 2pm. Spent the forenoon with Chief Stoker Barton going round the pumping, flooding and draining arrangements. Oil fuel sprayers again in the afternoon. Henderson, breaking from his torpor with a great effort, his first for weeks, succeeded in arousing Macmullen's righteous ire. Our hockey team beaten by the *Indefatigables* 2–7, but we had a very weak side out. The new cinema gave a show in the evening on the quarterdeck, but I was too busy to go. Heard from Aunt Jessie of dear old Aunt Do's death. I felt she had been doing too much lately, but didn't realise there was any danger. She was a wonderful old lady, a great patriot, and as kind as could be. I am sure that she got more enjoyment out of her last four years of life than the previous forty in strict retirement. I was awfully fond of her, as were all her relations.

Wednesday 24

Our rugger match with Loretto arranged for today scratched owing to the frost, fog, etc. Usual routine and work all day. Hutchinson is getting on my nerves terribly, owing to the way in which he continually copies everything I do. His notebook is an absolute crib of mine, and he seems incapable of originality, or, rather, all his original work is very inferior. Wrote to Rankine and Joko. The *Lion* proceeded to sea at dark; she is going to Newcastle to dock. Old Payne's four days' leave will be a perfect holocaust of festive orgies; no rules, regulations, or Provost Marshal will stop him. The vice-admiral commanding the Battle Cruiser force is shifting his flag and staff temporarily from *Lion* to the *Queen Mary*.

Thursday 25

The *New Zealand* returned at 4am and coaled ship. At 9am we went on board and spent the forenoon with her naval instructor, old Litchfield. This prevented anyone going on shore to lunch, but Hutchinson and

Johnstone went up to the skating rink in the afternoon. Johnstone has got his charmer in Edinburgh; she is a Red Cross nurse, going through a cookery course at the RAMC depot. I have not met her, but believe she is A1, only just eighteen. Katerina was there with the stolid and sphinx-like Miss Evans in attendance, and also the Milebank crowd, Sibyl, Betty Molyneux, etc. My 'day on', so I could not get ashore. Finished a lengthy description and diagram of an oil fuel sprayer. Old Macmullen returned on board very festive and wrote up the engine room artificers' workbook, singing blithely. ERA Pengelly left the ship, and the ERA's mess breathed freely again.

Friday 26

GQs in the forenoon and everything as usual. De Lisle very anxious over the personnel of 'A' turret, as we are losing so many of our reliable men, being drafted from the ship to barracks to man the new ships. Our guest night in the gunroom; a large number of guests; I meant to ask Self, but I got a nasty touch of flu, with a headache and diarrhoea, so I did not put in an appearance, but turned in early at seven. Had a rotten night, could not get to sleep, and had frequent fits of shivering.

Saturday 27

Coaled ship at 7am, taking in 400 tons from the collier *Mostyn*. I felt too bad to turn out till ten, when I lurched out of my hammock and waddled along to the gunroom. I meant to go up to Edinburgh today, but felt much too bad. Slept most of the day and ate nothing but a little soup. Very nasty rheumatism in my right shoulder. I wonder what has affected me. O'Reilly very kindly gave me the use of his cabin to sit in during the day. Heard from Joko.

Sunday 28

Feeling better. Intended to go up with Macmullen to lunch with the Crabbies, but the fates intervened, and at 11am we went to short notice, raised steam, and at 5pm proceeded to sea in company with the rest of the

Battle Cruiser Fleet. I kept the first watch below. Campbell-Cooke told some very funny yarns about Captain Judge d'Arcy of the *Africa* after dinner.

Monday 29

I kept the morning and second dog watches below. We represented the German battle cruisers, and the First and Second Battle Cruiser Squadrons represented our Battle Cruiser Fleet. We approached the Norwegian coast and then tried to slip up north unobserved, and escape to the Atlantic, but they scotched us; rather a dull affair. Full speed all the forenoon without undue forcing; we averaged twenty-five knots and touched twenty-six-and-a-half – much ado down below in the engine and boiler rooms. Old Weekes, the engineer-commander, the only one not to be flurried. Mogg sent me requesting the old boy to come down to the starboard engine room at once, as the vacuum was dangerously high or low, or both, I forget which; the dear old chap insisted on my squeezing into the engine room lift with him; he stopped it halfway down, and suggested that this was an ideal place for kissing the girls, and also recounted how he told this to Sir B Milne when the latter was inspecting the ship, Sir B answering: 'Go on, go on, Engineer-Commander, I am not a damned girl.' He is a fine old boy, old Weekes. GQs and sub-calibre firing at 10am. Everything in a hopeless muddle in 'A' turret; de Lisle in a philosophical mood; PO Bailey, the director trainer, is a useless ullage. Range-taking exercise in the afternoon. During the 'dogs' the sea got up badly, and we began to roll and pitch like old Harry, and the weather got worse all night. The whole Fleet proceeded north-west at eighteen knots between the Shetlands and the Norwegian coast. I dined with Macmullen after the second dog. We were both pretty tired, but some dinner and claret-cup bucked us up, and we listened with interest to some of Murray's Balkan yarns.

Tuesday 30

Passed the *Orcona,* armed merchant cruiser, of the old Tenth Cruiser Squadron on patrol during the middle. I wonder how the old *Alsatian* is getting on! The weather still very bad; all the galley fires put out, and the atmosphere in the gunroom rotten, as we were battened down. No cooked food going, and things reminded one of the old *Crescent* days last year. I kept the forenoon and first watches below with Findlay and Bull. Steaming steadily at from fourteen to fifteen knots. Going south in company with the rest of the Fleet, as it is too rough to fire at present, and we are supposed to be going to carry out some 4-inch practice firing.

DECEMBER

Wednesday 1

The weather moderated a good bit after daybreak, although a good big swell remained. Carried out 4-inch firing in the forenoon; being off watch, I went up in the foretop to watch the firing. After an hour's PZ exercise we formed line ahead in following order: Third, First, and Second Battle Cruiser Squadrons, *Invincible* leading the Fleet, and carried out the firing. To me our show seemed execrable, and the first BCS very good, but I could not see much of the other squadrons. I kept the afternoon watch below with Self; 12-inch sub-calibre firing in the afternoon, while I was below. The firing finished, we reformed the Fleet and proceeded back towards the Scotch coast, hoping to make the Forth early tomorrow.

Thursday 2

Turned out at midnight to keep the middle watch below with Findlay, but I regret to say that the attractions of the pages of a small volume called the *Adventures of an Irish RM* prevented me from taking a very close interest in the phenomenon attending the transference of heat energy to the propulsive energy of the ship by the medium of thirty-one Yarrow boilers and the Parson's reaction turbines of HM battle cruiser *Invincible*. I ensconced myself in a nook above the condensers, and was intensely amused by some very clever pictures of Irish life. Turned in at 4am after a very enjoyable middle. We entered the Forth and anchored at 5.15am in company with the rest of the Battle Cruiser Fleet except the *Australia, Princess Royal, Tiger* and *Indefatigable,* who have gone for more firing to Scapa. Commenced coaling and oiling at 7.30am, and took in 1400 tons of coal and 200 tons of oil. Finished coaling at 2.30pm after a weary and very dirty coal. I spent most of the day below with Macmullen superintending the cleaning of the boilers. Had a letter from Jessie Gedge. The detachment of marines in this ship is the rottenest impertinent lot of scoundrels I have ever met.

Friday 3

Went to the naval instructor in the *New Zealand* all the forenoon. My 'day on', working on the oil fuel system in the afternoon. Self said he would not want my valuable services after seven, as it was guest night. I had O'Reilly to dine; he is a very good chap, and took 21s. off us at Van John, rivalling Tollemache with his run of naturals. Other guests were de Lisle, old Fisher (a good old sort), Murray and SO. Owing to Campbell-Cooke having the first watch, I took president of the mess. I hear from home those carabineers, or anyhow Charlesworth and Fuller, are at home again.

3 December 1915   HMS *INVINCIBLE*

Dearest Mother,

Many thanks for all your letters; I am so glad to hear that you have quite got over your indisposition. (I probably said this in my last letter, but it fills up space.)

I am sending a parcel of collars home to be washed; please return them when finished. I am also thinking of sending some waistcoats, which you might get relined by old 'Stick-in-the-Mud' at Littlebourne.

As regards your Xmas arrangements, originally you
told me you had decided to visit the Duguid clan in
Aberdeenshire, and I suggested that if you did this you
should spend a night or two in Edinburgh, either going
north or when returning. I should strongly deprecate
your coming up to Edinburgh specially to see me, in
view of the heavy expense entailed and the fact that
the odds are that I should be unable to see anything
of you, as we might be away or I might be unable to get
ashore. I am afraid Aunt Jessie is going to Cannes for a
few months very shortly.

If you intend to give Xmas presents this year, I
suggest presents of utility; personally I should like a
nice new big sponge.

I was extremely cut up to hear of dear old Aunt Do's
death; I should have loved to have seen her once more.
She was a wonderful old lady. I am sure that the last
four years of her life were worth infinitely more than
the previous thirty. Poor old Izzie and the servants
will be rather adrift now, I suppose.

With regard to Harry Baird, as you know, I would
rather you did not send on my letters or extracts from
them to him, for various reasons, the chief one being that
I feel they would not really interest him, although he
would never be impolite enough to say so. Still, I leave
the matter in your hands. If he is very dull and bored,
I would try and write him a letter, but I feel it would
be very difficult to interest him. Are you absolutely
convinced that his enthusiasm over your letters is not
rather forced and the result of extreme courtesy and
appreciation of your eminently kind intentions?

Daddy seems to be having some good shooting now; tell
him to give my love to Kenneth Greig. The latter has

been appointed to the *King George V*, George Baird's ship, and I may possibly see him some day later on.

Please send my best love to Aunts Ethel and Maud; thank them very much for their letters which I love, and explain that I will try and write when I can, but that my time is extremely limited.

I am very sorry for Mrs Handfield-Jones, but more so for Dr, as it was probably her own fault. I wonder if Dr will live to usher your grandchildren into the world.

Please repeat the Auntie E and M. formula to Peg and Jim, and tell them both I am longing to have their company again.

We have just completed a very trying spell of North Sea November weather. All our galley fires were out for three days, and so no cooked food – quite like old *Crescent* days. The engine and boiler rooms are hell, at sea; one cannot realise the life of the stokers and other 'saints who toil below' until one actually experiences it. These men's work can vie with any, trenches and deserts not excluded; their whole life in wartime is a vivid succession of discomforts and hardships, unparalleled in severity and monotony.

Goodnight, 'Mammy', now.

Very best love to you and Daddy.

Toby

Saturday 4

Mugged up a few odd jobs in the forenoon and landed by the eleven boat and went up to Edinburgh. Very cold and snowing. Had a lobster with Campbell-Cooke at the Café Royal,* and then went on and had a

---

* The Café Royal restaurant on West Register Street.

mixed grill at the Waverley. We then went to 'Iolanthe' by the D'Oyly
Carte Company at the Lyceum. Very good show, old Henry Lytton
being excellent.* A big crowd of naval officers there, including 'Flags',
Fisher, Jones the 'Micro-doctor', O'Reilly, Cobb, Portal and Johnnie,
the latter with his latest love, nicknamed 'Cookery' by us, a very pretty
girl to whom I sat next. Betty Molyneux, described by O'Reilly as a
vision of golden hair, appealing blue eyes and 'come-into-the-office-
and-shut-the-door' lips, was there in a box with Lords Burghersh and
Wilton. She is a damned pretty girl. Bench and Chalmers from the
Lion, a young man whose experiences this war would fill a volume,
accompanied Marks I and II to lunch at the Caledonian, and then on to
a charity show under Lady Beatty's auspices, Miss Evans in attendance
as chaperon.

Sunday 5

A miserable wet day. Portal went to lunch with the admiral and family. I
was invited, but after a cag with 'Flags' and No. 1 I decided not to go and
spent the day working on board. Hutchinson and I went to dine with
Payne in the *Lion*, and we had the usual hilarious evening.

Monday 6

Wet again. Went over to the *New Zealand* naval instructor again
in the forenoon; we are supposed to go twice a week nowadays.
Superintending work on the test tanks in the afternoon and making
diagrams. Hutchinson and Johnstone are in the thick of a great burst
of energy at present, egged on by Macmullen, Mogg and the engineer-
commander. The *New Zealands* were quite hospitable this morning for
a change, and we all had cocktails in the gunroom. Bowlby, Poland,
and Rae were most affable, and old Annesley and O'Donnell were in
great form.

---

* Henry Lytton was a famous English actor and singer, and was the leading
exponent of the comic baritone roles in Gilbert and Sullivan operas.

Tuesday 7

A better day; bright sunshine, but a high wind. My 'day on'. Pretty busy all day on various jobs. The *Commonwealth* and some of the destroyers, who went out for practice firing yesterday, returned in the forenoon as it was too rough. The *Albemarle* also came in;* she was supposed to have left for the Mediterranean, but had a frightful 'doing' in the Bay, and so returned, lots of damage being done, including the loss of her bridge; five officers (including Commander Nixon) and fifteen men were drowned, and three officers and seventeen men were injured. Mott of the *St Vincent*, who was snotty officer of the watch, had a miraculous escape, being swept off the bridge and right aft on to the quarterdeck, where he was brought up with a round turn by a stanchion, with only a broken collarbone and a few bruises. Some of the Scapa light cruisers came in for shelter; they have been jiggering about round Heligoland.

Wednesday 8

A busy day for me; anniversary of the victory of the Falklands, so the ship's company piped down all day and did no work, and most of the officers landed in the afternoon. I took Johnstone's day on for him, as he wanted to lunch and play golf with the admiral. We lit up all night owing to the high wind, so as to prepare to shift billet if necessary, and so had to keep watch during the night till 8am. I had the devil of a lot of paperwork all day, drawing, writing, etc. All the Falkland veterans went over to celebrate in the *Inflexible*; on their return we had them in the gunroom and did great execution in the cocktail line, everybody very cheery. A ship's company concert in the afternoon, which, I believe, was very good, but personally I was swimming in work and could not go to it. At about five, after dark, in the middle of the concert an urgent signal arrived from the Rosyth signal station from Cobb in the first picket

---

* HMS *Albemarle* was badly damaged in heavy weather in November 1915 while in the Pentland Firth. The *Albemarle*'s bridge was swept away in the mountainous seas, with numerous lives lost.

boat, stating that he had been rammed by a mud barge at the entrance to the dockyard and was in a sinking condition and requested instructions. Much commotion caused. Murray, who was officer of the watch and was in the gunroom, rushed out in chase of an elusive boatswain's mate; the commander bawled orders from the poop, and in record quick time called away the second picket boat, and sent it in Tottenham's charge to assist the first. The second returned two hours later with the crew of the first and all the details. Cobb appears to have acted in the most excellent manner, and in spite of the sleepy inefficiency of the dockyard authorities, managed to arouse the King's Harbour-Master and get the boat alongside and hoisted by the big crane on the quay just before she sank. The accident occurred owing to the mudbarge being very low in the water at the end of a long tow and without lights. The accident did not prevent a rousing evening in the wardroom, where all gunroom officers and warrants were guests of the wardroom, in addition to Captain Beamish, who was the flag-captain, and Commander Bingham, another old *Invincible*. We had a quiet evening in the gunroom.

Thursday 9

Old Bull promoted to chief artificer engineer. Went over to the *New Zealand* naval instructor in the forenoon, but he was busy and very kindly gave us a day off, so we returned to the ship, and I did a few odd jobs before going ashore at 11am for a very welcome day off. Hutchinson, Murray and I motored up to Edinburgh with Payne and young Molyneux of the *Lion*. A whole deputation of Swedish journalists were at Hawes Pier awaiting a visit to the Fleet. They looked a weird lot of ruffians, mostly Hun spies, I expect. Campbell-Cooke got lured to go as our gunroom representative to a preliminary meeting of the Junior Officers' Club Committee, a club which is to be formed at South Queensferry; rather a poor show, I should imagine. Burghersh lured Selby to go from the *Lion*. Old Captain Gartside-Tippinge appears to be fathering the enterprise. Our party went to Gieve's after an adventurous drive up under the auspices of 'Spica'. We then went on and had a terrific ultra-jovial lunch at the Café Royal of crab, lobster, oysters, etc., sandwiches galore, cocktails and stout and liqueurs. Lieutenant Peploe, Captain of Cobbold's TB No. 36, a great rugger man and a friend of Louis, joined us; a very good sort; also an RNVR motorboat man from Leith and another friend of Bench's. Then we motored to the rink at Haymarket, stopping to do some 'tasting' for the mess at Ballantyne's on the way. A jolly good afternoon, excellent skating and a very good chocolate tea-party at the end, our guests including Mark I, a Miss Mary Scott, a Miss Foley, a Miss Stewart, a wet male creature in plain clothes, and Lady Mar. A thoroughly A1 time. Then we motored back to Hawes Pier, and came off, giving young Molyneux a lift to his ship, with a top hat of Burghersh's in which he is to do a 'Gilbert the Filbert' stunt à la Basil Hallam at Lady Beatty's charity matinée on Saturday. Incidentally I sat on the top hat. Payne came over to the *Invincible,* and he and I dined with Murray in the wardroom, and I again drank more than was good for me. I think I must go on the water-cart for a bit.

Friday 10

A miserable day. We had a gunroom rugger match versus the *New Zealand,* but scratched it owing to the damnable weather. GQs in the forenoon; nothing very exciting occurred. De Lisle went on leave owing to family troubles; something pretty serious, I suppose, otherwise they would not have let him go. It leaves me in charge of 'A' turret, so let's pray for a scrap while he's away. Franklin, the naval instructor from Dartmouth, joined the ship. Inspecting and making diagrams of boiler stop valves and feed check valves all the afternoon and evening.

Saturday 11

Heard from mother of Tootie and Humphrey's decision to secure themselves with a West Country whipping. I was very pleased to hear it and sent Toots a telegram. I am afraid poor old Dunk has gone back to the Front again. My 'day on'. The admiral asked me to accompany a party up to lunch and then on to Lady Beatty's charity matinée for her home for lost dogs or sailors or something. Unluckily I could not get anyone to take my 'day on', although I always seem to be taking other people's for them. Johnstone's mother is stopping here, and Bench had a previous engagement, but Henderson only refused out of pure 'cussedness'; Cobb went instead and thoroughly enjoyed himself. A big lunch party, including vice-admiral and Lady Beatty, Rear-Admirals Pakenham and Brock and Johnstone, and his mother. The matinée was a tremendous success, and they made £1000 or more. Margaret Cooper and Ethel Levey sang, and some damned prima donna and a Russian violinist performed, Corbett from the *Indomitable* sang comic songs, four *Indomitable* snots danced a hornpipe, Burghersh did 'Gilbert the Filbert' and 'The Constant Lover' and everyone said he was even better than Basil Hallam himself.* He and Corbett did a skit on 'The Watch on the Rhine' and there were a few other stunts. Burghersh in real life is just the sort of man typified on the stage by Basil Hallam. The whole show was an unqualified success. I had to spend the day mugging on board. Franklin came in after dinner and chatted over Dartmouth and Cornwall days.

Sunday 12

Heavy fall of snow in the night, and it snowed most of the forenoon. The new accelerated war promotions scheme came out. Under this scheme we shall come up for examination in May next year, four months earlier, which, added to the four months earlier due to recommendation, makes a total of eight months. Morse and Reid and all the 'highflyers' are to come up this January. It is rather sickening their being promoted over our heads, as we have been six years to their two-and-a-half in the Service, but as they are all well over twenty and none of us are yet nineteen it is excusable. In the afternoon Hutchinson and I landed at Rosyth and walked round to Admiralty House to tea. In the evening I

---

* Basil Hallam was an English actor and singer, whose comic creation Gilbert the Filbert was an inspiration for PG Wodehouse's Bertie Wooster. Hallam was killed at the Battle of the Somme on 20 August 1916.

had young Findlay from *Princess Royal* to supper. A most exemplary young gen'l'man, TT, non-smoker, and doesn't gamble.

Monday 13

Received a very sweet letter from Joko, which I answered with a hurried chit. The Fleet Surgeon told me that de Lisle's leave is due to a bad nervous breakdown. In his absence I am left in charge of 'A' turret, which is a big responsibility and entails much work. I can't help wishing we might go to sea and have a scrap while he is away, although it is rather horrid of me. Very busy in the afternoon evolving new schemes of organisation with No. 1. Life seems very much taken up just at present, but I am afraid I take things rather too seriously. Spent the forenoon in the boiler rooms superintending work in 'F' group which is being opened out. In the evening a superfluity of paperwork. Our engineering time is to be cut down to two months owing to lack of time. Rugger match v. *Lion* arranged for today scratched owing to snow.

Tuesday 14

The burst of energy aroused by the proximity of examinations combined apace, and practically no one went ashore. I had a very busy day again from 6.30am till midnight, with short intervals for meals. Hutchinson is getting terribly on my nerves. Everything I do he copies, damn him. I shall have a big row with him sooner or later, I can see. Campbell-Cooke gave a very amusing account of his views on marriage, just what one would expect of the slack, blasé individual.

Wednesday 15

Coaled ship, took in 350 tons. Morse, Reid and myself did not turn out till about 7.10. Old Borrett came along and had a frightful 'straf'; he saw me after lunch and talked glibly about getting us dipped six months' seniority, and finally stopped our leave for a fortnight, and told me to report in future every morning at 6.30 when the flat is cleared. I spent the morning in the boiler rooms with Macmullen. My 'day on' with Self. Inspecting armour belts with a view to a report in the afternoon; everyone seems extraordinarily ignorant about our armour. We borrowed the wardroom piano, which 'Recky' played to us in the evening. He is a beautiful pianist.

Thursday 16

I am seriously considering the advisability of specialising in engineering. I seem to have a bent in that direction. The pay is excellent, the work interesting, the conditions poor, and future problematic very, but with great possibilities. The question will have to be fully discussed with Daddy, Louis, old Finnis, Broadbent, and possibly Admiral de Chair. It transpires that de Lisle had a scene with the rear-admiral and the captain before he left; his nerves were in a terrible state, and I am afraid he will not be allowed to return to the ship. He will be a great loss, as he was an extraordinarily keen, conscientious, and capable officer, an indefatigable worker, a fine athlete, and a damned nice fellow. I hope he will absolutely recover and live to continue a distinguished career to an illustrious conclusion. Boiler room work all the forenoon, my last day in the boiler room, so I was pretty energetic. All the lucky ones gadded up to the skating rink in the afternoon, and I took Johnnie's afternoon so that he could go. Very busy with old Jennings' papers for the rest of the day. The padre dined in the gunroom in the evening with 'Heim', it being the latter's birthday. Murray is taking de Lisle's place in 'A' turret; he is a nice chap, but lacks his predecessor's zeal, and it will mean much more for me to do.

Friday 17

Down in the engine room all the forenoon, mucking round with Self most of the time. Superintending work on the evaporators and distillers in the afternoon. Then came up after four o'clock and did some more swatting. Gunroom guest night; I asked Macmullen, and he refused after an initial acceptance. No less than eight people refused from the wardroom. I wonder why? Tollemache and two clerks came. I played *vingt-et-un* and won a little.

Saturday 18

Ran through the turbine thrust arrangements and radial and facial
dummy systems with Self in the morning. Landed at 12.40 to play
rugger against the *Lion;* de Lisle, Cory, and Powell away from our side,
and we rather expected to be beaten, as AL Harrison,* the England and
Navy man, had been coaching his side, while we had not played for six
weeks. They started off well, and their scrum was far heavier than ours,
but eventually we beat them 18–5, to our great surprise. I managed to
get a try. All the popsies arrived from Northcliffe House, and George in
khaki. He hasn't wasted much time, as he only left Eton two days ago.
Worked all the evening.

Sunday 19

Very cold. All the family came off to church in the forenoon. I did a
certain amount of work in the afternoon, but not so much as I should
have done. My 'day on' with Findlay. Richardson's young brother from
Osborne and a friend named Tyrie, a chief cadet captain, both Blakes,
three below us, came off to tea. Young 'Shishishism' is a nice little chap.

Monday 20

In the port engine room all the forenoon, overhauling the evaporators
and distillers and their pumps, etc. The skipper came down about
eleven with the engineer-commander and Mogg to examine the new
auxiliary steering arrangements, which have been fitted to the port
steering engine. Spent the afternoon writing a description and report on
condition of the fresh-water distilling plant and making the necessary
diagrams. I have been told in confidence that poor de Lisle has gone
clean off his head and is now a raving lunatic. If true, it is very sad,
especially to me who saw such a lot of him, for he was such a splendid
man and officer in every way.

---

* AL Harrison won two caps for England before the war, and was involved in the
Grand Slam winning side of 1914. He was killed in action at Zeebrugge in April
1918, after which he was awarded a posthumous Victoria Cross.

DECEMBER, 1915.—52nd Week.

Lieut Fleming joined this ship vice de Hole.

Gore-Browne, the old Exmouth who showed up so badly & left the navy from Dartmouth 3 years ago, has just got the D.S.O. He was in the same battalion of the Rifle Brigade as poor old Mike, who loathed him.

Thursday 23 (357-8) Away in the E.R & B.R of the 2nd P.B all the forenoon, got to know all about the manning arrangements, ejectors pumping systems etc. O'Reilly invited me to lunch with him at the Edinburgh Services club & go on to the rink afterwards, but unluckily it was too late for me to shift so I took an afternoon off and slept till 3.30 & then worked for the rest of the evening till 6.30. Cobb & I dined in the W.R. with the Padre, & he was very cheery & we had quite an amusing evening considering all told.

Friday 24 (358-7) He is quite a broad minded priest anyhow & a good sort.

Sketching in the forenoon most of the time, although I paid a few flying visits to the Captain Engine flat to look after work going on there. Landed in the afternoon & the G.R Rugger team played the P.R's ditto. We won 16—5, altho' our forwards had an off day. Hutchinson & Henderson at the top of their form. A good supply of letters & cards for Xmas, included 2 cheques for "fivers". Spent quite a quiet Xmas Eve, everyone being too tired after Rugger to enthuse much.

Saturday 25 (359-6) *Christmas Day.* LESSONS.

Matins—Isaiah ix. to v. 8; Luke ii. to v. 15
Evensong—Isaiah vii. r. 10 to v. 17; Titus iii. r. 4 to v. 9

A very muddy day to start off with. Owing to the boisterous weather we have had of late we raised steam, in case the Boches try any games in the fog, so there was no leave. In the forenoon, headed by the R.A, we all went round the mess decks, which were wonderfully well decorated, as was the whole ship. The usual ships co. funny parties. The day dragged wearily on, at 3.30 in the afternoon the W.R challenged us to a cutter race, & some lunatics accepted & impressed a crew & got badly beaten by 2 lengths. Mrs Hood presented us with a plum pudding & a Xmas tree which was very good of her. We dined at 7.30 & about 7.45 things began to look up a bit, eventually we had an A1 dinner with heaps of everything to drink & we all got most hilarious & Xmassy. After the thing we had 2 solemn toasts in "absent friends" & fallen comrades" this crowd included "Falkland veterans" "Our visitors from the Inflexible", "The wounded", "helped of the push", "Our allies" enumerated by me & Gin No. "Sir D. Beatty" "the Hood family" "Scotland the Scots" "England wales the Irish" "The Army" (very popular that) "Lott's speech to the 6th D.G's copied the effort caused an uproar) "Sir J. Jellicoe" "the C.O" "the G.R staff" "the President" & lastly the British Empire. I made 3 speeches & we all got very biffed & sang & shouted till midnight, when we ended shouting on deck, & about 12.30 reached the W.R's men who joined in an another sing-song, & so to bed at 2.30.

Tuesday 21

Examined the steering gear, tiller gear, and hand steering arrangements, etc., all the forenoon, and did a lot of paperwork in the afternoon. I have had Borrett's permission to get a table and chairs rigged up in our flat forward during the daytime. It should be a great boon, as the gunroom is so cramped. The *Inflexible* sailed at dark; she is going off to dock. France-Hayhurst and Mercer came over to us, so that they can do their examinations for acting sub-lieutenants while the *Inflex* is away.

Wednesday 22

Went round the fire main, fresh-water and compressed-air systems in the forenoon with Chief Stoker Barton, and sketched in the afternoon. A cinema show in the evening on the quarterdeck; they have them every few days now when we are in harbour. The awning which was rigged up for the occasion was unequal to the occasion, and we sat there muffled up in overcoats, etc., with a torrential downpour dripping through on our heads. This was too much of a good thing, so I went below and did some more work. Stroma sent me a pair of gloves she had knitted for a Xmas present, which was very sweet of her.

Thursday 23

Lieutenant Fleming joined the ship *vice* de Lisle. Gorell-Barnes, the old Exmouth, who showed up so badly and left the Navy from Dartmouth three years ago, has just got the DSO. He was in the same battalion of the Rifle Brigade as poor old Mike, who loathed him. Away in the engine room and boiler room of the second picket boat all the forenoon. Got to know all about her manning arrangements, ejectors, pumping systems, etc. O'Reilly invited me to lunch with him at the Edinburgh Services Club and go on to the rink afterwards, but unluckily it was too late for me to shift, so I took an afternoon off and slept till 3.30, and then worked till 6.30. Cobb and I dined in the wardroom with the padre, and he was very cheery, and we had quite an amusing evening, considering our host. He is quite a broad-minded priest, anyhow, and a good man.

Friday 24

Sketching in the forenoon most of the time, although I paid a few flying visits to the capstan engine flat to look after work going on there. Landed in the afternoon, and the gunroom rugger team played the *Princess Royal* ditto. We won 16–5, although our forwards had an off day. Hutchinson and Henderson at the top of their form. A good supply of letters and cards for Xmas, including two cheques for 'flyers'. Spent quite a quiet Xmas Eve, everyone being too tired after rugger to enthuse much.

Saturday 25

A very mouldy day to start off with. Owing to the foggy weather we have had of late, we raised steam, in case the Boches try any games in the fog, so there was no leave. In the forenoon, headed by the rear-admiral, we all went round the mess decks, which were wonderfully well decorated, as was the whole ship. The usual ship's company funny parties. The day dragged wearily on; at 3.30 in the afternoon the wardroom challenged us to a cutter race, and some lunatics accepted, impressed a crew, and got badly beaten by two lengths. Mrs Hood presented us with a plum pudding and a Xmas tree, which was very good of her. We dined at 7.30, and about 7.45 things began to look up a bit; eventually we had an A1 dinner with heaps of everything to drink, and we all got most hilarious and 'Xmassy'. After 'The King' we had two solemn toasts in 'Absent Friends' and 'Fallen Comrades' and then crowds more cheery ones, including 'Falkland Veterans', 'Our visitors from the *Inflexible*', 'The Wonks', 'Ireland and the Irish', 'Our Allies' (enumerated by me and nine in No.), 'Sir David Beatty', 'The Hood Family', 'Scotland and the Scotch', 'England, Wales and the Jews', 'The Army' (very popular, but Cobb's reference to the Sixth Dragoon Guards spoiled the effect and caused an uproar), 'Sir John Jellicoe, the C-in-C', 'The gunroom staff', 'The President' and, lastly, 'The British Empire'. I made three speeches, and we all got very biffed and sang and shouted till midnight, when we rushed howling on deck, and about 12.30 reached the warrant officers' mess, where we joined in another sing-song, and so to bed at 2.30.

Sunday 26

Turned out very much the worse for wear after last night's carousal. One or two were fearfully tight, and everyone had the most awful heads this morning. Short notice was washed out at midday, and some people visited the beach. Personally I stopped on board and wrote letters and did some work, beginning to recover during the afternoon. Heard of Louis' engagement to Phyllis. Helped Campbell-Cooke with the mess wine books in the evening. An RNR AP joined the ship.

Monday 27

A miserable day, blowing like sin from the north-east. On board all day, employed on various jobs, but not feeling very energetic, and very cantankerous. Lieutenant Fleming is taking over 'A' turret *vice* de Lisle and Murray. He can't be more ignorant than Murray, anyhow. Received short notes from Tootie, Peggy and Joko. My 'day on'.

Tuesday 28

Examined air compressors and refrigerators in the forenoon and overhauled the fan engine's spare gear. The light cruisers went out at 4am and returned at 10pm after a short trip to sea for range-finding practices. After a long harangue I managed to induce Macmullen to arrange coaling duties for tomorrow, he being in an obstinate and argumentative mood.

Wednesday 29

Coaled ship at 7.30am. A cold job (note pun). Took in 350 tons from the *Frances Duncan* in just on the hour, this constituting a record for the ship, not only since she first commissioned, but since she was built. Accompanied by Chief Stoker Barton with the usual entourage, I went the rounds of the bunkers and made out the coal estimate. Had a bath, and worked in the gunroom most of the afternoon and evening. Heard from Denniston and Effie Robertson.

Thursday 30

A head schoolmaster has just joined the warrant officers' mess. Chief Artificer-Engineer Bull left the ship to join LB 35 as engineer officer in charge. Sorry to lose him, as he is an efficient and capable officer. He is relieved by Temporary-Engineer-Lieutenant A McL. Hine, an elderly, quiet-looking man, who has no previous naval or sea experience. Excitement among the 'knuts', as the Germans are reported to be preparing to 'sweep' the North Sea again. The light cruisers and destroyers rushed off to sea at 7am, and we went to short notice. Picket boat manoeuvres all the forenoon, the Battle Cruiser Fleet exercising 'concentration of fire' practice. 'Out nets' together by general signal at nine, followed by GQs. Old Tipples is very noisy in 'A' turret, now that de Lisle has gone. Short notice washed out in the afternoon. I was engaged making a list of all watertight compartments and particulars of them. A few people landed, Tottenham going to call on Mrs Townsend.

Friday 31

Went to 'general night defence' stations for exercise in the forenoon, and then I finished my drawings of a fan engine eccentric rod. Landed in the afternoon, and the gunroom took on the third watch of stokers at soccer. They beat us 5–0 in a howling gale of wind. We did quite well, notwithstanding the score, considering we have not played soccer seriously since Osborne days, and we had quite a lot of the game. Heard of the destruction of the *Natal*, which is a bad loss.* She was blown up

---

* Shortly after 3.20pm on 30 December 1916, and without warning, a series of violent explosions tore through HMS *Natal* while she was lying in the Cromarty Firth. She capsized five minutes later, killing between three-hundred-and-ninety and four-hundred-and-twenty-one men. The likely explanation was that a fire had broken out, possibly due to faulty cordite which ignited a magazine.

in harbour, apparently, but we have no details at present. Four hundred were saved, but poor old Havers and 'Charley' Chaplin were blown up. We had quite a convivial dinner, and then all went down to the warrant officers for a sing-song, and we performed in great style. At midnight Esmonde (the youngest officer in the ship) rang out sixteen bells in the traditional manner, and a huge gathering sang 'Auld Lang Syne', in spite of a very high wind, then on down to the wardroom for hot punch. CC very 'cheery to tight' and only with great difficulty we got him to bed. Finally piped down at about 1.30am. The gunnery training expedition for tomorrow in the *Prince Charley* has been postponed owing to the weather.

1916

22 January 1916   HMS *INVINCIBLE*

Dear Uncle Jack,

I am writing to answer your letter, and to say that
I think you are wrong when you say that you are not
a good correspondent. Personally I am extremely bad
in this line, which fact, coupled with our uncertain
mail system, makes regular correspondence very
difficult.

I agree very largely with your views on the
war, although impeaching sounds much too good. A
drumhead court-martial would be far swifter and more
efficacious. Nevertheless, I am no politician; they are
all the same to me, and I have no faith in anyone in
either House.

The country at last appears to be waking up to the
necessity of ruthless warfare. For eighteen months now
nearly we have maintained a strict blockade of Germany,
and not a ship has entered German ports from the North
Sea. Yet although we have starved Germany by holding
her neck, the neutral Scandinavian nations have,
metaphorically speaking, fed her through a stomach
pump.

Month after month the old Tenth Cruiser Squadron
maintain their arduous patrols from Scotland to the
Arctic Ocean, and not a ship reaches Europe from
America without first being examined by Admiral de
Chair's ships. Yet owing to the criminal weakness and
vacillating hesitancy of the Foreign Office they

cannot prevent huge quantities of foodstuffs and
raw materials being taken on to Norway, Sweden, and
Denmark for subsequent transshipment to Germany.
Even in cases where munitions are discovered on board,
and the ships are sent into British ports with prize
crews, yet the customs' regulations are so hopelessly
corrupt and futile that the ships often proceed to
their original destinations with their cargoes still
on board.

All the above is in confidence, of course.

The Admiralty are now mad on uniform alterations,
and have ordered that committees should be formed
in the various fleets and naval bases to consider
the question of alterations of officers' uniform. I
was very surprised to find myself called to sit on
the committee here, in company with a miscellaneous
collection of officers of all ranks and all branches
of the Service, Rear-Admiral Hood being president,
and the remainder consisting of one commodore, one
captain, one engineer-captain, one engineer-commander,
one lieutenant-commander, one fleet paymaster, one
staff paymaster, one surgeon, one sub-lieutenant, one
midshipman (myself), and one warrant officer. The 'hot
air' and 'balderdash' produced by this committee were
most amusing, and strongly enhanced my views that the
modern 'democratic' system of ruling by committees,
conventions, boards, etc., is hopelessly inferior to a
more autocratic type.

The loss of the *Natal* was peculiarly sad, in view of
the fact that she had just come into harbour, after a
long spell of arduous work, for a short rest. Several of
the officers' wives and children were on board to lunch,

and all were lost in the explosion. Both the captain
(a very brilliant officer) and his wife were killed,
leaving his mother, herself the widow of another
captain in the Royal Navy killed in action some thirty
years ago, in sole charge of three tiny grandchildren
under ten. It seems very pathetic.

As I dare say you may have seen in the papers, they
have evolved a new system of sending parties from the
Grand Fleet on periodical visits to the Front in France
and Flanders, ostensibly with the object of proving to
the Navy what a far worse time the Army are having,
a fact of which they are already very well aware.
Anyhow, all the people I have met who have come back
to the Fleet from the Front affirm that they would
willingly exchange our life of comparative comfort and
long months of weary waiting for the extra discomfort
of the trenches and the activity, excitement and chance
of distinguishing themselves. A man from the battle
cruiser *New Zealand* was wounded, blown up by a mine,
and worked a machine gun for five hours alone (for
which he has been awarded the Distinguished Conduct
Medal) before he had been in the trenches a single day.
Pretty quick work this, after months and months of
waiting for nothing in the North Sea.

I hear that Newcome has been mentioned in despatches
and been given the Military Cross. This is excellent
news.

Weddings seem to be de rigueur just at present, what
with Phyllis and Louis and Humphrey and Toots. What
a clannish family we are! There seems to be a perfect
horror of marrying anyone except a relation or close
connection.

Now I must stop.

Please give my best love to Cousin Sittie. With best
wishes.

Your affectionate nephew,

Toby

24 January 1916   HMS *INVINCIBLE*

Darling Mother,

Please thank P, J, and B for their letters, which I
loved getting. I suppose the first two will be off back
to school again now, before long. I expect they have
thoroughly enjoyed themselves.

How is the invalid? I hope he will soon be fit again.
I thoroughly endorse Uncle Jack's point of view about
Daddy still doing this ridiculous job in the AAC. I
think it is the supreme height of absurdity, and you
may please tell him so from me. If there is nothing for
him to do in the City, why does not he employ his time
at home, where, with all the men away, there should be
plenty of good hard pottering about to do, which would
be infinitely better for him. There is no necessity for
him to fritter away his health in a perfectly useless
job, which anyone could do; in fact, I consider it a
crime that a man of his abilities should waste his time
stargazing on London house tops.

If he feels it incumbent upon him to do something,
he should first regain his health, and then use
his ingenuity to find a suitable job. Personally
I suggest that when the weather is warmer a few
months later on a spell of deep-sea fishing in the
Cornish smacks would be a good thing. If he liked the
job, he might get something to do in a minesweeping
trawler.

By the way, it may amuse Daddy to know that my
latest duty at night when we are at sea is to control
the searchlights if they should be used; so we are both
on the same sort of job at present.

With regard to Auntie Jessie's request, it really
would have been far more suitable for her to have
written to Daddy instead of me. He, if you can arouse
his energies, will be able to give her far more
accurate details of the procedure necessary for her
to try and get her friend's son into the Navy than I
can. Please thank her very much indeed for her letter
to me, and ask Daddy to do what he can in the way
of supplying information (when he has recovered, of
course). By the way, if Jimmy intends still to enter
the Navy, which in wartime (in spite of whatever old
Roderick may say) he will have no difficulty in doing,
I should think it is about time Daddy did something
about it.

I had a fine letter from Burberry the other day,
and shall address an answer to Quaives, which I request
may be forwarded to him. He says that Bob has disgraced
himself and is not an ornament to the Army by any
means.

How is George getting on? I suppose he will be on
active service again soon.

The Admiralty have got a frightful craze on about
alterations of naval uniform. The RNVR officers have
been given a much thicker stripe, which is almost
indistinguishable from that of the Royal Navy. This is
probably at the instigation of a few influential and
singularly useless old 'Ullages' who have been given
temporary commissions as captains and commanders in
the RNVR, and who wish to appear as much like real NOs

as possible. There is no objection from our point of
view to these old buffers wearing anything from fur
coats to pyjamas, but the disadvantage lies in the fact
that the change affects the whole of the RNVR, and to
put those young temporary officers and gentlemen, who
evidently do not know how to behave themselves, in
uniform closely resembling that of the regular Service,
will tend to lower the dignity of the RN even more than
the behaviour of many officers of the RNAS has done at
present.

The *Natal* disaster was very sad, as she had just
come into harbour for a rest after a long and
weary job. A large number of the officers' wives and
children were on board to lunch, and all were lost.
I can't help repeating the story of the captain (an
extremely brilliant officer), which is very pathetic.
His mother was the wife of a naval officer, who was
killed in action about twenty-five years ago, and
she was left with three small children to bring up
entirely on her meagre pension. Two of these have
since died, I believe, but the late captain of the
Natal she managed to put into the Navy, and he was
the apple of her eye, and a most successful man. He
was married, with three children under ten, and when
the ship blew up his wife was on board and went too.
So now his mother is left in exactly the same position
as she was twenty-five years ago, alone with three
small grandchildren to bring up. This is quite true,
and makes you wonder how some people can have the
face to grumble.

Please thank Auntie Ethel very much indeed for her
most interesting letter. I might almost send it to you
as an example.

I hope that you have carried out all my instructions
about my clothes. Next time I come home I want all my
dress-clothes to be ready for me in London.

Now I must stop.

My very best love to all.

Toby

20 February 1916   HMS *INVINCIBLE*

Dearest Mother,

Many thanks for all your letters; I am afraid I have
not written for some time, but we have been on detached
service and have had fewer opportunities than usual
of sending mails, and this may be some time in getting
home.

I am afraid I was very remiss in not thinking of a
wish when I sent you the bead, so I will do it now, if
not too late.

May you live to enjoy the appreciation of your
children and grandchildren, and may that appreciation
develop into a more apparent and vital state (as at
present, in some cases, it may be in danger of passing
unrecognised).

Pride of ancestry and hope of posterity are both
very large factors in my views of life, although both
are somewhat subordinated to a firm belief in the
all-importance of self (not selfishness). Do your own job
and go your own way, and let the others go to damnation
by their own roads. Consequently the present generation
should not be overwhelmed by thoughts of the past or
glimpses of the future.

Enough hot air; I don't know what led me on to
produce all this bilgy vapouring of a diseased
brain.

Next time I come home I shall want two pairs of trousers (uniform) patched in the seat. I shall want two suits of mufti in London (one of them the one that used to be Daddy's), including my two mufti caps, overcoat, cape, etc. I have a large number of socks that want darning, and innumerable buttons missing, and holes in my pants. My servant is willing but unskilled, and, being a marine bandsman, wields the piccolo with more skill than the needle. Where are all my stiff collars? I sent them home to be washed and they have not returned – you only sent soft collars, many of them size fourteen; my minimum size round the neck is fifteen; I wear fifteen and upwards indefinitely.

Please send me an old pair of black uniform shoes which I left at Quaives, and have my black brogues brought to London (also one pair of grey flannel trousers).

As a final word to all these impending domestic movements in my clothing department: 'It is quite unnecessary to even spread rumours of the journeys or intended journeys of any of my clothes.' If your common sense does not tell you at what I am hinting, dear mother, try your conscience.

Are you in London permanently now?

If you have nothing better to do one afternoon, should you happen to visit one of those accursed cinema shows at the 'Empire' music hall, you may, I am told, have the privilege for a few seconds of seeing your first-born flash past on the film. A scene entitled 'Battle Cruisers at Work' depicts the *Invincible* steaming at full speed (the leading ship of a squadron of three), and on the foremost turret

your first 'trouble and worry' is standing. One of our
staff who has been in London saw the thing a few weeks
ago, otherwise I should never have believed that my
versatility would have led me to appear on a leading
London music hall stage, even on the film.

They must have taken the beastly thing from a
hospital ship or something, I suppose.

5 March 1916 HMS *INVINCIBLE*

Darling Mama,

I am so glad to hear that you are better again. You two
silly old things are always getting ill, first one, then
the other, like a Jack-in-the-box.

During your indisposition Daddy wrote me a
splendid letter – extremely interesting and amusing –
and this honour, one I seldom enjoy, was highly
appreciated. Thank him very much indeed for his
birthday present.

Tell him he is not so old as he thinks, and anyway
fifty is the prime of life.

I don't agree with his modesty saying that he hopes I
shall have a better life to look back on, when I am his
age. If I have a family of sons and daughters like his,
I shall be quite satisfied.

Apparently he thinks that having begotten us is
nothing to be proud of; just show the old devil the
error of his ways.

Many thanks for looking after my clothes. They
sent the wrong shoes from Quaives – *viz.*, patent
leather, when I said uniform. But don't bother.
Another item: please have plenty of white kid gloves
at the flat for me. I have got dozens of pairs
somewhere at home.

I expect to get some leave any time within the next
two months. It is getting on for six since I was home
now, and I am quite ready for another drop.

I shall be in London, if you can put me up, until I
am cleaned out, and then shall proceed as the spirit
moves me.

I promised over a year ago to stop with some people
named Culme-Seymour in Hampshire, so I might go there
for a night or two, although the shooting season would
be a better time.

I hope you and Daddy won't mind tying my ties, etc.,
when I am in London, otherwise I shall be helpless
without a valet. I really must learn to tie my own,
although it is a little eccentricity that I am secretly
rather proud of.

Have you seen that Sir Dudley de Chair has been
appointed naval adviser to the new Blockade Ministry?
He always struck me as being too polished for a sailor,
and would have been an ideal diplomat.

We have returned to our usual haunts again,
and everything is inches deep in snow at present,
although except for the cold the weather would be
very fine for this month, which is usually one of the
worst.

We spend most of our spare time now when in harbour,
and not able to get ashore, making munitions. And the
output of the Battle Cruiser Fleet is very considerable,
I believe.

Who is Nander engaged to? I thought he was the last
person to have been fooled by a woman.

There have been several little 'flaps' in the air
lately, which are kept very secret up here. Although

I expect the Stock Exchange and City are alive with
fantastic inventions almost before the C-in-C himself
knows that anything of interest has occurred.

Good-bye now.

Best love and kisses to you both, my revered parents.

Your dutiful (?) son,

Toby

19 March 1916 HMS *INVINCIBLE*

Darling Mother,

Many thanks for your letter, which arrived very
quickly after being posted, much more so than usual. I
am so glad to hear that you both are better. Is Daddy
still going to persist with his old searchlights? I
must confess to being rather disappointed that you
are having to give up the flat, as I should have
thoroughly enjoyed the use of it once more. I expect to
be on leave either the first or second week in April,
although one can never make absolutely certain, of
course. I suppose it would be quite impossible for you
to keep on the flat for a fortnight or three weeks
longer, although it does not matter very much, as I
can easily stop at my club. But I should have enjoyed
being in a 'home' more. It would be very convenient
if you could leave all my things, which you now have
at the flat, in a box or trunk or bag in London, as
it would be such a nuisance having to drag them up
again. Possibly Daddy could keep them with his things,
wherever he takes them, as I shall probably be home
quite soon now.

Please forgive all this, which is very selfish of me,
trying to add to your worries. But 'leave' comes rather

rarely nowadays, and I had made lots of plans for
this time, and have been looking forward to giving the
Invincible a short rest like anything.

How very funny your seeing Stewart's photo in the
Blunts' house.

I told him that my parents were very much struck by
his likeness.

When are Peg and Jim starting their Easter holidays?
I suppose I shall just miss them again. Is Auntie Maud
still with the Gedges at Strawberry Hill? As I shall go
down and look her up if she is.

No news for you at all, I am afraid. We are all very
sorry to lose old Tirpitz; he seems such a familiar
landmark.

How frightfully sad poor Harry Baird losing his
leg. You never told me yourself; I only gleaned it from
Grade's letter which you enclosed.

Best love now to all the family, and heaps of
kisses.

From

Toby

12 April 1916 HMS *INVINCIBLE*

Darling Mother,

Just a line in haste to thank you and Daddy
frightfully for being so long-suffering with me last
week. I enjoyed every minute of my leave to the full,
and am quite sorry to be back again. I enclose a letter
to Cousin Alex Thomson, and I should be pleased if you
would ask Daddy to put it in another envelope and post
it on.

I find that I have left a book in the shelves near
the fireplace in the sitting room of flat 69, and it

is called *The Admiralty Manual of Seamanship, Vol. II*
(a blue book). I should be pleased if you would send
it on.

Also I have left the yellow clothes brush that Jimmy
gave me behind (the one you said was a nail brush). I am
not sure whether it is at the flat or whether I left it
in Jerram's room at Westenhanger.

I hope you and Peggy enjoyed your dinner with the
Handfield-Jones, and that you are glad to be home
again. I envy you in the glorious sunshine of the south;
it is very cold and windy up here, and the snow is not
all melted yet.

Very best love to you all.

From

Toby

28 May 1916   HMS *INVINCIBLE*

Darling Mother,

Many thanks for the usual supply of letters. Did
you address my clothes to the *Indomitable* or the
Invincible? I have made inquiries and cannot trace them
to either ship at present.

I enclose the card of a weird old Canadian soldier
I ran across a short time ago. He does not know a soul
in this country, and in view of the unvarying kindness
and courtesy that is always extended to naval officers
in the colonies, I thought it would do no harm to offer
him a meal or a bed if ever he happens to be in our
part of the world. Funnily enough, he knows Francis
Alexander Carron Scrimger, the Canadian captain, who,
perhaps you remember, got the VC last year.

We have been away from our usual haunts of late,
and I have been ashore at Swanbister several times,

and managed to get some fishing at Kirbister in the loch.

For the first time for many months I have found time to enjoy the luxury of a book, and have just finished *Bleak House*. Have you read it lately? If so, does not 'Mr Skimpole' remind you vividly of a mutual acquaintance of ours? Some of this gentleman's characteristics are absurdly similar to the person of whom I speak.

No more now.

> Very best love to all.
>
> Toby

PS Please jog Daddy's memory regularly until he keeps his promise about the wedding presents.

5 June 1916   RNC Dartmouth

Dear Scrimgeour,

You will all be grieving at Alexander Scrimgeour's death, and I hasten to send a word of sympathy. You know already how highly we thought of him here – but we should like his parents to know. He was a most unusually strong, reliable character – and able; he is a real loss to the country. But such an occasion for death is enviable – here we doubt if the Germans will ever show themselves outside again – and in any case the battle was a complete vindication of all we believed the Navy to be. That the battle involved great self-sacrifice is to the everlasting fame of those who died. Such comfort there is, but I know it is inadequate to those who feel the loss most nearly; one can only state this point of view, and, please God, the comfort will come.

> Yours most sincerely,
>
> EH Arkwright.

7 June 1916   5 Clements Inn, Strand WC

Dear old Jim,

Mother and I are sending you two books for your
birthday. I have not been able to look in to them to
see if they are good reading so you must take them
for what they are. If you know one or the other or
both, and have read them already, post them back to
the booksellers they came from or to me - that is why
I did not write your name in them. If you like them
and keep them I will write your name in during the
holidays.

Mother and I have just had a call from Lieutenant
Sandford who was saved from Toby's ship. He was simply
splendid. He saw a lot of the battle before they were
scuttled and then a lot more from a raft to which he
and Commander Dannreuther were clinging and later on
again from a torpedo boat that picked them up. He told
us that Commander Onslow on the torpedo boat *Onslaught*
steamed right up close to a great German battleship and
sank her putting six torpedoes right into her as the
Germans' last shell swept the bridge of the *Onslaught*
and killed Onslow and everyone on the bridge - but
little *Onslaught* got home eventually. I will tell you
more when we meet.

I had a fine letter from Commander Dannreuther
which I will show you someday. He says, 'Your dear son
died as I am sure he would have chosen, full of fight
and giving the Derrflinger a good hammering with the
12-inch guns of "A" Turret. Commander Dannreuther is
coming to see me when he returns to town.

Heaps of love from us both.

Yours,

Daddy

16 June 1916   Woodside Cottage,

East Cowes
Isle of Wight

Dear Mrs Scrimgeour,

I must write you a line to offer you both our deepest
and most sincere sympathy.

The country has paid a heavy price in officers and
men, but she has lost no more promising officer than
your son.

He had many fine qualities, and one of his greatest
assets was his power of concentration on whatever he
was doing. Mr Culme-Seymour, who went new to Dartmouth
when the Drakes did, knew them very well, and he was
saying to me yesterday that he thought the best thing
Scrimgeour ever did was to go in for a special History
prize from 4-6.30 (and win it), knowing that he was
fighting the final of the heavy-weight boxing at seven.
Very few could have done it. I assure you it is very
hard to do one's work here just at the moment.

Everything reminds one of many we shall see no more.

Please don't answer this just now, but later on I hope
you will write and say that I shall have his brother
here. He will have a fine example before him.

Believe me,

Yours very sincerely,
FM Broadbent

Friday, 11 August 1916   Aldro School,

Eastbourne (Tel 205)

Dear Mrs Scrimgeour,

It was only last evening that I heard from Mr Fox that
Alex was in the *Invincible* when she went down in the

Jutland Battle. I have some slight glimmering of what
this loss must be to you, and I wish much that it were
in my power to do anything to lighten your sorrow.
May it be some little comfort to you to know that I
have always considered him one of the best specimens
of what a British boy really should be. We have the
very happiest recollections of him at Aldro. I have
never had a straighter boy, or one whom I would more
entirely trust in every way; he had the essence of the
true sporting spirit and always 'played the game'. I
have never had a boy who was more universally popular
with old and young alike. May the recollection of
his straight life and noble death help us all for the
future.

My very kindest remembrances to you all.

Yours very sincerely,

Harold R Browne

Wednesday   East Sheen Lodge

Sheen

Dear Mrs Scrimgeour,

My mother, Mrs Hood, asked me to send you a letter
which she received the other day, and which she is sure
you and yours would like to see. She was so comforted
by it.

The letter was written to her by the mother of an
officer who also went down with the *Invincible*, and
does make one feel how happy they were up to the very
second of their most glorious death.

I hope it will help you as it did us.

Yours sincerely,

(Signed) Eleana Nickerson

'I saw Commander Dannreuther, who was saved. You will
love to hear all that he has to tell us. I am writing
fully because I gather that you have not seen him yet,
and don't want you to lose a minute of the comfort
that I got from his story. He speaks of the glorious
excitement and happiness of the rush from Scapa to
the scene of action. They were so pleased that the
moment had really come. In the *Invincible* they did not
know that the *Queen Mary* and *Indefatigable* had gone
down. He distinctly told me that he only heard it after
he was saved. So they had nothing to damp them. Of
course, also, they knew that the Grand Fleet was near
behind them.

'I think they first became engaged with a light
cruiser at about 5.15 and sank it, then a pause, then
they took on the *Derfflinger*. More than one of our
ships fired at her - she sank. Your husband telephoned
up to Com. Dannreuther: "The firing is excellent. Keep
it up as fast as you can; every shell is telling." He
passed the message on to the gun turrets, and so my
darling in turret "X" knew that they were giving
satisfaction with their gun.

'Then the crash came, and Com. Dannreuther thinks
the shock of the explosion killed them. Anyhow, there
was no struggle, no minute to think, because the ship
sank (so he says) in ten to fifteen seconds. He was in
some high-up position with Leo, and was thrown into
the water some way off. He went down thirty feet and
came up again at once, and when he reached the surface
there was no one to be seen except the other five who
were saved.

'I am so thankful that they had no minute to grieve
or think of us. They were translated. I am writing

all this fully because I want you to have with me the
comfort of knowing that they were all so happy and
satisfied up to the moment when they passed without
feeling the passage into the next world. There is no
separation in spirit, and I know we shall feel that
more and more as the almost physical shock wears
off us.'

APPENDICES

INTRODUCING THE APPENDICES

The sudden end of Alexander Scrimgeour's young life demands rather more in the way of context than his diary entries. For example, how did he get on with his fellow officers, his contemporaries and his seniors? Fortunately he left a series of acute pen portraits of those he served with on the *Crescent*. It had long been common practice for Royal Navy officers to compile confidential character sketches of fellow officers, both their contemporaries and their seniors. The exercise developed the ability to assess character, a vital command tool, and provided considerable entertainment value from the increasingly fractious relationships that inevitably developed on extended cruises. Scrimgeour was no exception; his sketches retain a remarkable freshness, the men who emerge are instantly recognisable. In the case of Admiral de Chair the portrait is strikingly similar to those provided by admirals, statesmen and the officer directing his pre-1914 War course. Having read Scrimgeour's assessment it will come as no surprise to discover that de Chair spent the second half of the war working ashore liaising between the Admiralty and the Foreign Office on blockade questions.

The next four appendices present Scrimgeour's war from the perspective of journalists, boat crew, British naval officers and a German gunnery officer.

The British government enlisted every tool to make the blockade effective. The *Times* leader columns reprinted here are part of the war effort, and were intended to be read by American politicians, and fellow newspaper men, for whom the London *Times* carried real weight. The main problem was to keep the Americans neutral, while violating pre-war norms. Fortunately the Germans handed the British a massive propaganda coup by sinking the Cunard liner *Lusitania* without warning, killing more than one hundred Americans in the process. The legal niceties of using neutral flags to disguise British ships, under debate in February 1915, was quickly overtaken by the German decision to sink all shipping in the war zone. The March leader took a robust line when the Americans protested at British 'reprisals' and the food blockade. It stressed the far more heinous crime of the Germans – common piracy. Potent parallels with the Napoleonic Wars reflected growing acceptance that this was a total war of national survival, while the citing of Germans and American Civil War practice – a fruitful source of precedents for a common law legal system, was topped off by a scarcely veiled hint that the Americans should mind their own business. We might assume Scrimgeour's father would have been an avid reader of the *Times*.

While it might not carry the same international significance as a food blockade the basic tool of the Tenth Cruiser Squadron was the stopping and searching of neutral ships on the high seas. The relevant passage of the *Admiralty Manual of Seamanship* would have been Scrimgeour's constant companion throughout his training at Dartmouth.

The explosive events of Jutland bring the book to a sudden close, and Appendix IV reproduces the official reports of the senior surviving officer of the Third Battle Cruiser Squadron, the captain of the *Inflexible* and Commander Dannreuther, the senior officer of *Invincible*'s six survivors. These first-hand reports describe the last battle of the *Invincible*, as seen from the two ships astern, and her own gunnery control top, in great detail. The accompanying track chart provides visual reference to the myriad twists and turns of the action, but does not reflect the limited visibility that bedevilled both sides at various times. While the view from the other side of battle is equally important it is vital to remember that German times were two hours ahead of the British throughout the battle. Among the handful of German accounts of Jutland that appeared in English, Georg von Hase's narrative is the most significant for this book. As gunnery officer of the battle cruiser SMS *Derfflinger* he directed the guns that sank the *Invincible*. The *Derfflinger*, a new ship of 28,000 tons, was the exact antithesis of her victim, the extra 10,000 tons bought her the protection of a battleship, a powerful 5.9-inch secondary battery and two or three knots more speed. The best balanced, fast capital ship design of the era, *Derfflinger* was a very dangerous opponent for a decade-old ship with limited armour. *Invincible* had just crippled *Derfflinger*'s sister ship, Admiral Hipper's *Lützow*, when the smoke cleared from von Hase's sights.

– Professor Andrew Lambert

APPENDIX I

THE *TIMES* EDITORIALS ON
THE BLOCKADE, 1915

'BLOCKADE' AND THE NEUTRAL FLAG
(12 FEBRUARY 1915, PAGE 9)

Yesterday the State Department of Washington forwarded dispatches to London and to Berlin, dealing with the *Lusitania* incident and with the German proclamation of a 'war area' round the United Kingdom. We feel confident that the conversation which MR PAGE is instructed to have with SIR EDWARD GREY will be as friendly and satisfactory as our Washington Correspondent has foretold. He has assured us that nothing approaching a protest was to be expected, but that informal representations would probably be made as to the dangers to American shipping which an habitual use of the American flag by British vessels within the war area would involve. Any representations of the kind will, of course, be received in the spirit in which they are addressed to us. The fair and reasonable attitude which America has observed in all the problems raised by the war has strengthened our customary desire to respect, not only her rights, but her wishes and her susceptibilities. Both nations recognize the same general principles of international law, and both are anxious not to strain claims which are merely technical. As regards this particular question, which we consider the use of the neutral flag to avoid an enemy as an undoubted right, it is a right which we are most unlikely to exercise so as to expose the shipping of neutral States to serious peril or inconvenience. In these circumstances, and in view of the hearty good will which happily exists between both Governments and both peoples, a satisfactory accommodation should be promptly and easily reached. No doubt is felt in England, or amongst those conversant with maritime law and history in the United States, that the action of the *Lusitania* in coming into Liverpool under the American flag was perfectly lawful and in strict accordance with precedent. It continues, our Washington Correspondent tells us, to be much discussed in America, but both in Washington and in the Eastern Press the discussion is temperate and friendly to this country. The exceptional severity with which the censors deem it judicious to treat American news makes it difficult to learn American opinion so fully as we could desire, but the *New York Tribune* is, perhaps, right when it affirms that the interest of the flag incident would be academic, were it not for Germany's extraordinary version of the rules of warfare. That version, it is understood, is the subject of the American communication to Berlin. This document is also perfectly friendly, but it makes clear, we are told, that any German attack upon ships flying the American flag, without examination and proof that its use is for purposes of disguise, would be deemed to be a very grave event and might cause serious complications. It is clear that that whole incident of the *Lusitania* arose from the fact that the Admiralty had information of Germany's real intentions before these were proclaimed in the Memorandum of February 4. They knew that she intended to sink enemy merchant ships without examination and without warning to the crews. She had so sunk the *Tokomaru*; she had attacked the *Icaria*, and she had even attacked the hospital ship *Asturias*. With these instances of her contempt for law and humanity before them, they recommended our merchant shipping to use the neutral flag in order to avoid the wholesale sacrifice of non-combatant lives. The step was so regular as to be almost a matter of course, without necessity, gave the Germans a dialectical advantage. The advantage lay in the fact that just when American indignation at the German menace was very vehement the statement of the Foreign Office and the arrival of the Cunard liner under the American flag suddenly revealed that the Admiralty had, in fact, advised British merchantmen to resort to the familiar device of flying the neutral flag. There has not been any 'misuse' of that flag, as the Germans falsely asserted, but resort was had to the old custom of the sea at a time when the step was particularly likely to cause discussion, and to afford the Germans in the United States a fresh opening for misrepresentation. The cool sense of the American people and their respect for the recognized rules of international law have apparently prevented them from being misled. They are not pleased at the incident. But they are obliged to acknowledge that – unlike the German 'blockade' – it has a sound legal basis. The Foreign Office Statement establishes that beyond dispute. The practice is sanctioned alike by international law and by British municipal law. Ships of war of all nations have habitually sailed under all sorts of disguises in order to surprise enemy ships, whether armed or unarmed. The raid of the German cruiser *Emden* at Penang is a recent instance in point. Why, it may pertinently be asked of German critics, is it illegitimate and unfair for British merchantmen to sail under the neutral flag in order to avoid destruction, if it was legitimate and fair for the *Emden* to use false colours in order to destroy? We do no claim to make any use of the flag of neutral States which we do not allow belligerents, when we are neutral, to make of our own. The chief object of the ruse, in the case of merchantmen, is to compel enemy ships to comply with the recognized obligations of international law. It forces them to search the suspected vessel and her cargo before capture. That is just what the Germans have declared that they will not do within the 'war area'. They propose to sink all British ships at sight, and to take their chance of sinking neutrals. This, as the Foreign Office declare, is sheer piracy upon the high seas. But even 'friendly communications' with America might have been avoided, as it seems to us, had the Admiralty and the Foreign Office worked in this matter more closely together. We have no evidence that the use of the neutral flag, when the Admiralty advised it, had suddenly become so urgent as to override all other considerations. The Foreign Office are better judges of some amongst these considerations than the Admiralty possibly can be. It is the business of the Admiralty to look upon matters from one point of view, and the business of the Foreign Office to look at them from another. But the constant and intimate cooperation of both is essential in many matters if serious blunders are to be avoided. Nothing very serious has happened, or is likely to happen, this time, but the incident is an object-lesson in the disadvantages to which the independent action of separate Departments of the Administration exposes us. We hope that the less will be taken to heart.

NEUTRALS AND BRITISH REPRISALS
(4 MARCH 1915, PAGE 9)

We regret the general condemnation in the American Press of the policy of reprisals against Germany announced by the PRIME MINISTER. That policy was certain to provoke criticism, but the objections urged against it in the United States and in other countries whose trade interests it affects are largely founded, we fancy, upon misapprehension. Americans have been described as 'Pro-German' in England, and denounced as 'Pro-British' in Germany. It seems to us that their attitude on the reprisals question, like their attitude upon all previous questions, is intended to be quite impartial. Their sympathies, as we learn by a thousand signs, are very heartily with us, so far as the overwhelming majority are concerned. But they have not allowed their sympathies to deflect them from the 'real neutrality' at which they have aimed from the first. They have shown all along a natural and legitimate anxiety that their rights as neutrals should meet with due regard. That feeling was very manifest in the substance and in the tone of their Reply to the German proclamation of piracy. It obviously underlies and inspires a good deal of the newspaper comment upon the British counter-stroke. It is a feeling which Englishmen, with their long tradition in favour of the rights of trade, cannot but respect. We have been extremely careful, as SIR EDWARD GREY has pointed out in his Replies to the American Note of December 28, to safeguard those rights so far as the manifest necessities of our own military position have allowed. We do not intend to depart from the usage. But, while we are confident that the measure we shall adopt may be reconciled with the fundamental principles of international law, as applied to the wholly new state of circumstances which have arisen in the present struggle, and which have culminated, for the present, in the German claim to sink all vessels in the war area without examination, we admit, in the words of SIR EDWARD'S last dispatch, that we may have to take belligerent action 'in various ways which may, at first sight, by regarded as a departure from old practice'. Americans have studied the common law, which is part of their and our joint inheritance, too long and too well not to know that the adjustment of old principles to new conditions is of the essence of legal progress. That the conditions of the present contest are latterly different from those of the past wars, in which international law has mainly developed to the stage now laid down in the text-books, cannot be denied. A very large part of it was evolved before, or during, the conflict with NAPOLEON. Great armies were engaged on both sides, but it was only towards the very end of the struggle that SCHARNHORST'S idea of an armed nation was realized. In this war all the Continental armies are conscript armies raised in accordance with that idea. This single circumstance goes a long way to destroy the old distinction between the armed forces of a nation and the civil population. If the army is the 'people in arms', food for the people is necessarily, to a great extent, food for the army. Foods may be imported for the use of civilians, but it is quite certain that if the army wants them it will take them. The German decree of January 25, placing all imported grain and flour under Government control, introduces another element into the question for which there is no precedent. The subsequent modification of February 6 does not appear to be material. The decree in effect makes the German Government the ultimate consignee of all imported foodstuffs. How can any precedent, or any rule based upon precedent, for permitting consignments to civilians and for civilian use, be wrested to defend consignments which the enemy Government have announced that they will seize? Several Continental Powers have always maintained that foodstuffs are liable to seizure. When the present German Government denounces such seizure as 'murderous' and 'inhuman', neutrals should remember that two German Chancellors in succession, BISMARCK and CAPRIVI, defended it in the strongest and most comprehensive terms, that Germany, so far as is known, has never disavowed the practice, that she resorted to it ruthlessly in the siege of Paris, and that BISMARCK indulged his humour by talking of the starving Parisians 'eating babies' while he was at Versailles. The doctrine of 'continuous voyage', which the American courts did so much to elaborate in the Civil War, and against which England raised no protest, was just such an application of old principles to novel facts as is implied in our answer to German piracy. It might be extended, our Washington Correspondent suggests, to imports into Germany through neutral States.

The German answer to the 'suggestion' in the American Note of February 22 cannot lessen our difficulties in assenting to that project. Germany tells Washington, in substance, that she may suspend her piratical operations and refrain from endangering American ships and lives, if England will allow her to import all the food she needs, through agencies whose names are communicated to the United States, and who will hand it over to licensed dealers for consumption by the civil population only. We have already explained that a surrender by us to any proposal of the kind would be, in the circumstances, a surrender to blackmail. It would be an admission that German piracy had intimidated us, and a direct invitation to our enemies to resume the process at their convenience – say, when they had imported food enough to carry them on to the next harvest. But there are other objections to the project which should appeal to a practical nation like the Americans. What security should we have under such a scheme that the food would go to the civil population alone? Germany's word? The Americans know its worth, as well as we do. Are they going to guarantee it, and if so how, and how do they propose, in case of need, to enforce the guarantee? Are they to send, and is Germany to admit and to pay, a host of American officials who will supervise the German agencies in the ports, and the German licensed dealers in every town and village of the Empire? If disputes should arise between the German agents and dealers on the one hand, and the American inspectors on the other, who would decide them? Germany has pleaded 'necessity' as a sufficient reason for all her violations of treaties and of law. Why should we suppose she would refrain from urging it as a reason for breaking any new engagements she might make? We are satisfied that, on reflection, the utterly impracticable nature of this project will be perceived across the Atlantic, and that the plan will be seen to be a mere diplomatic trick. American opinion for the moment seems to have forgotten that in all great wars belligerents take action against which neutrals who chose to stand on the bare letter of the law might plausibly protest. Our Washington Correspondent reminds us that this was very markedly the case during their own Civil War. The victory of the Union was in great part due to the ruthless blockade of the Southern States, which it was one of LINCOLN'S first acts to proclaim. The blockade was certainly irregular, under the Declaration of Paris, for many months after it began. The Washington Government knew and confessed that it was irregular. All America knew the terrible loss and hardship which it inflicted on the whole population engaged in one of the chief of English industries. But LINCOLN'S Government appealed for toleration and for indulgence, and the appeal was not in vain. Under the guidance of men like BRIGHT and W.E. FORSTER, who understood the greatness and the value to mankind of the ideals for which the North was fighting, the British democracy did not scrutinize too closely the acts of a kindred people struggling for its life. Therein they showed the large wisdom and the large generosity of their race. May they not hope to-day, when they have been plunged against their will into a conflict yet more deadly, for aims which are not less high, that America will do unto them as, in the day of her visitation and of her trial, they did unto her?

APPENDIX II

EXTRACTS FROM CHAPTER VI BOATWORK IN *MANUAL OF SEAMANSHIP VOL. I,* 1905

(REVISED AND REPRINTED 1915)

Lowering a Sea Boat

On a sea boat's crew being away they man their boat instantly and put on their life-belts. The life-lines are crossed to prevent the boat surging in a fore and aft direction, and the crew on the inside stand by with stretchers ready to bear the boat off from the ship's side. No one is to be abaft the after fall or before the foremost fall.

The lee boat is always the one to lower, and in a rough sea a good lee should be made and, if necessary, oil used before lowering the boat.

Sea boat lowerers, consisting of a leading hand and two others, are told off to each fall; the leading hand slipping the gripes (with a hammer specially supplied for the purpose and secured to the davit with a lanyard) before starting the falls.

The officer lowering the boat as she nears the water gives the order 'Out pins', and then, watching his opportunity so as to drop the boat near the water, orders 'Slip', the coxswain slips (the inertia given the boat by the ship and the helm being over, she will sheer away from the ship), the crew at once get their oars out and give way.

Hoisting a Sea Boat

A lee is formed, and as the boat approaches, the boat rope should be passed into her as soon as possible by means of a heaving line, and manned inboard, and when secured, the boat hauled under the davits; a stern line is also passed into the boat if necessary and secured.

The foremost fall should be hooked on first, and then the after one, lifelines crossed, and stretchers used as in lowering. All the crew are hoisted in the boat, the falls being strongly manned.

When the boat is up and the falls secured, the crew get her weight off the pins by setting up the fore and after and griping her to, life-lines left clear and life-belts in place, tiller stopped over towards the ship, and boat-rope secured.

The coxswain reports to the officer of the watch that his boat is off the pins and ready for lowering. The falls are also reported 'clear for running'.

Boarding a Wreck, or a Vessel, under Sail or at Anchor, in a Heavy Sea

The circumstances under which boats have to board vessels, whether stranded or at anchor, or under way, are so various that it would be impossible to draw up any general rule for guidance. Nearly everything must depend on the skill, judgment, and presence of mind of the coxswain or officer in charge of the boat, who will often have those qualities taxed to the utmost, as undoubtedly the operation of boarding a vessel in a heavy sea or surf is frequently one of extreme danger.

It will be scarcely necessary to state that, whenever practicable, a vessel, whether stranded or afloat, should be boarded to leeward, as the principal dangers to be guarded against must be the violent collision of the boat against the vessel or her swamping or upsetting by the rebound of the sea, or by its irregular direction on coming in contact with the vessel's side; and the greater violence of the sea on the windward side is much more likely to cause such accidents. The danger must, of course, also be still further increased when the vessel on the lee side, if broadside to the sea, is the falling of the masts or if they have been previously carried away, the damage or destruction of the boat amongst the floating spars and gear alongside. It may, therefore, under such circumstances, be often necessary to take a wrecked crew from the bow or stern; otherwise a rowing-boat, proceeding from a lee shore to a wreck, by keeping under the vessel's lee, may use her as a breakwater, and thus go off in comparatively smooth water, or be at least shielded from the worst of the sea. If unable to approach a wreck in the manner above described, anchor to windward of the stranded vessel, and then veer down to 100 or 150 fathoms of cable, until near enough to throw a line on board. The greatest care, under these circumstances, has, of course, to be taken to prevent actual contact between the boat and the ship; and the crew of the latter has sometimes to jump overboard, and be hauled to the boat by ropes.

In every case of boarding a wreck or a vessel at sea, it is important that the lines by which a boat is made fast to the vessel should be of sufficient length to allow of her rising or falling freely with the sea; and every rope should be kept in hand ready to cut or slip it in a moment if necessary. On wrecked persons or other passengers being taken into a boat in a seaway, they should be placed on the thwarts in equal numbers on either side, and be made to sit down. All crowding or rushing headlong into the boat should be prevented, as far as possible; and the captain of the ship, if a wreck, should be called on to remain on board to preserve order until every other person has left her.

APPENDIX III

REPORTS OF SENIOR OFFICERS OF THE THIRD BATTLE CRUISER SQUADRON, BATTLE OF JUTLAND OFFICIAL DESPATCHES, 1916

Report of Senior Officer Third Battle Cruiser Squadron (Enclosure No. 8 to Battle Cruiser Fleet Letter No. B.C.F. 01 of 12/6/16. No. 363/16.)

HMS *Indomitable*

2 June 1916

SIR,

I have the honour to report that HM battle cruisers *Invincible*, *Indomitable* and *Inflexible*, HM light cruisers *Chester* and *Canterbury* and HM destroyers *Christopher*, *Ophelia*, *Shark* and *Acasta* left the Pentland Firth at 9.35pm on 30 May 1916, just ahead of the Grand Fleet, with which visual touch was kept by the late Rear-Admiral Commanding Third Battle Cruiser Squadron, The Honourable Horace Lambert Alexander Hood, CB, MVO, DSO, through *Chester* till we were in Latitude 57.49°N, Longitude 4.42°E at 2.23pm on 31 May.

2. At 2.23pm we received from *Galatea* our first intimation that the enemy were actually at sea; we were then steering 115°, speed of advance 14 knots; the speed of advance during the night had been 16.8 knots. Telefunken signals of strength 10 had just previously been heard. From then onwards many signals giving various positions of the enemy were received.

At 3.13pm the Rear-Admiral Commanding Third Battle
Cruiser Squadron increased speed to 22 knots; at 3.18pm
he ordered ships to 'Action stations'; 3.45pm he altered
course to 137°, the squadron was then in single line
ahead with *Canterbury* ahead distant five miles, *Chester*
on starboard side bearing 256° to 212° distant five miles
and the four destroyers ahead of the Battle Cruisers
as a submarine screen. By 4.12pm we were steaming at
full speed.

3. As usual, the positions of the enemy received
in the WT signals did not agree, but they all pointed
to the enemy steering 345° or 298°, and it is evident
that the late Rear-Admiral acted on this; at 3.57pm
we received signals from the Senior Officer, Battle
Cruiser Fleet: 'Am engaging enemy 1500.' At 5.30pm the
sound of gunfire was plainly heard. At this time the
visibility greatly decreased owing to the mist, the
density of which was various degrees; for, on some
bearings, one could see 16,000 yards, whilst on others
only 2000 yards. From then till dark the visibility
ranged from 14,000 to 5000 yards, which was, in my
opinion, a great handicap to us, the attacking force; in
fact much more of a handicap to the attacker then the
defenders.

At 5.40pm flashes of gunfire were seen on a bearing
about 215°, but I could not distinguish any ships. The
Rear-Admiral, *Invincible*, altered course to starboard
without signal, turning about nine points, thus
bringing the engaged vessels and *Chester* on the port
bow of the Third Battle Cruiser Squadron, and leaving
our destroyers off our port quarter; after a short
time we made out the engagement to be between the

enemy's light cruisers and *Chester*. The Rear-Admiral
led the squadron between *Chester* and the enemy's light
cruisers whom we engaged; at 5.55pm we opened fire on
the enemy with our port guns. Shortly afterwards some
more of the enemy's cruisers were seen following at some
distance astern of the light cruisers which we were
engaging, and I observed our destroyers developing an
attack on them. At the same time these enemy vessels
opened a heavy fire on our destroyers, and I am afraid
that *Acasta* and another destroyer were either sunk
or damaged for I only saw two of them afterwards,
nor did I again see either *Chester* or *Canterbury*. I
desire to record the fact that, when I saw them, they
were heading to make a determined attack. At this
moment my attention was called to the enemy's light
cruisers turning sixteen points; they were at that time
under a heavy gunfire from the Third Battle Cruiser
Squadron, and a few minutes later one was seen to be
heavily on fire and apparently she blew up. There was
also observed amongst them a four-funnelled cruiser,
apparently of the 'Roon' class. She was observed to lose
two funnels, to be steaming and firing very slowly and
heavily on fire amidships.

4. The First Battle Cruiser Squadron was then
sighted on our port bow, heavily engaged with some
enemy whom I could not see owing to the mist. At 6.13pm
Invincible turned to starboard, apparently stopped, and
large quantities of steam were observed to be escaping
from her escape pipes. At the same moment *Inflexible*
turned to port and tracks of torpedoes were observed
by *Indomitable* coming from the enemy's light cruisers
with whom we had been engaged. The range at which I
engaged them was about 12,000 yards. I turned away from

the torpedoes and increased to full speed. One torpedo
actually ran alongside this ship at a distance of about
20 yards, which we managed to outrun. As we turned, two
torpedoes passed close to the stern of the ship, but they
had run their distance, for I managed to turn ahead
of them and resume my place in the Squadron as did
Inflexible astern of *Invincible*, which ship was then
again going ahead, having turned to about 153°. In all
about five torpedoes' tracks were seen coming from the
enemy's light cruisers.

At 6.14pm *Invincible*, while steam was escaping,
hoisted the 'Disregard', but hauled it down at once
and followed it by hoisting 1 flag and the squadron
got into proper order again. About 6.20pm at a range
of 8600 yards the leading ship of the enemy's battle
cruisers was seen firing at the Third Battle Cruiser
Squadron. They were promptly engaged, and I realised
that *Invincible* could have sustained little or no
damage from a torpedo, as I had thought she had when
she stopped at 6.13pm, for I had to go 20 knots to regain
station in the line; 6.32pm shells were falling about
Indomitable from the enemy's battle cruisers, which were
distant about 8000 yards.

At 6.33pm *Invincible* was straddled by a salvo
and was hit in the after part; 6.34pm a salvo or one
shot appeared to hit her about 'Q' turret, and she
immediately blew up. Wreckage, etc., was thrown about
400 feet in the air. She appears to have broken in half
immediately, for, when the smoke cleared and we had
got to the position, the bows were standing upright
about 70 feet out of the water and 50 yards away the
stern was standing out of the water to a similar
height, while in a circle round was wreckage and some

few survivors. The visibility, which I have before said
was sometimes up to 14,000 yards, was now generally
much less than that.

5. The positions of affairs, when I took charge of
the Third Battle Cruiser Squadron on the lamentable
death of Rear-Admiral Hood, appeared to me to be as
follows:

We were steering 153°, as shown on attached chart (not
included). The enemy's battle cruisers were disappearing
out of sight, but were still firing on *Indomitable* and
Inflexible. The Director Gunner, Mr James H Moore,
reported that about this time one of the 'Derfflinger'
class fell out of enemy's line and he saw her sink. The
Lieutenant-Commander (G) in the Control top at same
period remarked that she was very low in the water.
The First and Second Battle Cruiser Squadrons were
coming up astern of *Indomitable*; *Inflexible* being about
three cables ahead of latter. When *Invincible* blew up,
Inflexible turned sharply to port, and I did the same
and eased the speed as I wanted to continue the action
in the same direction as previously and wished, if
Inflexible turned eight or more points to port, to turn
possibly under her stern, or, at all events, to get the
Third Battle Cruiser Squadron to resume their original
course and then alter it further to starboard in order
to continue the action. However, *Inflexible* quickly
turned to starboard and continued to turn towards the
enemy. By being compelled to ease my speed I had dropped
astern of *Inflexible*. I made no signal to her as she was
turning as I desired. You then ordered the Third Battle
Cruiser Squadron to prolong your line, which we did.
Shortly after this I saw the Grand Fleet astern of us
bearing about 340°.

6. Until 7.20pm none of the enemy could be distinguished owing to the mist; but at that time it commenced to lift, and at 7.26pm *Indomitable* reopened fire on the enemy's rear ship, the range being about 14,000 yards and decreasing. Towards the head of the enemy's line dense quantities of grey smoke could be seen and out of this came a destroyer attack, which was beaten off but caused our battle fleet astern to turn away from the enemy. At 7.40pm our fire was checked owing to lack of visibility. At 8.26pm ranges could again be got on the enemy, and *Indomitable* engaged the second ship from the enemy's rear, which, as the range decreased, appeared to be *Seydlitz*. The enemy very quickly straddled us and continued to do so, even after we ceased firing. I believe that *New Zealand* was also firing on this ship; at all events, *Seydlitz* turned away heavily damaged, and her fire lessened. At 8.42pm we ceased fire the enemy bearing 307°, but we could not see to spot.

7. The only damage sustained by *Indomitable* was a small hole in her middle funnel, though many splinters from shells fell on the deck, but no one was injured. At 8.44pm *Indomitable* received so severe a shock that I was knocked off the compass platform. I thought that the ship had been mined or hit by a torpedo, but no damage has so far been discovered. I assume that we either hit some wreckage or a submarine.

8. From then onwards I conformed to your orders and nothing further of importance occurred with the exception that at 3.12am on 1 June a Zeppelin was sighted on the starboard quarter coming up from the southward. At 3.17am fire was opened by 'A' and 'X' turrets, the Zeppelin then turned 101°, but had not been

411

damaged in any way. At 3.21am she turned to 10° and continued her course astern of us, but at too great a range to justify a further expenditure of ammunition. Several light cruisers stationed on our port quarter engaged the Zeppelin, but apparently without causing her any damage.

(...)

11. The following is amount of ammunition expended by this ship during the action:

98 rounds of AP Lyddite, 12-in.

66 rounds of Common Lyddite, 12-in.

10 rounds of Powder Common, 12-in.

12. I desire to emphasize the fact that, when *Invincible* blew up and sank, the Captain of *Inflexible* – Captain Edward Henry Fitzhardinge Heaton-Ellis, MVO – without warning such as he would have had in the case of a wounded ship, found himself leading the squadron, and he at once followed the highest traditions of our Service by closing the enemy.

13. As the Officer left as Senior Officer of the Third Battle Cruiser Squadron, I desire to record the sincere sorrow of all the Officers and men of the Third Battle Cruiser Squadron in the loss that the Nation has sustained in the death of Rear-Admiral The Hon. Horace LA Hood, CB, MVO, DSO, Captain Arthur Lindesay Cay, Royal Navy, and the Officers and men of HMS *Invincible*, many of whom were personally known to me and friends of mine.

Of Rear-Admiral Hood's attainments it is not for me to speak, but he drew from all of us our love and respect. The Officers and men of *Invincible* had previously been our chums in the Mediterranean.

14. Since compiling the above report, I have seen
Commander Hubert E Dannreuther, who was the Gunnery
Commander of HMS *Invincible* on 31 May. He states that
the cause of *Invincible* stopping at 6.30pm was that her
helm jammed when put 'hard-a-port'.

I have the honour to be,

Sir,

Your obedient Servant,

FW Kennedy,

Captain and Senior Officer,

3rd BC Squadron.

The Vice-Admiral Commanding,
Battle Cruiser Fleet.

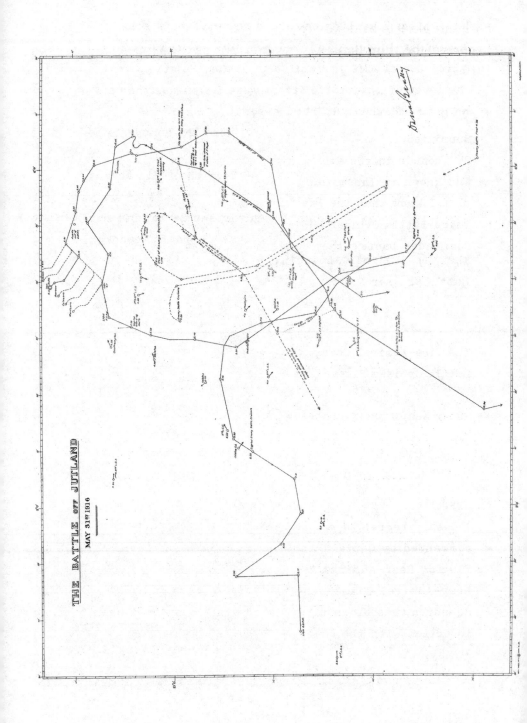

THE BATTLE off JUTLAND

MAY 31ST 1916

Enclosure No. 9 to Battle Cruiser Fleet (Letter No. B.C.F. 01 of 12/6/16):
Reports of the Third Battle Cruiser Squadron on the Action of 31 May 1916.

No. 20 S.

Submitted.

2. I concur in the attached reports as far as was seen and known in *Indomitable*.

3. I know that the late Rear-Admiral Commanding, Third Battle Cruiser Squadron, had a high opinion of Commander Dannreuther's abilities and zeal.

FW Kennedy,
Captain and Senior Officer of
3rd Battle Cruiser Squadron.

The Vice-Admiral Commanding,
Battle Cruiser Fleet.

Report of Senior Surviving Officer, HMS *Invincible*

HMS *Crescent*,

2 June 1916

SIR,

I deeply regret to report that HMS *Invincible*, commanded by Captain AL Cay, RN, and flying the flag of Rear-Admiral the Hon. Horace L Hood, Rear-Admiral Commanding the Third Battle Cruiser Squadron, was blown up and completely destroyed when in action with the enemy at 6.34pm on Wednesday, 31 May.

The total number of officers and men on board at the time was 1031. Of these only six survived. The names of the survivors are as follows:

Commander HE Dannreuther, RN
Lieutenant CS Sanford, RN
Chief PO (PTI) Thompson
Yeo. Signals Pratt (Walter Maclean), 216963.
Able Seaman Dandridge (Ernest George), 239478
Gunner Gasson, RMA

Of the above, all are free from injury with the exception of Gunner Gasson, who was severely burnt about the head and arms. They are now accommodated in this ship except Gunner Gasson, who is in the hospital ship *Plassy*.

The circumstances of the destruction of the ship are briefly as follows:

The *Invincible* was leading the Third BCS and at about 5.45pm first came into action with an enemy light cruiser on the port bow. Several torpedoes were seen coming towards the ship, but were avoided by turning away from them. *Invincible*'s fire was effective on the light cruiser engaged, and a heavy explosion was observed. A dense cloud of smoke and steam from this explosion appeared to be in the same position some minutes later.

Invincible then turned and came into action at about 6.15pm with the leading enemy battle cruiser, which was thought to be the *Derfflinger*. Fire was opened at the enemy at about 8000 yards, and several hits were observed. A few moments before the *Invincible* blew up Admiral Hood hailed the control officer in the control top from the fore bridge: 'Your firing is very good, keep at it as quickly as you can, every shot is telling.' This was the last order heard from the admiral or captain who were both on the bridge at the end.

The ship had been hit several times by heavy shell, but no appreciable damage had been done when at 6.34pm a heavy shell struck 'Q' turret and, bursting inside, blew the roof off. This was observed from the control top. Almost immediately following there was a tremendous explosion amidships indicating that 'Q' magazine had blown up. The ship broke in half and sank in 10 or 15 seconds.

The survivors on coming to the surface saw the bow and stern of the ship only, both of which were vertical and about 50 feet clear of the water. The survivors were stationed as follows prior to the sinking of the ship:

Commander Dannreuther (Gun Control Officer)

CPO Thompson Fore Control Top

AB Danbridge

Yeo. Signals Pratt Director Tower platform.

Lieutenant (T) Sandford Fore Conning Tower, hatch of which was open

Gunner Gasson 'Q' turret, at the range-finder

There was very little wreckage, the six survivors were supported by a target raft and floating timber till picked up by *HMS Badger* shortly after 7pm.

Only one man besides those rescued was seen to come to the surface after the explosion, and he sank before he could reach the target raft.

The *Badger* was brought alongside the raft in a most expeditious and seamanlike manner, and the survivors were treated with the utmost kindness and consideration by the officers and men.

> I have the honour to be,
>
> Sir,
>
> Your obedient Servant,
>
> HE Dannreuther

Captain's report, HMS *Inflexible*: Engagement on 31 May 1916 (No. 199W)

Inflexible,

2 June 1916

SIR,

I have the honour to inform you that *Inflexible* left Scapa Flow at 9pm on Tuesday, 30 May 1916, in company with *Invincible* (flying the Flag of Rear-Admiral the Hon Horace LA Hood, CB, MVO, DSO), *Indomitable* (Captain Francis W Kennedy), *Chester*, *Canterbury* and the four destroyers *Ophelia*, *Christopher*, *Shark* and *Acasta*. This Squadron, which left in advance of the main fleet, which sailed shortly after, under the command of the Commander-in-Chief, was stationed 10 miles ahead of the armoured cruiser screen; speed of advance of fleet was 17 knots.

2. At noon on Wednesday, 31 May, the position of the Third Battle Cruiser Squadron was 58° 7' North, 3° 55' East. At 2.20pm, the first reports of the enemy were intercepted by WT.

3. At 3.15pm speed of Squadron was increased to 22 knots and at 4pm to 24 knots, gradually working up to full speed, course being altered as necessary by

Invincible, presumably with the idea of joining up
with the Battle Cruiser Fleet, reports having been
intercepted that *Lion* was engaging the enemy.

At about 5.30pm firing was heard ahead, and at 5.40,
four hostile light cruisers were sighted on the port
bow, apparently engaging the *Chester*. On seeing the
battle cruisers, these ships turned away; fire was
opened on the second light cruiser from the right at a
range of 8000 yards, but was checked at 6 o'clock as the
ship fired at was enveloped in a high column of smoke
and was not seen again; it is presumed that she blew up.
Fire was reopened on the next cruiser, but after one
salvo was fired she disappeared in the mist. Meanwhile
the four destroyers in company had left the squadron
in order to attack the enemy and were last seen hotly
engaged.

4. At 6.15pm, two tracks of torpedoes were observed;
course was altered to avoid one which was seen to pass
down the port side at a distance of about 20 ft (the
torpedo was going very slowly – apparently near the
end of its run); the other torpedo passed astern. At
about this time another torpedo was observed to pass
underneath the ship, and emerge the other side.

5. At 6.20pm, enemy's heavy ships were observed
ahead, course was altered about eight points to port
and fire was opened at a range of about 8000 to 9000
yards. Owing to the haze and smoke only one ship was
visible, apparently a battleship of the Kaiser or König
class, and some direct hits were considered to have
been obtained on this vessel. At 6.30pm, the *Invincible*
blew up, apparently owing to being hit amidships
abreast 'Q' turret by a salvo. About 6.35pm, enemy
disappeared in the mist and firing ceased. During this

engagement, *Inflexible* was continuously fired at, and was straddled repeatedly, but the enemy ship fired at could not be determined owing to the mist. *Inflexible* was now leading the line and having passed the wreck of *Invincible*, altered course two points to starboard, fire having ceased, in order to close the enemy. At 6.45pm, *Inflexible* altered a further four points to starboard, when orders were received from *Lion* for *Indomitable* and *Inflexible* to prolong the line by taking station astern.

6. At 7.25pm, enemy's torpedo craft approached to attack, but were driven back by gunfire; the track of a torpedo passed 150 yards astern of the ship.

7. At 8.20pm, action was resumed at 6000 yards range with the enemy's armoured ships – believed to be of the Kaiser class. At 8.30, fire was checked, the enemy's ships disappearing in the mist.

At 8.35pm, the track of a torpedo was observed across the bows of *Inflexible*.

At 8.40pm, a violent shock was felt underneath the ship and a large swirl of oil was observed about 100 yards on the starboard beam: this violent shock was presumably caused by the ship coming into collision with wreckage.

8. *Inflexible* remained in company with the Vice-Admiral Commanding until arrival in the Forth AM on 2 June. At 2.24pm, 1 June, *Inflexible* passed a whaler of German pattern marked *V. 29*, and later, in about latitude 57° 2'N, Longitude 6° 13'E, passed large numbers of German bodies in life-belts and a lifebuoy marked SMS – (the name of the ship being covered by a body lying over it).

9. Except for the collision mentioned in paragraph
7, which must have caused an indentation of the outer
skin, no damage has been sustained, and no casualties
have occurred on board *Inflexible* during the recent
engagement, but the right gun of 'Q' turret, which was
cracked for a length of 30 ft during calibration, was
used and this appears to have enlarged the crack.

(...)

I have the honour to be,

Sir,

> Your obedient Servant,
> Edw. Heaton Ellis
> Captain

APPENDIX IV

ACCOUNT FROM THE FIRST GUNNERY OFFICER OF THE *DERFFLINGER*

FROM CHAPTER VIII, *KIEL AND JUTLAND*, BY G VON HASE

Third phase of the Skagerrak Battle (7.50 to 9.50pm). Heavy fighting against ships of the line, cruisers and destroyers. Destruction of the *Invincible*. *Derfflinger* forced to stop to clear her torpedo net.

By Commander Georg von Hase,
First Gunnery Officer of the *Derfflinger*

At 7.40pm enemy light cruisers and destroyers launched a torpedo attack against us. We therefore altered course to NNE, ie about six points to starboard.

The visibility was now so bad that it was difficult for us to distinguish the enemy ships. We were engaging light cruisers and destroyers. At 7.55pm we turned on an easterly course, and at 8pm the whole Battle Cruiser Squadron formed a line of bearing on a southerly course as the destroyers pressed home the attack. This brought us very effectively out of the line of the torpedoes that had been fired against us. At 8.12pm we again altered course towards the enemy. During this time we had only fired intermittently with our heavy and secondary armament. At 8.15pm we came under heavy fire. It flashed out on all sides. We could only make out the ships' hulls indistinctly, but as far as I was able to see the horizon, enemy ships were all round us. As I could not distinguish either the end or the beginning of the enemy line, I was unable to engage the second ship from the right, but selected the one I could see best.

And now a terrific struggle began. Within a short time the din of the battle reached a climax. It was now perfectly clear to us that we were faced with the whole English Fleet. I could see from her gigantic hull that I had engaged a giant battleship. Between the two lines light cruiser and destroyer actions were still raging. All at once I saw through my periscope a German light cruiser passing us in flames. I recognised the *Wiesbaden*. She was almost hidden in smoke, with only the quarterdeck clear, and her after-gun firing incessantly at an English cruiser. Gallant *Wiesbaden*! Gallant crew! The only survivor was Chief Stoker Zenne, who was picked up by a Norwegian fishing boat after drifting about for three days on a raft; all the rest, including the poet, Gorch Fock, who loved the sea above all else, sealed their loyalty to their Kaiser and Empire by a sailor's death. The *Wiesbaden* was subjected to a heavy fire by an English light cruiser. Again and again her shells struck the poor *Wiesbaden*. Seized with fury, I abandoned my former target, had the English cruiser's range measured, gave the range and deflection, and crash! a salvo roared out at the *Wiesbaden*'s tormentor. One more salvo and I had her. A column of smoke rose high in the air. Apparently a magazine had exploded. The cruiser turned away and hauled out at top speed, while I peppered her with two or three more salvos.

At this moment Lieut.-Commander Hausser, who had been engaging destroyers with his secondary armament, asked me: 'Is this cruiser with four funnels German or English, sir?' I examined the ship through the periscope. In the misty grey light the colours of the German and English ships were difficult to distinguish. The cruiser was not very far away from us. She had four funnels and two masts, like our *Rostock*. 'She is certainly English,' Lieutenant-Commander Hausser shouted. 'May I fire?' 'Yes, fire away.' I was now certain she was a big English ship. The secondary armament was trained on the new target. Lieutenant-Commander Hausser gave the order: '6000!' Then, just as he was about to give the order: 'Fire!' something terrific happened: the English ship, which I had meanwhile identified as an old English armoured cruiser, broke in half with a tremendous explosion. Black smoke and debris shot into the air, a flame enveloped the whole ship, and then she sank before our eyes. There was nothing but a gigantic smoke cloud to mark the place where just before a proud ship had been fighting. I think she was destroyed by the fire of our next ahead, Admiral Hipper's flagship, the *Lützow*.

This all happened in a much shorter time than I have taken to tell it. The whole thing was over in a few seconds, and then we had already engaged new targets. The destroyed ship was the *Defence*, an old armoured cruiser of the same class as the *Black Prince*, which was sunk on the following night by the *Thüringen* and other ships of the line. She was a ship of 14,800 tons, armed with six 23.4-cm and ten 15.2-cm guns, and carrying a crew of 700 men. Not one of the whole ship's company was saved. She was blown to atoms and all the men were killed by the explosion. As we saw the ship at a comparatively short distance in good visibility, magnified fifteen times by the periscopes, we could see exactly what happened. The whole horror of this event is indelibly fixed on my mind.

I went on to engage other big ships, without any idea what kind of ships they were. At 8.22pm we turned on a south-easterly course, but in the general confusion of the battle that was now raging I had lost all grasp of the tactical situation. Once the thought flashed across my mind: 'Can we be firing at German ships?' At that moment, however, the visibility, which changed from one minute to the next, but which on the whole was gradually growing worse, improved and revealed distinctly the typical English silhouette and dark grey colour. It is my opinion that our light grey colour was more favourable than the dark grey of the English ships. Our ships were much more quickly concealed by the thin films of mist which were now driving across the sea from east to west.

At 8.25pm Lieutenant von der Decken, in the after-control, recorded: '*Lützow* heavily hit forward. Ship on fire. Much smoke.' At 8.30pm he wrote: 'Three heavy hits on the *Derfflinger*.' Of these one hit the 15-cm battery on the port side, went clean through the centre gun and burst, killing or wounding the whole of the casemate crew. The explosion also knocked the first 15-cm gun off its mounting and killed or wounded several men. The other hits were aft.

I now selected my target as far ahead as possible, the leading ship of the enemy line, for I saw that the *Lützow*'s fire was now weak. At times the smoke from her burning forepart made fire control on the *Lützow* impossible.

At 8.24pm I began to engage large enemy battleships to the north-east. Even though the ranges were short, from 6000 to 7000 metres, the ships often became invisible in the slowly advancing mists, mixed with the smoke from the guns and funnels. It was almost impossible to observe the splashes. All splashes that fell over could not be seen at all, and only those that fell very short could be distinguished clearly, which was not much help, for as soon as we got nearer the target again it became impossible to see where the shots fell. I was shooting by the measurements of the Bg. man in the fore-control, Leading Seaman Hänel, who had been my loyal servant for five years. In view of the misty weather these measurements were very irregular and inexact, but as no observation was possible I had no alternative. Meanwhile, we were being subjected to a heavy, accurate and rapid fire from several ships at the same time. It was clear that the enemy could now see us much better than we could see them. This will be difficult to understand for anyone who does not know the sea, but it is a fact that in this sort of weather the differences in visibility are very great in different directions. A ship clear of the mist is much more clearly visible from a ship actually in the mist than vice versa. In determining visibility an important part is played by the position of the sun.

In misty weather the ships with their shady side towards the enemy are much easier to see than those lit by the sun. In this way a severe, unequal struggle developed. Several heavy shells pierced our ship with terrific force and exploded with a tremendous roar, which shook every seam and rivet. The captain had again frequently to steer the ship out of the line in order to get out of the hail of fire. It was pretty heavy shooting.

This went on until 8.29pm.

At this moment the veil of mist in front of us split across like the curtain at a theatre. Clear and sharply silhouetted against the uncovered part of the horizon we saw a powerful battleship with two funnels between the masts and a third close against the forward tripod mast. She was steering an almost parallel course with ours at top speed. Her guns were trained on us and immediately another salvo crashed out, straddling us completely. 'Range 9000!' roared Leading Seaman Hänel. '9000 – Salvos, fire!' I ordered, and with feverish anxiety I waited for our splashes. Over. 'Two hits!' called out Lieutenant-Commander von Stosch. I gave the order: '100 down. Good, rapid!' and thirty seconds after the first salvo the second left the guns. I observed two short splashes and two hits. Lieutenant-Commander von Stosch called: 'Hits!' Every twenty seconds came the roar of another salvo. At 8.31pm the *Derfflinger* fired her last salvo at this ship, and then for the third time we witnessed the dreadful spectacle that we had already seen in the case of the *Queen Mary* and the *Defence*.

As with the other ships there occurred a rapid succession of heavy explosions, masts collapsed, debris was hurled into the air, a gigantic column of black smoke rose towards the sky, and from the parting sections of the ship, coal dust spurted in all directions. Flames enveloped the ship, fresh explosions followed, and behind this murky shroud our enemy vanished from our sight. I shouted into the telephone: 'Our enemy has blown up!' and above the din of the battle a great cheer thundered through the ship and was transmitted to the fore-control by all the gunnery telephones and flashed from one gun position to another. I sent up a short, fervent prayer of thanks to the Almighty, shouted to my servant: 'Bravo, Hänel, jolly well measured!' and then my order rang out: 'Change target to the left. On the second battle cruiser from the right!' The battle continued.

Who was this enemy? I had not examined her carefully nor given much thought to her identity, but I had taken her to be an English battle cruiser. I described her as such in giving the target, as my gunnery log-keeper recorded. There had been no time to discuss her class while we were engaging her, for there had only been a few minutes in which to recognise her with any certainty. Only the gunnery officers and gun-layers and the torpedo officers had seen her blow up, the attention of the captain and his assistants, the navigating and signal officers being entirely taken up with keeping the ship in her station. It was difficult work navigating astern of the *Lützow*, which was hardly in a condition to keep her place in the line.

When, after the battle, the reports came to be drawn up, most of the officers were convinced that she was a ship of the Queen Elizabeth class. I was of the opinion that she belonged to the Invincible class, but I admitted that I was not at all sure. If you take a naval pocket-book and compare the silhouettes of the Queen Elizabeth and Invincible classes, there is at first sight a perplexing similarity. We therefore entered in our report that at 8.30pm we had destroyed by gun fire a battleship of the Queen Elizabeth class. Our report ran: 'The ship blew up in a similar way to the *Queen Mary* at 6.26pm. Clearly observed by the First and Third Gunnery Officers, and the First Torpedo Officer in the fore-control, the Second and Fourth Gunnery Officers in the after control and the Gunnery Observation Officer in the fore-top. Ship of the Queen Elizabeth class.'

After the battle, the following statement was made by English prisoners at Wilhelmshaven: 'One of the Queen Elizabeth ships, the *Warspite*, left the line, listing heavily, and hauled away to the north-west. At 8pm the English destroyer *Turbulent* received a wireless report that the *Warspite* had sunk.'

On the strength of our battle report and the statements of the prisoners, our Admiralty authorities were obliged to assume that the ship destroyed by the *Derfflinger* was the *Warspite* and, accordingly, the *Warspite* instead of the *Invincible* was reported as an enemy loss. That the *Invincible* was sunk we learned from the report of the English Admiralty, and naturally her loss was added afterwards to the previous report. As a matter of fact, it was the *Invincible* we had engaged and blown up and not the *Warspite*. The English reports soon made this quite clear.

On 3 June, the *Manchester Guardian* said that the German Admiralty report of the 1 June contained a detailed and frankly exact report of the English losses, except that it gave the name of the battleship *Warspite* instead of the battle cruiser *Invincible*.

The *Times* of 6 June 1916, reports on the evidence of combatants: The *Invincible*, flying the flag of Admiral Hood, Sir David Beatty's second in command, singled out the *Hindenburg*, and after a hot fight, in which some of our men claim that the *Hindenburg* received mortal injury, the *Invincible* went down.'

At this time the *Hindenburg* was still being built. The *Derfflinger* was her sister ship and the English account is correct but for the names: it was the *Derfflinger* and not the still uncompleted *Hindenburg* that engaged the *Invincible*.

The account of the engagement between the *Derfflinger* and the *Invincible* given by one of the two officers saved from the *Invincible* is perfectly correct with the exception of the time. The *Times* of the 12 June 1916, reports that the father of a lieutenant who went down with the *Invincible* received from the two surviving officers a letter, in which they say: Your son was with the Admiral and we were engaged with the *Derfflinger*. There was a tremendous explosion aboard at 6.34pm. The ship broke in half and sank in ten or fifteen seconds.'

On 13 June 1916, the *Times*, quoting a letter from the brother of the late Lieutenant Charles Fisher says: 'We learn from Commander Dannreuther, the sole surviving officer of HMS *Invincible*, that a shell fell into the powder magazine. There was a great explosion, and when Dannreuther recovered consciousness he found himself in the water. Ship and crew had disappeared.'

That they were the ships of Hood's Battle Cruiser Squadron that we had been engaging from 8.24pm onwards, at ranges varying between 6000 and 7,000 metres, is confirmed by Admiral Beatty's official dispatch. This reports as follows on the part played by the *Invincible, Indomitable* and *Inflexible* of the Third Battle Cruiser Squadron:

'At 6.20pm the Third Battle Cruiser Squadron appeared ahead, steaming south towards the enemy's van. I ordered them to take station ahead, which was carried out magnificently, Rear-Admiral Hood bringing his squadron into action in a most inspiring manner, worthy of his great naval ancestors. At 6.25pm I altered course to the ESE in support of the

Third Battle Cruiser Squadron, who were at this time only 8000 yards from the enemy's leading ship. They were pouring a hot fire into her and caused her to turn to the westward of south.'

A Reuter telegram of 5 June 1916 states that when the action had been in progress some hours the *Indomitable, Invincible* and *Inflexible* appeared on the scene; that this phase was chiefly a duel of heavy guns and that the *Invincible*, after fighting bravely and inflicting heavy punishment on the enemy, met her doom and sank.

My reason for supporting my own description of this event from the English accounts of the battle is that, hitherto, the German reports have left it open as to whether the sinking of the *Invincible* was due to gun fire or a torpedo. On historical grounds I consider it necessary to make clear that the *Invincible*, like all the other English ships lost in this battle, was destroyed by gun fire.

The Officer Commanding the Third Battle Cruiser Squadron, Rear-Admiral Hood, who went down in the *Invincible*, was a descendant of the famous English Admiral Hood, who distinguished himself brilliantly as a strategist and tactician in the North American War of Independence under Graves and Rodney, and later as Commander-in-Chief at the Battle of St Christopher (1782). During the Anglo-French War of 1793–1802 he was Commander-in-Chief (1793–94) of the Mediterranean Fleet and bombarded Toulon.

According to the record of my log-keeper the heavy guns fired until 8.33pm. At 8.38pm I gave the order: 'Heavy guns stand by!' There was no longer any enemy to be seen. At 8.35pm we had altered course sharply to the west. After the loss of their leader the remaining ships of the Third Battle Squadron did not immediately venture into the zone of our death-dealing fire. At 8.50pm the whole ship was ordered to cease fire. Then feverish efforts were made to put out the fires that had broken out in various parts of the ship.

At this time we noticed a destroyer slowly going alongside the *Lützow*. The flagship had a list, that is to say, she was leaning over to one side, and her bows were very deep in the water. Great clouds of smoke were rising from her forepart. Admiral Hipper boarded the destroyer, which then cast off and steered for the *Seydlitz*. While passing the *Derfflinger* the admiral signalled: 'Captain of the *Derfflinger* will take command until I board.' Our captain was therefore in command of the battle cruisers until nearly 11pm, for, owing to the headlong speed of the battle cruisers, which were almost continuously under enemy fire, it was not until then that the admiral succeeded in boarding another ship.

The *Derfflinger*, too, was now a pretty sorry sight. The masts and rigging had been badly damaged by countless shells, and the wireless aerials hung down in an inextricable tangle so that we could only use our wireless for receiving; we could not transmit messages. A heavy shell had torn away two armour plates in the bows, leaving a huge gap quite six by five metres, just above the waterline. With the pitching of the ship water streamed continually through this hole.

While we were steering west the commander came on to the bridge and reported to the captain: 'The ship must stop at once. The after torpedo net has been shot away and is hanging over the port screw. It must be cleared.' The captain gave the order: 'All engines stop!'

I surveyed the horizon through the periscope. There was nothing of the enemy to be seen at this moment. The *Seydlitz*, *Moltke* and *Von der Tann* were not in very close touch with us, but they now came up quickly and took their prescribed stations in the line. It was a very serious matter that we should have to stop like this in the immediate neighbourhood of the enemy, but if the torpedo net were to foul the screw all would be up with us. How many times we had cursed in the ship at not having rid ourselves of these heavy steel torpedo nets, weighing several hundred tons. As we hardly ever anchored at sea they were useless and, in any case, they only protected part of the ship against torpedo fire. On the other hand, they were a serious source of danger, as they reduced the ship's speed considerably and were bound sooner or later to foul the screws, which meant the loss of the ship. For these reasons the English had scrapped their torpedo nets shortly before the war – we did not do so until immediately after the Battle of Skagerrak and as a result of our present experience.

The boatswain and the turret crews of the *Dora* and *Caesar* turrets, under Lieutenant-Commander Boltenstern, worked like furies to lift the net, make it fast with chains and cut with axes the wire-hawsers and chains that were hanging loose. It was only a few minutes before the report came: 'Engines can be started.' We got under way at once.

The *Lützow* had now hauled out of the line and was steering a southerly course at low speed. The captain wanted to signal to the other ships to follow the leader, but all the signal apparatus was out of action. The semaphores and heliographs had all been shot away and the flags all destroyed by fire. However, our stout ships followed without signal when the captain turned on a northerly course and led the battle cruisers to a position ahead of the main fleet.

The lull in the battle lasted until 9.05pm and then suddenly fresh gun fire flashed out and once more the cry, 'Clear for action!' rang through the ship.

INDEX

Page numbers in *italic* refer to illustrations; numbers with 'n' refer to a footnote.

INDEX